D1234309

Temples of Grace

TEMPLES OF GRACE

The Material Transformation of Connecticut's Churches, 1790–1840

Gretchen Townsend Buggeln

UNIVERSITY PRESS OF NEW ENGLAND

Hanover and London

University Press of New England, 37 Lafayette St., Lebanon, NH 03766

© 2003 by University Press of New England

Printed in the United States of America

5 4 3 2 1

This book was published with the generous
support of The First Church of Christ in Hartford.

Library of Congress Cataloging-in-Publication Data

Buggeln, Gretchen Townsend.
  Temples of grace : the material transformation of Connecticut's
churches, 1790–1840 / Gretchen Townsend Buggeln.
    p. cm.
  ISBN 1–58465–322–1 (cloth : alk. paper)
  1. Church architecture — Connecticut. 2.
Architecture — Connecticut — 19th century. 3.
Architecture — Connecticut — 18th century. 4. Connecticut — Religion — 19th
century. 5. Connecticut — Religion — 18th century. I. Title.
  NA5230.C8 B84 2002
  726.5'09746 — dc21   2003000241

Contents

Illustrations

Preface

During the early nineteenth century, American religion was working out an accord with the material world that continues to shape both the material and spiritual lives of Americans today. In New England a Puritan heritage and an increasingly important culture of refinement came to coexist productively in an environment of economic growth and religious vitality. This process produced ecclesiastical architecture that both embodied and transformed the region's religious heritage.

Builders and congregations accepted and popularized an important style after the Revolution, a style that might seem more in keeping with Anglican precedent than Puritan principles. As the Reverend Henry M. Dexter explained in 1859: "About the beginning of the century there arose a disposition here [New England] to import the more modern forms of church architecture that prevailed abroad."[1] To Dexter, and to many since, it appeared that the "Puritan prejudice against costly and church-ly houses of worship had passed away." The old New England meetinghouse gave way to buildings that looked (and were) more expensive and more like churches. Outside, the main entrance was through a central projection or portico in one of the short gabled ends, surmounted by a tall tower capped with a steeple or cupola. Inside, the space was restructured. Long, front-facing pews replaced irregular box pews, and a lower pulpit stood at the end opposite the front door. Stylistically, these buildings seemed more "Anglican," and less like the former multipurpose New England meetinghouses. Urban congregations in particular began to refer to their buildings as "churches" rather than "meeting houses," and this signaled conceptual and functional as well as stylistic changes.[2] Just why these stylistic innovations were instituted and accepted is a question that has never been answered to satisfaction. Certainly, changing architectural fashion was a direct and important cause. But the establishment of a different religious context that chose, consistently, this new building type was key to the new churches' success and persistence.

Although builders erected these structures all over New England, there were regional differences. Because of the importance of understanding material objects in specific, historical contexts this study will focus on Connecticut. In this self-professed "Land of Steady Habits" a tenacious social conservatism was partly the result of a homogenous, largely white and Congregational population under the sway of a strong Puritan heritage, the continuing influence of Yale, and a handful of powerful leading families. Conservatism also derived from the state's overwhelmingly local and rural character; by 1810, for example, the whole of Litchfield County had only forty-one thousand people, and by 1820 Hartford and New Haven were only two of a handful of cities with a population over four thousand inhabitants. Yet Connecticut's educated citizens were far from unsophisticated country bumpkins. In the early nineteenth century, the state's small towns were rapidly re-creating themselves as lively and prosperous villages with up-to-date commercial and cultural institutions.

Many forces combined to challenge relentlessly the old ways of religion, politics, and society. Two broad trends were especially critical to the shape of Connecticut's religious culture at this time, one political and the other material. In the first decades of the nineteenth century the connection between Federalist political power and Congregationalism fell before a coalition of Republican dissenters. Religion was at the heart of much of the political conflict in the state; one of the most dramatic reversals in the new state constitution of 1818 was that Connecticut's citizens were no longer legally required to support local ecclesiastical societies. This had a powerful impact on the organization and vision of religious institutions. At the same time, a diversifying and strengthening economy allowed people to spend money and time in various new ways. Ideas about refinement and sensibility gave them the tools they needed to operate in a substantially different material world. Religion helped them make sense of these changes at the same time these changes shaped religion.

This study asks the question, What can the religious artifacts of federal Connecticut tell us about the relationship between religion and the broader culture of the early republic? These artifacts include not only buildings but interior furnishings, fixtures, textiles, artifacts used in ritual (such as communion silver), and graveyards. Such things are rich sources of information about the way faith became real in human life. As material embodiments of belief, they not only reflected religious experience; they actively shaped it. Yet they are also physical constructions that reveal all the worldly concerns of a community: style, money, power, and status. Religious artifacts are a special lens through which we can view the interrelationships of the spiritual and temporal dimensions of human life and locate the everyday meanings of the sacred. They have seldom been explored in their many dimensions, or properly mined for the historical insights they contain.[3] We need to ask pointed questions of these buildings and objects. What were the circumstances of their planning and creation? How were they used? What cultural work were they designed, consciously or unconsciously, to perform? Did material artifacts mediate tensions between the spiritual and the everyday? And, especially, what did people think about them? Religion in the early republic has been studied from several angles—evangelicalism, nationalism, and refinement among them.[4] A study centered on the material culture of religion can tie these various strands into a coherent whole. Religious buildings take us into a wide range of subjects—technical building knowledge, finance, property law, architectural design, theology, and social history. It is difficult to extract meaning out of objects that stand alone, but by putting objects at the center of an investigation, we ask different sorts of questions.

A good many Congregational and Episcopal buildings survive in this region.[5] Understanding this architecture and its interior accoutrements requires seeing the complete religious landscape, not just the better-known architecture of the dominant Congregationalists. Episcopalians, in fact, presented a rising challenge—numerically, politically, and architecturally—to the waning religious establishment, and their experience is central to the story. It is important to recognize that a clear understanding of the material religion of this period will require moving back and forth between artifacts and written documents. Looking only at buildings and church silver might lead to an interpretation too close to the myth of bucolic serenity. Ignoring the material evidence, on the other hand, would cause us to miss the desire for grace, elegance, and tangible stability that infused religious life.

The chapters to follow move from the mechanics of building to the meanings of religious architecture for both insiders and outsiders. Chapter one is a discussion of the process of building itself, the physical and mental effort required to put up a new house of worship. Chapter two investigates the financial situations that made building necessary and the fund-raising schemes that made it possible. Chapters three and four explain style: first that of architecture and then that of worship, or the manner of religious experience that took place within those spaces. Chapter five is a study of the buildings from the outside, the ways people envisioned churches as displays of virtue, republicanism, and prosperity in the landscape. The final chapter looks at the buildings from the inside, asking how new churches and their interiors shaped and intensified a sense of specific Christian community.

This study seeks to describe the contours of the complicated, yet *not*

false relationship between evangelical religion, a culture of sensibility, republican commitments, and the graceful and elegant federal style. How
did Connecticut's Christians of the early republic fashion a working relationship between the austerity of Protestant theology and the bounty of
the new nation? Throughout a wide variety of documents one finds the
period lexicon of fashion: grace, graceful, plain, simple, polite, decorous,
sensible, harmonious, and, above all, elegant. These terms applied both
to church buildings and to the religion practiced within. Grace was a
crucial element of Protestant theology; it was also a manner of practicing
those beliefs. A new material world of religion enabled even religious
enthusiasts to practice a religion that blended fervor and fashion, while
denying or diminishing neither.

It is a pleasure to thank the many people who have helped me through
the various stages of this long-term project. On my path through graduate
school I was blessed with teachers and colleagues who generously shared
their knowledge and love of history and artifacts. The world of early
American material culture is small and special, and I have been extremely
fortunate to have been taught by some of its most brilliant scholars: Mar-
garetta Lovell and Cary Carson, who first pointed me in this direction;
Kenneth Ames, Richard Bushman, James Curtis, J. Ritchie Garrison, Bernard Herman, Kevin Sweeney, and Barbara Ward, who made the Winterthur Program a wonderful, eye-opening intellectual experience. I owe
a special debt to Kevin Sweeney, my teacher at Winterthur and colleague
at Historic Deerfield. His work and professional example have influenced
me tremendously.

At Yale, Abbott Cummings and Jules Prown were superb teachers who
helped me continue my artifact studies. David Barquist and Patricia Kane
of the American Arts Department of the University Gallery were terrific
colleagues in the study American decorative arts. Jon Butler and Harry
Stout, through their energy and enthusiasm, drew me into the study of
American religious history and encouraged my forays into the little-
explored realm of the material culture of religion. I could not have found
a better dissertation adviser than Jon Butler, the perfect mix of inspirational and practical. I remember finding him in the library stacks one day,
thrilled at an old text he had found on the shelves; he reminds his students
that we are historians because we love history, and that is the only reason
to be in this business.

This project enabled me to put my interests in American religion and
artifacts together. I have been inspired and encouraged by colleagues in
that enterprise: David Morgan, Sally Promey, and Peter Williams espe-

cially. David and Sally invited me to be part of the Visual Culture of American Religions group, a three-year project that was a tremendously rewarding intellectual experience. They and the other scholars on the project strongly influenced my ideas about the visual dimension of religion. Peter Williams has been a supporter and friend since we first worked together at Miami of Ohio ten years ago. His expansive work in religion and architecture has opened up the field; his generosity and enthusiasm have brought us together.

Winterthur has been a supportive, resource-rich place to complete this project. My colleagues Gary Kulik and Pat Elliott have been patient and understanding, and it has been wonderful to work again with Ritchie Garrison and Jim Curtis. More than anything, I have learned from our research fellows and students. Although too numerous to name, I thank each one of them for the questions they have asked and the contributions they have made to the study of American culture. It has been exciting to work at an institution that is committed to understanding American life from the perspective of artifacts, and it seems that every day I am impressed by something said or done by one of my very smart colleagues or students.

In its various incarnations several people read the manuscript and offered helpful comments and suggestions. I am grateful to James Curtis, John Demos, Carl Lounsbury, David Morgan, Ritchie Garrison, Mary Ellen Hern, Louis Nelson, Sally Promey, Jules Prown, Kevin Sweeney, and Peter Williams for reading all or portions of this in process. Of course I am responsible for all the mistakes and failings of the product; I am certain any one of these scholars could have written a better book.

I am grateful to the Graham Foundation for Advanced Study in the Fine Arts for a generous grant to assist the publication of this book. I also thank the Pew Charitable Trust for a summer dissertation grant to complete some of the initial research. Phyllis Deutsch, Ann Brash, and the staff at University Press of New England have been enormously helpful, encouraging and efficient, and I am fortunate to have worked with a press that made the publication process so friendly for a first-time author.

In the process of research, writing, and gathering photographs I have been assisted by many librarians and curators. Help was given generously by the staffs at Winterthur Museum, the Connecticut Historical Society, Yale University Manuscripts and Archives, the New Haven Colony Historical Society, the Litchfield Historical Society, and various town halls and local museums across the state where I stopped in to look at a few documents or ask about a building. I especially thank Neville Thompson, Librarian of Printed Books and Periodicals at Winterthur, who is the very model of what a librarian should be.

A portion of this study was published as "Elegance and Sensibility in the Calvinist Tradition: The First Congregational Church of Hartford, Connecticut," in P. Corby Finney, ed., *Seeing beyond the Word: Visual Arts and the Calvinist Tradition* (Grand Rapids, Mich.: W. B. Eerdmans Publishing Co., 1999), and I thank Eerdmans for permission to reproduce portions of that essay in this book. I am also grateful to Corby Finney, the organizer of the associated conference and the editor of the volume of essays. *Seeing beyond the Word* opens up a world of questions about the relationships between a particular kind of Reformed theology and visual and material experience.

Although the beginnings of this project, the trials of doctoral work, are fading into a distant memory, I still remember fondly the friendships I made at Yale. I especially thank Suzanne Smith, my roommate, who cheerfully lived through a great deal of this project. For their humor and support, I also thank David and Margaret Bratt, Razmic Gregorian, Mary Habeck, Laura Mitchell Loretan, and Susan Treber. Many of these friends have left the halls of academia for other pursuits. They may wonder why they ever did Ph.D. work, but I am sure glad they were my companions down that road.

My mom and dad have always enthusiastically supported my academic interests, and I thank them for the freedom they have given me to take the most unpredictable paths. They are both astute cultural critics, and I hope they will appreciate the many dimensions of the story told here. My husband John and children Hannah and John Henry have put up with a lot for the sake of this book, and I thank them for their love and patience. John, a talented historian, has been more than helpful with the intellectual content and refreshingly practical when I needed advice. The kids asked questions that kept scholarship in perspective and made me smile. (Will it have pictures? Are you going to sell it? Will *Scholastic* publish it?) I told them months ago that we'd go out for pizza when the book was done. They are very hungry.

Temples of Grace

CHAPTER I

Builders and Building

I the sd. Thomas Dutton do Covenant & agree to . . . Build Compleat and finish Said Meeting House in all things . . . upon the same plan & after the Model and with as good workmanship as the Meetinghouse in Richmond lately Built is Done . . .
—Salisbury Congregational Society Building Contract, 1798

In early January of 1798, after several years of debate about what to do with its run-down 1751 meetinghouse, the town of Salisbury, Connecticut, voted to construct a new timber-framed building "in the modern stile."[1] The town, nestled in the northwestern corner of Litchfield County, sent an agent to ask the county court to affix the place of building and appointed a committee of three prominent citizens to manage the project from beginning to end. This committee negotiated with the master builder, "Captain" Thomas Dutton of Watertown, specifically asking that its proposed building follow the example of the wooden church recently built in Richmond, Massachusetts, and be sixty-four by forty-eight feet. (see Appendix)[2] Most of the work was completed during the summer of 1799, after the town had provided for the preparation of the ground and the building of the foundation. In June of 1800 the congregation formally dedicated its new building (fig. 1).[3] Dutton received, minus the cost of materials, just under four thousand dollars for the completed church.

A few years later, in December of 1804, the First Congregational Society in Hartford appointed a committee of nine men "to consider whether it be expedient for this Society to build a new meeting house."[4] The society's much-repaired 1739 building was crowded and no longer sturdy enough to support regular use. Three months later, on March 22 of the new year, the committee returned a recommendation that the society build a new meetinghouse of brick with a slate roof. The committee

1. Congregational Church, Salisbury, Conn., 1800. Photo by John Giamniatteo.

suggested dimensions of 102 feet deep by 64 feet wide, nearly twice the size of the old house. As for style, the committee suggested something "simple and decent."[5] The society approved the appointment of five society members, or "contractors," to the building committee; these men would oversee the project to the end. This new committee negotiated with the town for land, hired workmen, arranged for building supplies to be delivered to the site, managed pew sales, and kept a careful account of the entire operation, which eventually cost the congregation just over thirty-two thousand dollars. In December of 1807, Reverend Nathan Strong preached a dedication sermon in the not-yet-finished new building.[6] Construction continued through the following October (fig. 2).

The Salisbury and Hartford building projects provide telling and representative examples of post-Revolutionary church building in Connecticut. Salisbury's wooden, 1799–1800 Congregational Church is typical of small-town ecclesiastical buildings from the late eighteenth century through the 1820s. Hartford's 1807 brick church is a forerunner of a more flashy, expensive, durable style of building that wealthier city congregations preferred after 1800. This building of the First Congregational Society relates closely to later Hartford churches as well as the three churches New Haven's religious societies constructed on their central green a decade later. Both the Salisbury and Hartford buildings are unusually well documented and went up with great "expediency."

The growing Connecticut River city of Hartford and the rural hamlet of Salisbury were in some ways quite different places in 1800. Their individual building experiences reflect these differences; the cost and size of the churches differ dramatically. Yet certain similarities in process are evident: voting on the measure to build, asking the town or court to verify a building site, selecting a building committee, and formally dedicating the buildings. Although the creation of a new meetinghouse or church could be a highly idiosyncratic enterprise, legislation and tradition brought a measure of consistency to the procedure, and building in Connecticut did in fact adhere, if loosely, to a sort of "due process."

The manner in which a new ecclesiastical building took shape was both familiar and strange to builders and townspeople. Those who built them were joiners and carpenters skilled in the trades of woodworking, masons with expertise in laying stone and brick, glaziers who constructed windows, and painters, plasterers, carvers, blacksmiths, and day laborers. All regularly applied their building skills to the houses and barns of southwestern New England. Into the sameness of such projects would occasionally come the opportunity to work on a public project—a schoolhouse, an infrequent town house, or a church. Religious structures, with their large open spaces, towers, and often great expense, presented unusual technological problems and challenges as well as opportunities for workmen to display mastery of technique and stylistic flourish.

The actual design and construction process remains in some ways a puzzle. It is clear from the limited documentary evidence that the starting point, at least on paper, was much more like a suggestive sketch than a detailed blueprint. Building committees most often sent the master

2. First Congregational Church, Hartford, Conn., 1807. Photo by John Giammatteo.

builder on his way with incomplete design instructions, asking him to build it "like the new meetinghouse" in a neighboring town, with the added insistence that all be accomplished on time, within cost, in best "workmanlike" fashion. As a result the craftsmen, as they worked, had the opportunity to affect not just the quality of the building but the design itself. Primarily working with knowledge gained from experience, and not book learning, craftsmen proceeded as they knew how, making adjustments when faced with a new problem, such as the integration of a steeple into the roof frame of a building, with a conservative eye to stability. But often there was little in the construction itself that required extraordinary skills. A new church was just one more timber-framed, brick, or stone building.

At the same time, the construction of a house of worship was wholly different from anything else. Size and prominence alone meant construction was a public, much observed affair, and rare was the building committee that actually left a carpenter and his crew to their own devices once it signed the contract. The building committee members might have given vague instructions at the outset, but they watched carefully as the carpenters progressed, changing their minds and freely offering comments and suggestions. The duration of building, commonly several years from start to finish for a church, not infrequently stretched on for a decade or more. Everyone contributing money or time to the building had a stake in it, and from start to finish the erection of a church was a widely shared event. The construction of a new religious building could divide a town or unite it, place a town on the architectural map or be a source of embarrassment, prove the financial ability and generosity of supporters or, unfinished, remind them that their ambitions were bigger than their pockets were deep. And from the start, the construction of a church building could be charged with religious fervor. Standing on the foundations, a preacher might beg a blessing from God and plead with his people to let the project be a source of unity and harmony. Safety and speed in the building process were signs of God's favor.

Three primary arenas of work constituted the building of a new house of worship: planning, financing, and construction. These cannot rightly be called stages, because they all went on simultaneously throughout the life of the project and could even continue after the building was "done." Many congregations, for example, worshiped in buildings without pews or paint, or finally got their steeples or towers years after the new building was first in use. Delays often grew out of financial difficulties; debt sometimes began before the foundation was laid and stretched annoyingly on for decades after all the workmen departed. Changes to the building design, such as the replacement of a steeple with a cupola, the addition of a gallery for an organ, or a decision to hold off on building a portico until more money was available, were often the result of choices made after the building was already in process. The Winchester Congregational Society began its building in 1786 but as late as 1796 was still looking to "do something towards finishing off the inside" and voted to advertise for a carpenter "in the public papers."[7] The Roxbury Congregational Society started its new building in 1807, but by 1818, when it was finally ready to finish the inside, the society had to contract with "Mr. Bacon for the lower part of the church" excluding pulpit and reading desk.[8] Design and construction worked in tandem, flexing to the whims of the building committee, the talents of the workmen, and the fortunes of the society.

Into the nineteenth century, building a house of worship was never the job of the church proper.[9] The church took care of questions of doctrine and discipline only; issues involving money, even the payment of a minister's salary, were left to other organizations. First this would have been the town itself. In the colonial period and on into the early national period in some small towns, the Congregational meetinghouse served both as house of worship and as the place of assembly for the secular business of the community. The town technically owned the building, and this was only right, for the town had paid for it. Under colonial law all taxpayers, even those who did not participate in the religious life of the church, had to contribute to the financial support of the local Congregational society, including the building and maintenance of the meetinghouse.

This arrangement, however, soon had numerous exceptions. In the 1720s the legislature extended toleration to some other "Christian sects," which included the clause that if one could prove he were giving the allotted amount to another legally recognized religious society, he would be exempt from supporting the town's Congregational society.[10] Frequently a second Congregational group broke away from the first and had a separate minister and building. Such an arrangement was too complex for the town to manage, and each congregation formed a separate organization, known as an "ecclesiastical society" or "parish," for the purpose of managing its business affairs. Dissenters such as Episcopalians and Methodists generally went along with this format and created ecclesiastical societies to manage their business, too. Towns thus eventually surrendered all responsibility for the financial accounting of any of their religious groups. Despite this trend, at the end of the eighteenth century the small town of Salisbury was still operating as the business manager for its one Congregational society, and in that capacity oversaw the construction of the new church. The Hartford project of 1807, on the other hand, fell within the domain of the First Ecclesiastical Society, which had managed congregational business affairs since the 1670s.

In the course of their building projects, both the Salisbury and Hartford societies looked to the law for a guide. Eighteenth-century Connecticut law had standardized building procedures in specific legislation designed to stabilize what experience had shown could be a difficult or contentious process. A 1748 "Act directing how to proceed when it shall be necessary to build a Meeting House for divine worship" is typical. According to this law, the first step in building was that two-thirds of the "legal voters present" at a society or town meeting had to decide in favor of a new building.[11] Next, the society or town had to apply to the county court to "ascertain the place for it." Failure to do so would result in a fine of one hundred pounds. The reason for such harsh discipline on this point was that location could prove to be an extremely divisive, even explosive issue. The meetinghouse was the community center, and living several miles away could be a great inconvenience. The third step was for the society, at a publicized meeting, to appoint a building committee "for setting up, building, and finishing" the house. At the same meeting the society would decide the amount of tax necessary to support the project and appoint a clerk to take care of the financial record, which he would present in regular intervals to the county court. Although some of this, particularly the relationship between building and taxation, had changed greatly by 1818, when the Congregational Church was formally disestablished under the new state constitution, disestablishment did not end all state involvement in building projects. An outside authority was a useful and, it was hoped, impartial ruler, and congregations continued to appeal to the courts or legislature for guidance, albeit with declining frequency.

The General Assembly intended this legislation for its established Congregational societies, but the structure made sense to Episcopalians, who followed similar procedures and even occasionally appealed to the law to resolve conflicts encountered during the course of building. Although their specific liturgy and tradition called for some unique building features, Episcopalians ran their construction projects in much the same way, used some of the same builders, and adopted those Congregational procedures that could streamline their own endeavors. Many dissenting societies seemed unsure whether or not their buildings were to follow the same legal regulations that applied to Congregationalists. For instance, the congregation of St. Peter's Episcopal Church in Plymouth appointed a committee "to Examin [sic] and see whether the Episcopal Societys are obliged by laws to apply to the County Court for Building Churchs as the Presbyterians do to Building meeting Houses."[12] After a majority of the Plymouth Episcopal Society voted to build a new church, another faction within the church questioned the legality of the proceedings and called the vote "null & void of account of the elegality [*sic*]" of the meetings in question.[13] Here, as in many instances of building among dissenters and Congregationalists alike, church-building laws became useful when they could expedite a partisan cause.

Each project had its own ebb and flow. Even the very first step toward building, in which a two-thirds majority had to vote in favor of the proposed project, could take years to achieve, especially if the prospect of financing a new building was threatening to the taxpaying voters. It was important to bring up the issue before a representative collection of townspeople so that the vote would not be reversed at a later date. To publicize the fact that this matter was to be considered, a society or town gave notice stating when and where the meeting was to be. The announcement was either nailed to a regular posting place, often literally a wooden post or tree near the meetinghouse, or advertised in a local paper. The First Congregational Society of New Haven, for instance, ran an advertisement in the *Connecticut Journal* informing members that the annual society meeting on Monday November 23, 1812, at two o'clock would "take into consideration the expediency of building a new Meeting House for the use of sd. society (prepositions for doing which will be laid before said meeting for their approbation)."[14]

Once a congregation approved a new building project, it selected a building committee. Commonly, perhaps in part because of the significant threat of debt such projects posed, societies chose respected, trustworthy, and often wealthy men to lead them. It is not unusual to discover that there were several committees gathered during the process of building. Often a preliminary committee organized simply to ascertain the community's opinion on the proposed project. Subcommittees might be given specific tasks, such as gathering lumber. But there was a core committee that, especially after ecclesiastical societies took over church business from the town, might even take legal and financial responsibility so that the building would ensue "with no risk to the society."

After the building committee determined that adequate financial support would be forthcoming, it made basic decisions about materials, size, design, and cost. A concern with economy pervaded this stage of planning, and many societies did as the people of Christ Church, Sharon, did in 1812 when they told their committee to "Examine what size building and of what materials would be cheapest for building a church."[15] When the society or town reached some agreement on size and materials, it sent the building committee to look for a builder who could see the project through to satisfaction. In 1794, the Congregational Society of Roxbury asked its building committee "to enquire who will build a meeting House for us when we get the Bigness established and on what conditions."[16] It was customary for a congregation to advertise for a builder, and to accept the most qualified workman or workmen who presented a reasonable bid. The Winchester Congregational Society voted in March of 1796 "to advertise the doing off of the meeting house in the public papers."[17] This advertisement would have given the basic elements of the plan and presented the committee's desired timetable for building. In the *Connecticut Journal*, January 31, 1814, Trinity Episcopal Society of New Haven placed an advertisement "To Builders" informing them "Proposals will be received by the subscriber until the 14th of February next, for the building of an Episcopal Church in this city." The advertisement explained, "The building will be of the Common rock stone and built in the Gothic stile." Interested builders wishing to put in a bid could first "see the Plan or draft," by dropping in at the New Haven store of building committee member William McCrackan. McCrackan planned to accept proposals that were "in writing and under sealed covers."[18]

Despite great effort on the part of architectural and local historians, it is still difficult to match many of these buildings with a master builder, let alone identify other workmen. A smattering of names in church records and local histories leads to a few generalizations. Master builders usually came from the region, because committees were looking for not just a good price but some proof of skill before they would contract with a builder, and that required a firsthand familiarity with his workmanship. The country builders who worked on most of these churches had no specific training in church building, and the vast majority of their work went into undocumented domestic buildings. Many, probably most, workmen who were hired were not members of the church, or even the society for which they were building. Workmen did also travel from job to job, and particularly on the larger projects, such as the brick churches in Hartford, many would have been nonresidents or temporary residents of the city. Scholars are just beginning to identify the degree to which artisans in the building trades moved with peripatetic frequency across a broad region.[19]

Although a craftsman with standard on-the-job training might be adequate for a small wooden meetinghouse, a more ambitious project could call for a different sort of expertise. An unusual document left by the building committee of New Haven's First Church shows the trouble that congregation took to be certain that its new church would be of the best design and workmanship. After "much pains were taken to select a person whose architectural skill & experience, and whose fair character promised a faithful performance of his engagement," the committee selected Isaac Damon, on the basis of his reputation among "the most respectable gentlemen" and his recent work in Northampton, Massachusetts.[20] William Woolsey, a member of the building committee, went with Stephen Twining to Northampton to view Damon's work. Finding it "highly satisfactory," they prepared to enter into a contract with him. In February 1813 the committee contracted with Damon and his unknown associate Ithiel Town, and the assumption was that Town "was to be the assistant & not the principal" builder.[21] Much to the surprise and consternation of the committee, Damon never appeared in New Haven and Town, barely thirty years old, oversaw the entire construction. Once in New Haven, Town's skill, not to mention his proximity, earned him the contract for Trinity Church, to be built just southwest of the First Church site, and he worked on both buildings simultaneously.

United Church, on the north side of First Church, employed another well-known builder, David Hoadley of Waterbury. J. Frederick Kelly called Hoadley and Town "the only designers of early Connecticut Church edifices who are qualified to receive the title 'architect.' " Actually, in New Haven, both men based their Congregational churches on plans drawn by well-known architects elsewhere.[22] But in one sense Kelly was absolutely correct, and that is that Hoadley and Town had regional reputations and a finesse to their craft that were indicative of a shift toward professional training in architecture. Because these men had many visible commissions, and were marketing themselves as "architects," we know them. The many other builders and their workmen, whose hands did the majority of work on these buildings, tend to evade the light of historical inquiry.

As outlined in the 1748 law, progress reports on building and expenses, maintained by the society's clerk, went regularly to the society, the county court, or even the General Assembly. This not only kept builders and the building committee honest, but also, if the project was meeting with insurmountable difficulties, the court or General Assembly could step in with assistance, financial or otherwise. If all went according to plan and the congregation and committee were pleased with the outcome, the society officially accepted the building and extended thanks to the builder or builders. In reality, rare was the congregation that was able to follow the above steps, from making an initial decision to build to finally thanking the builder for a job well done, without mishap or idiosyncrasy. As the Salisbury and Hartford experiences will show, the appearance of a fashionable new church in town reflected perseverance, adaptability, and even patience, and depended on the interest and abilities of many persons.

Salisbury, 1798–1800

Citizens of the town of Salisbury, located in the very northwestern corner of Connecticut, met together at the end of the eighteenth century to discuss the condition of their 1751 meetinghouse.[23] Although not exactly a boomtown, there were some fortunes in Salisbury; its important iron foundry had been New England's largest supplier of cannon during the Revolutionary War.[24] With the war over, attention turned to the run-down building in the center of town. It was beginning to appear to the town that it was no longer enough to patch up the old meetinghouse, and that the wisest course of action might be to start again from the ground up. Salisbury had plenty of company in this predicament. Most of the Congregational churches standing in Litchfield County in the 1790s dated from the mid–eighteenth century, a time when a large influx of people settled and formed new towns. Of twenty-nine churches constructed in the county from 1800 to 1844 for which there is reasonable documentation, the majority replaced buildings that were over fifty and less than seventy years old.[25] It is clear that in Litchfield County very few mid-eighteenth-century ecclesiastical structures persisted beyond the middle of the nineteenth century. They were too small, too old, and unfashionable.

Looking at a century of changes in the Litchfield County landscape, one can see that two waves of building appeared: the first roughly in the middle of the eighteenth century, the second following the Revolutionary War, especially from 1810 to 1830. Because each of these waves followed a time of religious revival, it is tempting to conclude that renewed interest in religion led to greater church attendance and interest in church buildings. While this may in fact have been one cause of building, others are equally persuasive: the first wave coincided with regional growth, the latter with renewed fortunes following the economically stagnant and politically troubled time of the Revolution. For reasons both secular and spiritual, the town of Salisbury looked at its old meetinghouse and decided it was time to move on.

The 1790s had been a rocky decade for the congregation as it struggled to find, call, and keep a minister. In 1790 the town voted to call Fowler Miller, who apparently never came. A vote to call John Elliot carried the following year, but he also never appears as minister in the town records. James Glassbrook arrived to take the pulpit in 1792, but the town was dissatisfied with his service and voted to let him go just a year later. In 1795 the town called yet another minister, Timothy M. Cooley, who also appears to have stayed only briefly, if at all. Finally, a 1797 call resulted in the arrival of Joseph Warren Crossman, who stayed with the Salisbury congregation through the building of the new church. Crossman was a young preacher, by his own account encumbered by "youth and inexperience," yet he accepted the call within a month and was ordained in Salisbury.[26]

It was during this time of confusion over filling the pulpit that the town bandied about the question of whether or not to build a new meetinghouse. After being voted down in April of 1793 and again in October of 1794, the proposal finally met with majority approval in January of 1797, "after Considerable Discussion & mature deliberation."[27] It is perhaps significant that the long-hoped-for settlement of a minister and the decision to go ahead with the new building so nearly coincided after several years of uncertainty and indecision. One can speculate that the building of a new house of worship was an enticement to the young minister, or at least a reassuring sign that the citizens of Salisbury were committed to the state of religion in their town.

Hoping to build on or near the site of the 1751 house, the town sent Elisha "Sterly" [Sterling] to the Litchfield County Court to get approval, which he obtained.[28] A year later, little progress had been made, and the town voted again on the meetinghouse question, agreeing once more to "build a Meeting House in the Modern Stile."[29] An advisory committee of five men formed to determine the "Form and Dimentions of a Meeting House necessary & convenient for the inhabitants of this society" and to suggest "the probable expense thereof."[30] These men, Lot Norton, John Whittlesey, Esq., Colonel Nathaniel Buel, Samuel Lee, Esq., and Adonijah Strong, were, as might be expected, among the wealthier townspeople. In addition, all but Strong (the wealthiest man in town, according to the 1803 tax list) had experience in ecclesiastical affairs, serving on the pulpit committee, the ordination committee, or the committee to hire a singing master.[31] A combination of financial interest in the project and proven commitment to church business led the town to select these men to manage this important project.

Norton, Buel, and Whittlesey became the core of the building committee. The town entrusted them with the responsibility of raising money by subscription, an organized voluntary donation "towards Defraying the Expence of Building," money that the town agreed to take in two installments, one at the beginning of September in 1798 and the rest the following September.[32] An additional tax of twelve cents on the dollar augmented the building fund; the town made a point of noting that any person who subscribed at or above the amount of his tax was not obligated to pay the tax.

In January 1798 the town voted on "form and Dimentions" for the new building "necessary and convenient for the inhabitants of this Society."³³ The following month the committee of three received authorization to gather proposals from potential builders, and in April the town authorized the committee to contract with Captain Thomas Dutton, builder, of Watertown, a contract that it drew up the following November.³⁴ An earlier reference to a Thomas Dutton is found in the records of the town of Morris, in January of 1785, when its citizens voted that "Deacon Thomas Dutton be master workman of the Joyner work at the meeting house."³⁵ This was probably the same Dutton. He was without a doubt a builder of the Washington Congregational Church, about thirty miles south of Salisbury, begun in 1801 and finished in 1802.³⁶ Another Dutton, Daniel, also of Watertown, was being considered for joinery work on the Winchester meetinghouse in March of 1796, to finish off the inside of that building.³⁷

The contract between Thomas Dutton and the Salisbury building committee, signed November 21, 1798, is a formal, detailed expression of the responsibilities taken on by each party. (It is reproduced in the appendix). This contract, an unusual survival, illuminates the building process in a rural community. Although it is thorough in its own way, much of the details are missing—specifications of ornament, finish, interior configuration, and many other elements that we might relate to worship and the religious meanings of the building. Instead we have a sketchy plan that shows what was most important to builder and committee: dimensions, materials, and a schedule for building—all things related to convenience and expense.

Style was conveyed in one phrase: "of the form of the meetinghouse lately erected in Richmond in Berkshire County [Massachusetts]."³⁸ It seems likely that the committee was referring to a Richmond church modeled after one designed by Charles Bulfinch for Pittsfield (1789–93) (fig. 3). Out of that approximation Dutton was to pull the specific design and construction solutions that would make his building a reasonable copy; the building committee counted on his talent and ingenuity. As was common, the contract specified dimensions and materials, two important elements of the quality and cost of the building. The committee instructed Dutton to build a wooden structure "Sixty four feet in Length & forty Eight feet in width." In keeping with the Richmond church, Salisbury's building was to have "a projection of eight feet for the Porch & twenty Six feet at the base" with "a tower sixteen feet square & cupola" above. The length of the posts, which would determine the height of the building, was to be twenty-six feet.

The builders of the Salisbury church used their well-practiced methods of timber framing. Framed buildings earned their name by the employ-

3. "Winter View of Pittsfield, Mass.," earthenware platter, James Clews, Cobridge, Staffordshire, England, c. 1819–36. Courtesy, Winterthur Museum, 1958.1844.

Charles Bulfinch's Pittsfield church (1789–93) was a prototype for the regional style (see fig. 26). Here it appears on English export ceramics, the image derived from an unknown print source. To the left and rear is the Baptist Church of 1827. The large building to the left is the Berkshire Hotel, 1826.

ment of a heavy, joined skeleton, or frame, that provided the strength and stability of the entire structure (fig. 4). This frame sat on a masonry, usually stone, foundation, carefully prepared in advance to ensure that the wooden timbers would not be exposed to the damp, corrosive soil. Most of these Connecticut buildings did not have cellars, and the walls of the foundation consequently were not very deep. Below ground level, rough fieldstones were generally laid on top of each other without mortar, just as farmers laid New England's common stone walls. Above ground level, the part of the foundation known as the "underpining," more attention was paid to the visible wall. Here masons used quarried stones and laid them in an even, regular pattern.[39]

The builders prepared the heavy (generally eight-by-ten-inch mini-

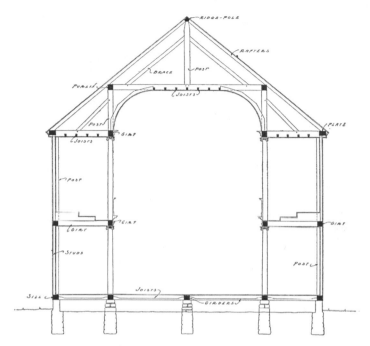

4. Framing section for church with central coved ceiling. From J. F. Kelly, *Early Connecticut Meetinghouses*, courtesy, Columbia University Press. Reprinted with the permission of the publisher.

The builders of Salisbury, South Canaan, and Washington churches used this type of frame structure.

mum) oak frame elements, such as the main vertical posts and horizontal beams, braces, girts, and roof framing elements on the ground before assembly. Because the whole was bound together by means of precise mortise and tenon joints and pinned with wooden pegs, extreme care in preparation of these timbers was crucial. First the wooden sills were assembled over the underpinning. The carpenter cut and partially assembled sections of the frame on the ground; then the frame and the rafters were drawn up together in the process known as "raising," which usually took place in the early summer.[40] As the frame was extraordinarily heavy, raising required additional labor at the site. Teams of extra men lifted the partially assembled sides of the building off the ground by means of long poles, and the carpenters then fastened them into place.

The process of raising brings to the fore one of the remarkable characteristics of building in this period: the combined efforts of community that it elicited. Obtaining and preparing materials, building the foundation, and raising the frame were all points in the construction where the

town and church members put not only money but some of themselves
into the new building. Reverend Thomas Robbins was much impressed
with the enthusiasm with which the members of his father's (Reverend
Ammi Robbins) Norfolk Congregational Society began laying a new
church foundation in 1813. "The people here are much engaged in building
their new meeting house," he wrote in his diary. "They are doing a great
deal of voluntary labor in preparing the ground. The old house is taken
down . . . the people are blasting many rocks on the green. I think it will
be much improved."[41] In New Haven in 1814, members of the United
Society volunteered their time toward preparing the ground for their
brick church. Charles Denison wrote to Senator David Daggett in January
to inform him of the progress. "As I know you to be most interested in
the affairs of our church," Denison told the senator, who was in Washington at the time, "I must inform you that a large quantity of Stone . . .
of the first quality are already delivered at the site of the new building.
[illegible] and Stephen Atwater & Levi Hubbard & Smith & I have laid
out the ground—If you had been at home, we should have made you
one of the party, being of the same sort."[42] Just before the raising of the
frame of its new church in June of 1828, the Litchfield Congregational
Society advertised in the local paper, "we are requested to mention that
the raising of the frame for the New House of Worship, will take place
on Thursday, 26th inst. and it is hoped there will be no want of expert
and able men on the occasion, that the business may go on safely and
expeditiously." This request went to all townspeople, but a special call
went out to "Members of the Society," who were "requested by the building committee to be present at eight o'clock in the morning."[43] The Morris Congregational Society in 1785 authorized its building committee to
"pick or choose the men that are proper and necessary to raise the meetinghouse."[44]

Hands-on involvement with the building process also shows in the
knowledge with which building committees discussed and regulated the
exact materials to be used. The most important element of a framed building was the wood, and the committee took great care in setting out types,
amounts, and cost. Builders, building committees, and townspeople had
a thorough (and to us, perhaps, remarkable) knowledge of both this type
of construction and the properties of wood, and discussed these matters
using specific terminology. In public meetings, some small towns even
considered the exact materials to be used and summarily voted on each
kind of lumber and its value. The Winchester Congregational Society in
1785, for example, voted "good pine shingles delivered at the place . . . 18/
p." and "thick stuff for sashes" at "£3:0:00/Thous." in a long list of enumerated items.[45]

More commonly the committee and the builder negotiated for the lumber, as set out in the Salisbury contract. The building committee delineated all the wood necessary, describing the amount, quality, and cost of timbers to be used for various elements: rafters, clapboards, shingles, and braces. Sills and sleepers, timbers resting on the foundation and providing the base of the first floor, could be left unfinished on some sides. The vertical posts, on the other hand, needed to be squared to receive the exterior boards and/or clapboards and the interior lath and plaster. The Salisbury committee specified that timbers used for the frame were to be "rough hewed except the sleepers which are to be hewed on one side." Wooden elements such as clapboards and floorboards came mill-sawn to the site; other larger timbers were "dressed," or finished, on site. The major frame elements were almost invariably oak; smaller lumber was pine, and the lath was to be of hemlock or chestnut. The properties of the varieties of wood were well known: oak was strong and durable, pine was light and cheap. The committee preferred high-quality materials, "white or yellow pine of the best quality," and "clear stuff" (no knots). The committee and possibly the town's "inspector of wood" kept an eye on the cost and quality of wood delivered to the site.

In October, even before the Salisbury contract was officially signed, the town and building committee began assuming their parts of the bargain. Most important, the town's obligation was to make sure that not just the wood but all materials be provided "in Suitable times & season" so that "Thomas Dutton or his workmen . . . shall not be put to any trouble Hindrance or delay in prosecuting the building of said house." The town invited inhabitants to provide building materials (wood, nails, lime for plaster) in lieu of taxes or cash payments on subscriptions, the cash value of such materials to be determined by two members of the building committee. Samuel Lee, member of the original five-person committee, took on the task of gathering the wood together after February of 1798, and the town requested that "a sufficient quantity [of lumber] for the Frame of sd. Meeting House Porch Tower & cupola" be on the site by May 1799 to ensure that the workmen had their materials in time to build during the warm weather.[46]

The town accepted responsibility for creating, literally, the foundation of the project. The contract specified, "At the towns Expense a good & sufficient foundation or underpining under the Sills of sd. House" be constructed "with sufficient Pillars or Supports under the Body of the House." At the October 1798 meeting, the town directed the committee "to procure material for the underpining . . . to lay the cells [sills] of said House—to be completed by the tenth day of June next." Dutton agreed to find the workmen necessary to finish the building; in turn the town agreed that "Thomas Dutton & his hands such as Carpenters Joiners & the whole of his workmen shall be boarded or found with diet Washing &c. at the Price of one dollar per week for each Man during the time that he or they shall be employed upon the Building sd. House." For the labor-intensive raising, the town would find "at the expnse [*sic*] of sd. Town of Salisbury a sufficient Number of suitable hands to assist."[47]

The contractual arrangement allowed Dutton and his crew to concentrate on doing the job of building without being bothered with the procurement of materials. Dutton, acting as master builder, headed his crew and probably subcontracted for some of the specialized labor such as masonry and glazing. He and his workmen were responsible for dressing timber, framing the building "sufficiently strong for such an House," and providing the ropes and tackle that would assist the raising. The contract directed Dutton to board the outside of the studs before clapboarding, and to plane (smooth) and lay the floorboards "in good and workmanlike manner." Dutton was to purchase glass and glaze the windows (or hire a glazier), lath and plaster the inside, find oil and paints and "Compleatly to finish said Meeting House from the sills and upwards finding all Necessary hangings and Trimmings for Doors Pews & with a Decent vane & Ball on the Top of the Cupola and a Conductor for Lightning." Only the bell and frame were left to the responsibility of the town.

In signing the building agreement, Dutton promised to finish the new building "after the Model and with as good workmanship as the Meeting House in Richmond lately Built is Done" by July 1, 1800. Construction must not have been much underway by the spring of 1799, when the town debated how far to raise the foundation above the surface of the ground, but the foundation most likely was ready by June, on schedule, for the builders had accomplished the raising and covering of the frame by the end of the summer. By December the town was discussing putting in stones for the front steps and painting the inside of the pews and seats; the building was shortly thereafter ready for occupation.[48]

The exterior of the Salisbury church has changed very little over time, so it is possible to compare the building as it exists to contract specifications. Its dimensions, sixty-four by forty-eight feet, with a shallow portico and square tower, are precisely as in the contract. The foundation built by the town includes three ashlar courses of marble above ground level, roughly finished. Although the contract specified that boards be nailed to the studs under the clapboards, apparently the builders omitted such a step to save time and expense, for they nailed the clapboards directly on the studs. The details—some large, such as the Palladian or "Venetian" window over the front entrance, others more subtle, such as the detailing of the cornice molding—Dutton either borrowed from the

5. Interior, Congregational Church, Salisbury, c. 1948. From J. F. Kelly, *Early Connecticut Meetinghouses*, courtesy, Columbia University Press. Reprinted with the permission of the publisher.

The gallery railings and columns are from a later renovation (c. 1845); originally the ceiling was raised in the center with a cove on each side, and the gallery columns ran up to the ceiling. The pulpit recess and large columns with heavy entablature are also not original.

Richmond example or took out of his own builder's vocabulary. The interior of the building has been altered significantly, and it is difficult to determine the original design features, pulpit, or pew arrangement (figs. 5 and 6). A second tier of gallery columns (extending from the galleries to the ceiling), for example, no longer exists. The church originally was fitted with box pews, replaced later with bench pews or "slips."[49]

The original ceiling was about six feet higher in the space between the galleries than the space directly above them, and the jump to this higher level was smoothed by quarter-round coves on the sides, giving the central space an arched, rounded feel.[50] Several other congregations indicated the desire to have an "arched" ceiling. In 1794 the Roxbury Congregational Church voted "to Arch the Meetinghouse & support the arch by pillars," but then voted again a month later to "reconsider the vote for Arching the meetinghouse."[51] Christ Church in Watertown similarly voted in 1792

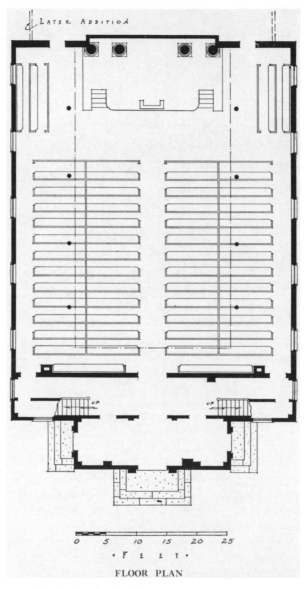

LATER ADDITION

FLOOR PLAN

6. Plan, Congregational Church, Salisbury, c. 1948. From J. F. Kelly, *Early Connecticut Meetinghouses*, courtesy, Columbia University Press. Reprinted with the permission of the publisher.

This shows a modern seating arrangement and a later extension beyond the pulpit.

that it would build "with an Arch over head in said House."[52] These sources suggest that arching the roof was a newly plausible idea, and that people approached it with both deliberate enthusiasm and some reservation, reflecting the extra work and expense involved.

The structure of Salisbury's original coved ceiling was probably similar to what Roxbury and Watertown had in mind and was a preliminary solution to the desire for an "arch'd" ceiling (fig. 4). The roof of the Salisbury church was supported in part by the upper tier of gallery pillars that continued to the rafters. The ceiling over the side galleries thus had to remain flat, but by raising a central tie beam between those gallery posts, the ceiling between the galleries and the raised, flat central roof could be plastered into a gentle curve, giving the whole a sense of reaching upward.

Technical advances of the early nineteenth century enabled later builders to span the entire width of a church with a dramatic, graceful ceiling hovering like a canopy over the whole sanctuary. David Hoadley and Ithiel Town, builders of New Haven's churches on the green, had engineering knowledge that moved them beyond makeshift solutions and enabled them to omit the intermediate posts without fearing that the roof would collapse. Town, who had worked on bridge design with Isaac Damon, developed and even patented a lightweight roof truss. He and Hoadley both used a divided tie beam that crossed at a central point, allowing the curve in the ceiling to begin at the outer wall. That central joint had to be strong enough to maintain the now-divided tie beam's tensile strength, thereby keeping the rafters from pushing the walls outward; the builders solved the problem by using an "X" or scissor truss, whereby the ends of the beams were lapped and joined to secondary posts (fig. 7). Town's trusses for Center Church in New Haven supported a ceiling that spanned a dramatic seventy-two feet.[53]

It is possible to recover a sense of the original interior of the 1800 Salisbury church by looking at the Washington Congregational Church built by Dutton (fig. 8) and also at another remarkably similar church built about the same time in South Canaan (figs. 9 and 10). No builder's name exists in the records for the South Canaan Congregational Society, but given the time of building (1802–4), the proximity of South Canaan to Salisbury (just a few miles), and extreme similarities in plan and detail, it may be assumed that Dutton at least influenced the building of this third church. All three have a large square tower, an identical main cornice, wooden quoins on all exterior angles, and a projecting entrance bay with an unusual arrangement of one large central door and a smaller door on each of its sides. The decorative woodwork on these doors is very similar in all three cases. The South Canaan and Salisbury churches have

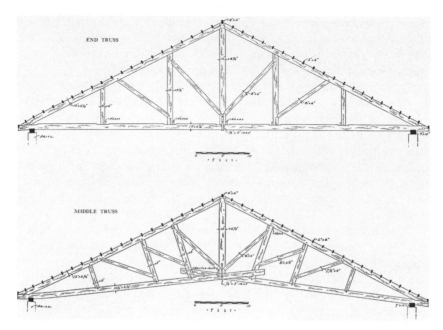

7. End and "scissor" truss, First Congregational Church, New Haven, Conn. From J. F. Kelly, *Early Connecticut Meetinghouses*, courtesy, Columbia University Press. Reprinted with the permission of the publisher.

The end truss (*top*) is of the typical "king post" type with a continuous bottom tie. To allow for the wide domed ceiling, the builders used a "scissors" truss (*bottom*) with two crossed beams joined and raised at the center.

elegant Palladian windows on the entrance bay and tower; in Washington the front bay has such a window while the tower has a circular clock face.

The Washington church has had some interior renovations over time, but the South Canaan interior is surprisingly intact (fig. 10). Both churches still have their original second tier of columns in the galleries. In the South Canaan church, these square, fluted columns are actually a continuation of the lower columns through the gallery floor. This may have been the case originally in the other two buildings, but the upper tier is now missing in the Salisbury church, and the lower tier has been replaced in the Washington church. The original upper tier of columns in the Washington church consists of graceful round fluted columns with elegantly carved Ionic capitals. While the Salisbury ceiling has been flattened, the South Canaan and Washington buildings still display the raised central ceiling between the galleries, eased into by a quarter-round vault on each side. The effect, while less open, is more interestingly modulated than that of the current interior of the Salisbury church.

8. Congregational Church, Washington, Conn., 1801–2. From J. F. Kelly, *Early Connecticut Meetinghouses*, courtesy, Columbia University Press. Reprinted with the permission of the publisher.

The front porch is an 1885 addition, and the steeple was rebuilt from the tower deck upward.

9. Congregational Church, South Canaan, Conn., 1802–4. Library of Congress, HABS collection.

AUDIENCE ROOM

10. Interior, South Canaan Congregational Church, 1948. From J. F. Kelly, *Early Connecticut Meetinghouses*, courtesy, Columbia University Press. Reprinted with the permission of the publisher.

This interior has changed very little from the original. Note the central coved ceiling and the floor-to-ceiling gallery columns with square paneling below and fluting above. The Palladian pulpit window is original; the slips are a later replacement. The original interior of the Salisbury church probably appeared much like this one.

In January of 1800, the town of Salisbury expressed its gratitude to the building committee, voting that the "Thanks of the Town of Salisbury be return'd to Lot Norton and John Whittlesey Esqrs. and Col. Nathaniel Buel for their faithful and liberal Services rendered."[54] The timber committee received a hearty thanks as well. The town decided at the same January meeting that it would not "take any Measures for Dedicating the Meeting-House antecedent to the finishing sd. House," so no dedication service was held until June of 1800. Although no mention of the dedication is found in the town, church, or society records, Reverend Thomas Robbins recorded on June 12, "My brother went to Salisbury, to the dedication of a new meeting-house, which is supposed to be the best in the state."[55] Apparently not having seen the finished building yet, Robbins himself reserved judgment.

The committee's final inspection of the building came just before the dedication, when it carefully looked over the finished church to determine "whether sd. House be completed according to Contract."[56] The building met with the committee's satisfaction, and Dutton was rewarded with complete payment. The town had contracted with Dutton for a total cost of $3,766.67, although, as was customary, it subtracted from that amount the cost of all the lumber and other materials that the town had provided. Dutton took his payment in four installments that allowed the town time to collect taxes and subscriptions and also to maintain some leverage. The town paid him $475 on January 1, 1799, then $410 in July of that year, and, on November 15, the rest of expenses and labor costs incurred by Dutton to that day. This was to enable Dutton to keep up with his accounts and pay his workmen. The remainder of his bill, "Deducting for timber Boards Plank Shingles Lime & other materials," Dutton could claim "at the foregoing stipulated prices" either on July 1, 1800, or "when the work is compleated," which, as it happened, was in May.

Hartford, 1804–1808

Hartford, like many New England towns, was coming out of a long period of relatively little public building in the 1790s. With just under six thousand inhabitants in 1807, the city was small by the standards of the early republic's larger urban areas. Yet in its own terms, Hartford was booming, and in the next thirty years the population doubled in size (fig. 11).[57] Its site on the west bank of the Connecticut River made it ideal for shipping and communication, and Hartford's citizens felt their city's increasing regional importance as a center for commerce and government. A new State House designed by Charles Bulfinch and finished in 1796 set the standard for three decades of building that would leave Hartford with one of the most impressive collections of city architecture in the state. In 1807 the First Congregational Society of Hartford dedicated its new building, the earliest nineteenth-century "modern" brick church in Connecticut (fig. 2).

As the continuation of the original congregation of Richard Hooker, founder of the Connecticut Colony, the society carried the weight of history and tradition. The ratification of the United States Constitution in Connecticut took place in its old meetinghouse in 1788, and many of its present and past members were economically and politically powerful citizens. Given its history, preeminence, and recent growth, it is no surprise that the First Society chose this time to build a substantial new house of worship, especially since its former house was no longer worth repairing.

11. *Hartford in 1824*, anonymous, oil on canvas. Courtesy, The Connecticut Historical Society, Hartford, Connecticut, x.1870.1.0.

This painting shows Hartford from the west, before the building boom of the later 1820s. First Congregational Church of 1807 is a focal point, with the original Palladian pulpit window clearly visible.

The society had moved into its third building in 1737 and dedicated it in 1739. This house, fifty-six by forty-six feet, was nearly on the site of the present 1807 building, but turned with a long side to Main Street and a steeple at its north end. It was a typical eighteenth-century meetinghouse, with three entrances, a canopied pulpit on the long side facing the street entrance, and box pews. Lightning had damaged the building in 1767; it was worn and too small for the congregation by November of 1804, when the society assigned a preliminary committee of nine to consider a building project.[58]

Despite the society's claim to preeminence, by 1804 it was hardly the only religious option in town. The Second or South Society, formed in 1670, worshiped in its own decaying 1752 building. Episcopalians held services in the newest religious structure in town, a wooden 1791 church with Gothic detail. Friends and Baptists worshiped regularly, although not yet in their own buildings, and Methodists were in the vicinity. Nevertheless, the ranks of the First Society seemed to be growing. One reason was the tenure of a very popular and effective minister, Reverend Nathan Strong, a Connecticut native and Yale graduate (1769) who served the Hartford congregation from 1774, when he was just thirty years old, until his death in 1816. Reverend Strong earned a reputation as a revivalist, leading several awakenings in Hartford from 1798 to 1815.[59] As more people came to hear Reverend Strong, the assembly of worshipers grew.

Three months after the society's December 1804 vote to consider building a new church, at a meeting "specially warned & convened at the Court House in Hartford," the committee returned with the opinion that a new building was necessary.[60] This building, the committee suggested, should be of brick, rather than the wood of the older house. The roof should be slate, fireproof and durable. The dimensions should be 102 feet deep by 64 feet wide, 18 feet wider and nearly twice as long as the old house. As for style, it should be "simple and decent." The committee estimated that such a building would cost between eighteen and twenty thousand dollars, a sizable expense.[61] After a vote "by more than two thirds parts of the inhabitants of said society, who were present in said meeting" the society made plans to go ahead with the project. Preliminary investigations by the nine-person committee showed there was sufficient interest among society members to support such a task, although the committee acknowledged that the greatest amount of money must necessarily come from "the more opulent class of the Society." The committee believed that "the urgency and importance of the object in view" would convince society members to subscribe to the building fund or promise to buy pews in the new church. Finally, the society approved the appointment of five of its men to the building committee, known as the "contractors," who would oversee the project to the end. These contractors promised the society that they would manage both the construction and the fundraising, and agreed that the society itself should never be responsible for any building debt.[62]

George Goodwin, Aaron Cook, Richard Goodman, Peter W. Gallaudet, and James Hosmer made up the building committee. Cook, Goodman, and Goodwin were sixty-two, forty-four, and forty-eight, respectively, at the time, older and established in Hartford. Because the church membership records are incomplete, it is difficult to know the exact relationship of these men to the worshiping congregation, but they were clearly involved with the business of the society and were not members of any other. There is no definite evidence, however, that any of these men were church members prior to the building, although the wives of Hosmer and Gallaudet joined the church before 1807, and Richard Goodman himself joined in 1822, at age sixty-one. These five men also led the roster for an 1807 building subscription, giving between $130 (an average donation) and $450 (George Goodwin's sizable donation). Although they expected to be paid for their services, there was much more to their involvement. All of them purchased at least a portion of a pew or slip in the new building.[63] These men acted as trustees of the congregation, taking responsibility not only for the work at hand but for its financial success.

Once the First Society's building committee set to work, it negotiated with the city to secure a slightly more convenient lot and petitioned the county court to fix the place. The First Society wished to build on or near its then current site, a fine location on Main Street near the new State House and in the center of the city. Its plan, however, necessitated a different sort of lot, as its new house would have its short side to the street, extending one hundred feet to the back. This presented some problems, as did the fact that access to the burying ground was through the land requested by the society. The city and the society resolved the situation quite easily at a town meeting in August of 1805.[64] Hartford agreed to give the society a plot roughly 65 feet wide and 131 feet deep in exchange for a portion of the society's old lot and a right-of-way to the burying ground.

Densely populated cities had problems determining building sites quite different from the problems faced by a rural parish. There, the picture was complicated by competition between denominations and the possibility that a proposed new building would require the obliteration of something old. Hartford was spared this sort of contention. New Haven, however, with its powerful Congregational heritage (perhaps the least ecumenically minded place in western Connecticut), had its share of conflict. In 1820, the city voted to allow the small and struggling group of Methodists "to Erect a meeting house to be built of Brick or Stone and to be placed on the north westerly corner of the public green."[65] The Congregationalists in town, recalled Harry Croswell, rector of Trinity Church, were "violently opposed" to the idea of Methodists "erecting this house in so public a place."[66] The Methodists doggedly pursued their object, however, even refusing a last-ditch offer of $1,200 from the Congregationalists as incentive "to select a more retired spot."[67]

Another New Haven site conflict occurred when the First Congregational Society planned to build a larger building in 1812, a portion of it directly over the old burying ground. The members of the society's building committee considered it "indispensable . . . to extend the proposed house upon a portion of the burying ground."[68] So as not to disturb physical remains, they suggested that trenches for the foundation be no deeper than three feet. As a memorial to the removed stones, they generously proposed erecting, at no cost to "survivors," a monument on the west side of the new building.[69] Some of these "survivors" were understandably disturbed with the society's brash plans and contested the supposed "indispensability" of building over their ancestors' bones. Despite an outcry of protesters claiming to be motivated by a sense of duty and respect for the precise resting place of their ancestors, the builders went ahead with their plans. To accommodate the graveyard, the builders constructed a crypt under the building, extremely out of the ordinary for New England ecclesiastical structures. Some of the graves were thereby undisturbed. In Hartford, the proposal was to work around the boundaries of the burying ground, and there was no such debate.

On Tuesday December 10, 1805, after a formal leave-taking by the congregation, Hartford First Society's 1739 meetinghouse was demolished. Some of the former building literally became part of the new in the form of salvaged stone and brick. Society member John Leffingwell purchased the old building for $305, but the society retained the rights to the bell, clock, and all the old brick and stone as well as some of the lumber for use in its new building. Leffingwell had essentially paid for salvageable lumber, not surprising since he himself was a builder. This conservative use of land and old church property was typical; durable materials and the accoutrements of worship, such as pews, were often removed to a new building.

The building process of Hartford's First Society is unusually well documented. A thorough record left by the treasurer of the building committee, Peter W. Gallaudet, in his account book from March of 1806 through December of 1808, allows us tremendous insight into the project.[70] First, the account includes a significant amount of information about the builders, their skills, and their relationship to the ecclesiastical society. Second, many of the entries refer to purchases of materials, and we get an idea of the amount and variety of raw material required to make a brick meetinghouse. Third, some sense can be made of the scattered dates of payment in order to determine a few things about the building schedule and the routine of the workmen.

From Gallaudet's account book, it appears that there was no master builder who took charge of the whole affair, as Thomas Dutton did in Salisbury. The aforementioned John Leffingwell, society member and master builder of the nearby 1799 State House, would have been a logical choice, but he appears to have had little to do with the building. Instead several master workmen were involved in the project. The man who appears most consistently in the records, leading crews of as many as ten men, was forty-three-year-old David Wadsworth, the master carpenter who worked on the framing and finishing of the building and who probably acted as supervisor of the building project. Although there is no indication that Wadsworth was a *church* member, he did take as payment seven pews in the new church, and the death of his infant child was noted in the records of the First Society in 1798, which indicates he at least was part of the society.[71]

The master mason, an important workman for a brick structure, was James Lathrop, a society member who joined the church after the revival in 1808. Daniel Danforth, a glazier, contracted with the church "to set the glass for the windows of the new meetinghouse at nine cents pr. light the glass to be bedded in putty & fastened in with tin, the sashes to have two coats of white lead paint—& to be finished in time for the building, the paint & putty I am to find & engage to have them well done."[72] Danforth later joined the church in the middle of another revival, in February of 1814. Peter Thatcher and Solomon Taylor, two joiners who led crews of workmen, were both church members prior to 1807. All these men purchased pews or portions of pews in the new meetinghouse.[73]

That a good share of the most important workmen had a relationship to the society suggests that the society preferred its own. One advantage to hiring its members either to work on the building or to furnish supplies was that the society could negotiate pew space in lieu of a cash payment. Glazier Danforth contracted to do the windows for two hundred dollars, agreeing "to take the balance" of his payment "in a slip or part thereof," which translated to half ownership of the slip he shared with Edward Danforth (possibly a brother), number thirty-three, on the main floor near the pulpit, worth $240.[74] Alfred Bliss, who joined the church in August of 1808, negotiated with the committee for "Plastering one Half the Meeting house." Bliss applied his payment of two hundred dollars toward the purchase of slip number thirty-eight.[75] Member and Deacon Aaron Colton was paid for making mortar boxes, "turning six Newels," "setting 204 squares of Glass in the Venetian window," inspecting boards, and for "6¼ days work staining & varnishing Pulpit & Stairs."[76] Deacon Colton purchased half of pew number ninety-three, for 30 years at a cost of $58.00.[77] Lemuel Swift, head of a crew of painters, may have had no relationship to the society, but "Lemuel Swift & Co.," received a gallery pew as a portion of its payment.[78] The majority of the workmen, however, have no documented connection to the congregation. They appear in the records of neither pew sales nor church membership, although that does not rule out the possibility that they were members of the society.

A total of fifty-seven men and two "boys" appear on the work records over the course of the project. These names include the heads of the various crews, such as Lathrop, Wadsworth, and Swift. They also include journeymen, such as the joiner James Anderson. Occasionally additional artisans contracted for a small piece of the work, such as Abel Buel, who earned forty dollars for "making the Large Capitals," probably the four carved capitals on the porch columns.[79] Many other workmen, however, were never distinguished by name. In the daily ledger of workdays, under the name of one of the leading artisans, for example David Wadsworth, a number such as "5½" indicates the total workdays he and his crew put in that day. The names of those in his crew are not generally noted, although we do know that David Wadsworth's son David, Jr., often worked for him. The fifty-seven names on the list, therefore, represent only a portion of the craftsmen actually at work on the building over two and a half years.

Among the workmen who appear sporadically, as if taken on as extra hands, is one Gallaudet designates only as "Timothy." Timothy probably was an African-American, and possibly free, although Richard Goodman was paid for some of Timothy's labor.[80] Gallaudet paid Timothy three shillings for a day of work, whereas David Wadsworth earned eight, and most of the laborers seven or seven and one-half shillings, depending on their skill.[81] Other African-Americans appear on the record. Some are discernible by their names: Wolf and Herod, for example. Another entry indicates that "a black man" was paid twenty-five cents "for assisting carrying window frames." And three dollars went to "four days work two black women."[82] Despite their contribution to the church, these African-Americans would not have been permitted to purchase seats; they may have attended worship.

The building committee paid day laborers or journeymen who were not working under other contract arrangement at the end of the week, on Saturday, for the number of days and portions thereof worked. Several of the workmen had individual accounts; most had their pay handled by team leaders like David Wadsworth. These men worked six days a week, and took a half day or a day off for the Fourth of July, the most consistently observed holiday. Those who worked under contract chose a payment schedule that worked for their needs. Sometimes payment was structured around the society's assets and ability to pay. Robert and David Collins, for example, who worked for the masons, put up rafters, and performed other carpentry tasks, agreed to "receive ¼ of their pay weekly and the balance when the Pews and Slips are sold," that is, when the building committee had more cash.[83] As was the custom, the society supplemented the workmen's pay with alcoholic beverages.

First Society's committee began gathering materials at the site during the winter of 1805–6, before the work on the foundation began. Foundation stone (red sandstone) was cut in the Rocky Hill quarries, several miles south of Hartford. A contract with Richard and Freeman Seymour specified that sufficient stone for "one side and one end wall of the foundation" be delivered in "large part" in the winter and the rest by the first of May. William Andres, also of Rocky Hill, supplied the other half of the foundation stone.[84] Brick kilns in the town of Windsor, north of Hartford, supplied the thousands of bricks necessary for the building. Thaddeus Barber and Samuel Lemon provided the majority, agreeing in January to provide 130,000 of them specified as "good lighter color red."[85] The committee asked Barber, Lemon, and six other suppliers to bring several hundred thousand more bricks to the building site that winter, purchased at an average of five dollars per thousand. It is not clear in the account book how many of these actually made it into the church walls, but we do know how many were ordered — over 313,000 by June for $1,515 and another shipment worth $753 to be delivered by late October.[86]

The other material that began to cover the ground was wood: chestnut, white, yellow, and black oak timbers, white and yellow pine boards. Although the walls were brick, the roof structure and interior woodwork were of course of wood, as was the scaffolding that enabled the masons to build the brick walls to their full height. Just as in Salisbury, wood was sometimes marked for a purpose: strong and durable oak for the joists of three floors, lighter chestnut and pine for floorboards, and wood for scaffold poles. The timber, the committee specified, was all "to be cut this winter" and at the site by late spring, giving it a chance to season. The cost of the wood varied according to type and cut, and no one person supplied a majority of the wood, although it came from local Hartford suppliers, including some society members such as Richard Goodman. David Wadsworth himself provided over four hundred feet of "plank" at one time. Other major suppliers included Samuel Brooks, Jr., and Thomas Bliss, who sold the committee floor joists and rafters at lengths and thicknesses specified. Additional building supplies included sand, lime, and hair for plaster; slate; and lime and sand for mortar. Dr. Isaac Bull, church member, provided white lead and "spirits" for painting. As mentioned above, some materials came from the old meetinghouse. The inmates of Newgate Prison, located about fifteen miles north of Hartford, were the source of casks of nails.[87]

The records make clear that supplies arrived constantly, even after the project was well under way, and members of the building committee or outside experts carefully selected and approved all materials. Hartford carpenter Robert Collins, Jr., whom the committee engaged for both supplying wood and laying the floors, judged that "the plank now piled is thought sufficient" and agreed "to get out the plank and lay the floors . . . in a good and sufficient workmanlike manner."[88]

The Hartford builders may have offered an array of used tools and both old and unused materials for sale as the building neared completion. After the 1815 dedication of New Haven's Center, or First, Church, the builder Ithiel Town advertised in the *Connecticut Journal* that he was selling a large quantity of unused or refuse materials, as well as good tools. "FOR SALE," the advertisement began,

The Lime-house and Work Shop used in building the new brick Church.—Also 2 or 3 sets of old step-stones, with two large top steps; a quantity of refuse and other Lumber; 30,000 of poor shingles, suitable for barns and sheds; 40 or 50 tons of pine Timber of various sizes and lengths, much of it clear and suitable for gutters and cornices; a quantity of pine and hemlock scantling and Plank of various sizes, clear and merchantable; a small Cable nearly new, and other small Cordage; a small pleasure boat with sails, &c; 200 feet of Connecticut river flagging and curb Stone; 600 lights of old sashes; a quantity of Lamp black and yellow Ocher; a large number of Carpenter's and Joiners tools, comprising almost all kinds used by workmen, and a great variety of moulding, cornice, and sash Planes, mostly English made and in the most approved style—Also, some Glass in half sheets. Inquire of JONATHAN LIVERMORE at the workshop near the new stone Church or of ITHIEL TOWN.[89]

Everything but the pleasure boat plainly relates to the construction of the brick church, and some of it, such as the "600 lights of old sashes," probably came from the New Haven society's previous building. The advertisement illustrates the practice of setting up a workshop at the site. Months later, Town was still advertising many of the same items for sale, with the addition of "500 Albany floor plank . . . 300 second quality floor plank . . . Pine logs, suitable for columns, vases, caps, and other turned work . . . 2 or 3 good ladders." The terms of sale would be "on approved credits of 3 or 4 months, if wished, and at the lowest market prices. . . ." In September, Town was still trying to get the materials removed from the site. His advertisement concluded, "The above lumber is all well seasoned and of a good quality, most of it lays on the Public Square about the new Stone Church (Trinity, where Town was currently employed, next door to the First Church site), and must all be removed from there within ninety days." Because of the urgency, "it will be sold at a price so reduced, as to make it an object to those who wish to purchase."[90]

Work began on the Hartford church, according to Gallaudet's accounts, with "the stone work for the foundation of the new Meeting House" on Thursday March 6, 1806.[91] On the Monday and Tuesday before construction began, four men worked half days, preparing the site. For three and a half weeks in March and two weeks in April, the account records the names of sixteen paid laborers, an average of five of them working per day. Several of these men do not appear on the lists after this initial period of construction, suggesting that they were masons involved in the foundation work and the construction of the cellar. The account of the master mason, James Lathrop, began that month. Lathrop was paid for "cleaning brick," "laying 755½ perch of stone, being the whole of the foundation & pillars," and for "laying underpining stone hewn stone in front &c., laying brick and stone gutters, and the foundation for the steps. He also participated in the "raising," and was the primary contractor for "slating Roof & finishing the same." Lathrop's bills totaled $2,686.25 for work done by December of 1807, the time of the dedication.[92]

Throughout construction, the record of how many men worked each day gives a good sense of the time and labor needed for each phase of the building. There is a gap in Gallaudet's account of labor from April of 1806 through July of 1807, although we know from a separate entry that David Wadsworth and three others, including his son, worked from April to December of 1807. Building in brick was a procedure different from that of timber framing. The building gradually rose up from the ground, the carpenters working along with the masons, constructing scaffolding and laying floor joists.[93] As early as July 1806, the society was purchasing scaffold poles.[94] Once the masons laid the walls to their full height, carpenters worked on framing the roof, enclosing the structure as soon as possible to protect the inside. Carpenters waited to lay the permanent floors until the roof was on. In his contract of August 4, 1806, Robert J. Collins, Jr., agreed to level the top surface of the joists and lay the floors, putting "the best & narrowest Plank . . . in the Isles." This he could not do, however, until "the building is under cover & ready for the flooring."[95]

The greatest concentration of effort happened in the summer of 1807, after the masons had finished the walls, the roof was on, and the floors were in place. At this time Wadsworth's crew, five other teams, and two individuals were at work on architectural details such as the portico and inside finish work. During July, an average of eighteen workmen worked daily. In August, the average number jumped to twenty-three; the most paid laborers ever at the site were the twenty-eight men at work one day in July. From September through November the teams worked steadily.[96] Some indications of particular tasks appear in Gallaudet's account, such as "[Solomon] Taylor at widows" in July. In August, Taylor was at work "raising venetian window" (the original pulpit window; see fig. 11). In June Abel Buel was paid for making the "four large Capitals." Buel also molded and cast plaster capitals for the columns supporting the galleries (eighteen pairs) and four small ones for the pulpit columns. Painter Lemuel Swift labored intermittently by himself or with another painter from time to time between June and December of 1807. James Lathrop at this time was busy "boiling plaster [of] Paris . . . for Plastering one half the meeting house." By September "he [was] still to finish the Plastering agreeable to contract." The other half of the plastering was completed by Alfred Bliss, paid September 30 for work that also included "laying stone in front of the building for the portico."[97]

Just before the Thursday December 3 dedication, the pace of work picked up. At least twenty men were at work two days before the dedication, and twenty-one the next. An unusually large group of five painters worked on December 2. Society records state, "The New Brick Meeting House in this Society was solemnly dedicated Dec. 3, 1807—The customary religious services being performed." Reverend Thomas Robbins, whose brother had attended the dedication of the Salisbury church, came himself to witness the event in Hartford. "One of the most solemn and affected scenes I have ever witnessed," he wrote in his diary, "a very great collection of people."[98] The large crowd gathered to dedicate the house no doubt breathed the aroma of fresh paint.

After the dedication, the number of workmen declined dramatically to just David Wadsworth, his team of five men, and an independent workman, Frederick Lathrop. Wadsworth and his team worked steadily until the following October, when the job seems to have finally reached completion. The workmen took no holiday for Christmas, but did have a three-day break during the election of May 1808, when the church would have been used for services. Gallaudet paid Ashbel Keeny for "4 days work on steeple July 1808," indicating that the steeple was completed after the dedication. Swift also worked from early September 1808 through the end of October, finishing the painting.[99]

The church of the First Society, 102 by 64 feet as the society originally agreed, is located at the present northwest corner of Gold Street and Main Street. It appears on the outside very much as it did in 1808, with the exception of a later pulpit recess (1851) on the west facade. James Lathrop's fine brickwork and much of the work of David Wadsworth and his carpenters have stood the test of time. There is a slight projection of the brick front wall under the portico, but the dramatic effect of the entrance comes from the projecting porch with its imposing triangular pediment and four smooth, round columns topped by Abel Buel's Ionic capitals (fig. 12). One can enter the building through the central door in this pediment or through one of two flanking side doors. The front facade, over the side doors, in the parapets, and in one of the lower steeple stages is decorated with unusual empty frames made of heavy wood moldings. The five-stage steeple is unique: Kelly calls it "an interesting but not altogether happy composition," rather awkward and overwrought.[100]

Inside, one enters into one of three separate vestibules, another idio-

12. Detail, First Congregational Church, Hartford. Photo by author.

13. Interior detail, First Congregational Church, Hartford. Photo by author.

The paneled gallery railings with carved egg and dart moldings and the large fluted gallery columns with their Ionic capitals are original. The seats, coffered gallery ceilings, interior window shutters, and gaslight fixtures are from a later renovation, c. 1852.

syncratic feature of the building. Stairs to the galleries lead from each of the side vestibules. The original side galleries and their round, fluted supporting columns remain; the galleries were slightly lowered in 1835 (fig. 13). The pulpit was lowered in 1816, again in 1835, and replaced entirely after 1852.[101] At midcentury long slips replaced some of the original pews, and the ceilings were brought to their present configuration: a barrel-vaulted central portion with coffered gallery ceilings. Originally, according to Kelly's close inspection of the roof trusses, the ceiling would have been very similar to that of the Salisbury, South Canaan, and Washington churches. While the Hartford church has both historical charm and beautiful aspects, evidence in both the construction techniques and the decorative details suggests that it is the work of men not accustomed to building such an edifice in this new style.

Both the Salisbury and the Hartford churches were ambitious projects that demanded the best work that artisans such as Dutton and Wadsworth had to offer. They were events that generated excitement in their communities as people shared in the creation of something new and watched with satisfaction as master workmen crafted something large and magnificent out of rough materials. In a process that followed a predictable pattern, towns or religious societies were able to get the job done, if fortune smiled, in a few years. The act of building allowed people of the community to share their talents and resources, becoming tangibly connected by and through this material statement of their community of belief. In its raw and practical essence, the building was something familiar and understood. The design, purpose, and expense of the building, however, inevitably set it apart. At the bottom of it all was money. It took fiscal optimism to initiate such an endeavor, and financial good fortune and ingenuity to see it through.

CHAPTER 2

Building Committees, Fund-Raising Schemes, and Churches as Capital

The privilege of taking a lease of a Pew at the rent aforesaid for five years, shall be sold to the highest bidder. . . .
—Trinity Episcopal Church, New Haven, "Plan for Disposing of the Pews," 1815

Ecclesiastical architecture is rarely studied from the perspective of cost, yet, as anyone who has ever been part of a church-building project knows, money is central to the endeavor. Connecticut's church builders of the early republic had to face this issue squarely because of two central facts of the period's religious life: the growth of competing denominations and the gradual decline of Congregational political power leading to formal disestablishment in 1818. Congregationalists could no longer count on the financial support of their communities. Fortunately, economic growth produced more available capital, and church building committees ingeniously pioneered new ways of capturing those resources for their purposes. This was especially important because buildings themselves were central to a congregation's financial stability.

After the Revolution, Connecticut displayed telltale signs of economic change: fast-paced business growth, diversification, capital development, and much new building. The economy of Connecticut, particularly in towns along major waterways, grew steadily throughout most of the early nineteenth century. Farmers producing a surplus tapped into a burgeoning export trade with the West Indies. Prosperous villages became commercial centers, providing jobs for a new class of merchants and professionals. Litchfield, a wealthy northwestern Connecticut town at the hub of no less than five turnpikes, served as a collection point for agricultural products then sent to New Haven, Connecticut's largest seaport, or Hartford, the center of the region's Connecticut River export trade. Until the Embargo Act of 1807 the region saw considerable prosperity. Embargo and war with Britain were devastating for many nonmanufacturing sectors of the economy, but in the end trade suffered only temporarily and rebounded considerably after the peace of 1815. Improved roads, turnpikes, canals, banks, and insurance companies made it easier for business to move forward. The population grew, notwithstanding significant migration west and north.[1]

The "market revolution"—this unprecedented growth of commerce, businesses, transportation networks, and banks—is at the center of questions about the restructuring of everyday life in the first half of the nineteenth century. Beginning as early as the mid–eighteenth century, the market undermined the barter system, broke down the semi-self-sufficient nature of rural life, built the fortunes of merchants, manufacturers, and professionals at the expense of a growing underclass, and spurred the creation of financial institutions that made possible the capital accumulation necessary to build roads and cityscapes. Moving in tandem with these economic changes were political and social forces that elevated freedom of choice and opportunity above conformity and tradition.[2] Religion, evangelicalism in particular, was a force that both molded and was molded by the market and its accompanying social change. Evangelicalism countered fears of the moral perils of economic frenzy at the same time it made Americans independent and bold enough to charge ahead with their capitalistic enterprises.[3]

The interaction of the market and religion is undeniable yet still puzzling and imprecise in the particular. Church-building projects offer a useful window that looks directly out over the confusing terrain where bankers, legislators, and businessmen drew on their many resources to bring their religious institutions toward solvency. In an altered economic and political environment, religious societies found themselves in a new position, freer yet more tenuous, with regard to both money and government. This prompted a reconfiguration of the economics and politics of congregational sustenance and growth. With ingenuity and adaptability, congregations survived by borrowing fund-raising techniques from the business sector.[4] Buildings, as advertisements and as capital, became crucial, central elements of a congregation's financial well-being in religion's open market. In the best of circumstances, a new building boosted the social and spiritual esteem of a society; in a worst-case scenario, an ill-fated building project was a financial sinkhole, a chaotic, never ending disaster.

Religious societies learned to think as competitive businesses. The more shrewdly a society planned its fund-raising and investing, the healthier its long-range prospects. Congregations began to recognize that buildings could be the keystone of their financial plans; buildings signaled the health of a society and attracted newcomers to worship. But they also served literally as financial capital. Under the system of pew rental that became standard in this period, a church building, specifically pew space, was the chief financial asset of a society. If a church's operating expenses were to be paid by the yearly rent of pews—better pews in better churches bringing higher rents—it proved wise to make an initially large investment in a building and thereby secure future income.

For practical and emotional reasons, pews were often at the center of debates about property and church community.[5] Plain and uncomfortable though it might have been, a pew placed an individual or a family in a religious community and gave material form to one's sense of belonging and status. Pew ownership goes back as far as the fifteenth and sixteenth centuries, when many European churches first admitted wooden seats for worshipers. Problems with individual claims to property also go back this far. Wealthier parishioners in English churches, desiring seats they could call their own, purchased pew space and fixed it up, sometimes to excess. In 1623 the Anglican Bishop Corbett of Norwich complained that

stately pews are now become tabernacles with rings and curtains to them. There wants nothing but beds to hear the word of God on; we have casements, locks and keys and cushions. I had almost said bolsters and pillows and for these we love the church. I will not guess what is done with them, who sits, stands, or lies asleep at prayers, communion, etc., but this I dare say they are either to hide some vice, or to proclaim one; to hide disorder or to proclaim pride.[6]

Some pews even contained fireplaces and special chambers for pets. Not surprisingly, notions of private property intruded on the public, worshipful character of religious space.

Abuse of privately owned pews was not a problem for the first Connecticut churches.[7] Although societies did assign pews to heads of households, and thereby reinforced a community's social order, pews did not become the private property of the sitter. Assignment was temporary and based on qualities possessed by the society members. Such an arrangement carried social weight, to be sure, but it was not a legal transaction. The real estate remained in the hands of the society. But as soon as innovative building schemes led to private pew ownership, in some cases dating back to the early eighteenth century, the nature of religious property changed. What was once a shared communal possession was divided into units that could be bought and sold like any other real estate. As we shall see, this could lead to unforeseen difficulties.

Religious communities responded to economic change in different ways at different times and in different places. Rural societies took longer to shake old patterns, partly because they retained a stability not enjoyed by many urban congregations; in the small communities across the state the old system of taxation and seat assignment succumbed only reluctantly to less personal arrangements. Denominational imperatives also played a role in church finances. Nevertheless, there was clearly an evolution in the way congregations thought about their religious property. Taxation gave way to voluntary giving. Government involvement shrank and business influence increased. The feasibility of individually, permanently owned pews declined in the face of a demand for "fair" and open pew rental. Religious societies recognized that maintaining legal possession of their property maximized its long-term value, and they began the sometimes tortuous process of trying to recapture pew property from private hands. Church buildings became emblems of a religious society's wealth, material success, and enterprise in a manner entirely congruent with the capitalistic energy of the young republic.

Building Committees

Church membership rosters of this time reveal an increasing preponderance of women, something noted by evangelical contemporaries such as New Haven's William Leffingwell, who wrote in his diary in 1815 that "the male members of our church are old & lifeless . . . indifferent to [ ] respecting eternal things."[8] Yet the financial business of a society was definitely the purview of men, generally respected businessmen, often members of a religious society without necessarily being full covenanted members of the associated church. Ninety-six of the ninety-nine pew owners in the new Hartford church were men, yet only twenty of them were church members by the end of 1808. Twenty more had wives who were members of the church. On the other hand, fourteen of these men joined the church after 1808, and at least seven were involved in other ways, such as serving as society clerk. Many Congregational men played an active role in the life of the society without experiencing a conversion and officially joining the church, and business affairs were a logical place to contribute time and talent.[9]

One such man was Daniel Wadsworth. Wadsworth's grandfather Daniel pastored Hartford's First Church from 1732 to 1747, a time of great revival, and preached the dedication sermon in the 1739 meetinghouse. His son, Daniel's father, the wealthy Jeremiah Wadsworth, died in 1804, leaving Daniel with a sizable fortune and a family tradition of community leadership. In 1807, at age thirty-six, Wadsworth purchased the most expensive pew in the new church, a large box in the corner to the left of the pulpit, for $1,100. He also purchased eight other pews and slips valued at over a thousand dollars additional, either for an investment or to support the building project, and was a major contributor to a general operating fund raised by the society in 1802.[10] In February of 1815, Daniel Wadsworth became a covenanted member of Hartford's First Church. His wife, Faith (Trumbull), was overjoyed. She recorded in her journal, "Blessed be God For his unspeakable mercies. This day I have had the long wish'd for comfort of seeing my husband profess his faith in our Lord Jesus Christ, and join himself in full communion with the visible church in Hartford."[11] Daniel was among the many who had been spiritually awakened as a result of revival in Hartford, but that awakening came long after he began contributing freely of his business acumen, vision, and money to the society. It would be wrong to argue that Wadsworth was not participating fully, even piously, in the life of the church community before he had his conversion experience.

As well as being predominantly male, building committees, pew owners, and contributors to such projects were, like Wadsworth, people of means. They were not the only people to use the building; when newspaper accounts describe a building as "overflowing," obviously there were many in attendance whose names have slipped through the record. But the more visible, wealthy men made the financial decisions of meetinghouse or church construction. Its members knew the marketplace well, so it is no surprise that, especially in the commercial cities of New Haven and Hartford, a building committee's financial schemes could take a distinctly capitalistic form. Connecticut's religious societies experimented with voluntary taxation, subscription papers, lotteries, and even stock holding as means of raising funds for building, keeping a building in repair, and paying salaries of ministers and other society employees. More often than not, they learned to bend to the demands of consumers who wanted both free choice and a good return on their investments.

The Legacy of Taxation and Subscription

The first New England meetinghouses were multifunctional buildings intended to serve both the sacred and secular purposes of all citizens. General taxation ensured that all propertied citizens contributed to a building they all ostensibly used. In reality, this happened only in the most straightforward circumstances: towns with one church.[12] The division of Congregational societies for theological or practical reasons frequently meant that the tax base quickly divided. Hartford raised taxes for one religious society only until 1670, when the Second Ecclesiastical Society formed; citizens then had the choice of supporting one of two Congregational societies. The situation became more complicated when dissenting groups, particularly Anglicans and Baptists, naturally objected to paying taxes to Congregationalists. The important Act of Toleration of 1784, the first act of toleration in Connecticut to be general and comprehensive, legally recognized dissenting Christian societies and thus gave them all the powers granted to Congregational societies, including the power to raise taxes among their own members.[13] By 1790, there were 307 incorporated religious societies in Connecticut: 203 Congregational, 58 Episcopal, 30 Baptist, 14 Strict Congregationalist, and 2 Quaker.[14] The figures for 1818 show the dramatic growth of dissenting congregations in the state: 75 Episcopal, 87 Baptist, and 54 Methodist, with Congregationalists holding steady at 205.[15] Less populous denominations, such as Universalists, were also occasionally making their presence felt, establishing congregations and building meetinghouses. Connecticut's more developed towns and counties, with a more diversified economy and social structure, tended to be the most religiously complex. New Haven or Middletown, for example, had a wider variety of congregations than did Chester or Durham. With fewer people to contribute to building and maintenance costs, taxation rapidly became a less successful means of paying a religious society's bills, especially those related to the large expense of building.

Eventually, the new State Constitution of 1818 wiped out any vestige of mandatory taxation. Section 3 of Article 1 stated: "The exercise and enjoyment of religious profession and worship, without discrimination, shall forever be free to all persons in this state." Section 4 of the law reiterates the new policy of the state with regard to religious choice: "No preference shall be given by law to any Christian sect or mode of worship." In practical terms, this law on the one hand codified what had already been true: one was free to choose a religious society to support. What was new was that no Connecticut taxpayer was required by law to support religion at all, eliminating all the taxpayers who supported Congregational societies by default. In fact, many churches had been forced to adapt to the reality of scarce funds much earlier. Taxation continued as a possible option, at rates agreed upon by each society, but taxation was virtually never sufficient, even for meeting a congregation's yearly costs for the minister's salary and property maintenance. To meet costs, societies had for decades been relying more and more on voluntary giving, usually in the form of an organized subscription, to augment the revenues from taxation. They frequently used subscriptions to establish ecclesiastical "funds," cash collections raised at one moment and added to (usually by additional subscriptions, legacies, or from the sale of church property) or borrowed from over the years.[16]

Religious societies joined canal builders, turnpike operators, and all manner of entrepreneurs in their use of the subscription paper. Banking on enthusiasm for the project and a timely generosity among parishioners, building committees found subscriptions to be an especially useful tool for raising funds. Under the plan of subscription individual givers "subscribed" their names on written documents and pledged a certain donation. When pledges were tallied, the building committee could ascertain whether or not it was wise to continue the project. The paper might include a payment schedule, indicating when the respective pledges would be due. In cities like New Haven and Hartford, pledges usually took the form of cash donations. In rural areas, subscriptions frequently were paid not in cash but in fungible goods — livestock, grains, even butter — or materials and labor directly applicable to the project, such as timbers, a cartload of stones, or hours of labor at a specified task. Subscriptions may be classified in two groups, "diffuse" and "concentrated," based on the number of initial investors and the involvement of the religious society in the financial business of building. Diffuse subscription required broad support of the society, with donations paid during the course of building, and often simply augmented taxation. The society or its representative committee managed the business affairs and assumed any debt incurred. Pews were not individually owned or rented, but assigned by committee; individuals could thus not claim ownership of church property.

The second type of plan, "concentrated" subscription, relied on small groups of men with resources and management skills who thought building could be more quickly achieved if they took matters into their own hands. This latter system resembles nothing so much as building on speculation, except that no profit was desired or expected; donors paid for the building out of their own pockets and banked on future reimbursement out of society income or subsequent donation. The society commonly specified that the committee proceed "at its own expense" (ensuring that the society would not be left with debt), gave the sponsors the right to sell the old building and property, and conceded ownership, excepting a few "society pews," until it could reimburse the sponsoring builders. The house, then, was temporarily the property of individuals who could sell pews to help pay expenses. If enough money could be raised to pay the debts incurred, the building committee would turn the building over to the society.

The choice to subscribe clearly gave contributors a perspective different from that engendered by strict taxation. A society tax for a building was much like any other tax, figured mathematically based on recent tax assessment lists and collected by a designated collector. It was also an unavoidable obligation. Subscriptions, on the other hand, were at the discretion of the subscriber, peer pressure notwithstanding, and it seems that when discretionary income was applied to church buildings, subscribers felt more than the usual shared interest in the material result. Donors who gave most generously felt a proprietary interest, a sentiment often made concrete in the ownership of specific pew space in a building. The largest advantage of a subscription plan was that it could expedite building, particularly if the subscribers quickly paid their promised sums. But pledges sometimes proved as difficult to collect as taxes. Good intentions at the moment of signing the list were not always translated into an ability to pay six or nine months later.

By far the most intractable difficulty of subscriptions, however, centered on questions of ownership. Was a church the property of the congregation that worshiped within, or did it belong to those who paid for it? Could the initial investors claim sole ownership of a building even after it had been the spiritual home of a group of worshipers for a generation? Such dilemmas of ownership reached a crisis point in the circumstances of New Haven's United Society as it attempted to dispose of two old buildings and build a new church in 1812.[17] The United Society's predicament illustrates the downside of too much private involvement in church building. Their misfortune also demonstrates the crucial importance of church buildings to both the social and the financial stability of a congregation.

The Problem of Religious Property in New Haven

The roots of New Haven's messy controversy went back to the United Society's genesis in the contentious religious environment of mid-eighteenth-century New England. In 1742, under the influence of revivalist preaching, a group of New Lights, calling themselves the White Haven Society, broke from First Society. Despite dismal finances and the relentless efforts of First Society to frustrate its plans, the White Haven Society quickly built a place of worship. In 1742, several of the wealthier members combined their private funds to purchase a lot and erect a small, nondescript meetinghouse. In 1769, disagreement over doctrine and preaching style resulted in yet another split. By 1771 this new society, called Fair Haven, was worshiping in its own newly completed building.[18]

Because of the partisan beginnings of these two societies and their relatively small membership in New Haven's congested religious market, supporting meetinghouses by general taxation would have been impossible. Instead, the two churches funded their buildings by concentrated subscription, and investors owned pews in the new buildings, representing a permanent share of the whole. The White Haven and Fair Haven houses were technically not the property of each society, but the collective property of the pew owners. Initially, this arrangement presented no problem; pew owners were satisfied and made room for nonowners for worship and other meetings. But, by the mid-1790s, the societies were in financial trouble, declining in members, and unable to pay their ministers' salaries. After 1795 both were without ministers, and doctrinal quibbles seemed trivial in the face of possible collapse. To many, reunification now seemed the only way to survive, and by November 1796 the two societies had successfully joined forces. Although the societies pooled their human resources, material resources did not become common property; ownership of pews remained as it was, and the United Society divided public worship equally between the two houses.[19]

As the society continued to struggle with its problematic finances, it became apparent that private ownership of the two houses was not helping matters. Money could be raised by annual pew *rental*, reasoned one committee, if the pew owners could be convinced to sell or donate their pews. The committee also suggested that the White Haven meetinghouse, more of a nuisance than an asset, should be demolished and the land sold. Some pew owners aggressively blocked this latter proposal, and the congregation continued to wander between the two dilapidated meetinghouses for over a decade. This unpleasant situation led to an 1807 report that "many valuable members of the United Society are strongly opposed to the mode of going from one meeting house to the other to attend Public Worship and this objection deters some good citizens from becoming members of said Society." Moreover, some members were unable to find pew space in one or the other house. The report further argued that the society "must surely decrease in numbers, wealth, and in respectability, unless some different arrangements can be made."[20] The stakes changed dramatically in December of 1812 when twenty members of the United Society proposed building a new brick structure on the Fair Haven site, on condition that they be given the former two houses and their lots. By general vote, the society swiftly accepted this proposal, and that was that: both former meetinghouses were slated for destruction.

The ensuing events were recorded in a clearly biased 1813 document presented by a group of disgruntled property owners. This pamphlet, "Report of a Committee Respecting White-Haven Meeting-House," was addressed to and attested by Dr. Levi Ives, a longtime deacon of White Haven Society.[21] In the eyes of the dispossessed, the December vote

clinched the illegal destruction of their property. They reminded their
readers that White Haven Society never owned its meetinghouse outright,
because private investors had paid for the building. Therefore, the general
society had no right to vote away its existence. The lamentable result of
this lack of due process was that "those who have continued for forty
years faithful to the society are to be deprived of land and house, of
minister, and society property and to be thrown into the open street!"
"We have surely as much right to prefer the houses, where our fathers
worshipped," asserted the writers, "as they have to prefer a new one."22
They requested that the White Haven house stand, be repaired at society
expense, and that those who would lose seats in the soon-to-be-razed Fair
Haven meetinghouse be assigned pews in White Haven, leaving the new
brick endeavor to those who were so inclined.23

Mingled with eloquent arguments for the sanctity and sentimental
value of the old houses, ample clues again suggest that the real issue was
one of property ownership. "A society, which cannot subsist without de-
stroying the pious monuments of the care, the industry, and the tender
affection of our ancestors, *and without violating our rights of property, as
established by the laws of this state* [italics mine] . . . can have no dependence
whatever on the protection of the Divine Head of the Church."24 "Where
property is the subject of vote," they continued, "the weight of property
should decide."25 Without denying genuine, sentimental attachments to
the old houses, what prompted such a vehement protest was primarily a
sense of dispossession, in crass, material terms. It should come as no
surprise that Deacon Ives held a large pew near the pulpit of the Fair
Haven church.

Dissent notwithstanding, the construction of the "new brick" progressed apace.26 The Fair Haven house met its demise, and the congregation temporarily worshiped in the White Haven building, still standing,
if precariously. A residual, divisive bitterness persisted among the congregation. December 21, 1815, the day after the dedication of the new meetinghouse, church member Ebenezer Foster wrote to Senator David Daggett in Washington. "It would seem," he wrote, "as though our society
might now be prosperous and happy but there are a *restless few* whose
obstinacy and inveteracy appear to increase." "Dr. Ives is irreconcilable,"
Foster continued, "and Mr. [Abraham] Bishop is boiling over with
wrath." Bishop was also talking about a lawsuit, and Ives threatened to
continue holding worship in the White Haven meetinghouse. But, as Foster related to Daggett, they were in for a surprise, for "the contractors
decided it most important to bring the thing to a crisis at once."27 Sure
enough, on the twenty-first "Col. Tilden . . . began to rip up the pews
and in a few days not a vestige will remain on the spot; this is a great

grief to Deacon Ives and his little band."[28] By January of 1816, White Haven was gone: "The old house . . . the hornet's nest of sedition was demolished. . . . This has evidently much disconcerted the opposition."[29] Eventually, even Deacon Ives came around. Written in the margin of the church records for January 5, 1815, is this short message: "Deacon Ives, after this, with some slight interruptions, continued to walk, worship and commune with the church."[30]

The appearance of Abraham Bishop in the fracas alerts us to another important dimension of the controversy: politics. Bishop was a Yale graduate and an articulate, ardent Republican, bitterly opposed to the Congregational order to the point of even being labeled an "atheist." Quite possibly the author of the "Report of a Committee Respecting White-Haven Meeting-House," he was known for his inflammatory orations and pamphlets, such as "The Extent and Power of Political Delusion," an address he delivered to fifteen hundred pairs of eager ears in one of the New Haven churches in 1800.[31] Here and in numerous other contexts Bishop decried the oppression of the Federalist clergy and spelled out the dangers of a union of church and state. New Haven was a difficult place to be a Republican; one can sense the exasperated frustration of the pamphlet's writer. "Deacon Ives and his little band" did appear to have cause for outrage over the destruction of their property, and their anger was no doubt increased by the dismissive tone of their adversaries. The New Haven controversy dramatically illustrates how church property could become a material focus for highly charged debates about the proper relationships between money, religion, and politics.

The Standardization of Pew Rental

Religious societies began to see their buildings as important financial assets. Meetinghouses and churches themselves became the financial bedrock on which a congregation could exist, as real estate to be parceled out, pew by pew, to investors. Individual pew *ownership* was increasingly seen as a situation to be avoided, for it did a society no good to have its greatest asset chopped up into small pieces and owned indefinitely. Pew rental was a far better system, because under the terms of leasing the pews would revert frequently to the church to be rented again for a period of one or several years. By this means, societies could raise sums equivalent to their expenses by assessing pews according to a predicted yearly budget. Pew rental also avoided the problem of the absentee owner: if a family had purchased a pew years hence, yet was no longer a society member, that family contributed nothing to the ongoing expenses of the society yet tied up assets. Although the sale of pews outright, or in "fee simple," did continue in some congregations, pew rentals eventually outpaced other means of feeding a society's treasury by virtue of the system's streamlined bookkeeping, parish control, freedom of choice for renters, flexibility, and predictability. But this shift to pew rental could not just happen as soon as its financial merits were evident. It was difficult to regain property that was privately owned and there was emotional resistance, especially in rural societies, to the notion of paying for seats in church. Some newcomer denominations, Baptists and Methodists in particular, were opposed to pew rental on principle. It was not a simple case of making the best financial decision, but of making practice commensurate with beliefs about the nature of worship and community.

Urban congregations most quickly accommodated themselves to the idea of selling or renting the pews. When a new church opened, the building committee advertised the time and place of public pew auctions. Building committees for all three of New Haven's churches on the green hoped to recover their expenses—in the vicinity of thirty thousand dollars for each building—through the sale of pews. The committee of Trinity Episcopal Church opted to rent pews for a five-year period. Trinity's "noble edifice," the *Connecticut Journal* recorded, "contains 224 Pews, of which no. 41 are reserved to the Society, leaving 183 to be disposed of."[32] The society hoped those 183 would bring in an annual rent of $2,775, the amount they reckoned it would take to pay clergy, building maintenance, interest on debt, and to chip away at the principal. Based on this predicted budget, the committee assigned a minimum value to each pew. Persons wishing to have a particular pew might bid a "premium" on top of the designated amount in order to beat the competition.

At an advertised December 13 auction, rents plus premiums bid for pews amounted to an annual rent of $4,621. Trinity's magnificent Gothic novelty attracted enough renters so that every pew was leased at a rate above the asking price. Copies of Trinity's pew deeds, listing name of renter, pew number, and cost, and the plan and conditions for pew dispersal, can be found in the parish records (fig. 14). Of the 41 reserved pews, 15 on the lower floor included one for the minister and family, several for prominent parishioners, and some to be held open for visitors. Twenty-six gallery pews consisted of 9 for the choir and 8 distant "wall pews for black people"—whom the society apparently did not consider capable or worthy of purchasing or renting pews. The committee assessed the remaining 183 pews at annual rents of from five to thirty dollars.[33] Most pews went to individuals such as Jared Shattuck, who agreed to pay thirty dollars a year for five years for the rent of a class one pew on the main floor. Shattuck also received a deduction for his previous

PLAN

For disposing of the PEWS in the New Episcopal Church.

1st. THE whole number of Pews on the lower floor is - 146
Of which are reserved - - - - 24

Leaving to be disposed of on the lower floor - - 122

Among the Pews reserved on the lower floor are
No. 5, 39, 41, 71, 72, 73, 74, 77, 78, 127, 143, 144.
The whole number of Pews in the Gallery is - - 80
Of which are reserved for the Choir, No. 147, 148, 149, 150, } 14
151, 152, 153, 154 and 6, in the Organ loft,
Wall Pews for black people, - - - - 16
For other purposes, No. 201, 202, 203, and 204, - - 4

34

Leaving to be disposed of in the Gallery, - - - 46

Total number to be disposed of, - - - - 168

2d. The Pews (except those reserved as aforesaid) shall be leased for a term of five years, at an annual rent, on the following principles :---

3d. There shall be eight classes of choices, each class to consist of the number of choices thereto affixed, and to be leased at the annual rent thereto annexed, Viz :—

Class No. 1 contains 24 choices, at $30 per annum.
2 do. 20 do. - 25 do.
3 do. 20 do. - 20 do.
4 do. 24 do. - 15 do.
5 do. 20 do. - 12 do.
6 do. 30 do. - 10 do.
7 do. 15 do. - 7 do.
8 do. 15 do. - 5 do.

4th. The privilege of taking a lease of a Pew at the rent aforesaid for five years, shall be sold to the highest bidder, taking the classes in their order, and beginning with Class No. 1 and Choice No. 1. The highest bidder on any choice may take any Pew which has not been previously chosen or reserved ; and any person entitled to a choice, shall immediately make his selection.

5th. In case there should not be as many bidders as there are choices in any class, the Committee appointed by the Wardens and Vestry for that purpose, may forthwith select as many Pews as there shall be choices unsold, before any choices in the next class are sold.

CONDITIONS.

A lease will be executed to the lessee for the term of five years, to commence on the first day of January, 1816, by one or more persons, to be for that purpose appointed, by the Wardens and Vestry ; and each lessee must execute an obligation to pay the rent annually, on the first Monday of January in each year.

In case the rent of any Pew be not paid within twenty days after the same shall fall due, it shall be in the power of the Wardens and Vestry, or a committee by them appointed for that purpose, to take possession of such Pew, and lease the same to any other person, until the expiration of the aforesaid term of five years.

Notes at thirty days from the day of sale will be taken, if desired, for the amount for which the right of taking a lease shall be struck off to any person.

The amount by any person subscribed, and paid towards the expense of building the New Church, and the interest from time to time accruing thereon, shall be considered as pledged by him, for the payment of the rent of any Pew, of which he shall have a lease, and the same may be retained by the Wardens and Vestry for that purpose.

December, 1815.

14. "Plan for disposing of the pews in the New Episcopal Church," Trinity Church, New Haven, 1815. Courtesy, New Haven Colony Historical Society.

subscription of one hundred dollars.[34] Under the conditions of the rental agreement, Shattuck's thirty-dollar rent was due on the first Monday of January each year for five years. If this rent was not paid within twenty days, the vestry committee had the option of repossessing the pew and finding a more reliable renter for the remainder of the term.

The sale or rent of pews never ended with the initial auction. Old church members left; new members came and wished to purchase seats. Or, individual owners might wish to dispose of some real estate. Notices of pews for sale and requests for purchase dot the pages of Connecticut newspapers. In May of 1810 Peter W. Gallaudet of Hartford announced that he had for "sale or rent several slips and pews in New Brick meeting house,"[35] Recall that Gallaudet was a member of the building committee for that 1807 structure; he had probably purchased extra pews at the initial offering in order to spur the project along. Three years later, Gallaudet was trying to sell off some of those pews. In 1824 Charles Hosmer advertised in the *Connecticut Mirror* that "the front PEW No. 137 in the South Gallery of Rev. Mr. Hawes' Meeting House, held in fee simple, will be sold on very accommodating terms."[36] Religious societies also regularly advertised their annual pew rentals. On April 13, 1810, the *Connecticut Courant* (Hartford) carried the notice: "Sale of pews in Episcopal Church for ensuing year, Easter Monday."

Confusion about the nature of pew ownership plagued religious societies, pew owners, and their creditors. Several resolves and acts regarding pews turn up in Connecticut legislation, testifying to their ongoing problematic nature. In May of 1810, a resolve "Regarding Pews and Slips in the Meeting House lately erected by the First Society in Hartford" passed. The law first attempted to standardize pew dispersion and ownership, granting pew owners the right to record "the evidences of title" in the society records "in the same manner as evidences of title to real estate are by law to be recorded." This title would operate just as any other deed, having "the same force and effect in the law, as the records of deeds and other evidences of title to real estate."[37] In 1814 and 1821 the Connecticut Legislature attempted to regulate pew sales further with two separate yet similar "Act(s) Relating to Pews."[38] Both acts stated that no right to a pew "in any meeting house or church belonging to a religious society, of any denomination of Christians in this state" for a period over one year be valid unless the deed was in writing, with two witnesses, acknowledged by a county official, and recorded by the society's clerk in a book specifically for that purpose. A pew, "being the property of any person or persons leaving a family who ordinarily occupy the same, shall be exempt, and not liable to be taken or disposed of by any warrant or execution, for any debt whatever." Pews were not to be a resource "to satisfy the demands of creditors when the estate of such owner shall prove insolvent." The law acknowledged that although pews were transferable property, they had a special, protected status. This legislation also shows that once pews became purchased or rented property, they entered a free market that was beyond the control of the church. This was all the more reason for churches to rent pews for a limited time only.

Once a church sold its pews, only with patience and persistence could they be regained as church property. The First Society in Hartford decided in 1804 to build its new brick church for an estimated $18,000–20,000. At that time, the committee took on the risk of building, expecting to pay for the building by a combination of loans, subscriptions, and, especially, advance pew sales. Potential customers had the choice of buying a pew in "fee simple" or buying for a period of thirty years, after which the society would reclaim the pew. More than a year after the church was completed, a March 1809 sale raised $27,723 from 116 purchasers and twenty-nine renters, but the final building accounts totaled a hefty $31,927.39.[39] After accounts were settled, the building committee still owed $1,800 to the Hartford bank and smaller debts to itself and several workers, the total amounting to over $2,000.[40] In 1815, the debt still outstanding, the society clerk recorded that although the original arrangement with the building committee was "a prudent means of precaution taken by the society that they might not become insolvent (as they otherwise might have been)," assuming the remaining debt, even if it resulted in losses, now seemed wise because "it would seem more equitable, that such loss should fall upon the society at large, rather than upon a few individuals."[41] Although this was ostensibly a generous gesture, it was also a practical necessity if the society was ever going to regain control of its property.

Annual pew rental was the obvious answer to the society's need for regular annual income. But with the majority of pews in the hands of scattered purchasers who had bought their seats years earlier, some of whom were no longer even members of First Society, this was easier said than done. By January of 1826 the situation was not improved. Parishioners were complaining about "the inequality . . . by which the present seats are held." First Society was clearly out of step with the times. The society noted "both the North and South Congregational Societies have elegant and convenient churches where seats may be purchased annually at auction upon perfectly equal competition." First Society's members wanted the same opportunity to occupy the most desirable pews. "It may not be improper to add," the recorder noted astutely, "the time seems fast approaching when the support of public worship must depend upon voluntary contribution or the sale of Pews."[42] Without a complete and equitable sale of all pews, First Society risked the loss of pew renters in a competitive environment. "Some individuals," the record states, "may have already certificated [that is, legally dropped their membership in the society]."[43] These accounts are remarkable for their frank assertion that pew rental was supposed to be an open competition based on money, and that the inability to claim a good pew was enough to send a Christian elsewhere. As late as 1838, the society was still trying to wrest back the remaining privately owned pews.[44]

Stock Holding Schemes and Banks

Although pew rental seemed to many to be the best option, congregations experimented with other innovative ways of raising funds as well. In several instances in Hartford and New Haven the investment nature of church building took on a more literal cast. Hartford's Second Society, North Society, and Christ Church and New Haven's Trinity Church raised money by selling shares in their building projects, not to subscribers, not to pew owners, but to "stockholders." Members of the community thus became investors in the building project, lending their free capital to a religious society in exchange for a promise that the investment would be returned and the society would pay them yearly interest on the borrowed money. Newly chartered local banks provided the model. The boom in capital in New England was largely the result of the positive balance of trade caused by foreign wars that bottled up the competition. Connecticut River towns such as Hartford were heavily involved in the West Indies trade, exporting livestock and agricultural goods, and importing West Indian products such as molasses. Merchants needed ready cash with which to pay their suppliers, and they desired a source of capital to fund trading ventures. In Hartford and New Haven, the number of banks grew with the demand. The refusal of the national government to authorize any banks but a few branches of its own did not stop state legislatures from granting charters to groups of local petitioners who could demonstrate sufficient stability and potential. From 1791 to 1811 alone, the number of state chartered banks in the United States rose from five to 117, and the capital invested grew tremendously from $4.6 million to $66.3 million.[45] Between 1811 and 1816 the number of state banks doubled again as did the amount of capital stock authorized. It was plain to Hartford's businessmen that the money was there. In an 1814 request that the General Assembly establish a new bank, the petitioners asserted that Hartford citizens had money to invest, even in the middle of a war. "The banking business in this city has been as good, if not better, since the war, than it was in the time of peace," they claimed. "The prodigiously great subscriptions to this [the Hartford] bank of late, whenever a new subscription to its stock has been permitted, prove the extreme desire of the public to possess it."[46]

Banks depended on the sale of subscriptions, or shares of stock, that provided the cash to back up paper credit; shareholders in exchange earned a portion of the bank's profit. Church building committees adopted a version of this procedure, selling shares for a small amount, usually fifty dollars. These committees used the terms "stock" and "stock-holder." In reality, the system operated more like a bond issue: churches borrowed money from investors who received interest (not dividends) on their investment, which was to be paid back entirely at a future, specified date. Trinity Church in New Haven tried stock holding to raise advance money for its 1815 building. In September of 1813 the society voted to pay for its new church in the following manner. First, "the amount of the expense of such building shall consist of stock which shall be divided into shares of fifty dollars each, payable by installments."[47] Construction was to begin when 400 shares, or twenty thousand dollars, were subscribed. Eventually 532 shares sold. The society used rental from the pews to pay the interest on the stock, and the surplus to pay off the principal.[48] In Hartford, North Church used a similar scheme to pay for its 1823 meeting house, raising sixteen thousand dollars by creating stock shares of fifty dollars each, earning 6 percent annually, the principal to be paid off within thirty years.[49]

Stock-holding schemes were not always successful. Hartford's South Church, planning to build in 1825, voted that "the best mode of effecting the object will be for the Society to borrow the necessary funds in stock to be put into shares of fifty dollars each," with 6 percent interest.[50] The report argued persuasively that "from the inquiries your committee have made, they have no doubt the stock would readily be taken up. The interest accruing . . . may easily be met by the rent of the pews in the meeting house, and have a considerable surplus in the treasury, which may be applied to the redemption of stock."[51] The shares were specified as transferable certificates representing "a proportion of land and building" and carried a promise of redemption within twenty years.[52] As caretakers of the investment, the society promised that it would keep insured an amount equal to three-quarters the value of unredeemed stock against fire loss, and would keep the property in good repair. At first the sanguine expectations of the society seemed well-founded. But, by 1832 the society had a miserable twenty-two-thousand-dollar debt and considered selling pews and slips in fee simple.[53] This they wisely voted down, creating instead a subscription fund to pay off debts.[54]

A much happier experience with stock holding and church finances was had by Christ Church, Hartford, perhaps because of the congregation's ability to tap into the wealthy and undivided Episcopal community. To finance its magnificent church, completed in 1829, the vestry depended on stock sales, generous gifts, and the state-supported Episcopal "Bishop's" Fund. The venture was remarkably successful considering that, at over forty thousand dollars, the structure cost more than any church Hartford had ever seen. Christ Church had certain advantages: denominational support, a lack of competition from other Episcopal congregations, and a base in the dramatic increase in number and respectability of Episcopalians in Hartford during the first few decades of the nineteenth century. Perhaps most important, Christ Church had among its members savvy businessmen.

Christ Church demonstrated its fine money management early in the nineteenth century. In 1807 a prominent merchant, Charles Sigourney, then serving as society clerk, and other members of Christ Church raised $800 by subscription and land sales and used it to buy two $400 shares of Hartford Bank stock. Sigourney, with foresight, predicted that with 8 percent interest, by 1831 the church would have almost $5,000 in the bank.[55] The ability of Christ Church to establish this fund rested in part on the fact that Episcopal congregations tended to have glebe lands, large property holdings for the support of the clergy. A strong denominational network also helped; over half of the subscription money in Sigourney's fund came from a paper drawn up in New York City in 1807, "for the purpose of representing the necessities of the parish and obtaining some relief." The Hartford parish presented itself as hopeful yet impoverished: "owing to removal, death, and failure in business, the congregation which was always small, has lost several of its best supporters, and the whole weight of its expenses now devolves on a very few individuals, who contribute annually . . . from fifty to $150 each."[56] The total subscription from New York amounted to $445, with forty-one subscribers giving from five to thirty dollars. In 1814 Sigourney was one of the founding directors of a new financial institution: Hartford's Phoenix Bank. Soon after, the vestry of Christ Church voted to take its investment, then $3,200, out of the Hartford Bank and transfer it to the Phoenix Bank.[57] This is no surprise, as Phoenix Bank backers were largely Episcopalians who anticipated that the bank could and would be a benefit to their church. As was common, the bank directors offered a bonus, in this case $50,000, to the Legislature in exchange for granting its charter. By agreement, $20,000 of this bonus was to go into the above-mentioned Bishop's Fund, the one non-Congregational state endorsed ecclesiastical fund.[58] Episcopalians thus directed a portion of their bonus back into a fund created for their own use.

Church stock-holding plans located architecture at the heart of institutional financial stability. A building plan had to rely on ambition and pizzazz if it was to attract investors in the first place; the pew rent necessary to pay interest on stock would be forthcoming only if both building and congregation had market appeal. Banks and religious institutions negotiated mutually helpful arrangements. As church budgets and debt grew, it was impossible that a society could manage the bookkeeping and interest payments without the help of a bank. And banks, to further their cause with the legislature, often promised friendly terms to churches, for instance agreeing to establish ecclesiastical funds. The state in turn helped Protestant churches when politically useful — promising that $20,000 of the Phoenix Bank bonus would go into the Bishop's Fund placated Episcopalians as they threatened to disrupt the political and social status quo. Churches, government, and business helped each other out, trading not in authority but in cash. Businessmen like Charles Sigourney connected the several worlds and specifically tied banks into church building. Both Sigourney and another director of the Phoenix Bank, Samuel Tudor, Jr., were members of the Christ Church building committee that had decided to use a stock-holding plan to pay for the church. They knew the money was available, for when their Phoenix Bank put its $1 million in shares on the market, there were seven applicants for every share.[59] As expected, stock in their church building also sold well.

Rural Churches

Rural communities, like the urban societies, may also have aspired to build in the "modern style," but these smaller congregations had severely limited means. Consequently, their buildings were of more modest size, almost always of wood, and much less expensive; church records show a common outlay of two to five thousand dollars for a new building. A close examination of the financial records of forty Litchfield County congregations demonstrates the rural pattern of church financing. These records convey some of the differences between urban and rural congregations. Two are striking. First, rural churches were reluctant to raise money aggressively and rent pews in an open market. Second, in the small hamlets of the Connecticut countryside, financial necessity often led congregations of different denominations to combine forces when it came to building new churches.

The colonial system of yearly pew assignment, generally based on wealth and age, continued to be comfortable for many congregations. Not only did it acknowledge community stature, it tended to reward those who had contributed the most to a building: those who had paid the greatest taxes and those who had been around the longest. That reward was assumed. For example, the Congregational Society in Roxbury, during its 1795–96 building project, kept careful accounts of who had contributed cash, materials, or time, to ensure that each would be assigned a seat in the new house.[60] The Roxbury society even used the promise of a seat to entice nonmembers to contribute; the society voted to invite members of "all denominations . . . to come in and pay their equal proportion towards building sd. Meetinghouse according to their lists & have a seat in said house appointed."[61] Scattered documents in the records suggest that some took the bait: Thomas and Daniel Weller, Jr., each signed agreements in which they promised "to pay taxes to the Presbyterian [Congregational] society in Roxbury . . . provided they give me a seat according to my age and list." At the same time Alvin Eastman made a "promise to pay the presbyterian soc. The sum of $8.12 within 1 year . . . and pay all taxes that shall arise in futer [sic] on sd. Soc. According to my list provided they give me a seat in their new meeting house."[62]

The Roxbury society used a combination of taxation and subscription to pay for its new building. A committee of five seated the meetinghouse for a three-year period according to the 1796 tax list and age.[63] For over two decades, the Roxbury society vacillated on the question of pew rental. As early as December of 1802 it voted to "sell" (rent) the pews, only to overturn the decision one week later, letting everyone "sit where they please."[64] The following December, the society voted to seat the house using a combination of age and wealth, and guaranteed that "all that ever paid anything toward building the meeting house" would be so seated.[65] In 1804 the society, referring to those contributors as "proprietors," gave them "the Privilege of sitting in what seats they please in this house."[66] In 1821 the society seems to have voted to rent pews to the highest bidders if $100 could be raised in this manner, but it is not certain that this occurred. Meanwhile, the society afforded "all persons of other denominations . . . the privilege of sitting in what seats they please in this house."[67] Not until 1823 is it clear the Roxbury society rented pews. In 1826 the procedure was carefully stated: "the person subscribing the largest sum shall have the first choice and so on to the person subscribing the smallest sum."[68] Unlike the previously mentioned urban pew sales, no exact sums were specified for each pew. The society indicated, however, that in order for the system to go into effect, the sale must raise at least $250. More evidence of ecumenical appeal follows in 1836, when the church embarked on yet another building project and voted that anyone who would subscribe at least twenty dollars to the project would be allowed to vote on all matters regarding the building, even if not a member of the society.[69]

The First Congregational Church of Morris never could quite figure out the best way to seat its church, and financial woes only aggravated the problem. In November of 1815 the society voted to "do something about selling the pews" for one year.[70] That vote apparently raised some disagreement, for the following month the society rescinded the decision and voted to tax its members three and one-half cents per dollar of assessed property. In November of 1819 the society not only voted to sell the use of the pews but asserted by vote that "this meeting consider it legal" to do so, and decided to sell outright some of the gallery pews.[71] Two weeks later the society decided against selling the gallery pews. It is unclear whether or not the pew sale occurred, but by the following year a vote for pew sale ended in a tie, causing the society to tax itself 1.7 cents on the dollar instead.[72] Again, two weeks later, the society modified the vote, deciding to rent the pews "except the two front pews and the widows pew" reserved for widows and men over seventy-five and their wives. Those people, the society agreed, could pay the society "what is just and right in their own opinion."[73] In 1826, the society decided to seat the whole meetinghouse by age only "without any reference to list."[74] This suggests that in the preceding years the seating was still according to wealth and age, and not pew rental as previously voted. As late as 1834 the society was still "dignifying" its seats.

Of twenty-five societies that clearly used pew rental in Litchfield County, the first was the Sharon society, which used rental briefly in 1807 before reverting to seat assignment. The Canaan society went to rental in 1808, Litchfield's First Society in 1811. Two more societies opted for rental in the 1810s, and six more in 1820s. Ten held out until the 1830s and the remainder even into the 1840s and 1850s. Just as with Connecticut's city churches, financial difficulties made the progression to pew rental inevitable. Yet for the time being, the new system was something to be evaluated carefully. In 1814 Winchester's First Society decided "to enquire of other Societies the success attending selling the pews in the meeting house."[75] The news must have been positive, for the society subsequently voted to "do something respecting selling the pews" on condition that enough was thereby raised to pay the minister's salary and society expenses.[76] The experiment failed, however, and it is clear from further records that the Winchester society continued to defer the selling of pews. By 1828, the society was using rental as a threat to pressure the congregation into making larger donations. A subscription paper circulated for two weeks "to see how much money can be raised to defray the expenses of the Society for the year ensuing." If the congregation pledged sufficient funds, each could "occupy such seat as he may choose." But they also understood that "unless money enough be raised to pay off Mr. Marshes salary and other necessary expenses the pews will then be sold. . . ."[77] The threat must have worked, for the society apparently never sold slips until it moved into a new house in 1842. The Congregational Church at Washington held out until 1839, when debt forced the society to go on a fundraising campaign. A society member made a motion that the society committee "try the minds of members of this society by giving in a vote the way each would have it done. By sale of the pews, By subscription or By a tax and the result was Subscription: 1, Taxation: 13, Sale of Pews: 20."[78] By 1839 the Washington society was finally ready for pew rental.

The source of hesitation is evident in the records of the Woodbury Congregational Society. As late as 1841, still vacillating on pew rental, the society sent representatives who "made enquiries on the subject, in various neighboring Societies, where the system of selling seats has been adopted." These neighbors were "unanimously of the opinion that the sale of the seats" would be "useful and advantageous" as long as well regulated.[79] But they recommended the procedure only if "the members of the society generally cheerfully and cordially concur in the measures," being "unwilling to recommend this or any other measure which should be found likely to disturb the peace and harmony at present existing."[80] To keep the peace, the Woodbury society made pew rental optional. But this situation, inherently unfair, led to a vote to "call on persons who were provided with seats in this house [without purchasing them] to contribute to the expenses of the society as far as they feel disposed."[81] It was a touchy situation, to say the least, for rural societies needed steady income yet were wary of alienating members. Pew assignment was personal; the committee associated a seat with a name, a personality, a history. Pew rental was democratic yet anonymous; pews were designated by number, and the right to a number was purchased at auction. For many rural societies, preserving "the peace and harmony at present existing" meant resisting, for a little while, the entrance of the market into a community's sacred space.

At the end of the eighteenth century specie was scarce, and rural congregations still used barter, chore sharing, and collection of noncash resources to complete their buildings. In 1796 Litchfield's Second Episcopal Society counted the labor of church members as their contribution to the cost of building, provided that they would work "as cheap as they can hire" outside labor.[82] When this parish united with the West Parish (Bradleyville) in 1799, the building tax arrived in the form of pork, beef, wheat, rye, Indian corn, bar iron, flax seed, cheese, oats, butter, and some cash.[83] The society's treasurer had the responsibility of turning those agricultural products into cash or goods suitable for paying carpenters and masons. Taxpayers to the 1792 collection for St. Peter's Episcopal Church in Plymouth delivered their allotted contribution in two installments: the first half in materials for building, the second half in cattle.[84] By the second decade of the nineteenth century, financial contributions to rural building projects were much more likely to be made in strictly monetary terms.

Just being able to put up a house at all was a mark of congregational pride. "A few, but zealous individuals" were behind most of the early-nineteenth-century Litchfield County building projects. Enthusiastic donors sometimes made the difference between building anew or putting up with the old meetinghouse. The Episcopal priest George B. Andrews gave nearly $1,000 to St. Andrew's in Kent in 1829 and also gave generously to buildings at Sharon, Salisbury, and New Preston.[85] Seth Thomas, the clock-making entrepreneur, donated a generous $2,300 plus a five-hundred-dollar building lot toward the first building of the Congregational Society in Plymouth Hollow, organized in 1836. Five other big donors gave a total of $1,765 to this project in subscriptions ranging from $200 to $605; the total raised was $5,917.[86] The subscription procedure followed in Plymouth Hollow was common for rural societies, although most villages did not have the benefit of a Seth Thomas. Such donors did not expect to recoup their investment, although they did retain a share of the property. Subscribers might waive their share once the building was complete. The subscribers to the Plymouth Hollow building voted in 1836 to "give up their right and interest in sd. house to the congregational society of Plymouth Hollow . . . except a lien on sd. house for such an amount as said subscribers falls short of paying the building committee, who are under contract to the builders for a greater amount."[87] They willingly donated the house to the society, but were not agreeable to paying off additional debt. In that way, they hoped to ensure that outstanding subscriptions would be paid. Societies were not shy about taking legal action if subscribers were not forthcoming with promised donations. In 1830 the North Congregational Church in Goshen voted that the society "forces a collection of such subscriptions as are not paid within a suitable time."[88] In 1841 Bethlehem's Episcopal Society hired an agent "to cause to be prosecuted in behalf of this Society such suit or suits as may be necessary to Enforce the collection of any sum or sums of money which are due from the delinquent subscribers to a certain 'Fund.'"[89] Subscriptions might have been voluntary, but building committees counted on that money once it was pledged.

Unpredictable finances led rural congregations to build as they could, often starting not with a polished plan but with a notion to cover a frame until money came to finish the church, or paint it, or build a steeple. Not thinking beyond the step at hand, societies assumed that if building began, it would eventually finish. So buildings grew up in tandem with the fortunes of a society. Seat-of-the-pants financing manifested itself in the makeshift character of building and the use of old materials. In 1801, for example, the Northfield Congregational Society voted to pull down its old meetinghouse and convert the usable remains into a new one "as far as they will go."[90] Rural societies often relied on independent initiative to improve their buildings. A society would vote to allow a certain change to its building, provided it cost the society nothing. Litchfield's First Congregational Society voted in 1808 to allow anyone to erect a porch at the east end of the house, as long as it could be accomplished "without subjecting the society to any expense."[91] Even necessary maintenance required donations; the Congregational Society of Colebrook circulated a subscription in 1821 to raise funds to repair the steeple and paint the church.[92]

If a society was desperate for a new building and doubted its ability to finance construction, it might bind together with other town societies to build a "Union" church. Such was the case in Colebrook, where the Baptists, Methodists, and Congregationalists together built a meetinghouse in 1815. Each signer of the subscription paper was to "insert with his name the denomination to which he belongs" in order to keep track of the respective donations.[93] Eventually, in 1829, the Methodists alone finished off the inside of the house, in return owning one-half of the house until the United Societies could pay back the cost. In Barkhamsted, although four congregations—Episcopal, Congregational, Baptist, and Methodist—constructed separate churches, they found themselves questioning the wisdom of pouring money into four minimally used buildings in a small town. In 1849 the Episcopal Society records declared that since members of all four societies had fit comfortably into the Episcopal Church for a recent funeral, it seemed ridiculous to have spent eleven thousand dollars on different churches in the last twenty years, especially since the village did not have a decent schoolhouse.[94] Yet, if a congregation planned to have its own building one day, and most did, then the wisdom of investing in temporarily shared housing was questionable. St. Peter's Episcopal in Northbury (Plymouth) hoped to head off this problem when getting subscriptions from the Walnut Hill section of the village in 1791. If those people, the society promised, "shall in the course of ten years Belong to any other Society within the limits of the Parish of Northbury . . . and they shall have occasion to Build an Episcopal Church for Publick Worship that we will Refund their respective sums which shall be paid by them" for the present project.[95]

The Litchfield County records suggest that church builders of smaller, rural congregations were operating under a somewhat different set of imperatives from those of their urban counterparts. For one thing, there was less cash to go around; many of these congregations were even without a settled minister and made the compromises necessary to stay afloat. In many cases, raising funds on a small scale could still be most efficiently accomplished through taxation, provided there was some additional subscription money. As these rural societies mulled over the possibility of pew rental, it became plain to them that, for all its attractions, the system did not come without a cost to community and tradition.

Lotteries

If a congregation balked at taxation, and if voluntary subscriptions or pew rentals could not equal a society's bills, another fund-raising option was a state-chartered lottery. Americans were in the habit of using lotteries for a variety of ends, generally to raise money for a public works project: the cleaning of the River Thames in 1804, Hartford's Retreat for the Insane in 1825, or the frequent lotteries granted to religious societies. Lotteries had several advantages over other means of generating funds for church-building projects. First, contributions could come from faraway places, thus broadening the base of support; local lottery tickets often could be purchased all over Connecticut and even in other states. Second, a society could decide it needed a certain amount of money, say three thousand dollars, and arrange the lottery to raise precisely that amount. But lotteries also carried several distinct disadvantages. Church societies generally gave the business of running the lottery over to lottery "managers," purportedly disinterested businessmen who ran the affair under the auspices of the society, paid out the prizes, and handed the proceeds back to the church. These managers in many instances proved either inept or corrupt, often leaving the church with disappointed ticket holders as well as unpaid bills. Ultimately, however, the decline of lotteries stemmed not from practical problems but was the result of a severe questioning of the morality of such enterprises, a criticism with obvious ramifications for churches.

The state, at least in principle, regulated all lotteries. If a church wanted to hold a lottery it first applied to the General Assembly for permission. Between 1800 and 1820 the Connecticut legislature granted thirteen lotteries for the benefit of twenty-two churches, designed to raise a total of $63,100.[96] Most often societies that applied for lottery rights were small and rural; sometimes a group of such societies would hold a joint lottery. Occasionally a lottery would be raised for general operating funds or the "support of gospel ministry," and in 1820 the legislature granted a large lottery to Episcopalians wishing to raise $15,000 for the Bishop's Fund. But more often religious societies requested a lottery for the specific purpose of paying for building or repairing a place of worship. Petitions to the legislature frequently reflect the congregations' pathetic circumstances and the need to raise fairly large sums of money. The Episcopal Society of Danbury received permission in 1800 to raise $1,800 by lottery to repair the damage done to its church in the late war, a war in which Episcopalians, in particular, suffered property destruction.[97] Beginning in 1801, the First Ecclesiastical Society of Norwich ran a $3,000 lottery to rebuild its "meeting house lately destroyed by fire."[98] In May of 1803, four societies in Preston, Canterbury, Voluntown, and Winsted together asked the state to permit a $6,000 lottery for "building and repairing the meeting houses in those societies respectively."[99] In two other instances congregations made joint applications for lotteries, congregations that did not necessarily have locale or denomination in common. What they did have in common was financial distress, and joining with other societies limited both administrative costs and risk. Most of these societies claimed that without a lottery, their building projects, and implicitly their societies, would fall into financial ruin. The Legislature legitimized their claims and their building projects by chartering lotteries.

Having secured legislative approval, the religious society chose managers who printed and sold tickets. In each "class," or distribution of tickets, a designated number of "chances" sold for set prices, generally from two to four dollars, and the lottery managers guaranteed prizes on lucky tickets drawn at specified times. Prizes ranged from just a few dollars to several thousand. Although the total proceeds from ticket sales equaled the total amount of prizes, when a winner claimed a prize he or she paid a deduction of about 15 percent. The bearer of a three dollar ticket, therefore, would put three dollars into the lottery winnings pot. If his ticket were drawn for a one-hundred-dollar prize, he would receive eighty-five dollars. It was that 15 percent deduction that went toward the sponsor's state-granted total and paid the manager's commission, usually amounting to between 5 and 15 percent of the winnings. Therefore, the lottery managers always sold tickets totaling far in excess of the state's grant. For a church to earn three thousand dollars, for example, the managers would need to sell twenty thousand dollars worth of tickets. Consequently, the schemes got very big, sometimes much too big to control, and often stretched to multiple classes of tickets sold over many years.

The sponsoring churches gained if the lottery went as planned, and also if winners neglected to claim their prizes. As a broadside advertisement for the Fairfield Episcopal Society Lottery declared, "All prizes not called for in one year will be considered as generously given to the Society, and will not thereafter be paid."[100] Although many took oaths of disinterest, lottery managers had much to gain as well. Lottery schemes blos-

somed in the private, free enterprise sector of the new republic, becoming
competitive businesses with extensions, new franchises, and statewide networks of ticket sellers. As suspicious a character as Phineas T. Barnum
sold lottery tickets at a 10 percent commission from his Bethel store, and
his grandfather Phineas Taylor was one of the four managers of the 1818
Fairfield Episcopal Society Lottery.[101]

It is difficult to know just how successful these lotteries ultimately
were. Church records tell the story quite incompletely and, with the exception of newspaper advertisements and hundreds of tickets and ticket
stubs, the details of management and execution are sketchy. It is clear that
managers and brokers sold tickets widely, and that portions of the profits
were distributed among a wide variety of players. In January of 1802
Hartford merchants Hudson & Goodwin wrote to Thomas Tracy, apparently a manager of the Norwich Meeting House Lottery granted in
1801, that "we are paying off the prizes as fast as they present the tickets—
the rage continues and those you have sent will doubly sell." Hudson &
Goodwin eventually sold 681 of these lottery tickets.[102] On January 19,
1800, Samuel Trumbull, who ran the Stonington Post Office, wrote to
the managers of the Goshen Meeting House Lottery, "I have been applied
to for Tickets or requested to write you to send some here for sale. I
believe were you to forward 1 or 2 dozen, have them advertised with the
scheme in the paper published in this place, a large number might be
disposed of."[103] Trumbull, no newcomer to the lottery business, added,
"If you think it proper I will sell on the usual commissions—I have a
Book Store and keep the Post Office which naturally draws a number of
people and which would probably have a good tendency in expediting
the sale. . . ."[104] "Chance" takers were generally anonymous, although a
detailed account of sales for the Fairfield Episcopal Church Lottery of
1819 found in the account books of the Lippit Manufacturing Company,
Providence weavers, sheds some light.[105] Buyers resided in Pomfret,
Woodstock, Abington, and even the Massachusetts towns of Shrewsbury
and Worcester. In this instance the buyers were almost all men, and many
names were listed as having made multiple purchases.

A lottery could be a disappointing fund-raiser, not to mention a major
headache, as illustrated by the experiences of the First Congregational
Society of Canaan. In 1770 the society voted thirty-three in favor and
seventeen against for raising a sixteen-pence tax to build a meetinghouse,
yet no evidence of building follows. Subsequent votes in 1784, 1785, 1789,
1790, and 1801 to either repair the old or build a new meetinghouse,
although passed, seem likewise to have resulted in no material changes.[106]
By 1802, the society appears indeed to have been in the process of building, yet doing so without any semblance of financial security, a combi-

nation of subscriptions and taxes proved inadequate for the task. Finally in 1804, the Canaan society resorted to a lottery, winning approval from the General Assembly to secure up to two thousand dollars "to discharge the debts of building a meeting house."[107] Even after the legislature granted the two thousand dollars lottery in 1804, however, the society's debt was unshakable, amounting to two-thousand dollars in 1806.[108] The Canaan society would not give up on its problematic lottery. It waffled on initiating a lawsuit against the lottery managers, and finally in 1808 decided to soothe its financial woes by selling the pews to the highest bidder for the year.[109] Yet after a further 1811 subscription to pay off the building debt failed, the society applied to the legislature to reappoint new lottery managers.[110] Although subsequent pew sales eased the debt, as late as 1828 the society was still stubbornly clinging to its recalcitrant lottery, and voted to "request the managers of the Canaan meeting house lottery to proceed to raise one or more classes the balance which is due the society by the original grant of the General Assembly."[111] Not willing, however, to stick its already well-extended neck out further, the society proceeded "upon condition that good and sufficient security is given to this society to indemnify them from the payment of all prizes . . . and from all other damages, losses, or injuries."

"The rage" of a lottery and the possibility of becoming one of the "Lucky Adventurers" quite naturally made it a successful means of ex-tracting money from some pockets. "Priscus," a writer to the *Connecticut Evangelical Magazine and Religious Intelligencer* in 1811, claimed that lot-teries were the best means of paying church bills because they, unlike taxes, were "voluntary and all cause of complaint . . . is prevented."[112] It is possible that some purchasers of tickets were genuinely motivated by a desire to further the beneficiaries' projects. An 1804 advertisement in the *American Mercury* for the Episcopal Academy Lottery spoke of "the en-couragement of literature," in which "all classes of citizens feel themselves interested."[113] And another letter from Hudson & Goodwin regarding the Norwich Meeting House Lottery mentioned the sale of a hundred tickets and asked for more "as our neighbors wish to help build your meeting house."[114]

Despite good intentions, lotteries could not shake their shady moral character. Unlike direct subscription, a lottery often pulled money from pockets much too shallow to afford the loss. To many of the antilottery agitators who began a concerted attack in the mid-1820s, lotteries were a dangerous means of tricking the laborer out of his few dollars and helping him along the road to dissipation. In 1830, petitioners from nine western Connecticut towns warned the General Assembly of the evils of lotteries. "The granting of a lottery is one of the most injudicious and unproductive sources of public revenue," they claimed, "so far from being the road to wealth, it is one of the most direct avenues to poverty, disgrace and ruin."[115] Reformers viewed lotteries as nothing but legalized gambling. By the 1830s, fund-raising lotteries were no longer an option for indebted churches, and an 1834 law finally prohibited all lotteries in the state of Connecticut.

Denominational Differences

Although Episcopalians usually went about their financial business as did Congregationalists, denominational differences were evident among Baptists, Methodists, and Universalists.[116] Initially their expenses were far less than those of established Congregational or Episcopal societies. The rough buildings they used for worship demanded minimal maintenance, and itinerant ministers asked for small recompense. Often congregations used what was available at little or no cost. In 1820 the Methodist congregation of Watertown-Bethlehem was meeting in the town's schoolhouse.[117] New Haven's Baptists worshiped in Trinity Episcopal's old church on the corner of Church and Chapel Streets and in 1822 met in the New Haven State House.[118] Yet as these congregations grew and strengthened, they eagerly built more costly houses of worship, and their finances, consequently, became more of a challenge. Voluntary donations had been the bedrock of their treasuries, and that continued to be true. The Baptist Church of New Milford resolved in its 1814 covenant that the members "agree to give of our temporal interest for maintaining the public worship of God and for defraying the necessary charges of the church."[119] But simply passing around the hat on Sunday morning could not supply the funds needed to build a new church.

Baptists, like the Episcopalians, could count on some support from their denomination. In 1821, while meeting in the State House, New Haven's small Baptist congregation proposed to build a new meetinghouse. After much discussion about the practicability of such an endeavor, the building's strongest advocate, Pastor Aaron Hill, promised to get financial support from outside the congregation. Hill traveled as far south as Savannah to get the money, collecting $2,319.59 for the building project.[120] The sixty-six-member congregation in 1824 found itself with a nice stone church worth $10,525.56, but also unpaid subscriptions and a bank loan.[121] Over the next decade the congregation constantly worried about its debt, usually between $1,500 and $2,000. In 1833, the congregation voted to "resume the circulation of the contribution boxes on the sabbath, as formerly."[122] The Baptists also gratefully acknowledged their "excessive obligation" to Nicholas Brown, of Providence.[123] The Baptist Brown had bailed out the New Haven church.

Baptists were uncomfortable with the idea of forced support of religion. As Hartford's Baptists understood matters, "the founder of our holy Religion and his apostles were supported by free gifts and voluntary contributions . . . and their disciples for some hundred years after followed the same example."[124] The context of this statement was an 1818 defense against general religious taxes required under Connecticut law. Yet the belief behind the complaint, a complete reliance on voluntary support, made building difficult. Hartford's congregation had voted in 1814 to raise a meetinghouse by subscription, the difference to be made up by 6 percent bank loan.[125] Only fifteen years later, the Baptists decided to build a new church and sell the former building to the newly formed Free Church, hoping to raise enough money by donation to stay out of building debt. Eventually, however, Hartford's Baptists gave in to pew sale. In 1831, after the deacons received authorization to "execute any acts that may be necessary to procure monies for the completion of the meetinghouse," they decided to sell the pews for a total of sixteen thousand dollars.[126] Income would then come from an annual tax collected on that property. If a pew owner ignored this tax, the deacons figured, one year after notice was given in writing they could repossess and resell the pew. "Free gifts and voluntary contributions" for Hartford's Baptists had given way to something that looked remarkably capitalistic.

Connecticut's Methodists had the most overt denominational direction regarding the construction of their meetinghouses. The denomination insisted that church buildings not present a distraction—financial or material—to the primary business of saving souls. The 1784 Methodist *Book of Discipline* called for buildings that were "not more expensive than is absolutely unavoidable; otherwise the necessity of raising money will make rich men necessary to us."[127] In 1820 a clause was added: meetinghouses were to be "with free seats." "It is contrary to our economy," the *Book* stated, "to build houses with pews to sell or rent."[128] This emphasis on free seats remained in the book until 1852, when the point was tempered to say, "Let all our churches be built . . . with free seats wherever practicable."[129] Despite this injunction, evidence suggests that New Haven's Methodists purchased pews by 1822.[130] The Methodists of Litchfield rented slips starting in 1837, the same year a new church was built.[131] The difficulty of raising enough money by other means is clear in the records of Woodbury's Methodists. Since building in 1839, they had been trying unsuccessfully to use monthly collections "taken up in the congregation to defray the continuing expenses." Additional subscriptions and taxes proved equally insufficient, and the congregation eventually took recourse to pew rental in 1851. Debt was a common problem, pew sale or rental the clearest solution.[132]

An unusual set of documents in the papers of New Haven's Methodists shows the effect the business world was having, even on them. An 1820 paper lists seventy-seven names of subscribers to a general fund for the congregation. An additional document, not dated but probably relating to this list, explains the situation: "the Society of the Methodist Episcopal Church in this city is in Debt about $4000 . . . to each of the banks in this city."[133] To escape from this debt, the Methodists chose a solution not unlike the building-stock schemes previously discussed. The society proposed "to change form of said debts by sharing them into stock in the following manner viz: Divided the whole into shares of $50 each, suppose 80." These shares would draw a 5 percent annual interest and were "Redeemable at the Pleasure of the Board of Trustees."[134] Like a bond issue, the Methodists asked investors to purchase their debt. Isaac Gilbert and his son bought twenty shares; Joseph Barber purchased four. Difficulty in paying the interest on the shares may be the reason that this group of Methodists, against denominational directives, decided to rent pews. An 1827 agreement for the sale of pew number fifty, at the cost of $150, included the condition that "sd. slip shall always be subject to the order and discipline of the [Methodist Episcopal Church] respecting love-feasts and class-meetings."[135] So, although privately owned, the pew was still "free" for certain specific meetings. This clause perhaps interprets the *Book of Discipline*'s insistence on free seats as something that applied only to certain meetings. In any case, this story again shows that, despite resistance, hard times forced congregations to see renting their pews as their most certain escape from financial distress.[136]

One final example shows the extremes to which the commodification of religious space might be taken. Hartfords Universalists had no qualms about commercializing their church property. In March of 1831, the Universalist Society agreed to hold a meeting to "take into consideration, some proposed alterations in said Meeting-House, by raising the main floor and altering the doors in such manner as will render the basement story more eligible for Stores."[137] This basement project, managed by church members, created two large stores and three offices underneath the church (fig. 15). Businesses, including a United States Post Office and a shoe store, paid rent to the Universalists. The congregation adapted its building with an eye deliberately set on making money from real estate, and it worked. Perhaps not so commercial, the North Church in Hartford had a basement school room that it rented to, among others, Catherine Beecher, probably for her academy.[138]

Most of Connecticut's religious societies did not go about marketing

15. "First Independent Universalist Church," *Geer's Hartford Directory*, 1852–53.
Courtesy, The Connecticut Historical Society, Hartford, Connecticut.

their buildings with the deliberate commercialism of Hartford's Universalists. Yet in virtually all cases market forces drew buildings and building committees into the competitive world of capital formation, profit and loss. The bottom line was that new churches were very expensive, whether four-thousand-dollar frame buildings or thirty-thousand-dollar brick ones. Only the most fortunate of congregations avoided some form of debt. In 1831, the new Free (Fourth) Congregational Society of Hartford asked the other Congregational societies of the city to spare a few families to help establish a core for its own congregation. The responses of the other churches to the request for families were telling testimonies of tenuous finances all around. The North Church said it had only 100 of 150 seats rented, and a debt of $12,000. The South Church claimed it was "embarrassed" with a $22,000 debt, in addition to owing $400 to its minister. First Church, after declaring its generally "prosperous state," excused itself because of large expenses and a debt of $11,000.[139] Three beautiful new churches, three indebted congregations. Had the societies been overly optimistic with their building projects? Or, were there other, longer-term considerations that outweighed the financial risks? To compete in the pew rental market, a congregation needed numerous and desirable pews in an attractive building. As we now turn to consider architectural style, it is useful to consider to what degree the market affected the very way church buildings looked. As free consumers listened to the arbiters of refinement and taste in choosing how to spend their dollars, church buildings, too, had to take account of those voices. Style was not a whimsical consideration but a practical one that affected not just the aesthetic and symbolic, but the concrete, material value of church buildings.

CHAPTER 3

Architectural Style and Religious Identity

For it is not the Bulk of a Fabrick, the Richness and Quantity of the Materials, the Multiplicity of Lines, nor the Gaudiness of the Finishing, that give the Grace or Beauty or Grandeur to a Building; but the Proportion of the Parts to one another and to the Whole, whether entirely plain, or enriched with a few Ornaments properly disposed.
— James Gibbs, *A Book of Architecture*, 1728

When the town of Salisbury asked Thomas Dutton to build a meetinghouse, it requested it be done "after the Model and with as good workmanship as the Meeting House in Richmond lately Built is Done." What did the town of Salisbury see in the Richmond, Massachusetts, building that it wanted for its own? In Hartford, the building committee of the First Congregational Society suggested that the congregation build something "simple and decent." The resulting 1807 church was highly fashionable and monumental. What relationship could that building have had to contemporary notions of "simplicity" and "decency"? These two communities of faith deliberately chose these particular buildings. In so doing, they equated architectural "style" with their spiritual and social needs.[1] Style was not merely fashion; it was a statement of congregational personality and purpose.

Builders and users operated in a visual world that brought together transatlantic architectural practices with regional and local innovation and preference. The builders and building committees of Connecticut's congregations took a general knowledge of European architecture, a superficial knowledge of the great ecclesiastical buildings of England and the Continent, and then leaned heavily on local idiom. Style was also a result of the compromise between what was desired and what was feasible — what materials available permitted, what local craftsmen could do, and what the congregation could afford. The realm of the possible had its limits, but within those boundaries choices were made, and it is those choices that reveal what the users and builders found important in their ecclesiastical architecture.

The notion of "style" raises questions of class and cultural authority. Who controls style? Who understands it? How does the shape of the visual world order human society? Work by Dell Upton, among others, stresses the close affinities between church architecture and "mansions," or the costly homes of the elite, in colonial Virginia as a means of reifying power relationships.[2] Churches in Virginia made a show of "hospitality," but the money and gentility implied by the insider-outsider codes in the architecture and the social rituals that took place within reminded those of the lower orders that they were not gentry. Churches worked, then, as instruments that replicated hierarchical social relationships. This was true in Connecticut's churches and meetinghouses, particularly with regard to seating arrangements that rewarded social position first, and later financial ability as displayed in pew purchase or rental. It should be constantly kept in mind that these buildings displayed a degree of taste and refinement far above that of the normal quarters occupied by ordinary persons.

But Connecticut was not Virginia. Even Connecticut's meetinghouses of the colonial period had communitywide significance as the center not just of worship but of town meetings and other civic gatherings. A tradition of participatory government—at least in rhetoric if not in reality— meant that the majority of (male) citizens had helped to pay for these buildings and felt they had some access to the political and social power they conveyed. There was a social structure, there was a power elite, but the barriers between insiders and outsiders were permeable.[3] Furthermore, by the early national period Connecticut's Christians had choices as to where they would worship. A church building could not afford to be simply a strict assertion of the standing order; the style of the building and the worship within had to be somewhat inviting to draw voluntary members and their financial contributions. Churches had to be advertisements as well as assertions.

A further difference between Virginia and Connecticut was one of religion itself. In colonial Virginia, Anglicanism, the established church, was formal and highly ritualized in a way that New England Congregationalism, despite its support by colonial governments, was not. Each congregation had a significant degree of autonomy. Furthermore, spiritual power was not the same as social power. This was formally delineated in the difference between ecclesiastical societies and the church proper. One became a *church* member not by bloodlines or social standing but through an unpredictable, individual, supernatural experience that was a result of the inexplicable workings of God, who perhaps paid attention to but was not bound by the pedigree of his children. Women, children, even

African- and Native Americans theoretically had access to equal standing before God.[4] The individualism implicit in Puritan theology, heightened by the religious enthusiasm of the nineteenth century, confuses our ability to pigeonhole the meanings religious buildings had for various people. Social standing alone did not determine how one felt in a church.[5] Houses of worship, even Puritan meetinghouses, engage the supernatural. History argues that people like their houses of worship to be distinctive, an impulse, we shall see, that was reasserted by Connecticut's latter-day Puritans.[6] The knowledge that worship would take place inside these community buildings led congregations to build special places, the best that local knowledge and skill made available. It would be simplistic to attribute the magnificence, or "otherness," of church buildings to forces that used religion for temporal purposes alone.

In a range of ways, secular and spiritual, members of congregations identified with the architecture of their visible churches. Style, I will argue, could become symbolic of doctrine or worship practices and delineate concretely the borders between one congregation or denomination and another. Competition between congregations or denominations, good-natured or otherwise, often influenced the construction of new church buildings. Many of Connecticut's congregations plainly used the occasion and style of building as an opportunity to make a statement about who they were to their neighbors near and far. Congregationalists tended to build in the "modern" style, fitting themselves in with the fashionable neoclassical architecture of the day. Other denominations, however, often preferred to build in styles that rejected "modern" fashion and the cultural accommodation that "modern" implied.

This chapter begins with a brief consideration of the transcontinental architectural history of which these buildings were a part. Some understanding of European architecture allows us to place these buildings in a wider architectural context. But the relationship between Connecticut's churches and the buildings of Europe was a distant one and will not be the focus of this discussion. Builders and building committees responded primarily to the architecture they knew and understood firsthand: regional, ecclesiastical buildings that grew out of a native architectural tradition. From the limited instructions to builders found in society records, and from evidence of competition between congregations, we can learn something about what society or church members found noteworthy or meaningful in those designs. Particular features of these buildings meant more than others; period remarks, for example, focus on proportion and technological innovation rather than the profile of a cornice molding. The final section of this chapter is a discussion of Connecticut's Episcopalians and how they used their architecture both to define themselves as a denomination and to find a place in their communities. This chapter will not present a comprehensive art historical review of the elements and genealogy of architectural form. Rather, it will investigate how the *idea* of architectural style was understood by the people of Connecticut, and how style was used by them to communicate with each other and outsiders.

The Architectural Context: International Fashion and Local Tradition

Taking a broad view, one can see how international liturgical and stylistic forces shaped Connecticut's religious buildings. First, these New England buildings were part of a tradition that responded to the practical worship demands of the sixteenth-century Protestant Reformation in Europe. Protestants of all stripes, from Scottish Presbyterians to English Quakers to German Methodists, created their places of worship according to a new order. However different these buildings may seem, they shared a need for an acoustically effective auditorium space for hearing the word of God preached in the vernacular and required room and fixtures to accommodate a shared communion service. For denominations with a preaching tradition, the pulpit assumed a central place while the altar frequently declined in importance, and side and/or rear balconies or galleries brought more of the congregation closer to the speaker. These worship requirements were the framework within which architects and builders experimented with style and ornament.

Connecticut's churches and meetinghouses responded to two primary, international styles: a revival of classical forms and details and a return to the medieval. By the later seventeenth century, the first of these influences, classicism, was at least subtly evident on many public and private buildings in New England. Classicism in its broadest sense was the Western world's attraction to the designs of Rome and Greece, an interest that began as part of the Italian Renaissance and continues to this day. Not just architecture but furniture, textile design, and even clothing reflected a taste for the classical world, felt and exercised among a small class of Europeans who had the time and money to make their material worlds into statements of learning and fashion. Classicism had a great variety of stages, each with its distinctive stylistic emphases, historical sources, and logic.

For clarity, art historians have divided the classical impulse into two phases. The first found its expression in the humanism of the Italian Renaissance. It was copied by admirers to the north, and was characterized by bold, elaborate forms and ornament such as shells and scrolls; the art of Raphael or the architecture of Andrea Palladio are typical. The second stage, often called neoclassicism, was more attentive to the actual forms and ornament of the ancient world. By the eighteenth century, archaeological discoveries, travelers on the Grand Tour, and the empirical thrust of the Enlightenment turned the eyes of European artists, architects, and intellectuals to the actual ancient relics of Italy and Greece for inspiration. Neoclassical artists and architects such as Robert Adam studied ancient Greek and Roman designs, which they found controlled, well proportioned, and geometrically satisfying, and then applied them to their own artistic creations, sometimes quite literally.[7] Eighteenth-century Connecticut churches and meetinghouses display classical features, however subtle. The Congregational buildings that are the focus of this study, those of the early republic, should be considered neoclassical.

The heyday of neoclassicism in Europe coincided with the birth of the American republic, where it took several distinct forms. Architectural historian William Pierson divides American neoclassicism into four stages, stretching from the early 1780s to the Civil War. One of the two stages with the greatest impact on New England church design was the earliest, a "delicate and refined," restrained mode of design, exemplified in the work of Boston architect Charles Bulfinch. This phase, sometimes called the "Federal" style, is characterized especially by imaginative interiors, with gracefully and playfully arranged delicate ornament and the creative use of geometric forms. The second stage was the "Greek Revival," a sentimental use of Greek forms that reflected the cultural self-consciousness of a country trying to be the next center of civilization and learning.[8] Greek Revival buildings lack the detailed ornament of the Federal style, have bold, readily identifiable classical elements (such as enormous front columns supporting an enormous front pediment), and rely on the use of flat, white surfaces that resemble the marble of the ancient world (even, as was usually the case in New England, if rendered in wood). Many Connecticut churches of the 1830s and 1840s display the Greek Revival influence, although purity of form in one primary way lost out to local tradition: the steeple or tower remains. The Meriden Congregational Church of 1830 is typical of a Connecticut Greek Revival church (fig. 16). The meaning of the neoclassical style in America, much more complex than it first appears, is further discussed in the following chapter.

The second stylistic trend, a return to the medieval, or Gothic, taste, did not have an impact on Connecticut's churches until the end of the eighteenth century. Then the Gothic was just beginning its American appearance in the details of Episcopal churches and occasional domestic buildings. The Gothic had reached its greatest brilliance in the European

16. Congregational Church, Meriden, Conn., 1830. Photo by author.

Roman Catholic churches of the middle ages; pointed arches, buttresses, complex spaces, and ceiling vaults were among its characteristic features. Englishmen of the mid–eighteenth century found themselves drawn to the Gothic's dramatic qualities. This early return to the Gothic (often called "Gothick") was based on the use of applied ornament rather than the replication of Gothic form, and left such whimsical monuments as Horace Walpole's generously arched and pointed Strawberry Hill (1749–76) (fig. 17). Advocates of the Gothick, such as English architect Batty Langley, were concerned with overlaying the features of Gothic design

17. Paul Sanby, *View of Strawberry Hill from the Southeast*, watercolor, c. 1783. Courtesy, Lewis Walpole Library, Yale University.

onto regular classical forms; the title of Langley's 1742 design book, *Gothic Architecture improved by the Rules of Proportions*, makes this clear. The Gothic style in New England—which appeared in the form of arched windows with trefoil muntins, or the use of stone rather than brick or wood—will be discussed at length in the final section of this chapter, a consideration of Connecticut's Episcopalians.[9]

Connecticut's church builders, when they did have knowledge of European design, followed English rather than French or Italian fashion. Until the great London fire of 1666, English Protestant churches tended to be either stripped-down, medieval buildings or, if built new, simple, rectangular structures with flat ceilings, white walls, wooden galleries, bench or box pews, and a combination of pulpit-altar-baptismal font in one central place along one of the walls. After the fire, the brilliant architect Christopher Wren (1632–1723) became surveyor general of the Royal Works and created new overall designs for fifty-two of the eighty-seven prefire London churches. Wren rejected the dark and narrow medieval chancel in favor of high, airy, barrel-vaulted plaster ceilings, classical proportions, and an infusion of light from large, clear windows. Although Wren often retained the Gothic tower and spire, he designed them with a delicacy of form and ornament that enabled them to be wed successfully to a largely classical building. Historically, spires had nothing whatsoever to do with classical architecture, but Wren made them work so well together that it is now hard to imagine an alternative.[10]

Considerable interest in church improvement continued in early Georgian England, and Wren's work was carried on by a new generation of architects, including Nicholas Hawksmoor and the Scotsman James Gibbs (1682–1754).[11] In 1720 Gibbs was appointed the architect for rebuilding the parish church of St. Martin-in-the-Fields (1720–27) (fig. 18). This building had far-reaching influence, and was especially influential in North America. St. Martin's is a rectangular block, heavily ornamented with classical detail; the delicately staged spire sits on the main body of the church, behind a large, temple-front portico with huge columns topped with elaborate, Corinthian capitals. The galleries inside, a vaulted and plastered ceiling, and a large Palladian window on the gable end further distinguish the building. The kind of roof system described in chapter 1, whereby builders could hang a plaster ceiling from wooden trusses, was first used in buildings such as St. Martin's.

This "elegantly poised" roof structure was fully illustrated in Gibbs's *Book of Architecture* (1728). The wide circulation of this book is the prime reason for the extensive influence of Gibbs's designs. Expensive as it was, it secured an international readership; multiple copies are known to have been in Boston, Philadelphia, New York, and Charleston libraries. Two of Gibbs's churches, St. Martin's and Marylebone Chapel (1721–24), both illustrated in the *Book of Architecture*, had a documented impact on American church design, as did Gibbs's detailed plates of steeple designs (figs. 18–20). Their influence can be seen on churches ranging from St. Michael's in Charleston, South Carolina (1752–62) to Christ Church, Philadelphia (1727–54), to First Baptist in Providence, Rhode Island (1775) (fig. 21).

American gentlemen and builders read with interest English design and pattern books such as Gibbs's *Book of Architecture* or Batty Langley's *Gothic Architecture*. These books reinforced artistic connections between England and its colonies. Until Massachusetts builder Asher Benjamin (1773–1845) published the first of his design books, the *Country Builders Assistant*, in 1797, carpenters who did have access to pattern books had only European publications. Even Benjamin's later book depended heavily on material he took from the pattern books of Langley, Gibbs, William Kent, and Robert Adam.[12] Despite the obvious influences, it is important to recognize that Americans were not making anything close to carbon copies of English buildings. Nowhere in the colonies were English designs used for much more than a source of decorative detail or proportion, a skeleton on which

Jacobo Gibbs Architecto.   The West front of St Martins Church.   H. Hulsbergh Sculp:

18. "West Front of St. Martin's Church," 1720–27, James Gibbs, *A Book of Architecture*, pl. 3. Courtesy, The Winterthur Library: Printed Book and Periodical Collection.

The West Front

The Section from South to North

Ja: Gibbs Arch: del.   H. Hulsbergh Sculp.

19. "The West Front" and "The Section from South to North," Marylebone Chapel, 1721–1724, James Gibbs, *A Book of Architecture*, pl. 25. Courtesy, The Winterthur Library: Printed Book and Periodical Collection.

20. "Five Draughts of Steeples made for St. *Mary le Strand*," James Gibbs, *Book of Architecture*, pl. 31. Courtesy, The Winterthur Library: Printed Book and Periodical Collection.

In the caption for this image, Gibbs wrote "Steeples are indeed of a Gothick Extraction, but they have their Beauties."

21. First Baptist Church, Providence, R.I., 1775. Library of Congress, HABS Collection.

American architects, builders, and building committees overlaid their own ideas and abilities, usually on a much smaller scale.

In matters of style it is a mistake to think of American architecture as simply the country cousin of elite British or Continental forms. Many scholars have considered the work of American builders to be primarily emulative of English style (mostly "unsuccessful"). To cite one historian writing in 1978, the colonial builder was "an architectural illiterate groping toward a fashionable idiom with nothing to work with but plain boards, a saw, and a hammer."[13] Individualism, creativity, and craftsmanship could thus be praised, but colonial design was something that at best approximated an elusive foreign prototype. Upton, in his work on Virginia churches, offered a different model: builders and even gentlemen architects had loyalties both to a "metropolitan style" but also to local preference. "Landmarks" of architectural design give us a good sense of the intellectual and artistic currents moving among elites, but are only a starting point for comprehending a collection of stylistic influences.

For Connecticut builders and building committees, what mattered more than pattern books or the influence of high-fashion English buildings was the tradition of the New England meetinghouse as it evolved from the seventeenth through the eighteenth centuries. New Englanders had a powerful sense of their own history, and in a landscape with few "historic" buildings, a distinctive old meetinghouse could be full of meaning. English Puritans who came to New England in the seventeenth century had an unprecedented opportunity to build ecclesiastical buildings as they saw fit. These buildings responded to several dictates of faith and politics. First, they were to serve both as religious spaces and as centers of community, literally "meeting houses" that held both Sabbath worship and town meetings. Second, they were to be centrally located, permitting colonists from all corners of a settlement to attend mandatory services. Finally, within the Calvinist tradition, they were to be well-built, decent structures that avoided unnecessary ornament and rejected "papist" pomp and show. Many seventeenth-century meetinghouses were roughly square, often with a hipped roof. The only surviving example of this type of building is the unusually large "Old Ship" Meetinghouse in Hingham, Massachusetts (fig. 22). Period illustrations indicate that this was a common form for first-generation buildings. Doors to the outside were on all walls except the wall with the high pulpit that dominated the interior. Seating was in the form of simple benches or box pews. These buildings, like Old Ship, might have had balconies, or galleries, facing the pulpit.[14]

Early in the eighteenth century, another form of meetinghouse appeared, a rectangular building that looked like a fine house. In spirit this was much like the earlier buildings—simple, multipurpose, relatively

22. Old Ship Meeting House, Hingham, Mass., 1681. Library of Congress, HABS Collection.

unadorned—but the architecture, like that of period houses, was Georgian classical.[15] Connecticut examples of this type still standing include the brick Congregational Meetinghouse in Wethersfield (1761–64), the Congregational Church in Brooklyn (1770–72), and First Congregational, Farmington (1771–72) (fig. 23). Classicism had an effect on meetinghouse design similar to that which it had on other public and private buildings in New England. This included a general sense of order, proportion, and symmetry; large sash windows, possibly including a Palladian, or tripartite, arched window; and details such as quoining (wood cut to look like staggered stone blocks) on the exterior corners of a building, pedimented doorways, and regulation plinth-column-capital arrangements of the classical orders. Many of these buildings had a bell tower or steeple tacked on the short side (a feature that was often a later addition).

23. Congregational Church, Farmington, Conn., 1772. Library of Congress,
HABS Collection.

A door through this tower gave access to the main floor of the house and sometimes to the galleries but did not replace the door on the long side as the primary entrance. This main entrance faced a high, often canopied pulpit; box pews were arranged around the main floor. Galleries made a second story of seats on two or three sides facing the pulpit. The rectangular glass panes, or "lights" in the sash windows were clear, allowing a good amount of light into the building. Inside, plaster and whitewash often contributed to the brightness. Outside, the buildings may have been painted white, although they also displayed surprising colors, such as blue, yellow, or green.[16] The controversial old White Haven meetinghouse in New Haven, for example, was painted blue.[17] Rather than pictorial decoration, beauty was in the form and details of the woodwork: elaborate paneled pulpits, cornice moldings, turned columns, and newel posts. Both the Farmington and Wethersfield pulpits were decorated with fancy floral carvings. These buildings clearly showed the impact of fashion. Nothing indicates that Connecticut's Congregationalists ever denounced these classical flourishes as too ornate or fashionable for Puritan meetinghouses, although they surely were stylish.

The next considerable change in Connecticut's religious architecture was the one following the Revolution. Beginning with modest buildings like Thomas Dutton's Salisbury and Washington meetinghouses, the style then produced uncertain examples such as Hartford's First Congregational, finally reaching full-blown neoclassicism in structures such as United Church in New Haven. The builders of these structures rejected the meetinghouse plan in favor of one with a different form and orientation, what we would now call a "church." Judging from the large number of very similar buildings that were built, this type was an excellent match for the needs of Connecticut's congregations. During the eighteenth century, Congregational societies had not made significant spatial changes to the inside of their buildings. Any changes that were made reconfigured a congregation's relationship to the outside, to the architectural landscape and to the community at large, responding to fashion without altering the congregation from the inside out. The early-national-period turn to churchly forms, on the other hand, was a thorough rethinking of Congregational worship space. That change was marked by three features: the integration of the tower into the heart of the buildings, the attachment of a large, columned front portico, and the reorientation of the plan so that the main entrance was through this portico on the short, gabled end of the buildings and the pulpit was on the opposite end.[18] Seats were increasingly benchlike "slips" facing the front in neat rows. A vote taken by the Roxbury Congregational Society in 1794 shows that these spatial changes required a deliberate, communitywide vote: the society voted "to build a Meetinghouse with a Door on the front side and the pulpit on the other side of the house."[19] Similarly, in 1801, before Dutton built its new church, the Washington Congregational Society voted that "all Doors to go into the sd. Building shall be at the South end [through a portico]."[20]

This apparently clean break with tradition demands explanation. From the preceding chapter, we know that this rebuilding coincided with renewed fortunes and attention to run-down buildings after the political conflict and economic uncertainties of wartime had passed. But why this new style? Was there, at this moment, a conscious rejection of a "plain style" to which Congregationalists, albeit with declining rigidity, had been adhering? Was this a capitulation to a seductive Anglican style?[21] Or, was this change in design simply the next step in an ongoing transformation that had constantly reflected fashion currents, fortunes, and the abilities of craftsmen? Can we read this move from the multifunctional meetinghouse to the church as declension, the last blow for the Puritan "plain style" ideal?[22] This important question about the historical meaning of architectural style will be discussed briefly here and then at greater length in the following chapter.

The idea of the "plain style" is itself problematic. While there was clearly a "plain style" as applied to preaching and rhetoric, the application of the concept to the material world was made not by Puritans but by their admirers or detractors who for good or ill wanted to link a perceived austerity to doctrine.[23] Historians have subsequently replaced the image of the gray, sullen Puritans with people who loved color, ate heartily, worshiped with more than occasional joy, and even experienced sexual pleasure.[24] This reversal came about through historical investigation into the material life of early Americans. A rereading of theology is also instructive. The only thing in Calvin's *Institutes of the Christian Religion*, for instance, that can be applied to religious space is a ban on material representations of things spiritual, and an insistence that no material thing should hinder the proper worship of God. Pictures of angels or Jesus, or work so elaborate that it gave glory to the craftsman rather than his creator, were strictly forbidden. But against beauty, Calvin had no injunctions.[25] Christians were to enjoy the beauty of the earth, and the beauty they could create out of their God-given talents and resources. Nothing was to prevent houses of worship from being beautiful. Now, there is no saying how much New England's Puritans looked to Calvin and how much they relied on their own interpretation of doctrine in the creation of their religious spaces. It is clear, however, that meetinghouses were among the most carefully crafted buildings in a town, and displayed a high degree of stylistic flourish.

Yet the meetinghouse has remained a kind of sacred cow that resists reinterpretation. Some of this may be attributed to the fact that the typical eighteenth-century New England meetinghouse is indeed, from our modern perspective, plain. These buildings were definitely not Anglican parish churches; they followed the forms of dissenters' buildings in Europe. To what degree that material reality was the direct result of a theological intention, a deliberate "Puritan plainness," is difficult to know, and is certainly not self-evident.[26] Such intentions are missing from the historical record, and the situation is complicated by the fact that these meetinghouses served multiple purposes, and so making them too specialized would have been impractical. But these buildings were not void of significant and costly ornament. They had special qualities that would not have been lost on contemporary viewers. Even first-generation, seventeenth-century meetinghouses displayed the best that colonial craftsmen had to offer, as Robert Trent argues in his provocative analysis of fragments of seventeenth-century meetinghouse interiors.[27]

It is important to note that a similar rectangular, towerless church form was used by Anglicans in England and its colonies. These churches, of course, did have different interior arrangements and stylistic flourishes. For example, Trinity Church in Brooklyn, Connecticut (1771), designed after the Anglican church of the same name in Newport, Rhode Island, is a thirty-by-forty-six-foot building with two tiers of windows and a hipped roof (fig. 24). Exterior features such as the round-topped lower-tier windows, and the single entrance on the short side, mark the building as Anglican. Inside, the box pews face forward on either side of a central aisle, the altar is front and center, and the pulpit and sounding board originally sat about a third of the way down the aisle. St. Matthew's Episcopal in East Plymouth (1792–94) is thirty-two by forty-two feet, has two tiers of round-arched windows, and originally had neither porch nor vestibule. The interior, with galleries and box pews, was originally probably much like the Brooklyn church. Although not Puritan meetinghouses, these Anglican churches nonetheless shared with them stylistic features of Reformed architecture, including decorative restraint and an interior space arranged to the advantage of preaching.

By the eighteenth century it seems likely that, for Connecticut's Congregationalists, the ubiquitous homelike place of worship had lost much if not all of the punch of visible dissent. There simply was no foil, no ornate churchly buildings for contrast. Meetinghouses and churches came to represent a local design integrity that had more to do with what looked "right," and with what was familiar to builders, than with what was considered theologically correct. If this has the effect of demythologizing the New England meetinghouse, it also will allow us to see the construction

24. Trinity Episcopal Church, Brooklyn, Conn., 1770. Library of Congress, HABS Collection.

of "churches" in the nineteenth century as a *reassertion* of the connection between Calvinist theology and the form and style of religious buildings. Interestingly, in this period in Connecticut it was the dissenters on the margins—Baptists, Methodists, and Quakers—who built the simplest, least-adorned churches or meetinghouses. This had theological and financial reasons, but also served them as a means of distinguishing themselves from Congregationalists and Episcopalians.

American Designers and their Sources

The complicated relationship between English design, American architects, and local tradition in the early republic is displayed in the career of the aforementioned Asher Benjamin and his designs for the 1814 building of New Haven's First Congregational Society (fig. 25). Benjamin was among the first native architects in the United States. Architecture as a profession, with specific training not just in design but in mathematics and engineering, was something new in the early republic. Self-designated "architects" like Benjamin were just beginning to make a reputation for themselves through their commissions and their self-promotion. Care is

25. Center Church, New Haven, 1814. Photo by author.

recommended when interpreting the use of the title "architect" in period documents. Especially in the late eighteenth century, "architect" as used in ecclesiastical society records was much more likely to mean "master carpenter" than "designer-draftsman." But evidence does suggest that the notion of "architect" had cachet. New Haven's well-heeled First Congregational Society made this clear when it went out of its way to purchase plans of Benjamin (who apparently had little or nothing to do with the actual construction of its 1814 building). Even in this case, however, we need to be cautious with the notion of sole designer, for Benjamin's plans (now missing) were altered during the course of the project.[28] This was also the case when the building committee of Hartford's Second Congregational Society, apparently working from a set of plans, "found . . . as the work progressed, that many alterations were necessary to render the House convenient and satisfactory to the society."[29]

Benjamin, a native of Hartland, Connecticut, probably trained initially with local Connecticut builders. He worked up and down the Connecticut River Valley, creating notable buildings from Suffield, Connecticut, to Greenfield, Massachusetts, to Windsor, Vermont. In 1795 Benjamin constructed the circular staircase in the Hartford State House. By 1803, when he was thirty, Benjamin was in Boston, working as a "housewright" and no doubt learning from local architects such as Charles Bulfinch.[30] Today Benjamin is known as much for his pattern books as for his actual buildings. For, in addition to the *Country Builder's Assistant* (1797), he went on to publish six other books in many editions. Benjamin learned his trade from local builders, from the masterful work of Boston architects, and from imported design books. His life, like that of similar carpenters, was one of "tramping," the yet little understood movement of artisans across regions, by which they both learned and transmitted their own designs to others.[31]

New Haven's First Congregational, or Center, Church, designed by Benjamin and built by Ithiel Town, is closely related to Gibbs's St. Martin's. This influence, however, was neither simple nor direct. Two decades earlier, St. Martin's and the Marylebone Chapel had influenced the design of Charles Bulfinch's important early churches in Taunton (1792) and Pittsfield, Massachusetts (1790–92) (fig. 3), which became the model for the 1794 Richmond church, which in turn influenced the building committee of the Salisbury meetinghouse (fig. 1). Other regional builders created their own versions of the basic design that became the regional norm: a three-door entrance through a pediment, a graceful staged cupola or spire, a double row of rectangular windows, and a reorientation to a "churchly" plan. By the time First Congregational was built, Benjamin's own highly influential "Design for a Meeting House" published in his

Country Builder's Assistant, had been circulating over fifteen years (fig. 26).[32] According to Abbott Cummings, it was a mélange of influence, "a powerful regional ferment in the 1790s" consisting of the work and designs of many builders, that popularized this church type.[33] Benjamin, Bulfinch, and their small-scale peers such as Thomas Dutton created a normative form that had a connection to European examples. But, by its modest size, frame construction, and relatively subdued decoration, it also had a stylistic debt to the New England meetinghouse.

So why, in 1814, would New Haven's First Society and Asher Benjamin reach back to Gibbs's 1727 church, by then nearly one hundred years old-fashioned? We do not know what the First Society's building committee told Benjamin, but the result is a reasonably faithful, if much smaller-scale, adaptation of the London church; the overall form, the spire, the templelike portico, and the banister rail along the roofline plainly evoke St. Martin's. First Church does, however, display the influence of later neoclassical design: the spire is taller and thinner, and the side windows sit in recessed arches. In addition, the designer placed a central, enclosed vestibule under the tower and portico. What these choices illustrate is the nonlinear progression of style and the multiple influences on design. The congregation was conservative, the oldest and most socially entrenched and politically conservative of the many New Haven societies. Perhaps it preferred, for the sake of tradition, a design that followed a known English example. Even so, when Benjamin chose St. Martin's as a model for First Church, he was not choosing a relic. The design may have been dated, but New Haven's citizens had never seen anything like it in their midst. Or had they? The basic elements of Gibbs's design had already been normalized by Benjamin himself and other local builders, and previously incorporated into local idiom.

Style and Meaning: Impact at the Local Level

Most congregations in Connecticut, unlike New Haven's large and wealthy First Society, did not have the luxury, or perhaps even the inclination, to buy church plans from an architect. The design of their buildings happened in the interactions between the builder and the building committee, and between the builder and his workmen. Design was often not something that was put down on paper, but was rather worked out in the process of building and finishing. When it came to questions of style, what really mattered? Was it the carving on a capital, the height of a steeple, the arrangement of pews? For the small congregations of Con-

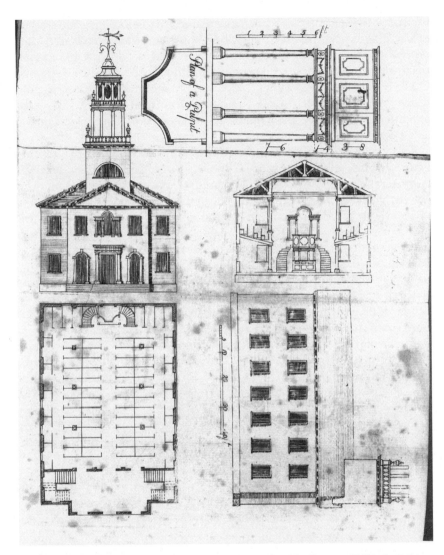

26. "Plan and Design for a Church," Asher Benjamin, *The Country Builder's Assistant*, 1798, pl. 27. Courtesy, The Winterthur Library: Printed Book and Periodical Collection.

necticut, certain elements of form or ornament had more significance than others. The limited instructions of building committees found in society records offer some clues as to what they valued; so do bare-bones contracts like the one between Thomas Dutton and the town of Salisbury. Other contemporary accounts of building, found primarily in correspondence, occasionally offer more complete information. Finally, some contemporaries freely gave their opinions, good or bad, about these remarkable buildings

Just as the Salisbury committee turned to the Richmond model, religious societies selected designs on the basis of what they knew locally.[34] A large portion of the work of building committee members, then, was getting acquainted with other local churches. St. Peter's Episcopal Society in Plymouth asked its building committee to take care of finishing the inside of its church "in a Decent and Elegant manner According to their judgement after viewing other churches as much as they think proper."[35] St. Peter's presumed its committee had a suitable knowledge of building, for it had previously asked the committee to "Draw a plan for a new church" itself.[36] In rural areas, the society as a whole played a role in design decisions. In a Roxbury Congregational Society meeting, the society voted "to make a portico to the new house something in form as was shown at the meeting or other wise in form as they see fit."[37]

In the case of larger, urban projects, it appears that the committee worked in conference with the builders, periodically approaching the society about significant design decisions or the need for more money. The building committee of Hartford's North Society reported in 1823: "They have prepared a plan, or rather parts of several plans, of a house, which they present herewith that the society may [select] from them the general outlines of such a plan for a house as they wish to build." The committee did offer its opinion as to what was best, picking and choosing elements from several sets of drawings: "that plan of a front for the house to which no Turret is attached, and to attach to it that form of a Turret represented on the front view of the other plan; and for the plan of the sides with a corresponding rear, that of the sideview herewith presented."[38] Buildings were composed of *units* of significance that each merited a vote: size of overall rectangle? Steeple, cupola, or neither? Porch or portico? Galleries on two or three sides? These units could be planned all at once or voted on in turn during the months or years of building.[39] Rural meetinghouses or churches in particular seem rarely to have been understood as "finished"; changes, additions, and repairs are constant topics in society records. Most changes made to existing buildings in the early nineteenth century were in the direction of added comfort, such as putting in stoves, carpeting, or slanting the backs of pews.[40]

An important consideration was the arrangement of seats, something that became all the more important as those seats began to represent revenue. The committee advised the North Society to work with "the floor plan now offered," which consisted of seating on the main floor but no side galleries, although those "may be erected hereafter, whenever further accommodations shall be needed." Finally, the committee asked the society to grant it some independence over the course of building "to make such alterations as they shall think will improve the comfort, convenience, or beauty of the house, without considering additional expense; preserving however the general appearance of the Building, as represented by the plan approved by the society."[41]

Salisbury found a building it desired to replicate completely. In most cases, however, design involved doing as Hartford's North Society did, taking specific elements from here and there and combining them in a way that suited the congregation's specific needs and taste. As the Cornwall society expressed in 1841, its new building should be "in such stile & form as they shall think best adapted to the taste of the Inhabitants of this society & the means they have to build with."[42] In 1794 the Roxbury society voted to model just the windows and steeple of its new house after those of the meetinghouse at Southbury.[43] The Morris Congregational Society preferred the fenestration of the Bethlehem meetinghouse.[44] The Woodbury Methodist Church wanted "as good materials and workmanship as the congregational Church in Roxbury," but wanted the plan to copy that of their sister Methodist society in Danbury.[45]

A mixture of considerations drew building committees to previous examples and guided them as they decided upon their own particular plan. "Proportion" was an important element. On the surface, this meant the physical size of the building, the size necessary to suit the community. Dimensions in this period were rectangular, usually between a 3:4 and a 3:5 ratio. Salisbury's building was 48 by 64 feet, exactly 3:4. Hartford's building was 64 by 102 feet, nearly 3:5. Size determined how large the lot would have to be, how many people could fit inside the building, and the gross impact the new building would have on the viewer. But "proportion" meant much more than simple height-width-depth dimensions. "Proportion" was the general sense that the design of the whole building fit together successfully with balance and equilibrium. James Gibbs had forcefully stated the importance of proportion in the introduction to his *Book of Architecture*.

For it is not the Bulk of a Fabrick, the Richness and Quantity of the Materials, the Multiplicity of Lines, nor the Gaudiness of the Finishing, that give the Grace or Beauty or Grandeur to a Building; but the Proportion of the Parts to one

another and to the Whole, whether entirely plain, or enriched with a few Ornaments properly disposed.[46]

Having "proportion" meant the building made visual sense to the viewer.
"Proportion" incorporated notions of "Grace," "Beauty," and "Grandeur."[47] It was what allowed a building to be elegant, even if small and
relatively unadorned.

A letter from Simeon Baldwin, a member of New Haven's United Society, to his son, a law student in Albany, illuminates these several notions of "proportion." Because of internal dissension, the United Society
was having a difficult time getting its building project off the ground. It
also faced competition from the First Society, which had published its
intentions to build a large, brick church in the center of New Haven.
The new First Church would be, according to Baldwin, "on the site of
the old one but much larger, the present one is 70 by 50 and they propose 70 by 100." Acknowledging competition between the congregations, Baldwin admitted that the plans of the First Society "rendered it
necessary for the United Society in self defence to agree to build also,"
and he told his son that his United Society was already busy "looking
about for the best plan." Baldwin had heard from his wife's brother
Roger Sherman of "the new Meeting House in Albany as one the proportions of which strike the eye very agreeably," and that brought him
to the point of his letter. Would his son send him some information
about the Albany Church (fig. 27)? "I understand that was an expensive
building," Baldwin acknowledged, "but as proportions cost little or
nothing we are desirous of obtaining the best and hope to build with
good materials in a plain manner." The size "will be about 96 by 70" (the
size of the proposed First Church), and the society was thinking it
would build the church "probably with a cupola instead of a steeple."
What Baldwin requested were the basics, "the dimensions and proportions of the house." "I should be glad of the length, Breadth, and
height—whether the roof is supported by pillars or not—is the ceiling
arched—what is the arrangement of the ground floor, are there wall
pews, or is the whole in slips, and anything else which you may learn
from their experience."[48]

Baldwin's concerns here were exactly those mentioned in many building records. Which dimensions are appropriate? Should we have a tower
or steeple? Should we arch the ceiling? Should we use slips or pews or
both? His particular interest in the support structure for the roof and the
use of slips accentuates the fact that these were two new features at the
time. Baldwin concentrated on these same details when he wrote, after
the three New Haven buildings were complete, to a minister in Fayetteville, North Carolina, who had requested information about New Haven's

27. Unknown artist, *First Presbyterian Church*, wood engraving on wove paper, c. 1900. Courtesy, Albany Institute of History & Art, bequest of Ledyard Cogswell, Jr.

churches. He gave the dimensions for all three: "Mr. Merwin's [United Church] 98 by 68, the walls 37 from the basement/Mr. Taylors [First/Center Church] 100 × 72, the walls 34 from the basement, The Church [Trinity Episcopal] 115 × 74, the walls 40 from the basement." Also interesting enough to mention was the "conference room over the entrance," a feature permitted by the typical enclosure of a portion of the entrance portico creating a vestibule with a room above at the level of the galleries. The ceiling, as usual, received considerable mention. "In the two North meeting houses," Baldwin related carefully, "the pillars support the gallery only the ceiling overhead is supported from the roof." This forms "a handsome elliptical dome of 10 feet elevation, ornamented with stucco radii from the corners (other stucco ornament) around its base and in the center." Baldwin was clearly impressed with the effect such engineering skill was able to produce. With regard to the seating plans, he remarked, "in Mr. Merwin's [Reverend Merwin of United Church] you perceive by the plan a part of the wall seats are in pews, in both the others the whole is divided into slips." Besides these features, Baldwin commented on the use of mahogany, particularly in the United Church pulpit. Of greatest interest to Baldwin, then, and to building committees in general, were the raw facts of the building's size and materials as well as features that displayed technical innovation. This by no means indicates that ornament was unimportant, but it does suggest that information about detail and style was readily available and understood and needed no communication. These Congregational buildings we call "neoclassical," but to contemporaries they were "modern," something new but not out of the ordinary.

A final note in Baldwin's letter to his friend in Fayetteville called attention to the remarkable total cost of these buildings, "not far from 100.000 Dollars." "This prima facie argues much in favor of the increasing attentions to the main objects of such building—and I think there is some reality in it." "But we must acknowledge," he continued, "that some part of our exertion is imputable to worldly pride and a spirit of rivalship."[49] This same spirit of competition was noted by Theodonia Woolsey when, on noticing that both the First and United Societies were about to build anew, she remarked that "I suppose a strife will commence which shall have the handsome's [sic]." [50] One product of the one-upsmanship in New Haven was a curious yet revealing Connecticut Journal column that appeared late in 1815 when the three buildings, First or Center Church, United Church, and Trinity Episcopal Church, were nearing completion (fig. 28). The writer, clearly amused by the hoopla over the new buildings yet obviously proud of them, too, pretended to have letters from a member of each of the religious societies, explanations why each writer's build-

28. *New Haven, Conn., Comprising a View of the Episcopal and Presbyterian Churches, Statehouse and Yale College*, 1831, hand-colored engraving, Illman & Pilbrow, New York. Courtesy, New Haven Colony Historical Society, 1973.342.

ing was the best. The column began with a tongue-in-cheek announcement of the "communications" and a confident claim that *all* the buildings deserved great attention:

The following communications shew the variety of opinion entertained respecting the new churches erected on our public square. Each one appears to possess an opinion in favor of his own, and we believe all have sufficient reason to be gratified. The connoisseur, the stranger, and the citizen will unite in admiring the beauty of the architecture and the grandeur of the view presented by these temples of devotion.[51]

The first "letter" was from a member of the First Ecclesiastical Society:

MESSRS. PRINTERS—It is a question often asked, which is the most elegant of the three new houses of public worship lately erected in this city. They are now so far completed that a correct [opinion] can be formed. I am one of the first society, and yet I am sure that my judgement is not biased at all by that circumstance. I candidly believe our House altogether superior to either of the others. It stands in the centre of the green, and in the centre of the others, and in the centre of the city. Now it is always known that the centre is always the place of respect and honor. From the sun, which is the centre of the heavenly bodies, down to the *center piece* on a splendid dining table, a central position is filled uniformly with the most beautiful and grand object—so it is with *our brick*. The spire, pillars, and corinthian and ionic columns, the arch, balustrade, and urns, are altogether superior to anything on the other buildings. Our bell also is larger, heavier, and more deep-toned than any of the others; and even the rope that rings it is made of the best hemp or flax. As to the Episcopal Church it is all over gothic—gothic inside and out—gothic from top to bottom. As to the North Brick, it is a pretty little box, but you will look at it in vain for the highly wrought and superb architecture which is every where conspicuous on ours; besides, our House stands on the sepulchre of the dead. Such situation cannot fail to inspire solemnity and veneration. In fine, our House, when compared with either of the others, is as sixteen dollar broadcloth is to eight. A BRICKITE

Next, a member of the United Society spoke:

MESSRS. PRINTERS: I am a member of the United Society. When the plan was laid for erecting two new Meeting Houses and an Episcopal Church, it occurred to me that there might be some competition between the societies as to the point which should be the best, and since they are erected I find it is often asked, which is the most elegant structure? I feel perfectly impartial on the subject and think I am able to judge very candidly, and I pronounce without any hesitation, that ours exceeds the others altogether. As to the *South Brick* it is quite disproportional— the steeple rises to the clouds—the body of the House is almost on a line with the burying ground on which it stands. The roof had such a monstrous break in it that a balustrade became necessary to hide its deformity. As to the ornaments which surround the tower, such as the bull's eyes, garlands, pilastres, &c., &c. why they are too gay and tawdry. The bell is too heavy, and one side of it is thicker than the other—it sounds awfully. Our house stands near the venerable elms which were set out in front of the house of the Revd. Mr. Pierpont; the spot seems consecrated, and it is, without doubt, one of the most pleasant in New Haven. The House is neat and elegant throughout, and the workmanship is perfect. The tower is low when compared with the South Brick, but it is symmetry itself. He is nothing of *gothic barbarism*, but the *style is after the best models of Grecian and Roman architecture*. Our pulpit is mahogany, and we have side pews instead of slips, which is a very important consideration. To be sure our House is not so large by two or three feet as the other Brick, but on actual measurement we have 15 feet more of seating, which will accommodate at least seven more persons. On the whole, I really think that it is the best house of the three. ONE OF THE UNITED SOCIETY.

Finally, "an Episcopalian" had his turn:

M.P.: It is quite surprising to me how the question can exist in any unprejudiced mind which of the three public buildings lately erected is the most magnificent. I have no partialities on the subject though I am a Churchman. Our House stands near the seat of justice where laws are made, expounded, and executed. It stands also near Chapel-Street, the greatest Street in this City, and on a gentle and beautiful declivity from the Colleges. It is built of stone taken from West Rock, and therefore, is literally (as it should be) founded on a rock. Its majestic tower and splendid turrets—its superb windows and pointed arches, and the most beautiful pulpit exhibit the finest proof of skill in architecture, and combined fill the mind with true ideas of magnificence. It is in the true Gothic style, and is uniformly so in all parts. It is, beyond doubt, the most elegant church this side of St. Peter's in Rome.

The two Meeting Houses, or more properly the two Conventicles, are neat, pretty little buildings; the brick and wood is put together with taste and judgement; but they are like four dollar cassimere compared to eight, when examined with ours. Those may answer till the fashion changes, and then down they will go, as the old brick did a few years since—but ours will be as noble and splendid ten centuries hence as it is now. I really think that I am free From all improper bias on this subject, and that I can say with truth, that those conventicles "hide their diminished heads" in view of the Episcopal Church. AN EPISCOPALIAN.

In these "letters" we find unusual access to a difficult question: what did *they* see when they saw these buildings? What design features made a conscious impression, and, therefore, clearly and easily could have *meant* something to the viewer? When we look at a building, what is ordinary or typical often escapes our consideration. We consciously process its unusual features. So, there are always at least two layers of "seeing" going on. On one level, a citizen of New Haven could have looked at these buildings and seen them as three rectangular boxes, nearly all the same size, with square towers, oriented with a gable end to the street, and full of pews and galleries facing a pulpit. But no one seems to have noticed the sameness of the structures.

Other aspects of the buildings had an immediate impact on the viewer, and some of these come out in the joke of the *Journal* column. The choice of site meant a great deal. This was evident throughout the colonial period as congregations weathered protracted struggles over the choice of a lot, despite efforts by the legislature to regulate the process. But now, even in urban centers, where a congregation was located, in relation to other buildings and the center of commerce, was significant. Whether the First Society actually gloated over its central location (it well might have), United Society valued its proximity to the Elms, or Trinity enjoyed edging up to the courthouse, is impossible to know. We do know from the mere mention here, however, that a church's relationship to the total urban environment was important. The "Brickite" boldly celebrated the location of First Church over a portion of the old burying ground, although the decision to build there had in fact been a source of much consternation on the part of "survivors" who resisted the desecration of their ancestors' graves. Site could influence a building committee's choice of design as well. When the Second Society in Hartford allotted funds for its new church, the committee suggested that "in justice to the character of the parish *and the part of the city where the house is to be located*, a less sum than twelve thousand dollars will not be adequate to the object" (italics mine).[52]

The text of the *Journal* column repeats some of the basic concerns that Simeon Baldwin's letter and the records of many ecclesiastical societies illuminate, for example, the use of materials (brick for the "Brickite," the West Rock stone of Trinity, the mahogany pulpit in United Church). The size and quality of bells and height of steeples also emerge as points of competition, two elements that immediately called attention to the structure. And seating is again something that holds interest. United Church's side pews were, after all, "a very important consideration," as they allowed more seats. Workmanship was consistently a concern of all the "writers," just as it was for building committees. All three were "highly wrought" and showed "proof of skill in architecture." Value in monetary terms, finally, was curiously expressed by the humorist: "As sixteen dollar broadcloth is to eight," he wrote, or "like four dollar cassimere compared to eight." Such thinking not only commodifies the buildings but reveals the fascination the writer felt at the simple material accomplishment of what he confronted.

We also see a general, if imprecise, academic knowledge of style and architectural terms. Terms such as "Gothic," "corinthian," "ionic," and "balustrade" might not be too difficult, but they are hardly common parlance today. Hints of some knowledge of correct neoclassical style also emerge. First Church, as mentioned above, closely resembled Gibbs's St. Martin's-in-the-Fields, London. Although this reference, and the church's bold three-dimensional ornamentation might have inspired "solemnity and veneration," such excesses of three-dimensional decorative details were out of fashion by this time. Hence "One of the United Society's" criticism of the ornament as "too gay and tawdry." United Church, on the other hand, was the most "modern" of the three. Built "after the best models of Grecian and Roman architecture," with a tower that was "symmetry itself," United Church reflected the current taste in neoclassical architecture. First Church, in fact, also demonstrates this influence in several details, such as the recessed wall arches that house all the windows (also on United Church) and the attenuated and more finely detailed spire. Nonetheless, there was enough awkward about First Church that the critic would think to use the word "disproportional" to describe it. And, although First Church was a bold architectural statement, the United Church may have had more direct bearing on the development of church architecture in the region. In 1826, for example, after examining "several plans and drafts which they think would be suitable and please the society," the building committee of South Church, Hartford, recommended that "the North House [United Church] in New Haven, reduced a little in size, would be as handsome and convenient as any that could be adopted in our case."[53]

Despite obvious overtones of ancient Greece and Rome, building a neoclassical church was, as the Salisbury committee put it, building in "the modern stile," the style of other public buildings of the time. It makes sense that Congregational societies, concerned about their increasing lack of political power, would choose to build in the modern style. This connected their churches visually with other neoclassical buildings that were the seats of political, economic, and social power—courthouses, banks, and academies, for example. This was fashion more than it was historicism, reiterated in the Episcopalian "Churchman's" comment that when fashion changes, "down they will go." A vague reference to the civilizations of Rome and Athens should not, therefore, be interpreted as a wholesale commitment to the heart and soul of those ancient civilizations. It is certainly a mistake to think that these buildings are "rational," in the fashion of the ancient Greeks, rather than "romantic," in the fashion of the nineteenth-century Americans copying them. More misleading still would be to presume that, because the architecture was neoclassical, the Enlightenment must have been producing empirical, classical humanistic thinking within. This was a time of emotional religious revival. Nonetheless, these buildings did reflect "taste and judgement," even to an Episcopalian. All three buildings, in fact, put in a claim for "elegance," the most widely used word to describe a successful ecclesiastical building in this period. "Elegance" had a direct relationship to "taste" and "gentility," qualities that, as Richard Bushman has shown, had greater value and were sought with greater urgency in the early republic.[54]

Trinity Church gave the writer something completely different. First Church and United Church were, after all, nearly the same building. Both were of brick; and they were the same size, had similar portico fronts,

29. Trinity Episcopal Church, New Haven, 1816. Photo by author.

The upper portion of the tower was rebuilt in stone in 1870.

parallel galleries and interior seating arrangements. But Trinity, regardless
of its obvious roots in the meetinghouse tradition, said something else to
our joker (fig. 29). Of dark stone, with a "majestic tower and splendid
turrets," "superb windows and pointed arches," Trinity conveyed "true
ideas of magnificence." We may find it way off the mark of "true" Gothic,
especially when compared with the later, careful work of ecclesiologists,
but the "true Gothic style," and "uniformly so," is what it looked like to
the people in New Haven. Searching for the supreme compliment, the
"Churchman" called Trinity the "most elegant church this side of St. Pe-

ter's," never mind that St. Peters was not Gothic at all. Slyly the writer reminded the Congregationalists that they inhabited two "conventicles," a reference to their dissenter origins and the rebellious nature of their existence. But it looked likely that they would lose out anyway in the sweep of history, whereas Trinity would be "as noble and splendid ten centuries hence." The First Congregational and United Churches were "pretty little boxes," but Trinity was a Gothic *church*. With Trinity, Christ Church, Hartford, and a handful of other early Gothic churches, American Episcopalians staked their claim to that medieval tradition and the respect it engendered.

Episcopalians and the Connecticut Gothic Church

Connecticut's Anglicans, a significant presence since the mid–eighteenth century, embarked on a slow but steady rise to respectability after the Revolution.[55] Naturally, the direct connection with the English Church had been a liability during the political conflict, as it was often assumed that a spiritual connection with Englishmen meant there was a political one as well, an assumption that was in fact often true. A presumed correspondence of Anglicanism and decadence also plagued American priests and their communicants. Congregationalists, even one as purportedly "gentle" as Ezra Stiles, could be merciless toward the Anglican Church, which Stiles once described as "an Asylum for polite Vice & Irreligion."[56] At the time of the Revolution, rabble-rousing patriots harassed Anglicans and destroyed their property. The Reverend Truman Marsh, rector of St. Michael's parish in Litchfield, remembered the trials of that time. "At the commencement of the American Revolutionary War most of the Episcopalians of this State were Royalists," Marsh recalled. "In consequence of their *political* opinions they experienced great hardships and persecution. Their characters were impeached—defamed—and ridiculed." These "Great prejudices" persisted "for some years after the war had ended." Marsh remembered when he himself was "ridiculed and insulted when going to, or returning from Church on the Lord's Day" in Litchfield. And the church building suffered violence: "the windows of the church were broken, and in the place of broken panes of glass, wooden and sliding windows were opened, to let in the Light of heaven to read the prayers of the Common Prayer-Book." "Thanks be to heaven," Marsh concluded with an audible sigh of relief, "for the great change in Public sentiment."[57]

This change in sentiment was partially the result of the metamorphosis of America's Anglicans into the American Episcopal Church. After American independence, official ties between American and English Anglicans became strained, and America's "Churchmen" and women had to look their fate squarely in the eye. Few of them wanted to lose their cultural connections with and goodwill vis-à-vis the English church, but the matter of political loyalty prompted the reorganization of the church here in new terms. Americans could not be declaring their allegiance to the British monarch each Sunday, as part of Anglican liturgy. As had been evident for decades, in order to thrive, the church in America needed its own resident bishop. Unable to convince the English Church to ordain one, American Anglicans turned to the bishops of Scotland, who quite agreeably consecrated Samuel Seabury, the American nominee, in November of 1784 in Aberdeen.

Bishop Seabury came home in 1785 to live in New London, Connecticut, and encourage the slow process of unifying the church in the United States. In 1789, the various state churches officially came together as the Protestant Episcopal Church in America. Anglicans in Connecticut had for the most part been socially and politically conservative, allying themselves with the Federalist Party. Yet by the second decade of the nineteenth century, it was obvious that their political interests lay with the Republicans. Despite the cultural and political power of Connecticut's Congregationalists, they had been significantly less than a majority for some time. Richard Purcell estimated that in 1787 in Connecticut as a whole perhaps one-third were Congregationalist or Presbyterian by name, and another third identified themselves as dissenters.[58] Statistics like this did not bode well for the continued dominance of Congregationalists in state politics, and indeed it did not take long for the dissenters and unaffiliated citizens to realize that if they banded together they could topple the old Congregationalist order. Episcopalians turned their growing presence into considerable political power by combining with Baptists and Methodists in the fight for religious equality under the law.

Somewhat ironically, America's Episcopalians, descendants of the state church of all state churches, were deeply satisfied with the hands-off policy of their new government. It took some rethinking, however, for proto-Anglicans to posit the relative advantages of such a position. The Episcopal bishop of New York, John Henry Hobart, sang the praises of disestablishment when he compared the United States with Europe in an 1825 discourse intended primarily for Episcopalian ears.[59] He found that Europe compared favorably with America in public squares and "large and imposing edifices" (public buildings), but when it came to "civil and religious institutions," Americans may, declared Hobart, "boast pre-eminence." The religious freedom Americans possessed, Hobart claimed, had the happy effect of genuine zeal in the support of religious institutions, and freed the church from the corrupt influence of politics. The Episcopal church here, Hobart declared, maintained faith, ministry, and worship "in their primitive integrity, without being clogged or controlled . . . by secular influence."[60] In an atmosphere of religious revival, Episcopalians, while not rejecting enthusiasm, preferred slow and steady growth. The *Journal of the Convention* in 1828 depicted the church thus: "Our church is, probably less subject to sudden fluctuations . . . look for no high excitements . . . no sudden and rapid growth . . . often as sudden in decay. To be steadily progressive in extent, in zeal, and in piety is what we most desire."[61] Despite its political involvement prior to 1818, the church in Connecticut did manage to remain somewhat aloof from the politics of the early republic, and, by identifying with its long, cross-cultural history, to present a bastion of tradition and stability in an era of change.

Hobart's choice of the phrase "primitive integrity" signaled an important aspect of Episcopalian identity in America. Here he referred not only to the primitive "true" faith but to its long-standing ally in the liturgy of the Anglican tradition. Hobart's was not a new church, but one with deep roots in centuries of English history. That much would not be sacrificed to the new freedoms of America. Bishop Samuel Jarvis made this connection clear in his 1814 address at the laying of the cornerstone for Trinity Church, New Haven. In blessing the spot of the new church, the bishop expressed his hope that it would be the home of the prayers of the congregation, and those of their children, and those of their children's children. The beauty of the Episcopal tradition, as he saw it, was that those prayers would not change, but would ring constant from generation to generation. "It is one of the distinguishing excellencies of our worship," Jarvis claimed, "that most of the prayers which it contains have been in use from the earliest and purest ages of the church."[62] "For fifteen hundred years at least," Jarvis reminded, "have many of them served to express the humble adoration of those saints, who are now uniting in the worship of the Church triumphant." The tradition was long and impressive, and the bishop reveled in these historical connections. "It is a delightful thought," he told his hearers, "that our children will be able to say of us, . . . 'These prayers our fathers have uttered; and this sanctuary, erected by their zeal, and their exertions, is the patrimony which they have bequeathed to us.' "[63] Also on the side of Episcopalians were the mystery and romance of Anglican ritual and history, which appealed to sentimental Americans who found a lack of decorum or depth of feeling in their own traditions. A priest from Newport, Connecticut, wrote to a friend in New York in 1818: "In this state, the church is rising in the public estimation, her numbers increasing, and her liturgy becoming very popular. This is believed to be the case generally in the Eastern diocese."[64]

One reason Episcopal liturgy was "becoming very popular" was its refined, decorous tone and manner. Simple matters like comportment had an impact on strangers. Theodonia Woolsey, after attending an Episcopal wedding, remarked that "they both knelt when the last prayer was made — I was pleased with that act of adoration—it is not customary that I know among presbyterians, but I think it *proper and looks well*" (italics mine).[65] Episcopalians had ceremonial, ritualistic events, such as Christmas services, that were attended by many non-Episcopalians and influenced even Congregationalists to adopt such practices in their own congregations. Thomas Robbins noted that on December 25, 1823, "the First [Congregational] Society in Hartford had a christmas [*sic*] meeting. I presume for the first time."[66] Another comment by Robbins shows plainly the mutual acceptance one frequently irascible Congregationalist found between himself and his neighbor Episcopalians. On December 25, 1827, Reverend Robbins related, "By invitation of Mr. Sherwood, the Episcopal clergyman here, I attended his Christmas meeting and dined with him. Kindly treated, I united with them in communion."[67] Baptist and Methodist revivalists made Robbins's hair curl (he wrote in his *Diary*, "I hope God will protect us from the machinations of the Baptists"), but the Episcopalians became less threatening to him as time went on.[68] Robbins knew that Episcopalians had more in common, culturally if not theologically, with Federalists like himself than with other denominations also challenging the old Congregational hegemony.

Alone among Connecticut's denominations, Episcopalians consciously chose one particular, historical, architectural style — the Gothic — to define themselves.[69] This choice of course had tremendous precedent in medieval English cathedrals as well as more modest parish churches, and in a few North American colonial churches, particularly those of the southern and middle colonies.[70] But Gothic was in no sense a given in America. The Gothic style at its most blatant had traditionally been anathema for Puritans in the Old World or the New. Preferring to avoid any aesthetic tainted by the corruption of the Roman Church and its equally sinister cousin in England, Puritans chose domestic styles, free of such associations, for their meetinghouses. As we have seen, that impulse was so strong in New England that even the Anglicans often bowed to such an influence by building what were more or less meetinghouses with an Anglican interior.

It is useful for us to attempt to look at the Gothic as early-nineteenth-century Americans saw it. From the frequency with which the term was used, we can gather that many people knew Gothic when they saw it; it was part of the common architectural vocabulary. Even the most "Gothic" of Connecticut's Episcopal churches of this period, Trinity and St. Paul's in New Haven, and Christ Church in Hartford, to our eyes look more or less like rectangular boxes with spires in the front—not so different from neighboring Congregational meetinghouses. Yet their stone construction and Gothic ornament made them seem wholly different to contemporary observers: dark, mysterious, substantial, and even *historically accurate*. Rather than critique these structures for falling short of "true" English Gothic, we should wonder why New England Episcopalians clung so tenaciously to this style in the early national period, how they changed it, and how and why they made it their own. Although it is perhaps not surprising that Episcopalians consciously owned the Gothic style after the Revolution, what *is* remarkable is the increasing amount of interest and praise that it won from "dissenters." Even the conservative Thomas Robbins could say, when he first saw the Gothic lines and ornament of Christ Church, Hartford: "It is magnificent."[71]

New England Anglicans had often used some reference to the Gothic style to distinguish their churches. Eighteenth-century designers were unschooled in the specific forms and ornament of medieval Gothic, so their use of the style consisted largely in surface flourishes. Before 1830 the use of the Gothic in Connecticut was restricted almost entirely to Episcopalians, and consisted of a few key constituent parts—broken-arch or round-topped windows (both called "arch'd" in the records), turrets, and thin spires—attached to a rectangular meetinghouse.[72] The Gothic impulse caused a group of determined Litchfield Episcopalians in 1796, although lacking both priest and tax base, to assert their presence with a small church having "13 Arch'd windows of the same dementions and one round window at the end where the pulpit is."[73] These Litchfield Episcopalians used architectural detail to mark a clear separation between themselves and other denominations, and so connected themselves to the European tradition. Episcopal churches built in Connecticut in the last half of the eighteenth century all had this distinctiveness. The wooden 1753 building that preceded Trinity, New Haven's Gothic stone church, was one of these (fig. 30). Harry Croswell, rector of Trinity after 1815, remembered the older wooden church's deliberate distinction. "It was built in the peculiar style of architecture, which, at that day, distinguished the churches from the so-called meeting houses of the congregationalists," wrote Croswell. "The long round-topped windows, and the corresponding forms of doors, vestibules, and entrances, were then held in great aversion by the descendents of the puritans, and was always pointed out, and sneered at, as peculiar to prelatical houses of worship."[74]

30. "Trinity Church in 1752." Courtesy, New Haven Colony Historical Society.

By the nineteenth century, Episcopalians in Connecticut chose the Gothic style not just for its mark of difference but for its heavily romantic overtones, a choice made simple by the ease with which Episcopalians accepted the emotional, aesthetic side to worship. As Jarvis stated in his Trinity Church cornerstone address: "Man is powerfully swayed by his senses. Of worship altogether mental he knows nothing." People needed material aids to devotion. "Hence it is essential to the homage of God" that churches "should be erected for his service, as will command the respect and veneration of those for whose use they are designed." The demand for historical and emotional cues was clearly best met by the Gothic style.

That style of building which is commonly termed Gothick, and which is distinguished by its pointed arches and its slender clustering columns, is peculiarly adapted to sacred uses. The experiences of ages has proved, that it tends, more than any other, to fill men with awe and reverence, to repress the tumult of unreflecting gaiety, and to render the mind sedate and solemn. Whatever tends in any degree to make men serious and devout when they approach the Divine majesty, is an auxiliary to his service; and the providing that which produces this effect in the greatest degree, is an act by which we doubtless honour and glorify our Maker.[75]

Bishop Jarvis recognized that not much of the Gothic existed in the United States. The building of Trinity Church was a landmark. "You, my brethren," he told his "Friends" in New Haven, "will set a laudable example to your fellow Christians, by erecting your church according to a mode of architecture, of which, as yet, there is not a perfect and pure specimen through the whole of the American republick."[76]

Trinity Church, by many accounts, quickly became one of the most notable public buildings in Connecticut. Despite the fine qualities of the two Congregational churches in New Haven, it was Trinity that claimed the most attention. The reason seems clear. Roger Sherman Baldwin wrote to his brother Ebenezer in Albany in 1816, describing the typical reaction to the three ecclesiastical structures on New Haven's green. It is "said by strangers that no town in the union can at a single view show three of equal elegance," he wrote. "I think the Episcopal church tho' by no means as neat and beautiful as the other, in point [of] grandeur surpasses them all."[77] In beauty, certainly in "modern" fashion, First and United Churches had Trinity beat. Yet Trinity's magnificent architecture— its "grandeur"—was extraordinarily compelling. The interior of the church, while displaying some complex Gothic stonework, was actually quite light, predating the darker Gothic interiors lavishly decorated with polychrome ornament and stained glass windows. Daniel Wadsworth, writing in 1833, described Trinity: "Although grave, and dark *without,— within*, it was as white as snow, and light as day, the workmanship being all delicate, and slender, of lofty pointed Gothic, the windows tall, unshrouded, divided into many tasteful compartments and admitting a flood of light" (fig. 31).[78] The exterior of Trinity Church today looks Gothic by virtue of its heavy stone construction, pointed windows, and massive tower with corner pinnacles. The building as originally seen, however, had much more delicately wrought Gothic detail, as seen in an 1831 image of the green (fig. 28). The original wooden tower was much more delicate and complex.[79] A wooden crenellation, or decoratively notched trim that looked like a castle battlement, ran along the roofline of the church and the top of the tower. Inside and out, the original effect would have been much lighter and more visually complex than it is today.

Reverend Croswell claimed outright that this grand building had the effect of drawing people into the Anglican communion. "Public attention had been for some time drawn to the church and it was noticed that there were daily accessions to the congregation, and to the society," he wrote. "It was also well understood that a large number of families, who had hitherto worshipped among the sectarians, had made up their minds to secure seats in Trinity Church, and to attach themselves, in due form, to

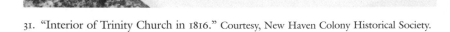

31. "Interior of Trinity Church in 1816." Courtesy, New Haven Colony Historical Society.

the parish."[80] The proof of the excitement generated by the building came on a rainy Wednesday in late February, when over three thousand people crammed themselves into and around the building to see Bishop Hobart of New York perform the consecration service. "The services were, in themselves, grand and impressive: and many circumstances conspired to render the occasion peculiarly interesting to the whole community," Croswell remembered. First, "it was the first attempt at the gothic style of architecture in church-building in New England." Second, "the building was one of the largest churches in the country." And third, Bishop Hobart was a celebrity and the consecration service an object of interest. With unmistakable and completely characteristic pride, Croswell stated that from "its very foundation, it [the church] had been an object of attraction to the people of neighboring towns, and when the day of consecration was announced they came together in crowds to witness the solemnities." In fact, many more came than could be accommodated. "At the opening of the services, not only were the sittings all occupied, but the aisles and galleries, were literally crowded with standing auditors, and the whole number was estimated at 3000! Although the seats were calculated to accommodate scarcely half of that number."[81]

Trinity was the first of several Gothic buildings erected by Episcopal congregations in Connecticut in the next few decades. St. John's in Salisbury (1823), St. John's in Kent (1823–26), and St. Andrew's in Marble Dale (1821–23) are good examples of the standard form these early Gothic churches assumed in more rural areas, rendered in brick or stone (fig. 32). St. Andrew's is typical of Episcopal churches built in the Northeast and Old Northwest. This building is "Gothic" by virtue of its pointed-arch openings and pinnacles. Episcopalians watched with interest as congregations continued to build, tallying up the number of churches on the Connecticut landscape, and always praising the propensity of their people to donate freely to the cause.[82] That "the liberality of our people has been proportionate to this increase (in numbers), is manifest from the great number of edifices which have been erected for the celebration of ordinances and worship of our church," Croswell wrote.[83] Buildings were evidence of denominational prosperity, and a gem like Trinity, Croswell acknowledged, was a particularly valued prize. "Trinity Church, in New-Haven, which was consecrated in February, 1816, is surpassed by very few, if any, in the Union, for size, convenience, or simple elegance."[84] One church soon to surpass Trinity was to be built only forty miles away, in Hartford. For the architect, Christ Church chose Ithiel Town, the architect of Trinity Church and a fellow Episcopalian.[85]

Perhaps the greatest benefit to be gained from the building of Christ Church was the boost the rector and congregation expected it to give the

32. St. Andrew's Episcopal Church, Marble Dale, Conn., 1821–23. From J. F. Kelly, *Early Connecticut Meetinghouses*, courtesy, Columbia University Press. Reprinted with the permission of the publisher.

reputation of Hartford's Episcopalians. For years, they had known that establishing a stronghold in that city was key to success statewide.[86] The parish was organized by Anglican missionaries around 1760–61, but had difficulty sustaining membership and maintaining a building. In 1786, the parish reorganized with more success, and one of its first acts was to build a church. This building, similar to the old Trinity, New Haven, was finally completed after 1795 and consecrated November 11, 1801, by the bishop of Connecticut, the Right Reverend Abraham Jarvis. Still struggling in 1807, the parish sent a plea to its comrades in New York, asking for money, for, as they saw it, "Hartford being the metropolis of Connecticut, the establishment of the Episcopal Church there is of the utmost importance to the prosperity of the Church throughout the State."[87]

The Reverend Philander Chase, onetime rector of Christ Church (1811–17) and later bishop of Ohio, remembered the pathetic state of Hartford's Episcopalians when he arrived there in 1811 from New Orleans. "Christ Church there was a small wooden building," Chase recalled, "and contained all the Episcopalians in the city. The minister who presided [Menzies Rayner, formerly a Methodist] joined the universalist denomination, and the congregation, containing only seventeen communicants, were disheartened."[88] But with Chase (who stayed until 1817) the fortunes of the church changed. Chase found Hartford to be a "lovely city" where, "in the bosom of an enlightened society, softened by the hand of urbanity and gentleness" and "crowned with an abundance of temporal blessings," the church began to flourish.[89]

In 1810, Christ Church first began its profitable association with Reverend Nathaniel Wheaton. Wheaton, a native of New Preston and a Yale graduate who had been teaching in Maryland, took charge of the church in 1821 and was instrumental both in pushing for the establishment of Washington (later Trinity) College and the building of Christ Church, both of which brought renown to Hartford. Wheaton was a smart promoter who had both a knowledge and love of architecture and a strong desire to see his church prosper without sacrificing the precious peace that he felt existed between Hartford's various denominations. In 1824, while fund-raising for Washington College in England, Wheaton saw and recorded what he could of English church architecture. In letters back home, he mentioned his trip to Ely "to view the stupendous cathedral, and the curious remains of ecclesiastical architecture, which date their origin from the Saxon Heptarchy."[90] He also spoke of his "antiquarian curiosity" leading him to Cotesback (to see the pulpit of Wycliffe) and finding "gratification in this spot, consecrated to the memory of the earliest reformer."[91] These letters introduce Wheaton as a man with finely tuned aesthetic sensibilities and historical knowledge, and one senses as well the connection Wheaton felt with the Church of England. After all, his mission there was to convince Anglicans of their vested interest in the education of American Episcopalians. That Reverend Wheaton was respected and admired in the larger Hartford community is evidenced in the fact that his safe return to Hartford was commended in the *Connecticut Mirror* of November 22, 1824: "we must be permitted to join our congratulations with the rest of the town, on the safe arrival of Rev. Mr. Wheaton" thus "restored to the church and congregation for which he has so long and so usefully labored."

Wheaton's elevation to the status of popular hero may be attributed to two things. First, his urbane, sophisticated presence brought to Hartford exactly the sort of cultural preeminence it desperately wanted. Second, Wheaton was hard at work both raising money for Washington College and trying to get its directors to agree to build the institution in Hartford, not New Haven or New London or the other towns vying for its favor. It was clear that a college in Hartford, even an Episcopal college, would bring both cultural and financial rewards similar to what Yale contributed to New Haven, its chief rival. The successful bid for the college had two necessary components: a convincing argument about the suitability of the locale for an institution of higher education, and a pledge of the citizens to contribute to the initial cost of land, buildings, library, and so forth. Wheaton was first a promoter for the college itself, regardless of location, but it did not hurt Hartford's cause that he was one of their own. For his part, Wheaton was characteristically circumspect about the whole affair, preferring the harmony of denominations to the college's establishment in any one particular spot. He wrote from England, "It appears that the course of the college subscription in our city has not been altogether unimpeded, a degree of prosperity which we indeed had no right to expect, & at the failure of which we ought not to be disappointed." Wheaton's larger concern was peace. "What I most fear," he wrote, "is that the harmony of the different denominations amongst us will be interrupted by these occurrences — an event which I should most seriously deprecate." "I do seriously hope," he continued, "that whatever location has been fixed upon . . . the discussions and events of which have transpired amongst us will have not tendency to prevent us from dwelling with our neighbors as brethren."[92] Largely due to Wheaton's efforts and diplomacy, Hartford won the college and good feeling prevailed.

Wheaton's other project, the building of Christ Church, came just as the *Episcopal Watchman* printed two illuminating articles about Episcopal church building in 1827, articles that Wheaton himself probably wrote. These articles show both the concern Episcopalians had for increasing the physical presence of their denomination, and their preference for the

Gothic style in stone. One article, titled "Church Edifices," draws a direct analogy between the growth of the American Episcopal Church and the number and character of its buildings. "It is the trial of the present generation of Episcopalians in the United States," the author insists, "to labour at the very foundation of their ecclesiastical affairs." This "foundation" consists of stone and mortar, and costs a great deal of time and money. Yet, the author urges, despite this burden, present Episcopalians should consider it "an honor and a privilege to lay the basis of a fair and stately temple, which, we have reason to hope, will hereafter be the joy and praise of our land." With such an expansive, noble goal, even "if it should cost us a little more trouble and expense," the writer persuades his readers, "it is our wisdom and indeed our duty to dig deep, and lay a wide and firm foundation." The writer gives his preference in material — stone — for if Episcopalians were to choose "any less permanent material we do not manifest that prudent forecast and noble disinterestedness, which ought ever to distinguish the management of Episcopalians." For this architectural observer, the character of the people should be revealed in their church buildings: "liberal and comprehensive," "permanent," and "prudent."[93]

This character will be best conveyed by Gothic churches. The writer is deliberately against modern fashion: "rather than build more airy and tasteful, but perishable houses, let us imitate the humble English country churches and chapels of the middle age: — snug, low, Gothic structures, with massive walls of rough, unhewn stone, adorned with a few plain windows and a decent and humble tower . . ."[94] This was both an explanation of the appropriateness of the Gothic for religious structures, and unqualified praise for Ithiel Town's plans and elevations for the new Christ Church, Hartford. Calling the attention of "the admirers of pointed architecture," the author recommends the Christ Church plans as "very tastefully executed" and displaying "a professional science which reflects great credit on the architect." This structure will be an improvement on Trinity Church, New Haven, the author claims, because it will "be on a somewhat smaller scale," the "walls are to be relieved from the tameness of a flat and even surface, by a projecting range of buttresses," and the windows will have two mullions rather than one. That is not to say that Trinity can be improved upon all that much, the author concedes. Trinity Church, with its prime location and commanding presence, "is the first object of attention that arrests the eyes of a stranger, and may probably challenge comparison with the most expensive edifices in New England." Trinity is imposing, its only flaw being that the size of the congregation required the building of galleries, which are inappropriate for a Gothic church and interfere with the "symmetry," and so diminish "the general effect."[95] (Nevertheless, galleries were put in Christ Church as well.) Gothic is good, the author asserts, because it is "picturesque" and has an "imposing air of antiquity," especially at its simplest and most severe.

American Episcopalians felt free to delve into the spiritual and aesthetic traditions of the Gothic for what was "picturesque." The picturesque was a category of aesthetic experience by the last third of the eighteenth century, and the term, far-reaching and flexible, appears frequently in period descriptions. Qualities of the picturesque included its naturalism, irregularity, and frequently its romantic, historical associations.[96] Often picturesque designs were asymmetrical and had a rough and mysterious yet nonthreatening caste. The historical and aesthetic qualities of the Gothic style met the requirements of the picturesque at a time when there was little of that sort on the American landscape. By the building of Trinity and Christ Churches, Americans were primed to respond positively to the visual effect of such Gothic structures. Episcopalians could be proud of their buildings, "so honorable to the Church, and so animating in the cause of piety."[97] The joy of their accomplishments was greater for the past hardships they had endured, and no building brought more satisfaction than Christ Church, where Hartford's Episcopalians first worshiped in 1829. The *Episcopal Watchman* described the structure as, "a faithful example of the ECCLESIASTICAL STYLE" from "the time of the last Henrys." Although no particular English building was the model, Christ Church bore details "almost all copied after drawings of the most approved specimens in England." This, according to the writer, was a vast improvement over most of the "attempts at" Gothic structures in America, characterized so often by "unseemly admixtures" of Gothic elements.[98]

On his travels, Wheaton had assembled a notebook of drawings of architectural details, probably the source for much of the embellishment of Christ Church. Various elements from English parish churches and cathedrals appear in the church: door tracery from Tattershall Church, Lincolnshire; a "rose" window "copied in part, but considerably enriched, from one in the Chapel of Magdalen College, Oxford"; and windows "copied from those in St. Mary's Church, Oxford, acknowledged to be one of the most beautiful specimens of the *perpendicular* style." A writer to the *Connecticut Mirror* extended the the approval of the city: "We must content ourselves therefore, with saying, that this building is one of the finest specimines [*sic*] of Gothic architecture in the country, and one of the greatest ornaments of our city. It has been erected at an expense of nearly $50,000 from a design of Ithiel Town, Esq., and in every particular, with the strictest regard to the rules of Gothic architecture."[99] Although Town did supply original plans, the master mason James Chamberlain, a parishioner, and Wheaton himself no doubt contributed to the design. In an 1829 letter to Bishop Hobart, Wheaton apologized for not having completed drawings of the church, explaining that he had "no leisure at present" and wanted to become reacquainted with his parish "before meddling again with scales and compasses."[100]

Christ Church, with its common form and uncommon ornament, embodies the compromise that Episcopalians found between what was locally acceptable and their own traditions (figs. 33–34). While obviously different in detail, it was still another rectangular, symmetrical meetinghouse and thus connected with Connecticut's indigenous, familiar style. But observers, like the writer to the *Connecticut Mirror*, noted not that similarity but the difference. What was unusual, the Gothic detail rendered in dark stone, brought renown to Hartford without jarring the viewer. Even in their interiors, Christ Church and its contemporaries were much more like the light, clean meetinghouse than later Gothic buildings. This did not go unnoticed by critics of American architecture, who increasingly demanded academic correctness and design integrity in American buildings. Henry Cleveland, reviewing James Gallier's architectural price book in 1835, sniffed that "the churches which have been erected within the last half-century, are, with few exceptions, rather modifications of the first plain-style meeting-houses, than imitations of the European churches."[101] Even Cleveland, nonetheless, found cause to give Christ Church modest praise as one of the "prettiest" Gothic churches in the United States, showing proof of "far better taste, as well as of greater knowledge, than appears in the construction of most of our churches."[102]

Christ Church, slightly smaller than Trinity, New Haven, was an eighty-nine-by-fifty seven foot dark red sandstone rectangle with a square, straight front tower and no transepts. In some ways Christ Church, with its massive stone tower and buttresses, was more authentically Gothic, and more "picturesque," than Trinity. Observers remarked most frequently upon the apparent strength of the building, the heavy stone construction, and unusual features such as the Gothic organ case bought in New York and, once again, Town's "ingenious" roof trusses.[103] Many observers, we have seen, apparently believed Christ Church to be close to an authentic example of the Gothic style in America. Reverend Wheaton, who had seen the glories of English cathedrals, had a more modest appreciation of the structure. Before its consecration, he wrote self-deprecatingly to Bishop Hobart, "If you look for a stupendous and magnificent church in the building we have been erecting, I must prepare you for a disappointment." Perhaps "as a specimen of chaste and pleasing Gothic architecture" it would "bear criticism." But, wrote Wheaton, "it pretends to nothing more."[104] Wheaton, for one, was not deluded, and perhaps his caution tells us that praise for the "true Gothic" by newspapers

33. Christ Church, Hartford, 1829; tower completed c. 1839. From J. F. Kelly, *Early Connecticut Meetinghouses*, courtesy, Columbia University Press. Reprinted with the permission of the publisher.

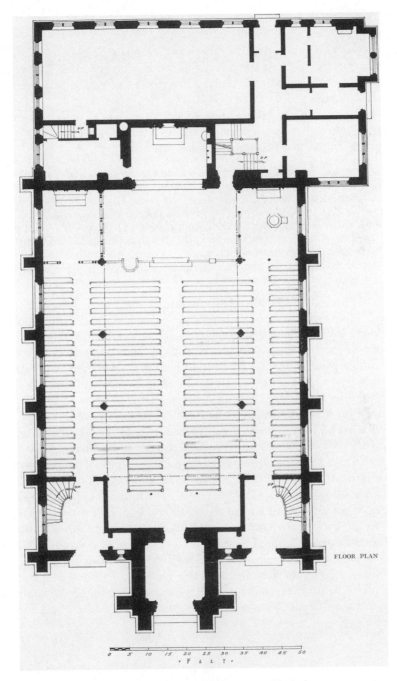

FLOOR PLAN

0 5 10 15 20 25 30 35 40 45 50
· F E E T ·

34. Plan, Christ Church. From J. F. Kelly, *Early Connecticut Meetinghouses*, courtesy,
Columbia University Press. Reprinted with the permission of the publisher.

This plan shows the new parish building, chapel, and recessed chancel erected c. 1879.
In 1919 Christ Church became the cathedral for the Episcopal Diocese of Connecticut.

and passersby was a conscious mixture of enthusiastic hyperbole and an appreciation for what Americans could do. It was, however, "chaste and pleasing," which sounds more like a description of neoclassical architecture than anything else.

What seemed to be an apparent ignorance of true style was the chief target of next-generation critics. Reverend Thomas M. Clark, in an 1855 sermon delivered in Christ Church, felt sure that

> when this church was built, ecclesiastical architecture in our country was at a very low ebb. There were a few seemly and some stately edifices scattered here and there over the land, copied for the most part from English models of the Sir Christopher Wren school, but there was not a pure and unadulterated specimen of Gothic to be seen anywhere. American architects, or those who called themselves by this name, were inflicting upon the church copies of the temple of Bacchus, with bacchanalian adornments; modified Puritan meeting-houses, buildings that were sometimes mistaken for banks; mixtures of pseudo-Gothic, Ionic, Egyptian, and native, at the sight of which we still continue to groan.[105]

Yet New Haven and Hartford Episcopalians knew exactly what they were doing: using architecture to better their position in their communities. Hartford's Episcopalians found a way of accommodating local preference without compromising their individualism, and the result was overwhelmingly positive for the parish. James Wells, a teenager, expressed in his journal in 1833 that "the beautiful Episcopal church of this city . . . is reckoned the handsomest Gothic Church in the United States."[106] The combination of styles berated by later critics was not invisible to the members of Christ Church itself—we have seen that in the remarks Wheaton sent to the bishop. In addition, society records from March 8, 1830, indicate that the parish believed it was "presenting to the scientific observer utility, strength, and beauty in a chaste combination of *Gothic* walls, with more than *Grecian* elegance" (italics mine).[107] Gothic detail was employed but not at the expense of a form that looked "elegant," proportionate and *right* to the eyes of the community. To the builders of Christ Church— as to the builders of United Church in New Haven, or even the Salisbury meetinghouse—what really mattered was not the close allegiance to a historical style but the attainment of "elegance," something that had the appropriate form of rectangle and steeple with some highly wrought ornament that distinguished the house of worship from other buildings.

CHAPTER 4

The Sacred and the Sentimental

. . . there ought to be not only room and convenience to accommodate the worshipers, but also dignity & elegance to assist devotion, and to express a respect for Divine institutions. . . . He who formed man with a taste for beauty, a love of order, and an admiration of grandeur, well knew that these properties, in the place and utensils of worship, contribute to inward piety and devotion; while, on the contrary, inelegance & disorder naturally tend to damp the fervor of devotion, and to repress the emotions of piety.
—Reverend Elisha Atkins, *A Sermon Delivered Nov. 18, 1818 at the Dedication of the Congregational Meeting House in the North Parish in Killingly.*

In 1832, a Professor Cogswell wrote to "Mssrs. Perkins and Marvin" of Hartford's North Church regarding a new psalmody. Cogswell noticed that in the preceding three decades "some changes" had "been produced in the state of feeling in the true church." These changes, Cogswell argued, demanded "a new selection of sacred poetry, better suited than any formerly known to the spirit and taste of the present age."[1] Just what, in religious matters, was "the spirit and taste of the present age"? Historians have often described the period of the Second Great Awakening, from the last years of the eighteenth century through the first decades of the nineteenth, as a time of religious fervor and intensified emotion, so Cogswell's reference to "feeling" is not surprising. Yet the context of this statement—a discussion of a new, regular, refined psalmody—indicates that Cogswell meant not religious enthusiasm and excess, but "feeling" in the sense of an appreciation for worship that was expressive yet tasteful. The changes wrought in church music came from practice and control, not spontaneity; they elicited predictable responses, not outbursts. An insistence that public worship be decorous and refined reverberates through Connecticut's church records, denominational publications, and newspapers of this period. This cannot be attributed merely to frightened Congregationalists wailing about the decline of the

status quo, for ministers and laity alike actively pursued rejuvenating religious revivals. Nor can the phenomenon be reduced to a secularization
process that brought social-climbing values into the sanctuary. A view that
considers broad cultural currents reveals "feeling" as an agent of change
itself. Connecticut's Christians—Congregationalists, Episcopalians, and
increasingly Baptists and Methodists—embraced a sensibility that not
only taught them how to feel but told them that those feelings were
vehicles of truth. The challenge for Connecticut's churches was to accept
and even encourage that desire for emotional experience, yet to contain
it within the bounds of orthodoxy and decency.

As noted previously, one of the most perplexing questions about the
buildings of this period is why they depart so clearly from the generation
of buildings that came before.[2] Early-nineteenth-century Congregational
buildings look like modern "churches," not eighteenth-century meetinghouses. They display more architectural ornamentation, inside and out,
and in greater variety. They are more orderly in their arrangement of
doors, aisles, and slips or pews. More expensive churches often have the
feel of fully unified design, rather than a makeshift combination of necessary elements. Numerous material and social explanations begin to explain this shift. Architecture emerged as a profession and design books
circulated. Once the Revolution came to a close and the economy recov-
ered, many churches had, all at once, both the need and the means to
build. As congregations grew, they needed bigger churches, and long
benches, or slips, provided more seating space than box pews. These explanations, however, can go only so far toward making sense of these new
buildings. They fall short in their failure to answer one important question: Why did New England congregations, supposedly coming out of a
Puritan "plain style" tradition, so swiftly and with virtually no protesta-
tion accept these architectural changes? What did they need these buildings to *do*? The answer lies in the new demands placed on worship: aesthetic and emotional fulfillment in a setting that was orthodox and
orderly.[3]

Worship practices are difficult if not impossible to reconstruct in their
full complexity. Church records reveal little beyond the skeletal structure
of a service, and sermons tell nothing about how the congregation listened
and participated. Fortunately, contemporaries had a lot to say about their
church buildings. Those comments, in dedication sermons and popular
verse, show theology combining with an emphasis on feeling to encourage
heartfelt piety and call for a new approach to worship in which the building played an important role. In a culture of sensibility, virtue took on a
crucial, aesthetic dimension that spilled over into the material aspects of
religion. We must look for the connection between the aesthetics of wor-

ship and the aesthetics of the space, pursuing this inquiry from a variety of perspectives. Dedication sermons and church records highlight the newly perceived "sacred" qualities of religious buildings. Increasing concern for better congregational music indicates both a desire for heightened pietistic feelings and a felt need to improve the aesthetic dimension of worship. An insistence on the special qualities of church buildings led to a mounting desire to protect them from secular invasions. All of these beliefs and concerns are revealed in the popular poems and hymns in which Connecticut Christians romanced their church buildings.

Religious Revival and the Culture of Sentiment

The rebuilding of Connecticut's churches corresponded to years of religious enthusiasm and optimism. Sporadic yet intense religious revival undulated through Connecticut and up the Connecticut River Valley in three waves from 1797 to 1822. This was most welcome to the Congregational vanguard, who lamented the lackadaisical religious attitudes of their fellow citizens and the pernicious slide from orthodoxy in other parts of New England, eastern Massachusetts especially. David Kling, in his chronicle of these Congregationalist revivals as they appeared in Hartford and Litchfield Counties, argues that they filled the need for "a clearly defined community in an age of uncertainty" and had a special appeal for middle-aged Congregationalists aware that the ground was shifting under them.[4] The mean age of Kling's converts was 31.5, five years older than the average convert of the eighteenth-century Great Awakening, and two-thirds of these converts were women.[5] Their new religious commitments tended to be deep and steady. Revival was so widespread and affected such different kinds of communities—from commercial centers like Litchfield and Hartford to small agricultural villages across the state—that it is difficult to reduce its appeal to a specific assortment of social or political conditions.[6] All across the region, the Yale-trained ministers who led these revivals had a message and preaching style that fell on receptive ears.

These "New Divinity" ministers held an orthodox Calvinist position: God has complete sovereignty, and his grace is the only means to salvation. They also stressed the importance of theological understanding, a solid grasp of doctrine based in scripture. These beliefs would have put them in some conflict with the temperament of the post-Revolutionary generation. The ethos of the era was one of individual self-determination and drive, not an abandonment of initiative. While ministers in the Calvinist tradition stuck closely to God's absolute sovereignty in human affairs, other forces pointed repeatedly to the ability of individuals to influence their own destinies. Furthermore, people were frustrated or bored with lengthy sermons and intellectual debates, and sought meaningful religious experiences. Congregational ministers were in a tight spot. The theology of Methodists and Baptists enabled them to encourage their followers to seize the moment for their own conversion. Calvinists simply could not declare outright that a person had the ability to work his or her own salvation; that would be heresy. But Calvinists could opt for a change in emphasis. While central doctrines could not change, New Divinity ministers could choose to stress aspects of their theology that were more sympathetic to the larger culture. Although they clung to doctrinal orthodoxy, in practical terms what stuck was their emphasis on the cultivation of piety. "Sensual spirituality," or "evangelical sentiment," was more compelling than theology; what had the greatest impact, Kling claims, "was a religion of the heart."[7]

One of the appeals of New Divinity revivals was a language of "sensual spirituality."[8] This can be linked to the metaphysical theology of the eighteenth-century American theologian and preacher Jonathan Edwards, who inspired many New Divinity ministers. Redemption altered the "religious affections," Edwards argued, thus prompting his followers to see the affections (emotions, feelings) as the seat and proof of true religious experience.[9] This did not deny God's sovereignty, but it defined religious experience in different, more emotional terms. Doctrine was a crucial foundation, but conversion ultimately happened in the heart, not in the head. In the 1820s, when New Divinity preachers were absorbed into a movement of general evangelical piety led by New Haven theologians Timothy Dwight, Nathaniel William Taylor, and Lyman Beecher, that emphasis on feeling persisted.

Two Calvinist theological tenets deserve attention because they potentially shape the meanings attached to religious spaces. The first is the Edwardsean notion of the religious affections or "religion of the heart." An emphasis on "sensual spirituality" heightened the potential of the physical worship environment to contribute positively to religious experience. The second theological tenet addressed the moment of conversion, stressing the value of preparation, or putting oneself in a state where one might be likely to receive the gift of salvation. That promising "state" was a receptive intellectual and emotional frame of mind. Could it also be a physical place? If worshiping in a church increased one's receptivity to spiritual experience, and if God made a church his special home, could the building itself be an instrument of grace? Ministers never addressed these questions in distinctly theological terms, but clergy and laity alike recognized the emotional power of a place of worship.

It is impossible to understand the relationship between people and religious practice in this period without acknowledging a broad cultural movement that valued heightened emotions. As noted, deep emotional involvement had been a component of evangelical revival since Edwards and the first Great Awakening. The value placed on highly charged sentiment was by no means confined to evangelicalism, or to religion in general. It affected aspects of life from art and literature to celebrations and politics. Cultural historians use terms such as sensibility, neoclassicism, Gothicism, romanticism, and the picturesque to describe the various and changing ways in which people used their imaginations—the way they thought and *felt* about beauty, danger, history, love, sorrow, and virtue.[10] In literature, by the mid-eighteenth century the ideal character, the hero or heroine, was the one who showed "sensibility," that is, a susceptibility to emotions with moral significance stimulated by his or her circumstances. Popular eighteenth-century authors judged the souls of their characters by the amount of suitable emotion they were able to display on cue, and their readers learned to value those same emotions in themselves. Such ideas were not inimical to Calvinists. Indeed, Protestants of many stamps were able not only to flock to sentimental and romantic ideals but also to be instrumental in their creation. Even the most austere incarnations of Calvinism were never devoid of intense emotional experience. Rather, Calvinists learned to listen very carefully to their emotions, even to relish the melancholy experience of a "Slough of Despond" that promised spiritual ecstasy on the other side. Feelings could in fact be indications of godliness. The optimism of the Enlightenment did away with some of the desperation behind these sentiments but did nothing to diminish the desire for feeling itself.[11]

While emotion had been tied to evangelical Protestantism for decades, what characterized the culture of sensibility in America in the later eighteenth and the early nineteenth century was the common belief that there were crucial links between feeling, morality, and *aesthetics*. Eighteenth-century Scottish moral philosophers first articulated this idea. By the end of the eighteenth century, their ideas had come to have a substantial impact on American thought and artistic practice.[12] These Scottish philosophers, beginning with the Earl of Shaftsbury in the early eighteenth century, taught that all people had an innate moral sense that guided them to correct behavior and an appreciation of the beautiful. These philosophers were Protestants, but their goal was not theological debate. Some of their ideas, however, did eventually shake down some long-held Calvinist ideas, partly because they so easily accommodated the structures and values of gentility and refinement. At the level of common understanding, Scottish philosophy elevated the value of beautiful things because of their affective power, their ability to elicit a correct moral response. Things that were virtuous and good would appear beautiful to the moral person (thus good taste equaled virtue). Beautiful things, on the other hand, could lead one to moral behavior. In 1790 Archibald Alison added an important element to the discussion of aesthetics and feeling when he published *Essays on the Nature and Principles of Taste*. In this work Alison set out his philosophy of associationism, arguing that beauty was subjective, or in the eye of the beholder.[13] The reaction one had to an aesthetic experience was not a mechanical reaction to concrete aspects of the thing itself, but depended on the way it connected to what was already in the viewer's mind. The more powerful the associations, the stronger the emotional response. Associationism accommodated a greater range of emotional reactions to aesthetic experiences; two people would not necessarily react the same way to the same stimulus. It also highlighted the importance of keeping associations correct and pure if one were to have the proper emotional reaction to a thing, a person, or an event. People acquired taste—and learned how to be virtuous— through their experiences in the visual and material world.

By the late eighteenth century, the cult of sensibility had swelled to excess. Sensibility found its critique among European upper classes who in reaction to late Baroque extravagance turned to a neoclassical aesthetic that, on the surface, appeared to be about logic and restraint. Neoclassicism became the dominant literary mode in early-nineteenth-century America. It was optimistic about society, confident in the order and proportion of nature, and highly suspicious of enthusiasm, religious enthusiasm included. Yet criticism was not leveled against feeling per se, but *false* sensibility, emotion that seemed to be nothing more than an end in itself. Although scholars, particularly in the decorative arts, have tended to equate the classical allusions, subdued decoration, and balance of neoclassical design to an intellectual respect for classical order and democratic ideals, the style was much more richly complex.[14] It allowed one to be highly fashionable by what appeared to be stylistic *restraint*, thus exhibiting both taste and morality at the same time. As Neil Harris argued decades ago, "Somehow, neoclassicism met and conquered luxury."[15] Harris argued neoclassicism was perhaps more emotional than rational, a "romantic idealization of the past." The style contained within it the possibility of a wide variety of emotional responses. Hundreds of courthouses and other public buildings across America may testify to neoclassicism's powerful evocations of classical models of government and civil society. But the style meant other unexpected things as well. In Charles Brockton Brown's frightful gothic novel *Wieland; or, The Transformation* (1798), all sorts of nefarious deeds took place in a neoclassical garden pavilion.[16] Neoclassical motifs regularly show up among the artifacts of the deeply emotional and sentimental culture of mourning in nineteenth-century America (fig. 35). The Enlightenment, after all, could go only so far toward rationalizing the world, for people had come to enjoy and expect emotional experience. Neoclassicism permitted a more restrained emotionalism that accepted feelings as vehicles of moral insight yet tolerated no effusion. This was evident in a pervasive insistence on proportion as a key to aesthetic beauty, a call for harmony and balance in art and architecture.[17] Putting things together, we have a culture that valued harmony and proportion yet also yearned for emotional experience. This was reflected precisely in the character of Connecticut's nineteenth-century revivals and its church buildings.

In December of 1807, revival came to New Haven. Amos Townsend, a young boy at the time, sixty years later recalled the lively and compelling preaching of the young Moses Stuart, who began his work at New Haven's First Congregational Church in 1806. The Reverend Stuart cried "like a live policeman. . . . Fire! Fire! and the congregations were assured a new life!"[18] Townsend remembered "the whole city was moved. Men stood at the corners of the streets and with deep emotion and interest conversed about religious things." Evening meetings in "halls and large parlors . . . were opened almost every evening and crowded to their full capacity in all parts of the city."[19] Abraham Bradley and a number of other First Society members "took a dwelling house on Orange St. . . . removed all the chamber partitions and improvised a room for religious meetings." This room, Townsend claimed, "was crammed night after night."[20] Although Townsend admitted that such meetings "were denounced by a few conservatives," he also insisted that the spirit of revival had transformed the city.

Despite the vigor Townsend describes, these revivals were notable for their more measured qualities: harmony and proportion. Their nature is revealed in personal papers and published accounts that stress the exciting yet altogether dignified demeanor of the events. A writer to the Congregational *Connecticut Evangelical Magazine* described the first New Haven revival, one that brought many younger people into the Congregational churches. "Everything has been regular, grave, and solemn. There has been nothing light, nothing ludicrous, nothing extravagant. Nothing incompatible with refinement of manners, delicacy of feeling, or sobriety of deportment."[21] Meetings were "particularly crowded and serious."[22] New Haven as a whole endured nothing of the disruption brought by other revivals: "The community at large is more peaceable, orderly, sober, and considerate."[23] An insistence on restraint is suggested in a Connecticut

35. Mourning picture, Catherine Butler, Hartford, 1806. Courtesy, Winterthur Museum, 1958.2876.

This picture commemorates Henry Butler, Jr., who died at age 19, apparently at sea:

> Delusive hope with flatring [*sic*] pencil drew
> His safe return oe'r Ocean's rolling stream
> But soon the prospect faded from our view
> & hope disappear'd for death has clos'd the scene

Mourning pictures were typically loaded with symbols of sentiment: willows, obelisks, black-clothed mourners, classical drapery. To the far right is visible the spire of the village church.

woman's memory of her conversion in a different 1806 revival. "Tears flowed without control. The language of my heart was, O my dear Savior, come, and take everlasting possession of my soul. . . . My emotions were so great, that *I found it difficult to keep myself from immediately kneeling upon the floor and extending my arms where I then was in the meetinghouse* [Italics mine]."[24] This statement seems to imply that, while this woman reveled in the emotional wash of saving grace, she was not quite sure what the proper public expression of that feeling should be.

As clergy and laity mused over what was proper churchgoing behavior, they considered the character of the space itself. The dual nature of the colonial New England meetinghouse was a legacy bequeathed to the nineteenth century. A rethinking of that multipurpose status began as early as the first half of the eighteenth century, when the creation of town houses first allowed some communities to remove business from religious spaces.[25] This may have been the result of uneasiness over the incongruence of worshiping God and debating town politics in the same space. The Puritan aesthetic did not preclude a perhaps innate human desire to separate certain material places and things as more "sacred" than others. Yet it was not until the period following the Revolution that Congregational societies appeared everywhere frustrated with being forced to let their churches moonlight as assembly halls. Was a meetinghouse a "sacred space?" New England's iconoclastic, plain-style Puritan tradition said no, yet common intuition and sentiment suggested that there was indeed a qualitative, spiritual difference between a church and a secular assembly hall. The nineteenth-century specialization of religious spaces may be attributed to circumstances both practical and ideological: the existence of other meeting places, financial self-reliance, the example of Episcopalians, and a rhetoric as much sentimental as ideological about the special qualities of a house of worship.

Building Dedications and the "Sacred"

Dedication and consecration sermons directly reveal attitudes toward church buildings. Anglicans, now Episcopalians, had always consecrated new churches using a specific liturgy. Consecration turned the building into a sacred house of God; the congregation asked God to be always present there and committed itself to keeping the building holy. In the eighteenth century, Congregationalists began similarly to gather to ask God's blessing on new meetinghouses increasingly set aside for worship alone. Congregationalists called the service "dedication" (although the word consecration does appear occasionally, even within dedication ser-

mons). By the nineteenth century, virtually all Congregationalists and
Episcopalians in western Connecticut launched their new buildings into
service with such a solemn ceremony. According to Anglican doctrine,
consecration was an act of God that fundamentally transformed the nature
of a space. Dedication was subtly different, as Congregationalists did not
formally believe that their prayers permanently altered the character of the
space. Congregational dedications were simply an important event in the
life of the congregation and a promise to respect and cherish the building
for its spiritual purposes.

Doctrinal differences were not sufficient, however, to keep consecrations and dedications from being in effect the same thing: a pious act in
which the minister and congregation thanked God for the gift of a new
building and asked his blessing on it. This is further confused by the
tendency of Congregational ministers actually to use the words "sacred"
and "holy" to describe their new buildings, or "temples." In the context
of a culture of heightened emotion, we can understand the use of these
terms in two ways. First, there is a "sacred" in the sense that Professor
Cogswell had a collection of "sacred" songs—something, in this case music, that was designated for a specific spiritual purpose and set apart by
human action. Understood this way, a building could be "sacred" simply
if its users agreed that it would serve only spiritual, or "sacred," purposes.
"Sacred" was a valued religious quality, intended to evoke a special emotional, spiritual, human response. But there was also another understanding of the word "sacred," and that was that the thing—generally a place—
had been removed from the ordinary by an act of God. Moses' burning
bush and the temple in Jerusalem were sacred in this second sense. In
sermons and poems we see Connecticut's religious culture yearning for
"sacred" in the mysterious second sense by using it in the first; the emotional quality preceded the hoped-for metaphysical reality.

Ministers preached dedication sermons with earnest seriousness. Dedications were ritualized reviews of the congregation's accomplishments
and prospects, and a reminder of the solemn duty of Christian worship.
The service followed a pattern not very different from Sunday worship:
prayer, scripture, a sermon, perhaps a hymn or two. The primary difference between these services and Sunday worship was the degree of pag-
eantry and attendance; celebratory dedications drew many curious onlookers as well as regular worshipers. Newspapers often reported that
dedication services were "filled to overflowing" by a crowd of persons
susceptible to the charms of pomp, circumstance, and novelty. Ritual performances at the opening of new buildings were, according to William
Ellery Channing, natural to human character. "Nature has always taught
men," he preached at the 1826 dedication sermon for the Second Unitarian

Church in New York City, "on the completion of an important structure, designed for public and lasting good, to solemnize its first appropriation to the purpose for which it was reared, by some special service."[26] Channing was careful to avoid conferring "any peculiar sanctity or any mysterious properties" on the Unitarian Church.[27] "We do not suppose," he explained, "that in consequence of rites now performed, the worship offered here will be more acceptable, than prayer uttered in the closet, or breathed from the soul in the midst of business."[28] Unlike Channing, many of Connecticut's Congregationalist ministers felt sure that there was something special about a place of worship. Moreover, ministers argued repeatedly, the place of worship must not be a shop for business or a parlor for society.

The idea of a special place for worship was not inimical to the Reformed tradition. John Calvin himself wrote, "As God by his work ordains common prayers for believers, so ought there to be public temples wherein they may be performed."[29] Yet there was often the reminder that that worship space should absolutely not be seen as qualitatively different from any other; Calvin and his followers strongly emphasized that believers must avoid the temptation to believe that God would be more present to them there than anywhere else. "We must guard against taking them to be God's proper dwelling places, whence he may more readily incline his ear to us." Calvin stressed, "let us leave this stupidity to Jews and pagans, for we have the commandment to call upon the Lord, without distinction of places."[30]

English Puritans took this to an iconoclastic extreme in their moment of power, smashing idols of popery wherever they were found and taking delight in the desecration of churches; Puritans used churches as stables and prisons and even turned dogs loose to hunt a cat in Litchfield Cathedral.[31] But this particular intense aversion to the notion of sacred space was a reaction to what had been before, a means of distancing from Jewish, Roman Catholic, and pagan ritual rather than a concrete program for what should be. Puritans rarely built new structures for worship but used parish churches stripped of iconography. In England, in the long run, the Puritan injunction against sacred art—icons, idols, visual representation of the spiritual realm—did take hold. Yet the buildings themselves retained the look of a church.[32]

New England Puritans had the unique opportunity to build their religious environment in complete conformity to their doctrine. It has been argued that New England meetinghouses stated emphatically the Puritan insistence that their houses of worship must not be qualitatively different from any other structure.[33] It is true that no angels danced on their ceilings and no icons of Christ or the Apostles flanked their altars. But in their original architectural context they had much in common with the finest public and domestic buildings (see chapter 3). Cotton Mather's oft-quoted statement that there is "no place which renders the worship of God more acceptable for its being there performed" expressed the infusion of God's presence into all spheres of life; it did not prohibit the ornamentation of meetinghouses.[34]

The meanings of these buildings, of course, were never wholly secular, despite their multiple uses. Kevin Sweeney noted that early meetinghouses assumed "a certain holiness or even sanctity" as an emblem of the prayer and worship of the community.[35] In his study of seventeenth-century piety, Charles Hambrick-Stowe found the same thing: the tendency of supposedly iconoclastic Puritans to fasten on images and symbols, such as meetinghouses and communion silver, that could give religious meaning to their lives.[36] This all indicates, perhaps, that Mircea Eliade was right when he noted the unavoidable tendency of religious persons to look for "hierophanies," or places in the physical world where they can find the transcendent. According to Eliade, spiritually inclined human beings look for cosmic order ("cosmos") behind the disorder ("chaos") of the visible world, and that order is most often centered on religious spaces that become the center of their spiritual, or "real," experience.[37] In the eighteenth and nineteenth centuries, perhaps as the "chaos" of society mounted and it became more difficult to locate the sacred, New Englanders grew more inclined to look to the meetinghouse or church as a visible center of spirituality. It is tempting to consider the domed or arched ceilings of this period's church architecture as markers of sacred space. We have seen the technical prowess that was required for such curved, open surfaces, especially ceilings, such as those at Center Church and United Church in New Haven, which spanned the whole width of the building. Such a graceful canopy might have represented the sky or the heavens, and at any rate gave a sense of expansiveness to the interior, altering its mood.[38] Art historians have commented on the numinous, spiritual quality of the pure light that filters into these and earlier New England meetinghouses.[39] Besides having much evidence that contemporaries *desired* these features, it is frustratingly difficult to know what they *meant*, in spiritual terms, to worshipers.

The meaning of religious space became a tricky puzzle for Congregationalists and other inheritors of Puritan iconoclasm, Quakers, Methodists, and Baptists in particular. In official doctrine they insisted that God was present in believers, not in buildings, and consequently there was no physical place that God would call his home on earth. Yet both the culture of sentiment and the desire for a physical center for spiritual life coaxed them into certain feelings about worship space, official doctrine notwithstanding. It is evident that many worshipers and clergy, too, saw church buildings as the house of God, and the place that God was most likely to meet his people. In one sense this was nothing new; Puritans believed that public worship was a means of grace, and that saved and sinners alike hoping to be touched by the Holy Spirit did well to attend. But for Puritans, it was the assembly of the faithful that drew God's presence; the building itself was supposed to have nothing to do with it. Nineteenth-century Christians wanted to make worship space a place where God resided, a place he made his earthly home, a place where they could inevitably feel his presence. For them, the idea of a transcendent, omnipresent God and their emotional insistence on persistent "sacred" qualities of worship space could be held simultaneously only in tension.

Dedication sermons illuminate how ministers and people managed to hold apparently conflicting beliefs. With familiar dexterity, New England ministers jumped back to the Old Testament in order to link themselves with Israel, this time an Israel that reveled in the glory of the temple. Despite Calvin's remarks about the stupidity of "Jews and pagans," Connecticut's Congregationalists almost without exception used Jewish examples when discussing the house of God, for in the Hebrew Bible they found enticing images of God in his sanctuary. While recognizing official doctrine ("of course we know God is not *really* more present here . . ."), ministers freely attributed Old Testament holiness and majesty to present architectural accomplishments. They praised their congregations for building something suitable for the awesome God they then implored to bring truth, dignity, and even terror to worship. Ministers hoped this intensity would contribute to the seriousness with which the congregation pursued the duties of Christian worship. Dedication ceremonies were opportunities for renewal. The achievement of a building was proof that God was with a congregation, and would, if the people did their part in worship and kept the sanctity of the building, remain there.

Three Hartford dedication sermons show precisely these concerns. In 1806 in the midst of a bustling city center, the First Congregational Society began to raise the brick church previously discussed, a building of bearing and elegance that many citizens had never beheld before. Reverend Thomas Robbins, in town for the building's dedication in December of 1807, wrote that it was "one of the most solemn and affecting scenes" he had ever witnessed.[40] On the day of its official deliverance to God, the Reverend Nathan Strong looked down on a "very great collection of people" — church members and other, less familiar faces. Strong chose the word "consecration" rather than the less imposing "dedication" to describe what he was about to do. The text he selected was from the Old Testament, Psalm 93:5, "Holiness becomes thine house, O Lord, forever."

There should have been no question as to what Reverend Strong was going to say.[41]

He began by asking his audience to prepare to enter into the task ahead "with reverence, and fervent prayer" and proceeded to set forth both the special nature of the place of worship and the reverential behavior it demanded. "There is a sanctity in the place where God reveals himself," Strong declared, where "we draw near to him in the duties of devotion." The psalmist knew the sanctuary as "the most delightful and solemn place" to seek God's presence. In houses of worship Christians drew together in the fellowship of saints, "which raiseth them above the power of temptation and the afflictions of the world." Here God heard them, guided them, strengthened them, protected them, blessed them, and, finally, sanctified them. Strong declared that the house of God demanded diligent attendance, "deep mourning on account of sin," and real devotion. The patriarchs proclaimed the awesomeness of the house of God, Strong reminded, and "whoever comes with a light mind into the place where God is usually worshipped, or a heart filled with the pleasures or enmities of the world, doth not know how glorious Jehovah is." The Christian's attitude in church must therefore be one of reverent expectation with a resolute singleness of purpose.[42]

It was completely inappropriate, Strong claimed, that churches be used for other than worshipful ends. "The house of God is not a place for us to mingle earthly and holy joys," Strong warned, "for they are not in their nature capable of being united." He made direct reference to New England's multipurpose meetinghouses, claiming "the impropriety of applying our churches, as is the custom in many places, to other uses beside the worship of God. Thus mingling things holy and unholy has a powerful influence to destroy Christian reverence."[43] Strong insisted that "certain times, places, and things" must be "appointed to God's service, in such a manner, as not to be united with secular interests, or the common works and pleasures of the world." Christians were to guard jealously the sanctuary as "an entrance into heaven," the place where God would meet them. From these comments it appears that while God may not have needed churches to make himself known, the sanctuary was of crucial necessity to worshipers. The maintenance of "Christian reverence," by guarding against worldly associations and maintaining the spiritual overtones of the place, was essential to right worship. Strong ventured to use the word "holy" to describe the church, claiming that the idea of "holiness, when applied to inanimate things, means that they are appropriated to some use in the worship and service of God." Strong meant "holy" or "sacred" in the first sense, in which the actions of people set material objects apart for spiritual purposes.[44]

The whole point of worship was to make *people* holy, and that could be done only through an act of God. The outcome of devotion should be that a Christian possessed "a conformity of the will and affections to the moral character of God." Only the Holy Spirit was capable of making such a transformation in people in their "natural state," but this change was always worked with the assistance of various "means," the very greatest of them being worship in the sanctuary. Strong noted worship was a less effective means if intrusions were allowed that tended to "destroy Christian reverence." Concentration on right feelings was essential. The sinner, argued Strong, must take on a "holy disposition" in preparation for eternal life, and worship was a key way to ensure the development of such a character. Worshiping in God's house was not only for his glory but also for the eternal good of the worshiper. It was of crucial importance that the atmosphere of worship had nothing that would "destroy Christian reverence."[45]

Although Strong believed that his God was everywhere, he also was firmly convinced that God was more present some places than others. Strong pointed to the "sanctity in the place where God reveals himself," indicating that God's expected presence in the building made it, like the temple, "holy" in the second sense. God has "promised a special blessing," Strong stated, "in the sanctuary where he meets us to hear our prayer and praise." This is the sort of mildly unorthodox notion that appears in most dedication sermons. Its sentimental, even magical content was made clear in the customary warnings preached by Strong and others about wrong use of the sanctuary. Worshiping God was a duty, insisted Strong, and too many worshiped erratically or with a frivolous attitude. What one did or did not do inside a church had consequence on the magnitude of salvation or damnation. Those who did not attend worship at all risked not only their own eternal situation but that of their children. Strong threatened such slackers in his own congregation, who were "not only endangering their own souls, but devoting their offspring to ruin." "Many spend the Sabbaths in vain conversation, in a secret attention to secular interests or in amusement and their faces are rarely seen in the congregation of God's people." Poor attention to worship was a curse on the congregation, and interruptions, such as a newspaper or a too-fashionable hat, could serve to turn God's concern away from his people. Strong's sermon served, as did the new building itself, to remind people of the duty of reverent, consistent Christian worship.[46]

Nearly twenty years later, Hartford celebrated the completion of its second brick church, North Congregational, with a similar ceremony. The pastor of Hartford's First Church, Reverend Joel Hawes, was the speaker. His sermon, using emotionally charged images and phrases, openly expressed the desirability of a sentimental attachment to the new building. Hawes, like Strong, chose a text from the Psalms, 122:7–9: "Peace be within thy walls, and prosperity within thy palaces. . . . Because of the house of the Lord our God I will seek thy good." After reading his text, Hawes began, "these words breathe a tenderness of religious feeling and sentiment. . . . They are expressive of the warmest love to the Church of God, and the sincerest attachment to the place consecrated to his worship." Hawes noted, as Strong had done, that the psalmist, a character capable of great and admirable emotion, felt a warm attachment to the temple in Jerusalem: "it was the seat of his fondest desires and most grateful recollections."[47]

The purpose of the meetinghouse, according to Hawes, was *"the glory of God and the salvation of men."* The house was worthy only insofar as it satisfied both purposes. "The beauty and grandeur of the temple in which you assemble" was not in itself enough to "sanctify your services, nor make your sacrifices of prayer and praise ascend acceptable to heaven," Hawes told his congregation. "It is the presence of God in his earthly temples that constitutes their true glory." Hawes's sermon, in common with many of the period, served as a warning of what would happen if worship was not regular and honest. The occasion of a new building allowed the minister to mark the progress of the congregation and to stress that the building itself, however beautiful, was meaningless and useless if the teaching inside was heretical or poorly attended. Hawes insisted that only a commitment to the doctrines of the fathers would keep this new building full and flourishing. If his congregation were to fail, he threatened, "The sacred shades of the pilgrims will testify against you . . . God himself will testify against you, and, provoked by your dereliction of truth and duty, will inscribe on the walls of this temple,—the glory is departed." Reverend Hawes, with relish, employed the drama of the Old Testament tradition, freely using the word "temple" to describe his Georgian brick church in Hartford. Given his Puritan roots, Hawes's evocation of both the "temple" and "glory" is remarkable. Yet those roots were not at all forgotten, for Hawes urged the continued allegiance to the doctrines of the "pilgrim" fathers and in curious fashion suggested that their ghosts were drifting around the church monitoring orthodoxy.[48]

Despite this reliance on Old Testament text and imagery, Hawes, like Strong, had to mediate between that driving need to make the church sacred, or at least emotionally foreboding, and a Puritan tradition he plainly revered. "God is greatly to be feared in the assembly of the saints," he told his audience, "for there he is in a peculiar sense present." In worship God hears and answers prayers and forms his people into saints. In worship we should leave everything else behind as "utterly inconsistent with the holiness of God's house." Regular worship, undertaken with a humble spirit, deportment, and "the utmost seriousness and reverence" was essential. Although Hawes had to admit, finally, that nothing could contain God, he believed God condescended to dwell with his people; even the New Testament promised Christ's "special presence, wherever two or three gather together" in his name. Hawes ended his sermon with a litany of consecrations for each part of the church—walls, pulpit, and "altar"—and made a special plea that the walls never "be profaned with unholy services."[49] Finally, he told the congregation that the church was a special place of refuge, where worshipers might feel the presence of God and practice holiness. The building would be "a resting place of the soul— this retreat from the cares and burdens of earth—this asylum for the weary and heavy laden." Day-to-day life in Hartford, apparently, was less than conducive to spiritual experience and growth. Those yearning to feel the presence of God might need to come inside his house.[50]

The idea of the church as God's particular dwelling place formed the core of the Reverend Joel Linsley's dedication sermon for Hartford's Second, or South, Congregational Church in 1827. Linsley's text was the Genesis passage (28:17) in which Jacob dreams of the ladder to heaven, "the angels of God ascending and descending on it." "How dreadful is this place! This is none other but the house of God, and this is the gate of heaven." Linsley resolved the theological sacred-secular dilemma with a typical answer that kept Puritan doctrine intact while allowing for human intuition and feeling. True to his formal creed, Linsley, referring to the New Testament message of the priesthood of all believers, first acknowledged that the church was present not in buildings but in believers. "Enlightened as we are by the radiance of the Gospel," he told his congregation, "we may it is true perceive that we are not now authorized to attach any postive [sic] holiness to the particular sanctuary in which we worship, in distinction from other places." Yet, he continued, "certainly it is proper that a house designed for the worship of Jehovah, should be regarded as sacred to this object. It is not meet that a house of prayer be made a house of merchandise, or converted into a theatre for secular business of any kind." Furthermore, "it should ever stand in our view, and live in our associations, as the consecrated habitation of the Most High . . . the holy and beautiful house—the sacred and venerated place where our fathers worshipped." Linsley could not argue for the special qualities of worship space from any tightly reasoned doctrine. He was able, nonetheless, by a sentimental, emotional appeal to propriety and the memory of Christian forebears, to maintain the distinctly majestic and spiritual overtones of the space.[51]

Linsley organized his sermon around the question: How does a building become and remain God's house? First, the building must be built for God only, not for worldly gain or praise. If the builders were "prompted to the undertaking and governed in its execution by the influence of custom, or by pride and the spirit of display," God would not deign to descend; he would not be happy with "the mere exterior decorations and splendours of his earthly courts." But with prayer, sound doctrine, and zeal, the sanctuary would become, in a sense, "the presence chamber of the King of Kings."[52] Linsley recognized the temptation to build a showy, expensive church for the wrong reason—human pride. But he also spoke about the building as being "the consecrated habitation of the Most High." Wasn't it only right, then, that the building would attain a certain degree of splendor that would mark it as special? Ministers warned their people about putting more resources into their own homes than they put into the house of God. Hartford, its citizens noted with pleasure, was becoming a fashionable city. Stacks of bricks and timbers from dozens of new building projects lined the streets. If such exertion were going into construction and ornamentation of stylish new homes, how could Hartford's citizens, in good conscience, worship God in shabby, old, or plain buildings? "It does not become them," chided Linsley, "to live in their ceiled, adorned, and well furnished houses, and yet exclude from the sanctuary of the Most High, those fair fruits of human genius and skill, which might render it at once convenient and attractive." This was imperative because of the "dignified and important ends" the church was to serve. Linsley, looking around at the fine detail of the expensive new church, reassured his people that he could not "learn from the scriptures . . . that it is unlawful for those to whom God has given the ability, to spend their substance liberally in providing handsome accommodations for his worship." Because worldly treasures were a gift from God, it was only right to give them back to him, packaged as a stunning and costly place of worship.[53]

Congregational ministers knew they were walking a thin line between appropriate material display and the treachery of fashion. Richard Bushman has pointed out the tension inherent in the position they shared with their congregations.[54] On the one hand, tradition demanded that their faith be one of the plain word of God, unencumbered by fashionable ornaments. The specter of a false gentility that impoverished spiritual life haunted their dreams of worldly success. Such had always been the case for Puritans with a disposable income. Colonial Americans so burdened chose either to avoid shows of extravagance or to justify display by convincing themselves that wealth and possessions were essential signs of God's favor. Yet most colonists, certainly those in Connecticut, inhabited a world where options for show were not that great. With the vast majority of Connecticut's people scratching a living out of recalcitrant soil, opportunities for material display were limited to a small range of small-town possibilities. Meetinghouses, as already mentioned, were often expressions of the best a community could build, but that was not much.

Nineteenth-century Connecticut was a different world. As Bushman argues, gentility, including the attainment of a proper sensibility, was becoming less of an adornment for a privileged few and more of a general code of behavior for people in the know, middle-class folks who, with proper education and accoutrements, could walk into a room with the confidence that they were doing so the "right" way. Gentility, in Bushman's view, was internalized and, ultimately, spiritualized. By the 1820s, Connecticut's people could view refinement not as a threat to spirituality but as an essential element of it, even as a sign of sanctification. When God touched a human heart, of course that heart became more sensitive to beauty, whether in the character of others or in the material world. It was, therefore, proper to put a premium on good manners and beautiful things, and on the sensibility to appreciate them.

Simply appreciating beauty, however, was not enough reason to throw resources into a beautiful house for a New Testament God who was known to be comfortable lying in a manger or traveling with a gang of misfits. Beauty had to be assigned a didactic, spiritual function before inheritors of the Puritan tradition could be truly comfortable celebrating magnificent houses of worship. The Reverend Elisha Atkins put this succinctly in an 1818 dedication sermon:

. . . there ought to be not only room and convenience to accommodate the worshipers, but also dignity & elegance to assist devotion, and to express a respect for Divine institutions. . . . He who formed man with a taste for beauty, a love of order, and an admiration of grandeur, well knew that these properties, in the place and utensils of worship, contribute to inward piety and devotion; while, on the contrary, inelegance & disorder naturally tend to damp the fervor of devotion, and to repress the emotions of piety.[55]

These sermons indicate clergy and people alike felt it was important that places of worship keep a significant distance from the world and its cares and corruptions, which could interfere with the spiritual associations the building could convey. In other words, the spiritual *feeling* a building evoked needed to be protected.

A proper, beautiful atmosphere could focus the piety of worshipers. It could also manipulate the congregation to act in a respectful, devout manner. But behind these assumptions was the idea that by creating a beautiful space and a respectful atmosphere, a minister and congregation could, in effect, call up the presence of God and perhaps even bring down grace to the sinner. The idea of God's "special presence" in the sanctuary was not so comfortable that ministers could say so without a disclaimer. "We are not now authorized to attach any postive [*sic*] holiness to the sanctuary in which we now worship," preached Linsley. "Inanimate things cannot be holy in the most strict understanding of the word," preached Strong. "God is essentially present in all places."[56] "Heaven and the heavens" cannot contain God, declared Hawes, "how much less the walls of temples made with hands?"[57] Such were the protestations.

Yet far more prevalent in their sermons were indications that on some level most believed that God would do something special in a house of worship. And that something, aided by the beauty of the building itself, was that he would bring sinners to a heartfelt knowledge of their neediness and save their souls. In 1811, a writer to the *Connecticut Evangelical Magazine* argued that private religious meetings, while useful, lacked the power of worship in church: "the houses consecrated to [God's] public worship . . . the place in which he uses his great and leading means of convicting and converting sinners, of building up his church, and preparing it for the glory of heaven."[58] Church buildings had a unique power. By 1831, Episcopalians could call "the house of God" itself an "auxiliary . . . means of grace."[59]

The ability of church buildings to be "means" not only to devotion, but to salvation itself, depended on their success at arousing the required emotions. Nathan Strong noted that human beings are moved by emotional responses to the stimulation of their senses. "Our weakness is such," he explained, "that we need every assistance in devotion. We are so affected by sensible things, that without their aid we fail in that warmth of the affections which is due to a great subject." Churches, with a wealth of beauty and positive associations, have "a powerful tendency to elevate our affections to divine things."[60] If devotion and "warmth of affections" were so valued yet at the same time fragile and elusive, it is no wonder that ministers and worshipers sought to create a worship environment conducive to heightened emotion.

This sheds more light on the confusing use of the term "sacred" in the second, metaphysical sense. People at some level needed, or at least wanted, to believe that God actually descended into a house made by human hands and condescended to make a home there. An article written by an Episcopalian, titled "On the Sacredness of Churches," reveals some disagreement about the purpose of church consecration and defends the belief in consecration and sacred space. The writer claims that "of late years, it has been customary to decide that veneration which the greater part of Christians feel for those places which are particularly devoted to the service of God." Critics might "ask with a sneer, whether a greater degree of sanctity can be attributed to one pile of wood and stone than another," but the answer is obviously yes.[61] Examples from biblical and ancient history shore up the author's argument that God promised to be more present some places than others. "Sacred" seemed to mean, for Congregationalists and Episcopalians both, that God had agreed to make of their physical church building a special home. "He hath promised a special blessing in the sanctuary," Strong told his audience."[62] "The sanctuary becomes," Linsley promised, "in a sense the presence of the King of Kings." God will "fill this temple with his presence; record his name here," preached Hawes, "and here dwell to animate and accept your worship."[63]

The degree to which Connecticut's Congregationalists were willing to forget their doctrine for the sake of feeling is made perfectly clear in a remarkable passage from Joel Linsley's 1827 dedication sermon. The practice of setting apart a religious space, Linsley preached,

has been deemed an appropriate religious solemnity, in all ages and among all nations, whether christian or pagan; and therefore we may presume that it is a dictate of reason. Some of the ancient heathen attached such sacredness to their gods, that they accounted it a sacrilege afterwards to convert them to any secular use. In this sentiment we may perhaps discern something of the influence of superstitious devotion; and yet it is impossible not to yield our respect to feelings so worthy to be cherished.[64]

Worthy "feelings" were in themselves proof of piety—sentiments even capable, perhaps, of excusing a pagan from wrongheaded doctrine.

These Hartford ministers argued for a fresh and watchful attitude toward church buildings and worship. Two developments in particular illustrate changes in the style and tone of public worship. First, there was a new attention to music in the worship service, music of the sort that Professor Cogswell advocated, music that was not just an expression of praise but a calculated performance. Second, there was a persistent attention to proper deportment in worship. In sermons, articles, and private papers, we find the belief that unrefined worship might interfere with the work of God. Both the renaissance of church music and the insistence on proper behavior reflect the changing nature of worship toward a practice that demanded deep but controlled emotional work by the worshipers. This was not a doctrinal decision of ministers but the response of religion to cultural trends that valued sentiment, beauty, and emotion, here centered on public performance. I do not mean to say that the move was wholly secular; it was not. But spiritual experience itself, as Colin Campbell described it, changed to rely more and more on setting—that is, piety existed in a frame of sensual experience. Ultimately, such emphasis on the special nature of the worship experience gave a hearty push to the movement to separate religious spaces from the corruption of the world.

A New Style of Worship: Music

Music was a tool that could both heighten the expressiveness and maintain the dignity of worship.[65] A pronounced change wrought in the worship service by the culture of sentiment was the introduction of what Professor Cogswell described as "beautiful, touching and spiritual lyric effusions." New church music changed the sound of worship, altered its organization, and placed new demands on church buildings.[66] There were two important components to church music, the vocal and the instrumental. The character and place of each had been hotly contested within the Reformed tradition. Instrumental music did not come to play a major role in Connecticut's Protestant churches until the later nineteenth century, although the role of instruments in worship, pipe organs especially, was a concern much earlier. These Connecticut congregations were greatly occupied, however, with the problem of congregational singing. It is clear in Connecticut's church records that post-Revolutionary singing was rarely satisfactory and certainly not inspirational. From the late eighteenth century on, religious societies, one after another, recorded votes to "hire a singing instructor" or, simply, "do something about the quality of music in our society."

Based on the authority of the New Testament model, seventeenth-century New England Puritans sang unaccompanied psalms in unison. The first book published in America, *The Bay Psalm Book* (1640) was the fruit of the careful labor of New England ministers intent on a correct, metrical translation of the original Hebrew into rhythmical English poetry. The melody was selected from a repertoire of generally well-known tunes. Typically the psalms were "lined out," meaning that a precentor would sing each line before it was sung in turn by the congregation. Although this ensured that all present could participate, it led to a certain jarring awkwardness. To add to the confusion, the melody often wavered at the mercy of the precentor and was set either too high or too low; many of the singers strained to follow.[67] As early as the 1720s some New England clergy and laity recognized, if not the fundamental insufficiency of this type of psalm singing, at least the pathetic manner in which congregations often performed it. This led to the formation of singing schools designed to teach both how to read music and how to sing, including three-part harmony. These schools provided a formal setting for instruction in "sacred" music. Traveling "singing masters" taught their pupils, men and women together, in a regimen of evening lessons.[68]

By the late eighteenth century church music had changed dramatically with the introduction of more melodious and heartfelt singing, a core component of evangelical revivals. The hymns of the English nonconformist Isaac Watts dominated through the antebellum era in America. His *Hymns and Spiritual Songs* and *Psalms of David* were the most frequently published American imprints of the eighteenth century. The historian Stephen Marini has argued that these hymns were the single most important vehicle for the transmission of evangelical beliefs at that time.[69] Now familiar hymns, such as Watts's "Oh God our help in ages past" or "When I survey the wondrous cross," or the Methodist Charles Wesley's "O for a thousand tongues to sing" or "Come thou long expected Jesus" hardly seem revolutionary today, yet at the time they promoted a dramatic reconceptualization of Protestant congregational singing. Nathan Hatch, in *The Democratization of American Christianity*, argues that another wave of lively and nontraditional religious folk music swept through America between 1780 and 1830. This he calls "another aspect of the democratic impulse" in American religion.[70] Methodists, and particularly rural New England Baptists, seem to have participated in such democratic music making, as Hatch suggests. But what was heard in Connecticut's Congregational and Episcopal churches, and the urban congregations of other denominations under their influence, was music of a different tone. The attractions of popular religion called for a response from traditionalists. The passionate, dramatic, mobilizing, seductive hymns of camp meetings had no place in Connecticut's Congregational churches.

In an unusual ceremony in 1807, Reverend William Lyman dedicated the new church organ in the Congregational Church of Lebanon-Goshen. Lyman's sermon, titled *The design and benefits of Instrumental Musick*, was a tentative yet considerable apology for quality church music, specifically that made by instruments. The organ in question was a "barrel or hand organ—of uncommonly large size," made by "the self-taught and ingenious" Mr. Erastus Wattles of Lebanon.[71] Although quirky, this published sermon gives insight into the position of Connecticut's Congregationalists on the subject of church music. Simply the fact of its existence indicates the debatable nature of church music at this time. The arguments against it were well known to Lyman's listeners. Didn't church music interfere with true worship? Didn't a fine performance divert the praise of God to the praise of men? Turning to the Old Testament, Lyman was able to find ample evidence of God's people worshiping with instrumental music. The psalmist himself sang "Praise him with stringed instruments and organs." The psalmist, of course, was not talking about a pipe organ, but neither was Lyman.

Solicitous subscribers to the organ fund had no doubt encouraged Lyman to perform this peculiar dedication. Lyman rose to the occasion, beginning with a biblical validation. As written by the prophet Zechariah, "In that day there shall be upon the bells of the horses, Holiness unto the Lord." If horse bells will be consecrated in the last days, Lyman asked, why not church organs? "I have little doubt, my brethren, that in the Millennium, to which, I suppose, the words of the text have reference, there will be a surrendery [sic] to the service of God and the benefit of the church of many things." Even those things which now produce "sensual merriment, and enliven the giddy throng in the airy mazes of nocturnal hilarity, shall captivate, warm, and enrapture the soul of piety . . . to burst forth in the language of praise." Certainly one did not have to go so far as this to legitimize the organ, "a noble instrument which hath generally been considered as among those which are sacred to the use of the church," and not usually "ranked with the incentives to carnal mirth."[72]

According to Lyman, many churches already used organs in worship. "We find it in use with a respectable class of Christian worshippers, in many of their churches; and by degrees, gaining admission into the temples of those who are of a different denomination." The "respectable class" here mentioned was probably Episcopalian, for England's Anglicans cum Episcopalians had long worshiped to the accompaniment of organs. Congregational churches, however, were just coming around to see the value of the organ. The ultimate triumph, Lyman proposed, would be if all musical instruments could be rehabilitated for the use of Christian worship. "I should rejoice if the time were to come when this and other instruments of Musick, shall be taken from the perverted use to which they seem destined, and made the sweeteners and enlighteners of God's worship." Music, as Lyman saw it, could "sweeten" or palpably improve the quality of worship, and it might also instruct or "enlighten" the worshiper.[73] Lyman told his audience that music "charms, elevates, and enraptures their souls." It could "remove gloom, despondency, and deadness from the soul," with the spiritual effect that "animated devotions" take place. It could even "keep up the attention" of worshipers liable to snooze.[74] The first argument for the use of high-quality music in worship was that it would "elevate the souls" of the worshipers, spurring them on to greater piety.

But Reverend Lyman's concerns were also quite practical. Worship simply had to change, he insisted, if it had any hope of overcoming the enticements of popular entertainments. Because church music could awaken the affections, declared Lyman, young people in particular would be persuaded to forgo "the assembly and ball-room" and "choose the house of God as the place of highest entertainment and delight." Lyman's hopes in this regard were obviously too high, but his easy use of the word "entertainment" in connection with worship is telling. There was nothing wrong, it seemed, in making worship pleasurable. The proceedings in Lebanon did not go uncriticized. Lyman alluded to his critics' derision of the organ dedication as "a low business, and undeserving such solemn parade." He confessed that he himself was uncomfortable with the dedication and preferred to think of the event as a meeting to worship with the assistance of the new instrument.[75] The events at Lebanon-Goshen were a harbinger of the vocal and instrumental music that would soon alter the worship of most of Connecticut's Congregationalists.

Episcopalians, long accustomed to avowing the desirability of choirs and organs, were their most articulate and prolific advocates. In an 1808 article titled "Thoughts on the singing of Psalms and Anthems in Churches," an anonymous, conservative contributor to the *Churchman's Monthly Magazine* analyzed the use of music in worship. The only reason to have music, he declared, was "to excite and increase devout affections." In contrast to Lyman, this writer believed music should not be used as a means of luring people into a church. That would be horrible, a "deplorable insensitivity to the sanctity of the place." Yet pleasure, he argued, was "instrumental to devotion." The choice of music was the issue. Psalms were acceptable anthems; hymns "out of some insipid hymn book" were not. The singers, he said, should master the music before the church service. The author dismissed prejudices against instrumental music as the result of negative experiences, agreeing that organs could be "nuisances to serious people, by being played on improperly." Bad, or inappropriate music, such as the "light airs which are calculated to send people dancing out of church," was another unfortunate affront. The overall tenor of the article was strongly in favor of church music, yet insistent that music be appropriately solemn and well performed.[76]

Hartford's Baptists declared in March of 1809 that "it is the duty of the Members of the Church to whom God has given the ability to sing his praises To improve their talents in that way at stated times when the Church meet for worship."[77] Certain Baptists did have trouble accepting the inroads the world was making into Baptist worship. By January of 1811, Elder Henry Grew "had withdrawn himself from the Pastoral care and fellowship of this church, on account of some existing differences of sentiment respecting the order of Christ's House."[78] A society discussion that June considered whether "a connection existed between the church and people of the world in society . . . which was productive of undue influence on the church in regard to the order and disapline [*sic*] of Christ's House." Three voted yes, eleven no. The following week the society voted that as regards singing, "it is the duty of the church to maintain that part of worship in our social meetings."[79] It is quite possible that the two references in the Baptist records are related. Mary Treadwell Hooker, an elderly member of the Farmington Congregational Church, expressed tentativeness when she wrote in her diary: "I have once more joind. the choir to celebrate the praises of God in his House, it laboured long in my mind, I was fully satisfied that it was the duty of every one that could sing, to join in that part of the publick worship of God."[80] Singing schools proliferated, and special pews, often in the galleries of churches, became "singers' seats," meaning that the worshipers would not see the singers as the music wafted over their heads. Music was intended to contribute to making worship more refined, more sensual, more beautiful, and more *effective*. Hymns could soften hearts stubbornly resisting the gospel. Harry Croswell records giving Susan Barnett, a young unbeliever, a book of hymns. I "presented her with a little book of easy hymns," he recorded in 1821, "in hopes to draw her mind to some realizing sense of divine things."[81] These hymns were evangelistic not because they brought church music to the level of the common people, but because they encouraged them to rise to a higher level of sensibility.

Critics grumbled not over the existence of choirs per se, but their exaggerated importance. In 1840 members of the South Congregational Church in Hartford wanted to dissolve their choir because of its inflated pride. Perhaps the choir was a bit puffed up, considering that it had its own set of written records and in them claimed "sacred music is a highly interesting and important part of public worship."[82] Choirs were the target of one critic who claimed that disputes within choirs, "whistling and talking and levity so often observable in the singers seat," not to mention the "thoughtless and even blasphemous manner in which the name of God is often used" by the choir, degraded the quality of worship.[83] Another apparent problem with vocal music was that a singing master could be "vain and intemperate," a mere "bloat of vanity," and those characteristics could infect worship.[84]

The most common criticism leveled against church music, however, was that untalented musicians gave a dreadful performance. Reverend Samuel Gilman, in his good-natured *Memoir of a New England Village Choir*, parodied this situation. "Nothing . . . could be rougher than the Stentorian voice of Mr. Broadbreast and nothing more piercing than the continued shriek of the pale but enthusiastic Miss Sixfoot. I shall not disclose the name of the good man who annoyed us a little with his ultra-nasal twang, nor of another, who had the ungainly trick of catching his breath violently at every third note. . . ."[85] Reviews were not always bad. When at the Hebron church in 1799, Thomas Robbins noted, "They sing here excellently. At evening went to a singing meeting."[86] Proof of the desirability of good singing is found in the willingness of congregations to commit funds or even raise subscriptions for that purpose. These sums most often were in the range of twenty to fifty dollars. The Winchester congregation, for example, voted in 1809 to spend thirty-five dollars for "a teacher of Psalmody to Instruct the youth & others in the art of sing-ing."[87] It is rare for any substantial information about congregational singing to appear in society records, although occasional references do show the seriousness with which it was pursued. In 1812 the First Church in Hartford appointed a committee "to make a selection of tunes of such number and variety as shall be sufficient for the purposes of public wor-ship in the society." The society asked the choristers to then choose the music, but insisted that no new tunes be introduced without the approval of the music committee.[88] This degree of control indicates not only the importance of music but the potential pitfalls if singing went out of control.

On June 12, 1791, Reverend William Bentley of Salem, Massachusetts, recorded in his famous diary, "I preached in Mr. Clarke's congregation [Boston]. It is not large, but very liberal in opinions. They have an organ, the first introduced into dissenting Meeting Houses. The example is se-ducing, Not merely from the fondness of parades, which leads religion as well as follows easily in its train, but from the great inconveniencies, & real difficulties attending the support of vocal music."[89] His comment speaks not only to the trials and tribulations surrounding singing and choirs, but suggests the practical function that organs could fill. Even for Congregationalists, the joys of organ music proved hard to resist. In his memoir Reverend Gilman admitted, "I cannot find in my soul to dispense with the glorious majesty of sound with which an organ fills the house of prayer. In the tones of this sublime trophy of human skill, there is something that wondrously accords with the sentiment of piety . . . the connection between religion and the organ is something more than fan-ciful. Who has not felt at once inspired and subdued by the voice issuing from that gilded little sanctuary which towers in architectural elegance over the solemn assembly below, and seems to enshrine the presiding genius of devotional praise?" (fig. 36)[90]. The Reverend Bentley kept tabs on the progress of church organs in Massachusetts. In February of 1809 he noted that "the change of manners in our Order of the Church be-comes every day more visible. An organ has been presented to the

36. Rear gallery with organ, First Congregational Church, Hartford. Photo by author.

The society installed its first organ in 1822 and replaced it with another in 1835. This photo shows an 1883 organ in the 1835 case. The woodwork on the gallery railing dates from a later extension to accommodate choir and organ. The coffering on the vaulted ceiling dates from the 1852 renovations.

Congregational Church at Pittsfield under the pastoral care of a good republican Mr. Allen by a Mr. Shearer. Organs are now used in our principal towns and in several towns in the County, perhaps as many as 12 in this state in Congregational Churches. 3 in Boston, 2 in Salem, 1 in Newbury Port."[91]

At the end of the eighteenth century, there were only about twenty church organs in all of New England, most of them in Anglican churches.[92] Three-quarters of those were imported from England, adding to their already great expense. Qualified organists were few and far between. Yet, as Reverend Bentley noted, dissenters were beginning to see the advantages of organ music. The first dissenting congregation in New England to acquire an organ was the Congregational Church of Providence, Rhode Island, in 1770. Connecticut's Congregationalists were slower to acquire organs, although by the middle of the nineteenth century many congregations had them.[93] In 1819 the United Society in New Haven paid Mary Salter "for playing on the organ."[94] In 1822 the First Congregational Church of Hartford agreed to "cheerfully accept of an organ now offered to be procured and put up by individuals of this society."[95] Six years later, its neighbor the North Church voted to purchase an organ costing one thousand dollars from Thomas Appleton of Boston.[96] Jabez Huntington, William Thompson, and a Dr. Sheldon gave a New York–made pipe organ to the new Litchfield church in 1829.[97] The First Congregational Society of Norwich acquired an organ in 1824; Thomas Robbins, preaching in Norfolk in 1825, noted "they have a good organ."[98] Perhaps the primary obstacle to obtaining a church organ was the great expense. Most congregations could hardly afford not only the initial outlay of funds, but the cost of maintenance and the organist's salary. Frequently, when it came to music, churches agreed that if there were members in the congregation who wanted to pay for improvements, they were welcome to do so. After the completion of the new church in Salisbury in 1801, the society voted that "liberty be given to such persons as feel disposed to subscribe towards procuring instruments for church music to be used in the Meeting House."[99]

Meetinghouses and churches were natural sites for well-attended concerts of sacred music. The size, the lively acoustics, and the arrangement of pews facing forward made new churches excellent concert halls. Often these concerts were organized and presented by the choirmasters. In 1829 Hartford's North Church voted that its organist, Benjamin Barclay, could use the "church and organ, under the direction of the committee, for the purpose of giving two concerts of sacred music in the course of the year."[100] Barclay also agreed "to give two concerts of sacred music for the benefit of said society whenever requested." On May 22, 1822, Harry Croswell recorded a concert of "sacred music by the Philharmonia Association—composed of choirs of the several congregations" at "Mr Merwin's meeting-house."[101] Newspapers often printed notices for these concerts. All were open to the public, and most were free. An 1825 notice in Hartford's *Connecticut Mirror* promoted a "Sacred Music Concert" to be given by the Singing Society of the North Congregational Church. The Wednesday evening concert included "Anthems and set pieces, most of which have not before been performed in this vicinity." The twenty-five-cent admission charge would go "for the further improvement of music."[102] That these concerts were expressly devoted to "sacred" music is significant. Church buildings were available for concerts, but almost always only if the music to be performed had a spiritual content. Yet this was not a purely spiritual event. People attended for the social outing, for the novelty, and to hear beautiful music. Music built a bridge between church buildings and polite society.

A New Style of Worship: Decorum

Debates about church music made manifest an overarching concern that worship be decent, refined, controlled, and *elegant*. "Elegant" buildings and worship worked together to create an atmosphere appropriate for desired spiritual experience.[103] That ambience demanded respectful conduct. The woman who stopped herself from kneeling on the floor and raising her arms in the 1806 revival knew that there was a code of acceptable behavior. Congregationalists and Episcopalians both believed that church attendance called for manners. In 1804 an Episcopalian instructed readers in the proper method of showing devotion. First, he wrote, be contemplative when you approach church, taking special heed to your posture and gestures. Be sure to arrive early, and do not leave until the final blessing is over. Once in church, fall to your knees and pray silently. Work on listening actively to the scriptures and the sermon, and when you take the sacrament, do so "with a penitent and obedient heart."[104]

With some dismay, critical observers noted that many worshipers were not at all attuned to propriety. Writers to Connecticut's public press recoiled with horror at the apparently mounting disrespect for public worship. People talked, slouched, stared, and slept during worship—hardly correct conduct for the house of God. When the people of God acted in such unsuitable ways, the "beauty, the order, and the solemnity of the service are destroyed."[105] Another writer was shocked by the irreverence of such as "sit at their ease, as if they were hearing an idle tale." Even among Episcopalians, it was alarming how "greatly this irreverent and irreligious practice has spread itself." Few knelt to humble themselves. "If you look into the well-lined, seated, and finished pews," he claimed, "the elegant worshippers think it sufficient to lean a little forward" in prayer. During praises, one should stand, not sit. The whole problem, the writer asserted, was that "too many persons . . . have mean notions of public worship and go to church rather to hear some admired preacher, than to join in the devotional services." Some were so impatient with the service that they would "Purposely absent themselves till the service is nearly finished." You could learn a little doctrine in private, he conceded, such as the evangelical "night meetings" offered, but "public worship is a blessing and a duty."[106]

The chief criticism pointed at careless worshipers was a lack of respect for God's house, and here is evidence that concern over proper worship had religious as well as social purposes. A light attitude destroyed any possibility that the worship service could make a spiritual impact on the worshiper. "The sanctuary is God's Holy Temple, and he who enters it with such earthly feelings as to forget the place and the occasion, will not be very likely to go away with any serious impressions." One writer was surprised that such disrespect existed. "It is not unfrequent [sic] that we see many, whom a self respect and moral dignity should teach better things, passing up the aisles of the church, talking and laughing." Social distractions were everywhere. "Should they meet the vacant glare of an impenitent companion, a scene of winking and blinking ensues." Young people in particular were guilty of such inattention, and ought to know that worship "is no place for the perusal of irreligious Books, no place for amusement, and of all others, no place for the indulgence of levity."[107] A writer to the Litchfield Enquirer claimed to have seen, during an 1829 worship service, "as the minister was announcing the text, the congregation was disturbed by the entrance of a young gentleman, & 2 young ladies, all dressed in *full fashion* — Instead of occupying seats near the door where they entered, they marched forward, giggling & talking as they advanced, nearly the whole length of the church" to a pew where they would most easily "see and be seen."[108]

Fashion was a special enemy of Sabbath piety. "Custom seems to have made it necessary," complained one churchman, "that the attention of females should be more turned to dress on the Sabbath than on any other day." First, "the greater part of the morning is spent in thinking what gown, belt, shoes, &c. will do to wear." Then "the rest of the time is spent in dressing and parading before the glass." Where is the Bible or a devotional book in such a display? Their place on the dressing table is usurped by "combs, brushes, perfumes, and jewels." Once in church, this "fashionable female walks up the aisle, thinking much more of the presence of man than the presence of God." All the while she eyes her competition, "looking at this one's bonnet and another's dress—and thinking what an effect her own appearance produces."[109]

The Sabbath provided the perfect opportunity to "see and be seen," a devilish trap for those easily swayed by public opinion. It provided an occasion for heterosocial enjoyments, despite the efforts of the religious societies to keep young men and women apart. The church in Morris was reduced to voting "to appoint some person whose duty it shall be to prevent the young men from taking a seat upon the girls side of the gallery."[110] Eliza Brainard, a sensitive Haddam girl, wrote often about the Sabbath in her diary. On a Sunday in May of 1817, fifteen-year-old Eliza experienced the transformation of her conception of true worship. "I went to the house of God careless as ever," she confessed, "but my mind in the morning was made very solemn."[111] As was her customary practice, in the intermission between services Eliza "mingled with rude company," and she admitted that she was "very rude" herself. Yet her conscience "was not easy." By the afternoon she "felt condemned" for her behavior and, she recorded, "I was struck with a deep sense of my awful situation as a sinner. I could not lift up my head. Tears flowed freely. The preaching never before appeared as it did then, and when returning from meeting, and hearing the young people talking about balls and parties, as I used to do, it shocked me." In a later diary entry, Eliza mourns missed Sunday worship as "a trial, for the house of God is my delight. I have staid from it but two or three times in three years."[112] The publication of Eliza's diary indicates that the public valued her as a model of piety. It is notable that her conversion, as it were, to proper worship took place in the emotionally charged atmosphere of the church interior.

Specialization and Isolation of Religious Space

Worship actively competed with the world for attention. Eliza Brainard was tempted by society before she recognized the special nature of time spent in church. Clergy and laity admitted music partly for its spiritual value, but also because it was "interesting" and "entertaining." Worship had always been removed in form and "feeling" from everyday experience, but in the early national period a generalized emphasis on emotion and feeling upped the sensibility ante. Worship, to maintain its special, reverential tone, had to be distinguished from day-to-day life. It did so by taking place in a building with special qualities, containing God's special presence and offering the promise of spiritual rejuvenation. Churches, more than undistinguished meetinghouses, provided a contrast to, even a refuge from, life in the world.

Shortly after Hartford's First Church dedicated its 1807 building, the congregation voted that "it is the opinion of this society that it is improper that the Meeting house belonging to this society should be appropriated to any other use than that of religious worship."[113] As Nathan Strong had proclaimed in his dedication sermon, "The house of God is not a place for us to mingle earthly and holy joys, for they are not in their nature capable of being united." Strong had noted and denounced the practice of "applying our churches, as is the custom in many places, to other uses beside the worship of God." In 1818, Joel Linsley's Second Church, still in its old building, agreed with Strong's sentiment when it voted that it would no longer "consent to the town of Hartford holding their meetings in the 2nd Ecclesiastical Society's House of Worship."[114] Both practical and ideological reasons contributed to the resolution of religious societies to remove secular business from their meetinghouses. The records of the Roxbury Congregational Church reveal the problem in its complexity, and illustrate how one rural society understood and used changing conceptions of "sacred" space.

At the time of the erection of the Roxbury meetinghouse, 1794, the Congregational Society was not in a position to finance the building entirely and called on the assistance of outsiders. In 1794 the society invited "all denominations . . . to come in and pay their equal proportion towards building . . . and have a seat in said house appointed."[115] It is evident that this Roxbury building was less of a building for a distinct religious unit than a structure for the community at large. As a reward to contributors, the society voted in 1803 to reward seats to "all who had ever paid anything toward building the meetinghouse" and subsequently referred to such "proprietors" as those who had a right to vote in any manner respecting the use of the building.[116]

By the 1820s, the Roxbury society could no longer count on general support from the village and grew protective of its resources, particularly its building. Yet the society could not argue in practical terms that the meetinghouse belonged only to them, for others had contributed as well. Hence they resorted to an ideological argument about the proper use of a house of worship. Some of the problem was purely practical. In 1821, in an urgent petition to the society as a whole, the church pleaded for some respect, "having been deeply pained at the great injuries which their house of worship has sustained by the repeated meeting of a public and secular nature."[117] Among these public meetings had been "Training,

Proxies and Town Meetings," any of which might have been capable of significantly stressing the building.

Not only did these meetings burden the society because of the wear and tear on the building, but the church claimed that the business of the town had shut down the business of God. The congregation had cause "to regret the encroachment of meeting of a public and secular nature." This flew in the face of the intent of the original builders, the petitioners argued, because "their Fathers have told them, that this house was erected for the express purpose of worship and has been consecrated to the service of Almighty God." Biblical precedent was a useful tool; they called "to mind, that the tabernacle and Temple were considered holy." Jesus Christ himself had angrily chastened, "Make not my Father's house a house of merchandize, for it is written, my house shall be called a house of Prayer, for all nations." These Roxbury Congregationalists were aware that the local Episcopalian church escaped the abuses their own building suffered, and they claimed to "most cordially unite in the belief of some of their brethren of different denominations, that to use the house for any other purpose than that for which it was erected and to which it has been solemnly consecrated, is a gross profanation of the sacred place."[118]

The Roxbury congregation was not alone in its belief that secular business constituted "a gross profanation of the sacred place." For practical but also for definite spiritual reasons, Connecticut's Protestants decided that their places of worship demanded a separation from the secular, corrupting influence of the world. The architectual plan of Connecticut's new churches facilitated this separation by the inclusion of a vestibule, an intermediate space between the sanctuary and the outside world. The associations between the space and God's work needed to be protected and the vestibule acted as a buffer zone. The result of new attitudes to worship, however, was not just the separation of the "sacred" from the "secular," but the transformation, in material as well as ideological terms, of the "sacred" itself. The spiritual power of religious buildings rested in their ability to make worship a special, rewarding emotional and spiritual experience. Architectural form and ornament that elicited worshipful sentiment was not only permissible but desirable. Ornament bespoke not pride and the inroads of the world, but the majestic character of God's house, adorned, as the temple of Jerusalem had been, with the best artistic embellishments the society was able to offer. Michael Zuckerman writes of the separation between religious experience and daily life in the nineteenth century: "Just because daily life did not resonate through religious experience, religious experience became more difficult to sustain."[119] Steepled, fashionable churches encouraged worshipful attitudes by declaring the needed difference between the spiritual and the day-to-day. These decorous buildings were one place where Christians could expect an experience that was both emotionally and spiritually fulfilling.

Religious Space in "Lyric Effusions"

In poems and popular hymns, Connecticut's Christians romanced their meetinghouses. Popular verse reiterates the ideas found in dedication sermons and even takes those ideas further. Poets, unlike orthodox ministers, felt less of the restraint of doctrine and freely unleashed their sentimental appreciation for church buildings. In a culture of sentiment, anyone who could combine the right feelings into the flow of rhyming stanzas could become a published poet. On the pages of Connecticut's newspapers, particularly by the 1820s, we find hymns to predictably emotion-laden occasions, such as the tragic death of a young and saintly girl, and unexpected hymns to more mundane events—the New Haven Agricultural Fair, for instance.[120] Poems and hymns to religious buildings drip with sentiment, as the mode of expression required, but they also convey some important truths about the way people thought about these structures. That people invested their meetinghouses with a variety of meanings—historical, sentimental, and metaphysical—is evident from the descriptions, memories, and hopes set out in these poems.

In these poems, more so than in dedication sermons, the church itself became not just an emblem, but an instrument of salvation, "A modern Ark!" that would "guide our footsteps to a world afar," and "bear our souls above."[121] Poem after poem attributes a saving power to the building itself, as does this stanza from a poem by a Yale alumnus describing Trinity Church: "I see my own dear mother church, that warned me from my sin."[122] "This house of prayer doth teach," penned another poet, "that all are sinners—all have stray'd / Like erring sheep."[123] Naturally, ministers and congregations had more to do with spiritual nourishment than the mute walls of a man-made church, yet it was more than the dictates of an inferior sort of popular poetry that made these lines so common. Poems and hymns indicate an anthropomorphism of church buildings that allowed them to assist the Word of God, actively "warning" and "teaching." Meetinghouses were "friends" because they had witnessed so much of the lives of the worshipers. In 1813 New Haven's Theodonia Woolsey informed her nephew James Hillhouse that his sister Rebecca was saddened when an old New Haven meetinghouse was torn down to build a new. "Have you heard Rebecca's old friend [   ] meeting house is down and vigorous preparations are made to build another?" she asked her nephew.[124] One poet sang to his soon-to-be-demolished house: your "walls have given meek hope a home, / And tearful penitence, repose." It was like watching the demise of an old friend, one who had helped him in his spiritual life, an "ancient nurse of holy thought."[125]

The most valued physical parts of the meetinghouse, as these poems indicate, were distinctive elements capable of releasing a stream of heartfelt associations, those readily available to carry metaphorical associations. Steeples, "the holy spires of prayer," received much of the poets' attention.[126] A steeple breaking through the horizon, reaching toward the skies, pointing the way to heaven, was the most obvious sign that here was a house of God. "Pointing to heaven—our resting place— / The spire its ancient form uprears."[127] Spires could seem like arms, reaching up to the heavens from whence the church came. "See the proud spire, a shining pageant rise, / Like virtue, pointing to her native skies."[128] In the hands of poets, spires actively participated in the spiritual work of the faithful. "Devoutly looking into heaven / Like mortal telegraphs to bear / the upward thoughts of the forgiven."[129] Like supernatural phone booths, churches took the prayers of the faithful and through the steeple sent those messages winging to God's ears.

Church walls symbolized the memory of past worship and worshipers: ghosts of the departed, shadows of moments of spiritual satisfaction, echoes of praises there offered. The walls contained God's presence. "This is his chosen dwelling place," one poet exclaimed, describing sensations on entering "the house of prayer" in 1827. "Then enter, oh my soul! with fear / This holy place, for God is here."[130] A hymn written for dedication ceremonies, appearing in the Congregational *Hartford Selection* (1810 edition), proclaimed with awe the mystery of a house of worship:

> And will the great eternal God
> On earth establish his abode?
> And will he from his radiant throne
> Avow our temples for his own?
>
> These walls we to thy honor raise,
> Long may they echo with thy praise;
> And thou descending fill the place
> With choicest tokens of thy grace.[131]

Congregations who sang this hymn expressed their belief that their earthly constructions were "temples" of the Most High. With wonder, they expected God to "fill the place," and promised in return to provide honor and praise.

Creating a church was, in a sense, setting the stage on which God would deign to fill the starring role. A beautiful house of worship was a congregation's enticement for the "great eternal God" to leave his "radiant throne" and live among his people. An Episcopal consecration hymn of 1829 formally invited God to dwell in a new church: "Supplicate / That favouring presence which doth condescend / From the pavilion on high heaven to beam / On earthly temples."[132] This hymn pictured God's presence wafting down from "high heaven" to fill churches, like beams of light. Light, the stark, clear sunlight that came through the tall windows of Connecticut meetinghouses, evoked a sense of purity. One poet, writing about "A New-England Village," described the feelings aroused as he saw "the sun-gilt windows gleam / in their unstained transparency." "Chaste thoughts came o'er me," he sighed, remembering "the grey haired pastor" who touched his brow with baptismal water, and the religion of his youth.[133]

In this latter poem and many others it is the remote and weathered country church that the poet describes. Country churches emblematized, perhaps, all that was wholesome in a life that many new Englanders had forsaken for urban pursuits by the 1820s. The old meetinghouse in Tariffville called up the poetic talents of Hartford Episcopalian Lydia Huntley Sigourney in 1832, becoming the centerpiece of her ode to country life, "The Lonely Church."

> It stood among the chestnuts—its white tower,
> And slender turrets pointing where man's heart
> Should oftener rise.—Up went the wooded heights
> Abruptly beautiful, above its head,
> With verdant screen, shutting the waters out
> That just beyond, through deep, sequestered vale,
> Wrought out a rocky passage.—Clustering roofs
> And varying sounds of village industry
> Swell'd from its margin,—while the busy loom
> Replete with radient fabricks, told the skill
> Of the prompt artizan.[134]

Mrs. Sigourney's church provided a visual contrast to the bustling textile mill nearby. She identified the church with the slow and steady pace of nature in that "sequestered vale," offering a stillness to contrast with the hum of the looms. The church was wrapped in a hushed peace that settled over the gravestones in the churchyard. Human voices were absent, but the epitaphs spoke eloquently of those gone before.

> But all around
> The solitary dell, where meekly rose
> This consecrated Church—There was not voice,
> Save what still Nature in her worship breathes;

> And that unspoken love with which the dead
> Do commune with the living—There thy lay,
> Each in his grassy tenement—The Sire
> of many winters, and the noteless Babe
> Over whose empty cradles, night by night,
> Sat the poor mother mourning—in her tears
> Forgetting what little span of time
> Did hold her from her darling.[135]

The church and gravestones taught Mrs. Sigourney a lesson in mortality, "the little span of time" separating living Christians from those already in heaven. The place also reminded her of her own spiritual journey and her own inevitable death.

> And methought
> How sweet it were, *so near* the sacred house,
> Where we had heard of Christ, and taken his vows,
> And Sabbath after Sabbath, gather'd strength
> To do his will—There to lie down and rest
> Close 'neath the shadow of its peaceful walls,
> And when the hand douth moulder, to lift up
> Our simple tombstone, witness to that faith
> which cannot die.[136]

The little church witnessed all the critical moments in the life of this Christian, and ultimately might be her final resting place. In the final stanza, Mrs. Sigourney addresses the church as if it were a silent evangelist: warning, protecting, nourishing, befriending, guiding, and guarding.

> Heaven bless thee—lonely Dome!
> And duly may'st thou warn a pilgrim-band
> From toil, from cumbrance, and from strife to flee,
> And drink the waters of eternal life.
> Still, in sweet fellowship with trees and skies,
> Friend both of Earth and Heaven—devoutly stand
> to guide the living, and guard the dead.[137]

The church had been there for all the weighty events of many lives and promised to outlive the present generation.

It may seem strange that "the mournful mantle of decay" had such appeal in a fresh, young America. Yet, lugubrious as it might have been, Mrs. Sigourney's poem brought to the author, and presumably the nineteenth-century reader, a delicious sense of pathos. New England's educated girls, in particular, learned how to cultivate and appreciate such emotions from their friendships and their schools, and such sensibility was an important badge of refinement.[138] Thousands of them spent long hours reading popular sentimental stories or carefully working elaborate silk needlework pictures of weeping maidens draped over tombstones (fig. 35). These literary portraits of New England's churches suggest that many people had strong personal ties to their houses of worship and thought of them in distinctly romantic terms. This fueled expectations about how a church and a worship service should act on one's emotions.

The attitude of a certain refined English class toward religious architecture is nicely summed up in this passage from Jane Austen's 1814 novel *Mansfield Park*. Fanny, the poor but virtuous heroine, has left her dismal London life to live with her uncle and aunt Bertram at their country estate. In this scene, she and her cousins are visiting the magnificent estate of the Rushworth family. Mrs. Rushworth gives her visitors a tour of the house, and at length they come upon the private chapel. Fanny, sensible as she is, is disappointed with its aspect.

They entered. Fanny's imagination had prepared her for something grander than a mere, spacious, oblong room, fitted up for the purpose of devotion—with nothing more striking or more solemn than the profusion of mahogany, and the crimson velvet cushions appearing over the ledge of the family gallery above. "I am disappointed," said she, in a low voice, to Edmund. "This is not my idea of a chapel. There is nothing awful here, nothing melancholy, nothing grand. Here are no aisles, no arches, no inscriptions, no banners."[139]

Fanny, by far the most spiritually tuned of the group, was hoping to find something visual to transport her, but it did not happen. In Fanny's case, we can assume that such an effusion of feeling would have pointed her in the direction of the Supreme Being. For many, perhaps including Lydia Huntley Sigourney, it seems that a vague sense of well-being and peace was the result of encountering something spiritual and sentimentally beautiful. One British critic, quoted in the *Episcopal Watchman* in 1833, noted, "we never entered into a place of worship without feeling a quiet and delightful serenity diffused over our senses, like a traveler suddenly turned away from the busy and dusty road into the cool and refreshing of the forest. The animosities of our heart, and the evil prompting of our passions . . . rapidly dies away."[140] The church calmed his soul, refreshed him, and banished evil from his heart.

It is not surprising that America's Episcopalians would have taken quite naturally to the sentiment being felt and expressed by their spiritual cousins in England. Certainly the adoption of the Gothic style is good evidence for that. It is more unexpected that such modes of expression would be taken up by Congregationalists and as formerly materially restrained a band as the Methodists. In 1836, the dedication of a new Methodist meetinghouse in Goshen prompted the writing of a hymn. This hymn shows just how far the culture of sentiment had pervaded the evangelical domain by the 1830s. "This *temple* to thine honor raised / We *consecrate* in love to thee," sang the Methodists (italics mine). "Let incense from this altar rise / And hallowed fire perpetual burn."[141] This oddity is not just the result of poetic convention. It signals a change, not in theology, but in *feelings* about religion and religious spaces.

The dates on these poems and hymns suggest that this revision affected Episcopalians and Congregationalists by the turn of the century, and its influence mounted until even Methodists felt the pull by the 1830s. The material result was the creation of church buildings that took notions of the sacred and sentimental and translated those ideas into a physical worship environment that reinforced emotional tendencies. In sum, a religion of feeling and a culture of sensibility allowed and even encouraged a degree of ornamentation and polish that would help demarcate the space from others. Hence the descendant of Thomas Hooker's congregation, First Church in Hartford, invested unapologetically in plush pulpit furnishings, somewhat to the surprise of onlookers. Kendall, in his *Travels*, remarked after visiting First Church in 1809: "what is still more modern, and still more worthy of regard, this puritan church contains a pulpit of which the furniture is of green velvet, with cords of green and gold, fancifully entwined round the supporting columns."[142] Connecticut's Calvinists were learning to use the riches of the modern material world to their full spiritual advantage.

CHAPTER 5

Religious Architecture and Republican Community

Whether we respect the present life or that which is to come; whether we regard the peace, order, and happiness of community or the higher considerations of religion, whether we wish the welfare of the age we live in, or look at the interests of posterity; in whatever view we consider the subject, we must be sensible that it is all important to guard the outworks of religion, namely the Sabbath, and the public worship of God.
— Writer to *Connecticut Courant*, January 17, 1810

T he place of religion appeared especially unstable to many of Connecticut's citizens in the early republic. In colonial New England, Puritans had assumed that their religious concerns and beliefs would permeate all aspects of the public sphere, including politics and moral order. There was no this-worldly/otherworldly dualism; rather, the workings of the spirit were expected to infuse and direct the workings of society. This social order reflected invisible cosmic order; people had suitable stations, and rulers, chosen for their wisdom and moral leadership, listened to the dictates of divine order rather than heeding the whim of the people. Ministers had a right, indeed an obligation, to preserve the political and social order. Christian community was, in a broad cultural sense, identical to the sum of the people.[1] But even in the seventeenth century, this ideal rarely held up when matched with the complicated reality of human society. The rise of party politics, the assertion of individual freedoms, and the apparent decline in public morality in the early national period further challenged the former understanding of Christian society. Ministers, drawn into ugly partisan politics, were no longer speaking for the whole, and the moral arm of the church seemed unable to reach far enough into the dark corners of the community to prevent the alarming propagation of irreligion and vice.

Yet dissent and even the disestablishment of religion altogether under the 1818 State Constitution did not signal a decline in religious fervor.

The increasing variety of religious options was an outgrowth of strong religious sentiment. The aim of Connecticut's concerned Protestants was to harness that energy and diversity in ways that would assist their own social and political agendas. Congregationalists especially sought ways to maintain their social influence and the Christian moral qualities of their communities. In his recent study of New England clergy in the early republic, Jonathan Sassi convincingly argues that rather than floundering around hopelessly as their political power waned, Congregationalists in New England transformed their vision of a Christian America.[2] Realizing that the state could no longer be counted on to foster or even support their programs, the clergy saw this was now the responsibility of the church alone. Despite the growth in numbers and power of Episcopalians, Baptists, and Methodists, Congregationalists still had the advantage when it came to money and influence, and used that to establish a program for a godly society. In part they accomplished their goals by initiating or taking the reins of social projects designed to impart or protect a general sense of Christian morality and virtue. The church had to educate Christians to assume the responsibility for shaping a moral society. Christians now put up barriers against the world, sent their soldiers out to fight the devil, and brought the wounded back to the safety of the church. The church recognized that to prepare its members to resist the decidedly *un*-Christian world, it had to build up their identities as *Christians*. Educational programs and religious publications grew by leaps and bounds. Churchgoers had many opportunities to meet together during the week, including night meetings, small Bible studies, home discussion groups, and participation in a growing number of moral societies.[3]

Anxious Christians were eager to keep track of the moral state of society. In 1800 members of the infant Connecticut Academy of Arts and Sciences, most of them Congregationalists, sent a circular to all the towns in Connecticut, requesting responses to a series of questions.[4] Most of these questions were directed toward natural history, manufactures, and the practical aspects of daily life. Yet one question concerned the state of religion, and the respondents, primarily Congregational ministers, paid considerable attention to it in their reports. In article twenty-four of its circular letter, the academy asked respondents to note "Places of public worship; their number, and the denomination to which they belong—the rise of congregations and various sects, the names of successive clergymen, the time of their settlement and exit—notices of any eminent clergymen; the salaries of clergymen and the funds by which religious worship is maintained."[5] In their responses, writers numbered the members of the different religious societies, recorded ministers' salaries, detailed church funds and budgets, counted meetinghouses or steeples, and noted the number and location of graveyards. These statistics reveal a great need to *see* and *count* the impact of religion on society, underlining the importance of visual evidence of religious vitality on the landscape.

The Middlesex County statistical and narrative reports submitted by Haddam's Congregational minister David D. Field are the most complete accounts of the state of religious affairs provided by these town reports.[6] Like most of the writers, Reverend Field was a clergyman with a vested interest in the ongoing health and wealth of his church. It is no surprise, then, that religion plays a dominant role in his account of the public life of Middlesex County. Field precisely counted and briefly described religious buildings, detailed funds for the support of the ministry, listed ministers of the different denominations, and recorded the number of members of the various congregations. He was particularly thorough with his assessment of the financial situation of the many congregations in his county. Given that church finances are a relatively private and uninteresting business today, it is notable that the respondents answered that part of the query with such regularity. This was because the affairs of religious societies, corporations chartered by the legislature, were a public matter; how they fared was a matter of public concern, from both an economic and a social point of view. In the narrative reports, Field did not conceal his sadness that the people of Middlesex were no longer "of one heart, and of one way to serve God."[7] Yet religion was surviving, even thriving in the county. Field noted not just the present buildings ("generally convenient but plain structures"), but the ones they had replaced, indicating both a celebration of progress and a sensitivity to history. He recorded their dimensions, and whether they had bell towers (cupolas) or spires. Field's Middlesex account reveals the age of these buildings: only six of the eighteen Congregational structures in the county had been erected since 1790; ten were built prior to 1750. On the other hand, of the seventeen structures dissenters had built in the county (six Episcopalian, six Baptist, four Methodist, and one Strict Congregationalist), all but five had been erected since 1790. Some of these were, of course, early nondescript barnlike buildings of Methodists and Baptists. Nonetheless, this sort of survey made it plain to Congregationalists that it was time to build anew.

By 1800, a considerable variety of religious and civic buildings dotted the landscape — meetinghouses and churches, town houses, courthouses, alms houses, schoolhouses, and academy buildings. These structures shared the many functions originally united in the Puritan meetinghouses. But this was not the end for Congregational visibility, for as the meetinghouse lost its role as symbolic center of community life, a new breed of grand church buildings claimed to be something equally important to the community: the home of a Christian civility based in refined worship, a generous public spirit, good manners, and good taste. Monumental religious buildings impressed nearly all who saw them. Distinctive churches had a visual effect different from that of the old, quaint meetinghouse; immediately, they proclaimed an undeniably religious presence. Religious buildings were the flagships of Christian society, the public markers of religious life. Building committees, ministers, town boosters, and cultural critics recognized the didactic potential of churches and attempted to fashion and direct it toward their particular social and educational purposes. Religious architecture, as a symbol of virtue, proof of a community's taste and wealth, and a site for moral instruction, became a key element in programs of civic identity and civil religion.[8] Protestant Christianity was a pillar of the republic; impressive churches on the landscape proved the new nation was thriving—artistically, economically, and, most important, morally. Church buildings became the tools of social engineers who used them to shape the character of their country, their cities, and their citizens.

The Necessity of Public Worship: Morality, Taste, and Religious Architecture

Implicit in early Americans' definition of republicanism was the intimate and necessary connection between virtue and power.[9] Republican citizens were not born virtuous, and they were in desperate need of moral education. Public worship was a logical place to learn and to practice right attitudes and behavior. Not surprisingly, those preoccupied with monitoring the signs of virtue and vice used church attendance as a barometer of American morality. Concerned Christians worried unceasingly that a decline in public Sabbath observance would sabotage the moral future of the republic. Between 1810 and 1830, a Sabbatarian movement called attention to this gross neglect. Sabbatarians did have concerns about the state of souls, but their movement was not simply addressed toward adherence to Christian doctrine and religious practice. Churchgoing would teach morality, refinement, and even good taste; the behavioral lessons learned in church could lead one down a path of middle-class respectability.

During the first decades of the nineteenth century, Sabbatarians conducted a wide-ranging campaign to restrict work, travel, and recreation on Sunday. Recently, historians have seen Sabbatarianism as more than the defensive "priestcraft" of conservative clergy on their way out, or the work of conservative politicians desperately trying to reinvigorate their waning cultural hegemony.[10] The Sabbath was part of "a cherished cultural and religious heritage" that shaped the rhythms of community life.[11]

Using the tools of anthropology, Richard R. John saw the New England Sabbath as an important community ritual, a "liminal moment," that offered a chance to enter sacred time for "collective self-renewal."[12] Anti-Sabbatarians were *not*, as one might suspect, opponents of religion, but frequently evangelicals from newcomer denominations, such as Baptists, Disciples of Christ, and Methodists, who respected a Sabbath themselves but were highly suspicious of anything that reminded them of the legislative power of the previously (and, in some cases, still) established church.

The Sabbath was a widely valued institution for Christians of many denominations, and Connecticut was among the most ardent states in giving it legislative protection. Certainly the Sabbath seemed a venerable institution to Elbridge Gerry, Jr., who, irritated by his inability to travel through Connecticut on a Sunday, wrote: "Here we are in the centre of Connecticut, whose inhabitants are bigoted and strict in their tenets."[13] Mary Camp, a student at Miss Pierce's school in Litchfield, wrote in her notebook the promise that she would "attend public worship every Sabbath unless sickness or some unavoidable accident should befall me and will behave with reverence in the house of God."[14] Sabbath observance was a means of maintaining a familiar geography of space and time in which public piety was central to community experience.

In January of 1810, a writer to the *Connecticut Courant* set forth a lengthy argument in favor of Sabbath observance. "None but atheists," the writer proclaimed, "will deny the fitness of public worship, and its conduciveness to moral and religious improvement. It is actually found," the writer continued, "that civilization, social order, and pure morals are most conspicuous in those places where public worship is most steadily and seriously attended."[15] Although "infidel and atheistic principles seemed, a few years since, to be taking root and spreading everywhere," bringing "an avowed contempt of public worship," things were looking better, at least to this advocate. The arid religious climate of the Revolutionary era was changing by revival and renewal. Sabbath observance was not simply a vehicle for spreading salvation, the writer insisted, but had tangible, earthly value as well.

Whether we respect the present life or that which is to come; whether we regard the peace, order, and happiness of community or the higher considerations of religion, whether we wish the welfare of the age we live in, or look at the interests of posterity; in whatever view we consider the subject, we must be sensible that it is all important to guard the outworks of religion, namely the Sabbath, and the public worship of God.[16]

This was not primarily a plea for piety. This was an argument for maintaining a religious sensibility to ensure that the "interests of posterity" would be upheld.[17]

The most tangible of "the outworks of religion" were places of worship. In 1816 Senator David Daggett of New Haven expressed his pleasure at the recent completion of three new churches on his hometown green. "I rejoice at the interest which is excited in N-Haven by the public buildings," he wrote to his wife, Wealthy Ann. "Such displays of munificence in so good a cause show a sound state of society, and, at least an external respect for religion highly honorable to our citizens."[18] Daggett's appreciation of "at least an external respect for religion" suggests on the one hand a cautious optimism about the reality of religious fervor in New Haven. But Daggett's remarks indicate that visible religiosity was an important first step, if not an end in itself. The hoped-for correlative of such respect for worship was "a sound state of society," and an "honorable" citizenry. "The interests of prosperity," as the *Courant* journalist had argued, would naturally be furthered.

A strong advocate of both public worship and fine church buildings was the Reverend Timothy Dwight, an old-order Congregationalist who firmly believed that Christianity, public worship, morality, and prosperity were all inexorably entwined. Dwight, a prolific Sabbatarian, insisted that "religion cannot exist . . . without public worship," and religion "increases common prosperity."[19] Dwight chose the metaphor of architecture to describe this relationship: "with the loss of religion, therefore, the ultimate foundation of confidence is blown up; and the security of life, liberty, and property buried in the ruins."[20] The critical issue for Dwight was the maintenance of public morality, and he believed that the consistent, public exercise of religion was the only way to be certain that Christian mores would pervade the new nation. "Morality, as every sober man . . . discerns with a glance, is merely a branch of religion: and where there is no religion, there is no morality."[21] Conversely, where there was no moral behavior, Christian belief could not exist.

Dwight's idea of morality was much more complex than a list of rules for godly living. Morality was a sense, operating in the realm of *taste*, that included the visible as well as the invisible world. "Taste," a term commonly used by Americans in the early nineteenth century, should be understood as meaning "appropriate understanding," rather than simply "an appreciation of the finest things," as we would tend to grasp the idea today. Raymond Williams noted that by the eighteenth century taste was an active quality that referred to the general character, rather than a specific trait, of a person.[22] Today, Williams explained, "taste" has become "a matter of acquiring certain habits and rules" and "cannot now be separated from the idea of the consumer." But "taste" as understood by Americans who referred to their fine churches, for example, as exhibiting the "good taste" of the community meant the active faculty of mind that preferred the good.

This was precisely the same mechanism as described by Jonathan Edwards in his *Religious Affections*.[23] Taste was the link between desire and action; good taste led to moral behavior. Dwight recognized that some people did not come naturally to morality and that religion, to reach them, must do its best to pull them out of their moral stupor. The way to do this, Dwight argued, was to set an example of good taste. A sense of taste was an essential part of human nature, but in some it was grossly underdeveloped. If one could appeal to a latent sense of taste, encourage and shape it, then one had a good chance of raising that person up from moral infancy. "The first thing powerfully operated on, and in its turn proportionately operative, is the taste," Dwight explained. "The perception of beauty and deformity, of refinement and grossness, of decency and vulgarity, of propriety and indecorum, is the first thing which influences man to attempt an escape from a grovelling and brutish character; a character in which morality is chilled or absolutely frozen."[24] It was a developed sense of taste, Dwight believed, that enabled a person even to know right from wrong.

This sort of thinking burdened the churches with the responsibility not only for religious instruction but for instruction in taste, or, more particularly, refinement. In 1823, Reverend Gardiner Spring put this role succinctly in a sermon promoting Sabbath keeping, noting the "neatness and cleanliness which it [public worship] promotes, especially among the lower classes of men, the softness and civility of manners, which it diffuses throughout a community."[25] Dwight's choice of language seemed to show more concern for beauty, refinement, and propriety than it did for the Ten Commandments. But then such aspects of character were elemental Christian virtues in the minds of aspiring new republicans.[26]

Reverend Dwight, on realizing the connection between taste and morality, puzzled over the best means of arousing a slumbering, redeeming sense of taste. How does one elicit taste from a person of "grovelling, brutish character?" The best vehicle for such a task, he decided, is architecture. "This perception is awakened by what may be called the exterior of society," Dwight argued, "particularly by the mode of architecture."[27] In this instance Dwight was writing primarily of domestic architecture, but the message was clear and transferable: architecture has a didactic, moral function. Slovenly buildings promote slovenly manners. "The dress, the furniture, the equipage, the mode of living and the manners, will all correspond with the appearance of the building." Inject beauty into a city and everything changes. People will necessarily see the advantage of more tasteful objects and will wish to emulate the possessors of such things, not as mere consumers of objects but as owners of taste, and hence, morality.

This was not an invitation to extravagance, Dwight cautioned. "There

are virtuous cottages," and "sound morals can be found where there is
neither polish nor splendor." Yet, how much more so a truly elegant
home? It is wrong to think that fine things are "dangerous to piety,"
Dwight insisted. "But the debate is not between cottages and palaces, nor
between poverty and opulence. It lies between taste and the want of it,
between grossness and refinement."[28] Dwight promoted a style of architecture that was "neat, tidy, and convenient." When it came to public
buildings, he agreed that a certain impressive quality was desired. "I am
still willing, with Demosthenes, to have public buildings assume a style
superior to this and am not afraid of seeing them even splendid."[29]

Part of the building strategy of Congregationalists and Episcopalians
was just this: their ecclesiastical buildings should be at least as fine as the
finest architecture in town, and preferably more so. With an increase in
prosperity after the Revolution, the homes of Connecticut's wealthier set
improved in style and magnificence. Old meetinghouses often lagged behind in the parade of finery. This incongruity disturbed those who
thought that the house of God ought to be the most glorious residence
in a community, or at the very minimum keep pace with the finest local
architecture. In part this was due to a growing sense that the people of
Connecticut were a people of taste, which ought to be reflected in their
religious, as well as their social, life. As early as 1772, Elizur May, preaching in Haddam, although cautioning his hearers that nothing was more
glorious than the presence of God in a building, nonetheless insisted that
houses of worship should have a certain distinction. "I don't mean so
much as to intimate," he hedged, "that people should not be solicitous
what kind of houses they build for public worship, these ought to be
decent and elegant, and at least more magnificent than our common
dwelling houses." When such buildings were created in harmony with a
community's piety and economic ability, then even a house that was
"stately, magnificent, and ornamental" could be "truly a laudable temple."[30]

In 1815, when Episcopal Bishop Samuel Jarvis laid the cornerstone of
Trinity Church in New Haven, he took the opportunity to remind his
listeners that propriety demanded they show the same attention to their
religious buildings as they gave their private dwellings. Because people
associate ideas with things, he argued, care should be taken that the physical features of a house of God command respect in a given community.
There is nothing inherently wrong with worshiping in a "church built of
logs and covered with thatch," Jarvis preached. That is, if one is a "*savage*."
"A savage might look with veneration," he acknowledged, on such a
building. But that was altogether impossible in the New Haven of 1815.
"We live in a refined and civilized society," Jarvis told his audience, "when
all the arts and sciences seem to vie with each other in rapidity of im-

provement." "The structures of our churches must, therefore, keep pace with the extension of our wealth and the progress of our refinement." A rude church in this modern community would be an insult to God. It is our obligation to take the gifts of God, "the elegances of life and the refinement of taste," and "devote them to his service." Jarvis then congratulated the congregation on its decision to build a church of distinguished, awesome, appropriate Gothic proportions on the New Haven green.[31]

The bishop's concerns were the same as those of Joel Linsley, whose Hartford sermon of 1826 was discussed in the previous chapter. Reverend Linsley argued that, despite traditional restraints on material extravagance, it was important that houses of worship attain a certain splendor to mark them as special, to distance them from the world. Beautiful churches were gifts to God, a return on the material success he had given his people, and provided a suitable atmosphere for worship. It was important, as Reverend Joel Hawes claimed in his 1824 Hartford dedication sermon for North Church, that a church building reflect the best taste and ability of a congregation. The "grandeur and elegance" of his own building proved equal to that "demanded by the taste of the times" and comported well with "the dignity of public worship."[32] Bishop Jarvis's words reveal a further concern: churches should emphasize the progress of society. Remarking that "all the arts and sciences" were vying with each other in "rapidity of improvement," Jarvis proudly hailed "the progress" of New Haven's "refinement." Church architecture—and, by association, Christianity—should reflect and proclaim the progress of civilization and refinement.

White Steeples and the Progress of Civilization

Public character was of crucial importance to New Englanders of the nineteenth century. They were well aware that they were being scrutinized by visitors from other towns and nations, strangers who would report back on what they found, and they were anxious to make a good impression. Promoters of the new nation took great pleasure in seeing churches springing up in America's towns and villages, evidence not only of Christianity but the progress of civilization.[33] "Thus we see, and cannot but be impressed with gratitude and admiration at the sight," wrote one correspondent to the *Churchman's Monthly Magazine* in 1806, "places of public worship rapidly increasing with our increasing population and prosperity, in the very heart of our country, which, but a few years hence, was a rude and howling wilderness."[34]

The association of religion with civilization and progress was nothing new. But the physical evidence of religion had a heightened importance in the vast expanse of the new republic's landscape. Church steeples were immediate, reassuring evidence of the "right" kind of civilization moving westward. Timothy Dwight commented with pleasure and delight when he found "cheerful and brilliant" white steeples as he traveled throughout New England. (fig. 37).[35] A poem written for the *Danbury Recorder* in celebration of a new western canal in 1826 described the transformation of the landscape.[36] "Fields luxuriant" teeming with grain replaced "barren waste," and settlers vanquished "the lurking beast." Far more important, however, was the replacement of native chaos with Christian order:

> No more is seen the savage train
> Lurking like tigers for their food.
> No more is seen the desert plain
> Where once the native hovel stood.
>
> But where they stood may now be seen
> The stately house of God;
> Where christians all may worship him,
> The Father of all good.[37]

The nomadic disorder of "the savage train" and the impermanent "native hovel" were obstacles to be overcome, and this poet rejoiced as they became a thing of the past. In their stead was "the stately house of God," where Christians could worship the deity who made such progress possible. This astonishing lack of sympathy for the predicament of Native Americans is in part explicable by the new Americans' need for order, stability, and permanence, needs met by a church building's physical declaration of a community's intent to plant itself and prosper. White steeples became part of New England's regional identity. Reverend Joel Hawes of Hartford, in his 1835 "second century" speech, prayed, "may the time never come, when the sons of Connecticut, into whatever part of the world wandering, on returning home, shall not be greeted from the distant hills and smiling valleys of their native State, by the church-spire . . . pointing the soul to heaven."[38]

In New England, highly visible white churches stood out among the dense forests and announced the presence of community. Some preachers and writers saw the buildings as individual elements in a vast network, their steeples points of transmission of a religious culture that enfolded the region. White, steepled churches, as Reverend David Austin claimed in an 1815 dedication sermon in Franklin, Connecticut, formed a chain of lights across New England. "In all this christian land," he preached, "palaces of celestial record do raise their turrets towards the heavens." In

37. *N. Eastern View of South Cornwall 1 mile distant*, John Warner Barber, ink and wash, c. 1835. Courtesy, The Connecticut Historical Society, Hartford, Connecticut.

Connecticut, "in the neighborhood of our present station, how frequently, within how few miles distant, do these celestial palaces hold fellowship with one another!" Church buildings were a connection between independent congregations and individual believers in different communities. "Stretch your gospel sceptre to the east or to the west—to the north or to the south," Austin claimed, "and it is met by the greetings of the children of the kingdom on every side." With the erection of its new house, Austin's congregation was "enabled to take [its] station; and to hold the rank of visible fellowship with the places of celestial record" that surrounded it.[39]

Timothy Dwight had expressed a similar vision fifteen years earlier, even before much of the church rebuilding in his native state. Dwight's fondness for white, steepled churches or meetinghouses, old style or new, appeared in his "Prospects of the United States" when he rhapsodized about New England's future, steeple-filled horizon. A traveler will "easily anticipate the rise of temples," he predicted, "consecrated to the worship of God, diffusing, like so many stars, light and splendour over the whole horizon of his view."[40] In Dwight's well-known 1794 poem *Greenfield Hill*, a paean to the glory of America, he sets the church spire, not surprisingly, at the center of his picture of the virtuous republican hamlet. "In every

village, smil'd The heav'n-inviting church," he penned. The spires of Connecticut towns splash light into his image: "New Haven's spires, in sculp-
tur'd silver rose"; "sky-encircled, Stratford's churches beam; and Stratford's turrets greet the roving eye."[41] Dwight's prescient vision explains
part of the impetus behind the great rebuilding of Connecticut churches;
congregations were not just building for themselves, but participating in
a regional, even national, assertion of faith and progress that would be
marked by white steeples.

A coda to New England church building, reflected in the poem above,
is the march of the white, steepled church into newly opened western
territory after the Revolution (fig. 51).[42] It is clear that this readily identifiable building was an important emblem of American civilization, and
New Englanders, in particular, brought it with them when they emigrated. Frederick Marryat, a British tourist who published his *Diary in
America* in 1839, was both fascinated and puzzled by these western church
buildings. They were not, he concluded, impressive buildings, but rather
"clap-board and shingle" affairs that hardly compared to English ecclesiastical architecture. Yet Marryat noticed that Americans were tremendously proud of these buildings, particularly their great proliferation.
Marryat was convinced that the buildings went up even before the congregations existed to fill them, as a sort of advance guard of civilization
and also as a bulwark against the potential gains of rival denominations
who might get to a new settlement and build a church first.[43] The American drive to build churches that Marryat found somewhat incomprehen-
sible, even ridiculous, was based in a need to see evidence of faith — and
republican civilization — on the landscape.

Church Architecture and Community Pride

As cities and towns fashioned "prosperity" out of the "rude and howling wilderness," they competed with one another for preeminence. The
citizens of Connecticut's towns and cities engaged in an ongoing game
of architectural one-upsmanship in which church buildings were highly
valued marks of achievement and critical to urban self-esteem. Timothy
Dwight, among others, constantly referred to churches as "ornaments" to
towns. Dedication sermons, although inevitably containing warnings
about taking pride in architectural achievement, just as inevitably managed to sneak in praises to the building and the builders. "To the benefactors of this laudable work, some notice is due," Reverend Pitkin
Cowles told the Congregational Church at North Canaan in 1823. "He

who so skillfully devised the plan, and faithfully executed the structure, is held in high estimation."[44] Those the minister most often thanked were the building committee, the builder(s), and often the congregation. Such praise might come in the form of a lengthy footnote to the published sermon, as when the promoters of the new meetinghouse in Ellington in 1806 noted with pride that the building "equals, and perhaps exceeds, in point of elegance, any of the kind in Connecticut." The builder, Samuel Belcher, "has discovered an excellent taste, and superior skill in architecture: and he is justly deserving of the thanks of his employers."[45]

Because building projects often began with an investigation of recently built structures in other towns, comparison and competition were inevitable from the outset. Beyond the obvious interest of a particular congregation in its building was the interest the *town* felt in its ecclesiastical marks of achievement. At a time particularly tuned to growth and building, fine architecture was an important, distinguishing ornament of a community. The cities of Hartford, New Haven, Middletown, and Litchfield competed with each other not just for economic preeminence, but for leadership in taste and respectability. Church buildings served both as noteworthy architectural monuments and as indications of the morality and character of a town's citizens. Hence, city boosters were carefully attentive to the quality and acclaim of religious structures, sometimes with little regard to which Christian denomination a building represented. Congregationalists could be as delighted with the Episcopalians' stone, Gothic buildings as they could be disgusted by the plain and poor Baptist "barns" in their communities. It seems that occasionally this ecumenism (or simple community pride) turned into financial support across denominations. The Congregationalist Reverend Thomas Robbins, for example, contributed twenty-five dollars to the subscription for the Episcopal Washington College.[46] Such references are infrequent, but they do suggest a larger reality of tolerance and even mutual support. By 1830 a small band of Roman Catholics were building a substantial new church on Talcott Street in Hartford, which the local paper rather nonchalantly noted. "We understand that the Catholic Church in this city will be solemnly dedicated to the service of Almighty God" "and a collection will be taken up to aid in liquidating the debt of the Church."[47] This does not suggest that Protestants were openly linking arms with Catholics, but it does demonstrate that matters of buildings and finances were a common concern.

At Trinity's consecration, the *Connecticut Journal* published a short poem that praised all three of the recently erected churches on New Haven's central green: Trinity Church, Center Church, and United Church.

The writer was gratified that a stranger would know, immediately, upon seeing these churches, the upstanding religious character of New Haven's inhabitants.

> Let strangers walk around
> the city where we dwell
> Compare and view the holy ground
> And mark the buildings well.
> The orders of thy house
> The worship of thy court
> The sacred song, the solemn vows
> And make a fair report.[48]

The poet assumed that strangers would come to New Haven and would be passing judgment and then telling others what they found. The architecture was as much for the good opinion of strangers as it was for the good use of residents. The poet's use of "thy house" and "thy court" is somewhat confusing, but seems to indicate that the poem was also directed to the Almighty, perhaps as a sort of apologia for the spiritual state of the town. "Sacred" and "solemn" worship was part and parcel with the architecture, and the town green itself had been transformed into "holy ground." New Haven exuded a sort of spirituality and, perhaps more important for its image, the city could claim to be picturesque.

Published news of New Haven's church buildings indicates that simply the magnificent material accomplishment of building three expensive structures generated a great deal of notice. In November of 1815, William Leffingwell, a member of the First Society of New Haven, noted in his personal diary (which primarily concerned his spiritual life) that "North Brick Church sold for 33,850," interesting news for a man attuned to the progress of religion in his city.[49] Newspapers assumed their readership, like Leffingwell, had an interest in the financial affairs of the buildings, and frequently cited cost, debt, and amount raised by "the munificence" of citizens. After the initial pew sale for United Church in November of 1815, the *Connecticut Journal* reported proudly that the pews "went off readily at very high prices, producing $33,875," which "after paying the expense of the building, will leave a handsome surplus." The article noted that First Society's pew sale the previous year had produced "upwards of $32,000" and cheerily assumed that the new Episcopal Church, the cost "probably exceeding $30,000 will be as liberally remunerated as that of either of the others." The writer was certain that such buildings were evidence of the strongest "public spirit and honorable munificence" of New Haven's citizens.[50] New Haven was building its reputation.

Downtown New Haven was in the middle of a remarkable transfor-

38. *View of NH* [New Haven] *in 1800*, William Giles Munson, oil on canvas, c. 1830. Courtesy, New Haven Colony Historical Society, 1971.182, gift of the Botwink Foundation, Inc., in memory of Harris and Hyman Botwink, 1952.

mation at the completion of these three ecclesiastical buildings. In 1800 the green had borne the mark of a past generation (fig. 38).[51] The 1763 brick statehouse and two wooden meetinghouses, First Congregational Society's 1758 building and Fair Haven Congregational Society's 1771 building, represented the old-fashioned Georgian style popular in the eighteenth century, begged for extensive repairs, and insufficiently demonstrated the civic and cultural aspirations of New Haven's elite. A haphazard collection of straggly gravestones crowded the yard behind First Society's meetinghouse, and the cattle of local farmers grazed and dozed on the green. This city still wore the aspect of the country.[52] By 1814, the center of New Haven was in the middle of a great metamorphosis, the three church buildings gradually attaining their great size and height. In August, Sophos Staples wrote to his cousin Emily in Hartford, describing the state of things in New Haven. "Temple Street [bisecting the green, fronting the new buildings] looks forlorn & forsaken," he wrote. Building materials cluttered the ground: "the rubish about the three meetinghouses, or rather two meeting houses and one church presents no very interesting appearance." Yet all this would change soon. "The brick meeting house is almost finished and begins to present a better face. The spire is 190 feet high said to be one of the highest in the United States and the building when completed and the rubish cleared away will be one of the handsomest buildings in the city." Staples liked superlatives such as "the highest" spire, or "one of the handsomest buildings," and had a personal interest in the look of the green. "I have an office directly in front," he related smugly, "a very pleasant place when these houses are finished off."[53]

When all the building was done, trees planted, walks laid, and grave-stones moved, New Haven did have a dramatically different look (fig. 28). In the shade of mature elm trees stood Trinity's Gothic church; at the center and right were the new brick churches of the First and United Societies.[54] Up the gentle slope behind these buildings was Ithiel Town's 1831 Greek Revival statehouse, and behind that the buildings of Yale College. The green became a manicured "park," crossed with geometrically balanced pathways, providing the perfect setting for an afternoon prom-enade. "We think we can safely assert," wrote an anonymous contributor to the *Connecticut Journal*, in reference to New Haven's public buildings, "that no town in the union can present their elegance of situation, no-bleness of architecture, and beauty of perspective."[55] Not only were these buildings each impressive, but together they displayed the whole range of architectural styles, Gothic, Greek temple, and "modern" neoclassicism that heralded the stylistic eclecticism to come. New Havenites such as Roger Sherman Baldwin internalized such paeans to their fair city. Writing to his brother Ebenezer in Albany, January 9, 1816, Baldwin sounded just like the writer to the *Journal*. Regarding New Haven's ecclesiastical build-ings, it is "said by strangers," he claimed, "that no town in the union can at a single view show three of equal elegance." Again, superlatives were the goal, and New Haven, especially in its own eyes, became like "no town in the union." New Haven earned praise for its splendid prospect, particularly the green with its three churches, and New Haven's citizens won renown for their generosity, public spirit, and taste. A favorable com-parison with New Haven became the ambition of other Connecticut towns.

New Haven's chief rival was Hartford. The two cities warred for nearly a century over which would emerge as the sole state capital, investing large sums in duplicate statehouses, and sharing the responsibility as co-capitals until Hartford eventually captured the distinction in 1880. There were more subtle arenas for competition, and perhaps the most irksome to Hartford was the issue of its appearance. New Haven enjoyed wide-spread fame for its parks and buildings, but also for the character and manners of its inhabitants. Although there is no way to calculate the extent of Hartford's inferiority complex among its citizens, by the mid-1820s newspaper editors were leading a charge for improvement. It is clear from these editorial columns that many people assumed the depth of public virtue of Hartford would be read in its appearance. Chastising the citizens for the amount of unnecessary rubbish in the streets, one editor reminded his readers that "we had occasion once before to remind the good fold of this city of the neatness of New-Haven and the comparative slovenliness of our own."[56]

Garbage was just one problem. More irritating was Hartford's lack of a public square or green, particularly since this was a feature of New Haven visitors so often lauded. By 1827, however, the editor of the *Connecticut Mirror* could write with satisfaction about the changes made in Hartford's physical *and* moral environment.

The improvements which have been made in this city within a few years past, reflect the highest credit upon our city authorities, and upon the public spirited individuals who have contributed to them. We believe it may safely be asserted that more has been done toward improving the appearance of the town within ten years past, than in any thirty years previous. A change seems to have been wrought in the sentiments of our citizens on this subject, corresponding to the alteration in our streets and buildings, which is alike creditable to their good taste and honorable to their character.[57]

Changes included a center square and a new town hall, an Asylum for the Deaf and Dumb, a college, and, significantly, "three new churches, and another . . . soon to be erected, which for architectural beauty, are equal to those of any of our sister cities" (fig. 39). These new churches — First Church (1807), North Church (1824), South Church (1827), and the plans to build Christ Church (1829) — helped to put Hartford back into competition with New Haven. They added not just architectural dignity but proof of Hartford's character. The physical character of a town had a direct relationship to "the sentiments" of its inhabitants, and those were conveyed most clearly in material evidence of a healthy religious life. The "public spirited individuals" who made such progress possible were those who contributed by subscription or purchased stock to further building projects.

One of Hartford's inhabitants, James T. Pratt, wrote from home in 1823, four years before the *Mirror* saw its desired results, already delighted with the amount of building in progress. "The buildings on Pratt Street flourish very fast and will soon be completed. The one also on Caldwell's corner is fast advancing. The Retreat for Insane is sd. to be allmost completed, & the Universal [Universalist] Church is progressing. It is as large on the ground as the Brick Church in the City — also — the New Society Building is in fair condition and will unquestionable be a splendid edifice, differing very considerably from other churches in the vicinity. The plan is like one in New York which is said the admeration of admirers. . . ."[58]

39. *View of the City of Hartford,* Robert Havell, painting and engraving, 1841. Courtesy, The Connecticut Historical Society, Hartford, Connecticut, A-1723.

This reasonably accurate view illustrates, following the towers and steeples from left to
right: Second (South) Congregational Church (1827), First Congregational Church
(1807), the State House (1796), First Baptist Church (1831), the Free Church (Fourth
Congregational, 1832), Christ Church (1829, the dark tower), the Catholic Church
(1830), and North (Park) Congregational Church (the tall steeple to the right, 1824).
Nineteenth-century prospects such as this tended to exaggerate the size and height of
notable public buildings.

Pratt compared Hartford's buildings with each other ("as large on the
ground as"), and compared them with buildings in other cities ("like one
in New York"). It seems likely that observers of buildings thought about
them according to what could make them bigger than, or better than, or
as admired as, other buildings in other cities. Ultimately, what was important was the way the city's architecture reflected its citizens' character.
This connection is evident in the newspaper accounts of new buildings.
On April 16, 1827, the *Connecticut Courant* celebrated the completion of
South Church, claiming "the building itself is furnished in elegant style,
and the society deserves credit for the laudable spirit and enterprise manifested in its erection."

Just as a fine building could be a source of pride for a town, a neglected
church could bring shame. Dedication sermons claimed inadequate
church buildings could be humiliating before God; they could also be
embarrassing before some very human critics. In the late 1820s, the hill

town of Litchfield suffered a small crisis of self-esteem as a result of the completely unacceptable state of its old Congregational meetinghouse. Litchfield was no ordinary country town. Although nestled in the hills a good day's journey from Hartford, Litchfield was a growing commercial center and a popular stopping point for travelers on their way to Albany, Boston, or New York. It was also, and certainly in the eyes of its inhabitants, one of the most politically and culturally important locales in Connecticut. In 1810 Litchfield's population of 4,639 made it the fourth-largest city in the state; then began a drop in population reflecting a decline in agriculture that led to outmigration.[59] As home to Tapping Reeves's law school (which instructed, among others, Noah Webster, Samuel F. B. Morse, John C. Calhoun, and the educator Horace Mann) and Miss Sarah Pierce's progressive Female Academy, it was an important center for law and education. Reverend Lyman Beecher arrived in 1810 to take the helm of First Congregational, bringing to Litchfield the distinction of having "one of the greatest divines in Connecticut."[60]

In the 1820s, Litchfield was in its prime, buoyed by its successful schools and an economy charged by the rise in market agriculture. The village prospect consisted mostly of farms, but also contained several factories and mills and an array of fine domestic buildings. A traveler from New York State noted the streets "containing about 100 houses well built and generally painted white." "Gardens are large and highly cultivated," he wrote. "Excepting New Haven, it is the pleasantest place we have seen in Connecticut, there is every appearance of affluence and politeness." The only flaw he found was that Litchfield needed "a little more vital religion."[61] Others were less enamored with the town's polish. Litchfield tailor Elmer Booth wrote to his brother in Mamaroneck, New York, in 1831, "The people" are "the most distant and formal in every respect (here on the hill) and are proud and hastey." Litchfield, in his opinion, lost "all its charms by their particularity and jealousys and none but the rich can move in the first circle."[62] While revealing his own sense of inadequacy, Booth's complaints portray the rigid structure of Litchfield's exacting society.

At the time Reverend Beecher brought his family to Litchfield from Long Island, the congregation of the First Society was meeting in the old red meetinghouse of 1762 (fig. 40).[63] Reverend Beecher's daughter Harriet Beecher Stowe remembered this church as "an awe-inspiring thing—Its double row of windows, its doors, with great wooden quirls over them; its belfry, projecting out at the west end; its steeple & bell."[64] Mrs. Stowe described a typical example of a New England eighteenth-century meetinghouse, embellished with the "wooden quirls" decoration of a Connecticut River Valley mansion house. Back in 1807, when E. A. Kendall passed through Litchfield, he found the "church or meeting-house . . . a

40. *Congregational Church at Litchfield, Conn., Erected in 1762. Taken down in 1827,*
Mary Ann Lewis, drawing. Courtesy, Litchfield Historical Society, gift of Mr. Floyd Thoms.

handsome wooden building, placed in the centre of the little plain that is
on top of the hill. . . ."[65] But this old meetinghouse was sorely out of
place in the swanky Litchfield of the 1820s and tarnished an otherwise
pristine self-image.

A "Stranger in Litchfield" wrote to the *Litchfield County Post* in 1826,
summing up the remorseful condition of Litchfield's meetinghouse. First,
he concurred with the glowing reports of Litchfield's beauty and polished
society. "Litchfield has long been considered one of the most beautiful
Villages in New England," he reported. "It contains much wealth, and
has, for years, been, and still is the resort of many young persons of both
sexes, for education. The inhabitants are generally of a superior grade of
character for information and a polite demeanor, and many of them, of
exalted talents." But there was a glaring incongruity smack in the middle
of this rosy picture. Although "few congregations in New-England assembled for public worship, appear as well in every respect as that of the
Presbyterian Society," its church building was not nearly so pleasing to
the eye. This ill-kempt "meeting-house, standing conspicuously in the center of the village, 'like a city set on a hill, *unfortunately* cannot be hid.' "
The writer bemoaned the fact that this "old, decayed, shabby building

pains the eye of every stranger." Such an embarrassment was "a reproach to the taste, the opulence, and the good sense of a large and respectable society of worshipping christians," especially when contrasted with the "neat, ornamental and convenient" Episcopal Church, St. Michael's, built by private investors in 1812. Litchfield's numerous Congregationalists had lapsed into a very public breach of good taste, made all the more galling by the visual superiority of the rival church.

Just as ministers often did in their dedication sermons, this writer reminded residents of the necessity of showing at least as much concern for God's house as they did for their own and for their places of business. Neglecting God's house while their private dwellings flourished was not only incongruous but damning. When all other buildings, "even the jail," were tasteful and even magnificent, how much more the affront to God?

Yes, in the midst of these splendid edifices, one the theatre for the wrangling of litigious parties [the courthouse]—another the seat of money changers [the Litchfield branch of the Hartford Bank] and scores of residences of private farms, stands a House dedicated to the service and worship of the Glorious Being who directed the building of Solomon's Temple, and dictated the solemn dedication in the 9th verse of the 1st chapter of the Prophet Haggai [" 'You look for much, but behold, it comes to little; when you bring it home, I blow it away. Why?' declares the Lord of hosts, 'Because of My house which lies desolate, while each of you runs to his own house.' "66] The cupola of this house reminds one of an inverted hornet's nest—the stoves and stove pipes resemble the furnishings of the linto of an old iron-mongers shop; the chandeliers of greasy wood, look like the candle moulds of a tallow chandler's cellar. . . . Presbyterian Christians67 of Litchfield, did you never read the pathetic exclamation "The foxes have holes . . . but the son of Man hath not where to lay his head!" Your houses, your furniture, your gardens, your equipage, your dress, are elegant—your cattle and your horses are conveniently housed, but the divine place of the King of Kings is a mean, shabby, decayed and neglected old meeting-house!68

This windy scolding suggests several things. There is an attention to the broader architectural context provided by other buildings and a mockery of old styles. But the harshest criticism is directed at the the Litchfield Presbyterians for their failure to provide a suitable place for the King of Kings *despite* the evidence that their own homes, gardens and dress were so fine and even their *animals* were well housed. What impression, then, would one would thereby garner about the importance of religion in Litchfield? Attention was lavished on the buildings of commerce, law, and banking. Not only that, but all aspects of private life reflected an attention to refinement. But that refinement, without the commensurate attention to religion, was flawed. Litchfield's Presbyterians needed to put money and energy into the house of God if they were to justify the high style of their private lives.

Not surprisingly, a new building project was soon under way. The congregation had realized two years earlier that it needed to consider carefully the state of its present building. In January of 1825 the society voted to remove the decayed steeple, and the records also show that by that time the society had agreed that it was expedient to build a new church, provided that it could be done by independent money at no cost to the society as a whole. A subscription list circulated in October of 1827 and succeeded in raising the minimum commitment set by the committee, six thousand dollars. Many of the building decisions were left to the committee, but the society was in on a vote that the new church be "adjoining or near the public green," highly visible in the center of town. By November the building committee had set out to build a fifty-by-seventy-five-foot wooden building with galleries. In June of 1828 a notice in the *Post* called for "Expert and able men," particularly society members, to help with the early morning frame raising. A week later the *Post* announced the successful raising and claimed that as soon as the old meetinghouse was removed, Litchfield would have "as large and handsome a green as can be found in any town in the state."[69] Litchfield's Presbyterians had redeemed themselves (fig. 41).

Buildings for Outsiders: Free and African Churches

By the 1830s the public face of religion in Connecticut's larger settlements was not only refined but diverse. Hartford's first city directory, published in 1828, listed eight established religious congregations in the city: three Congregational, one Episcopal, one Baptist, one Methodist, one Universalist, and one "African" church whose structure was Congregational.[70] The three Congregational societies worshiped in large brick buildings extending in a line down the west side of Main Street. Gothic Christ Church, officially opened in 1829, had an equally prominent site on the west side of Main Street, between First Church and North Church. Hartford's Baptists, gathered since the late 1780s, were worshiping in 1828 in a small church on Dorr Street, but were soon to move into a new brick building on the east side of Main Street, across from Christ Church.[71] The Methodist congregation formed in 1820 worshiped in the refurbished old State House from 1821 until 1860.[72] And the Universalists, led by a former Episcopal priest, Menzies Rayner, built a brick church on State Street by 1824.[73] All these buildings were in the middle of, or at least close to, the central commercial areas of Hartford (fig. 39).

Despite these numerous and growing congregations, mathematical genius was not necessary to conclude that all of Hartford's approximately

41. Photograph of the Litchfield Congregational Church, c. 1880, prior to its being relocated to Torrington Road. Courtesy, Litchfield Historical Society.

nine thousand inhabitants were not being effectively served by these churches. With the future good of the city so closely linked in the minds of many to church attendance, it is not surprising that citizens were attentive to this problem. Hartford's Congregationalists, in particular, were aware that their churches, however spacious and numerous, did not serve (or did not welcome) certain segments of the population, and this was cause for concern. Pew rental systems served as an obstacle to those who either could not pay or chose not to pay the annual premium. Harry Croswell of New Haven noted with frustration that one of his parishioners, a Mrs. Bunnel, had conflicted priorities. She worried about her fifteen-year-old daughter's lack of religious sensibility and attributed this in part to the fact that "they were obliged to occupy a very cheap seat at Church, on account of their inability to pay for a better." Yet, as Croswell noted disdainfully, Mrs. Bunnel managed to find the money to send this daughter to dancing school![74] Some citizens clearly had no inclination to shell out money for a fine seat in church, yet without one were loath to attend public worship.

Other groups of people were not welcomed into the free market competition for seats. Students and African-Americans, for example, were allowed only designated seats in the least desirable and more marginal regions of a church: the back rows and rear galleries. Because a social hierarchy persisted in the seating of the churches, albeit one now based on the heft of one's pocketbook as much as community status, some potential worshipers opted to stay out of the ranking. Worries about this unchurched lot led Congregationalists to assist outsiders in creating their own religious spaces where they would learn both Christian doctrine and republican virtue. Architecture would not only serve churchgoers, but also draw outsiders under the umbrella of republican civil religion. Socially prominent citizens supported the construction of appropriate religious buildings in the less respectable regions of the community. Hartford's African Church, mentioned in the city directory, was one response to the problem. In African churches, free blacks could worship somewhat on their own terms, segregated from white worshipers.

African-Americans, while accepted among New England Congregationalists as part of the invisible church, were expected to be a separate part of the visible one. Certain pews were available for "blacks" according to pew rental schemes, such as that of Trinity, New Haven, whose pew plan specified that eight "wall pews for black people" in the gallery were to be kept out of the rental market.[75] Trinity New Haven, also offered specially designated meeting times for African-Americans, for example an "evening lecture to blacks" given by the rector in the New Haven schoolhouse on April 19, 1821.[76] Unfortunately, nothing is known of the content of these lectures, but presumably the sense that African-American Christians were different was reflected in the subject matter and tone of such presentations. Not surprisingly African-Americans soon sought to form independent congregations.

In Hartford, some African-Americans organized themselves into their own religious society and broke away from First Congregational Society in 1819. Hartford's African-American community was not large but it was significant. Kendall, in 1807, noted that in Hartford "Negroes and mulattoes are numerous," and "the greater part are free" (although Kendall recorded that there were sixty-seven slaves in Hartford County in 1800).[77] In 1826 the African-Americans who were practicing Congregationalists officially formed a separate religious society in Hartford. By 1833 the African-Americans had joined the African Methodist Episcopal Church; initially they were supported by Hartford's Congregational community.[78]

The fortunes of the African Church in Hartford were of enough general interest to be covered in the local press. This was no doubt due in part to an uneasiness about the activities of the free blacks in Hartford. In December of 1816 the town of Hartford had voted "to cause the Conduct of the Negroes in this town to be inspected," indicating no little suspicion about the activities of independent African-Americans.[79] A separate church was a reassuring measure of the morality and respectability of that segment of the community. As the *Connecticut Courant* explained the church in 1826, "an association was formed by many of the most respectable coloured people of this city, some years since, for the purpose of maintaining the public worship of God amongst themselves."[80] The emphasis on the respectability of the African-Americans was in keeping with the customary desire to find refinement among Hartford's citizens, but the stakes were no doubt raised when African-Americans ventured out on their own. "This association has now become so numerous," the writer to the *Courant* continued, "that it has been thought expedient by themselves, and their active friends, to organize them into a distinct and legal society; which was done last week." The new society, called "The African Religious Society of Hartford," quickly set about solidifying its independence with its own place of worship, a plan which had the support of the press.

They have purchased a lot of ground on Talcott-St, on which they intend erecting a house for public worship, and after obtaining all the aid which they can among themselves, they propose making an appeal to our citizens at large for donation sufficient to raise the sum necessary to accomplish their object. The persevering zeal which the society has manifested, from the time of their first association, to maintain the stated worship of God, is a pledge of their future stedfastness and success. Those remarks are thrown out at this time, to prepare the public mind to decide upon the merits of the case, when their subscription paper shall be presented.[81]

Hartford's citizens responded to the request for financial help. The *Courant* reported in November of 1827 that the African Society had been worshiping "in a room procured for this purpose near the river." But now, by "their exertions, aided by the liberality of our citizens," they will worship in a "Handsome brick building" fifty-six by thirty-six feet, "Furnished in a plain but neat manner, with a basement story designed to accommodate a Sunday School (fig. 42)." The building was a very simple rectangular meetinghall, but its brick construction and subtle neoclassical details, such as fanlights, were congruent with the surrounding buildings.[82] Ostentation would have been inappropriate. Still missing, due to want of funds, were "suitable seats," so the congregation made do with "temporary benches." The continued involvement of the larger Congregational community is made clear by the fact that different "clergy of this

42. Talcott Street Congregational Church, Hartford, 1833, *Geer's Hartford Directory*, 1858. Courtesy, The Connecticut Historical Society, Hartford, Connecticut.

This simple African-American church resembles many early, economical Methodist and Baptist buildings.

city" preached in rotation at the African Church, and Reverend Joel Linsley of South Church delivered the building's dedication sermon on November 15.[83]

The newsworthiness of Hartford's African Church sped its reputation elsewhere. A Litchfield paper, for example, informed local people that a "church has been erected at Hartford, for the colored people . . . by exertions on their part aided by the liberality of the citizens."[84] The uniqueness of the church alone might have been enough to generate interest, as was the benevolent paternalism exhibited by Hartford's white Congregationalists. Also noteworthy was that the African-American congregation performed in a manner worthy of republican virtue, building a "plain but neat" church by its own initiative, adding something respectable to Hartford's religious landscape. There was no doubt relief among Hartford's white Congregationalists that their African brethren were removing themselves from congregations where second-rate status was inevitable, and creating a mission church for their "own people." Supporting a respectable African church may have seemed more pleasant to Hartford's Congregationalists than sitting next to an African-American in public worship.[85]

African-Americans were not the only ones not being reached by Hartford's Congregational churches. As an attempt to take down the financial and at least some of the social barriers to worship, a group of Hartford Congregationalists from the three societies decided by 1831 to create a "free" church, in which seating would be free and open. This Free (later the "Fourth") Congregational Church in Hartford organized officially and obtained its own building in 1831. The three preexisting Congregational churches in the city were reluctant to release members to the Free Church and thereby increase the already problematic competition for members. But a determined committee pushed forward the plans for providing the new congregation with a building, a mark of establishment solidifying a congregation that already existed.

The rationale for the Free Church was fourfold. First, Hartford's population was rapidly increasing. Second, there was the threat of an increase in popery and heresy: "efforts made by the Catholics and Universalists to get into their churches strangers and others not attached to any religious society" endangered the fidelity of Hartford society to its Puritan forebears. Third, a free church would welcome the poor. The lower classes "might be gathered into the Free Church" even though they "could not be induced to go to one of the other Congregational churches." Finally, there was already a makeshift congregation of free worshipers, and they wished to continue in that manner. The building itself would be a critical element of the church's evangelistic program. Opponents of a free church claimed that the other churches were in debt and far from full, and that a new church would draw away "especially useful and active members."[86]

This last concern, the loss of "useful and active members," suggests that those interested in the extension of the work of the church further into the Hartford community were motivated in part by a sincere zeal for the cause of Christianity Puritan-style. These families voluntarily left the prestige and social network of First, South, or North Churches to evangelize their city. In 1831 a group of members, "gentlemen on their own responsibility," purchased the old Baptist meetinghouse on Dorr Street (the Baptists by this time had moved to Main Street) and "opened it for public worship, calling it the Free Church," with a view of "gathering in that part of the population who did not avail themselves of the privileges of the Gospel." They hoped that this congregation in its new building would "bring within the influence of the gospel, that class of people, who, from various causes have habitually been absent from the sanctuary on the sabbath." This would provide "to the poor, to seamen, and other transient persons the means of religious instruction, and a place of religious worship free of expense, and to advance the cause of Christ and evangelical religion in the City."[87]

One reason for desiring the new building was that the Free Church "had not been as successful as they expected in collecting the poor."[88] The trustees of the church requested that a small number of families leave the other Congregational churches to "form a nucleus about which converts and strangers might from time to time be gathered."[89] The plan was for seats to remain free, although those who could were encouraged to support the preaching. A new church-building project began after the church voted unanimously, "and after much conversation," on April 12, 1833, "that it is expedient for us to build a new House for Worship if it can be done without embarrassing the church."[90] Despite its good intentions, the church soon succumbed to renting its pews.

The Free Church and the African Church of Hartford were extensions of the civilizing power of a church building into territory that needed evangelization. These building projects proved the interest of the religious community in magnifying the visible strength of religion in Hartford and increasing the space where Christian worship—and instruction in republican civility—might take place.

Religion in Community Life

Just after noon on June 10, 1816, members of the Lyme Congregational Society, local clergy, and artisans met outside Mrs. Parson's Inn to solemnize and celebrate the building of their new house of worship. The entourage included young men and women, "elderly ladies" and men, and "singers" of both sexes. The masons and carpenters were there, carrying "the implements of their profession." Toward the end of the line members of the building committee assembled together, clergymen and deacons on either side. After forming in parade fashion, the marshal led the company in a march up the street to the northeast corner of the foundation. There the procession halted, splitting at the middle to allow the dignitaries unobstructed passage to the cornerstone. The marchers then closed a circle around them, and the singers fanned out in formation. Assisted by the master mason Ebenezer Smith, the pastor, Reverend Lathrop Rockwell, plumbed and squared the cornerstone. Reverend Rockwell solemnly led the audience in a prayer before the choir sang an introductory hymn. Reaching to the sky, the pastor held up and read a copper plate inscribed on one side with a dedication; the other side listed the members of the building committee. Pastor and master mason together placed the plate in a hollow in the cornerstone, cemented it in place with beeswax, and sealed it with an upper stone. Another short invocation, another hymn, and then it was Reverend Rockwell's chance to deliver a "short address." A concluding hymn and benediction preceded the marshal's attempt to "proceed up street and return to the inn."[91]

Although evidently of great importance to those involved, it is impossible to know how the community at large received such dramatically choreographed public ceremonies. But it is certain that hundreds of similar ceremonies spread religious culture throughout communities and emphasized the exceptional nature of religious practices and events. Although the specialization of church buildings and their uses created spaces that specifically functioned as religious, this did not imply a banishment of religion from the rest of community life. From these buildings emanated a religious sensibility that brought the sacred, even sacred artifacts, out into other public and private spaces. Early nineteenth-century churches gave a focus to the spatial aspects of Christian culture, but that culture did not simply begin and end there. Citizens might view a "copy of da Vinci's Last Supper" in the State House, read "sacred" poetry in a newspaper, or attend a popular revivalistic "night meeting" or midweek religious lecture in a private home or lecture hall.[92] Even church bells had the effect of extending religious sensibility outward from the building. As one writer to the *Connecticut Mirror* penned in 1827, "nothing sounds so sweetly as the tone of a distant bell."[93] "There is something exceedingly impressive in the breaking of church bells on the stillness of the Sabbath," wrote another enthusiast. "I doubt whether it is not more so in the heart of a populous city than anywhere else. The presence of a single, strong, *feeling* [italics mine] in the midst of a great people, has something of awfulness in it."[94] These things made religion materially manifest throughout the community. The church was the central node of religious culture. As Mircea Eliade wrote, "In the last analysis, *it is by virtue of the temple that the world is resanctified in every part*. However impure it may have become, the world is continually purified by the sanctity of sanctuaries."[95]

Urban churches held or participated in many important public events that were not specifically worship occasions: college commencements, secular concerts, Election Day festivities. Churches were frequent stopping points in urban processions. This was not simply because of the large size and convenience of the buildings, because by this time alternate sites existed. Hartford and New Haven both had other available public buildings, and increasingly small towns had a commodious schoolhouse or town house. But there was a significant symbolic purpose to bringing a parade of people into and through a religious building in the process of a primarily secular event. Fourth of July celebrations frequently included a processional into a religious building where speeches, sermons, and prayers gave a religious cast and legitimacy to the political and social

events. Even New Haven's Agricultural Fair included exercises in a Congregational meetinghouse. Rector Harry Croswell, Reverend Nathaniel
Taylor, and the Baptist preacher Aaron Hill made part of a parade that
"proceeded from the front of the court-house, round the square, to the
North meeting House," where all three of them were joined in the pulpit
by an orator, Burage Beach, of Cheshire. After speeches and prayers, presumably for the fortunes of Connecticut's farmers, clergy and people
marched up to Hillhouse Avenue to view the cows and hogs.[96]

Susan Davis, in *Parades and Power: Street Theater in Nineteenth-Century
Philadelphia*, discussed at length the social purposes of the various street
parades in Philadelphia. Davis found that these processionals created and
shaped tradition, drew hierarchies and distinctions between groups of
people, and, by their notions of "respectability," set standards for private
as well as public behavior. In Philadelphia, the working class marched in
its own alternative parades, mocking the neat, precise, and respectable
processionals of the upper classes by their own disorderliness and row-
diness. Given this separation of styles of parading based on occupation
and class, Davis was able to explain Philadelphia parades as an arena of
contest more than a show of consensus, a "legitimization of the power of
the propertied, and challenges to that legitimacy."[97]

Hartford and New Haven, despite the precocity of having themselves
declared incorporated cities, were certainly not cities on the order of Philadelphia. Philadelphia, with over eighty thousand people in 1800, had a
much denser urban population and a more complex social structure than
any Connecticut town of that period. Davis's interpretation is nevertheless
useful in regarding Connecticut's processionals as events that did confirm
the standing order and the values of the Congregationalists (together with
an increasing number of respectable Episcopalians) who ran Connecticut.[98] Connecticut's public performances underlined what was important
to a community, and one thing that stands out is a religious sensibility,
enhanced by the presence of clergy and the centrality of religious buildings.

The emotional importance of using religious space in what we might
consider secular affairs emerges from a discussion about the location of
Yale's commencement exercises in the fall of 1815. Commencement was an
event of some magnitude, marking the departure of graduates, many of
them ministers-to-be, from New Haven into the wider world. Commencement was not just for graduates and families, but an event that
engaged the town as a whole. By a 1757 vote, the First Society of New
Haven had agreed to hold commencements in its brick meetinghouse.
After the completion of the new brick church in 1816, there was some
question as to whether the society would allow this practice to continue.

A separate society meeting was called to resolve the issue on the second Monday of September. William Leffingwell, who attended the meeting, was happy to find that the society agreed to stick with tradition. "The Soc. voted that they wd. not do anything to impair that vote or to do it away," Leffingwell wrote in his journal. "My mind is much relieved for I was afraid the Society would by a vote prohibit the use of ye House to College—which I should consider a reproach to it."[99] For Leffingwell and others, holding commencement in the church of the First Society ensured the religious character of the exercises and continued the society's important relationship with the college. Tuesday of the following week, Yale began its commencement exercises at nine o'clock at the college, and then "the procession moved to the new church of the First Society, where the following exercises were exhibited before a large and brilliant society."[100]

Election Day was an optimum chance to orchestrate a stunning processional. E. A. Kendall recalled the two days of Hartford Election Day festivities he witnessed in 1807.[101] Governor John Trumbull arrived by boat on the Connecticut River. In early evening voluntary companies of guards, on horse and foot, met the governor at the riverbank and escorted him to his lodgings. Kendall recalled that the timing of his arrival, just before sunset, was as dramatic as it was picturesque. The "beauty of the river, the respectable appearance of the governor and of the troop, the dignity of the occasion, and the decorum observed, united to gratify the spectator." The next morning the foot guards "were paraded in front of the state-house" showing off their "military demeanor." "About eleven o'clock, his excellency entered the state-house, and shortly after took his place at the head of a procession, which was made to a meeting-house or church, at something less than half a mile distance." Kendall and other observers followed the trail of governor, lieutenant governor, assistants, high sheriffs, members of the lower house of assembly, foot and horse guards, and, "unless with accidental exceptions, all the clergy of the state" as they made their way on foot to the meetinghouse. The crowd of "gazers," according to Kendall, "considering the size and population of the city, may be said to have been numerous."[102]

Kendall found the meetinghouse itself less impressive than the occasion warranted, for in 1807 the First Society was in the middle of its building project and the company had to resort to an old meetinghouse, a wooden "small one . . . alike unornamental, within and without; & when filled, there was presented to the eye nothing but what had the plainest appearance." The military remained in the street, but much of the rest of the parade squeezed into the building. Kendall was surprised at the black-robed clergy, who "had no canonical costume." As in the case of New Haven's Agricultural Fair, no less than four clergymen filled the pulpit, "a number which, by its form and dimensions, it was able to accommo-date." One preacher offered a prayer, another a sermon, another a prayer, and the last the benediction. "The sermon, as will be supposed," wrote Kendall, "touched upon matters of government." Kendall reported that the service was respectable: "A decent order was the highest character that presented itself." Following the service, the parade processed back to the State House.[103]

The religious character of such political occasions was marked not only by content but also by atmosphere. To Kendall's eyes, accustomed to Anglican churches and "canonical costume," the Election Day events had a provincial aspect. But to Connecticut's citizens, who linked the events of the day with the best and most impressive people and spaces their world had to offer, Election Day made sense, and connected the world of religion with that of the political order. By bringing the processional into a religious space, the participants and the crowd were able to make not only intellectual but sensory associations with the work of God. The practice of holding worship in connection with Election Day continued until 1831, when Reverend Thomas Robbins noted with disappointment that he attended his first election in Hartford that had no associated wor-ship service.[104]

Fourth of July, commencement, and Election Day ceremonies drew observers and participants into and around church buildings to mark events and passages. The impressions made by the religious landscape — a church spire, a processional — reminded Connecticut's citizens of the dominant faith and were part and parcel, as well, of their character and citizenship. Connecticut's religious landscape was also evidence of a unique kind of architectural and spiritual taste. This explains why the terrain in other parts of the United States could so disorient New En-glanders. Philadelphia and Washington, D.C., in particular, often threw them off balance. Reverend Thomas Robbins, on a visit to Philadelphia in June of 1806, remarked that he found the city "exceedingly defective in turrets and spires."[105]

Fifteen years later the Reverend Harry Croswell traveled to Philadel-phia for the first time. He had imagined what the city should look like and was surprised by its unimpressive plainness. "Never was I more dis-appointed," Croswell sighed to his journal, "of a place which I had en-deavored to form an idea." Chief among Croswell's complaints was the uninterrupted skyline: "no spires save that of St. James Church — nothing to relieve the eye." With "neither steeple nor tower to direct me," Cro-swell wrote, he felt quite lost.[106] Croswell's hometown, New Haven, was a place with a definite center, a parklike town green acclaimed by visitors from far and wide. And in the center of that center were three monumental church buildings, their tall spires visible for miles around. Any stranger could follow those spires to the the heart of New Haven, and to the heart of New Haven's public character. Harry Croswell's experience in Connecticut had built in him a strong sense of what was proper in a cityscape, and distinctive church buildings sat squarely in the center of that vision.

CHAPTER 6

Church Interiors and
Christian Community

That the house may prove a blessing, and a bond of union to the Soc. And be the means of the future growth & peace & prosperity of the same.

—United Society Records, 1815

After a protracted time of trial, New Haven's United Society finally had a new church (figs. 43 and 44). The building project caused, as we have seen, dissension within the congregation and embarrassment in the New Haven community, resolved only by the careful diplomacy of church leaders and the salve of time. The 1816 neoclassical church, greatly admired, widely known and even copied, brought renown to the congregation. Together with other New Haven architectural masterpieces, it encouraged the worldly pride of New Havenites and furthered the sociopolitical goals of the old Congregationalist order. United Church was one more tower piercing through Connecticut's treetops, one more sign of republican character and progress. But was the building more than simply a social and political coup for Congregationalists?

The Reverend Samuel Merwin, minister to the United Church, addressed that very question in a letter he wrote to United States Senator David Daggett five months after the dedication. For Merwin, the new building was plainly an event of spiritual importance for himself and his flock. "I think some how or other," he wrote, "it takes me longer to write a sermon than it us'd to—especially since we have met in the new church." "I feel that I am in a new place," Merwin explained, "and can hardly be satisfied with old things." Religious experience had taken on a new character. Reverend Merwin perceived that the new building offered an opportunity for renewal. "I hope indeed that I feel more the worth of souls & am more faithful to my Master. It is high time for me to awake out of sleep." He found the completion of all three New Haven buildings a

43. United Congregational Church, New Haven, 1816. Photo by author.

cause for rejoicing. "As a citizen, especially as a Christian minister," he told Daggett, "I view & think of them with pleasure." But most of all, Merwin was pleased with the affect his own new building was having on the members of his particular congregation. Not only did they "feel very happy in it"; the event of building had been energizing their spiritual lives for several months. "The Church," Merwin thought, "are more [mark'd] upon the subject of religion than they have been for years. This encour-

44. Interior, United Congregational Church. Library of Congress, HABS Collection.

ages me. They are more united perhaps than they have been—they have more confidence in each other & act more promptly when called to act."[1]

Merwin's feelings about his brand-new church help formulate a final set of questions for these buildings and their artifacts: What impact did these buildings have on Christian community? How did these new churches and their fittings encourage and express the nature of a community of faith? As Christian churches searched for ways to maintain their moral influence in society, they found it useful to blur denominational lines when working together on civic problems such as temperance. Here the Congregationalist's enemy was not a wild-eyed Baptist, nor was the Baptist's foe a wooden, spiritually dead Congregationalist—both fought against vice to save the dissipated sinner. Evangelical moral crusades thus transcended some of the old divisions of doctrine and practice, and mutual tolerance among believers with slightly different interpretations of key doctrines was regarded as a necessary virtue.[2] But the new religious climate also emphasized the bond between an individual saint and his or her freely chosen "sanctuary," as churches were increasingly called.[3] Membership in a body of believers protected one from the world, and congregational gatherings reasserted inclusion in a church family.

A shift in communion practices illustrates this change. Connecticut's colonial Congregational societies in principle had encompassed the entire community, saints and sinners, and attendance at worship was the legally enforced duty of all citizens. The important division between church member and nonmember came at the time of communion, in which only the saved, or "regenerate," shared the bread and wine.[4] A communion service (called "The Lord's Supper" by Congregationalists) followed worship on four to twelve Sundays per year, at which time the nonmember worshipers left the church. Communion thus marked a sharp division between saved and unsaved, in spatial and material as well as spiritual terms. By the 1820s Congregational churches were dropping this spatial distinction. The Morris Congregational Church, for example, opted in 1827, "upon the recommendation of the Consociation, to have the Lord's Supper incorporated as part of publick worship and administered in the presence of the whole congregation."[5] Although this was not meant to undermine the necessity of grace and faith, it did reduce former structural divisions between "saved" and "unsaved" worshipers. The dividing line between insider and outsider increasingly was found not in distinctions of Christian ritual but at the doorway of the church. Simply being inside marked one's distance from the world; crossing the threshold could itself be a profession of faith and an assertion of belonging.

Turning inward to the spiritual and social dynamics of particular, self-determined congregations, we can observe how artifacts worked as primary bearers of both congregational identity and history. Buildings, their interiors, and communion articles were important representations of the life of the church family; they stood for what had gone before and for what was hoped to lie ahead. We can view the problem of community from several material vantage points. First, evidence of increasing "homelike" comfort—and the reaction to it—tells us not only what congregations grew to prefer, but how they justified "progress" and change by telling increasingly dramatic stories about the physical hardships of former Puritan worship. Second, communion vessels, their acquisition and use, illuminate the meanings of a specific ritual that was at once an individual profession of faith, an assertion of the covenant between God and the community, and a joint declaration of membership in that body. Finally, controversies over pulpit control reveal that congregations felt an association between their particular proclamations of faith and its material manifestation: churches stood for a specific group of people following specific doctrine. Congregations struggled over rules as to what doctrine could be preached inside, and at what point heresy desecrated the space. In all of these instances, religious artifacts mediated between individuals and the community, past and present.

Comfort and Convenience

The focus of previous chapters has been the crucial significance of elegance and refinement in architecture and worship. We have seen how the post-Revolutionary rise in deliberate elegance and order in church exteriors and interiors affected and reflected spiritual concerns. By the 1810s, this trend was joined by another critical change in the material culture of worship: a growing insistence on comfort. Many churches underwent major interior revisions in the 1830s or 1840s that were the culmination of discussions initiated in the 1810s. The addition of cast-iron stoves, carpet in the aisles, an increasing use of textiles, slanted seat backs, the removal of awkward box pews and high pulpits, the installation of oil lamps and chandeliers — all made churches more physically welcoming and more homelike. For the individual believer, such changes in the church interior may well have been more profound and spiritually meaningful than a new style of architecture. Architecture provided a setting, but a newly warm and comfortable environment more forcefully affected each human body present.

John Crowley, in his excellent recent study, demonstrates how "comfort," originally a spiritual and psychological construct, grew increasingly to indicate a material reality in this period as people equated a pleasant state of being with physical ease.[6] Connecticut's church builders frequently used both "convenience" and "comfort" to refer to spaces they intended to provide physical satisfaction. Bit by bit, congregations did away with the fabled discomforts of the Puritan meetinghouse by warming, lighting, and softening the interiors of their new houses of worship. Jane Nylander, writing about alterations of nineteenth-century churches, noted that developments in church interiors paralleled domestic innovations and should be seen in the context of changing technology and increased wealth.[7] Alterations could be spurred by a competitive spirit that made an issue out of which congregation had the most elaborate pulpit or the richest textiles. But the choice to incorporate what was modern and fashionable into the worship space was not a given and, if scattered and somewhat mythical accounts are to be believed, the "Demon of Progress" occasionally faced spirited resistance from the "Angel of Conservatism."

Nylander argued that the "home-like" qualities of the meetinghouses of this period corresponded to a softening of theology: "The stark physical setting of Puritan worship was replaced by a much more comfortable place in which to find sustenance for a heartwarming personal religion."[8] Although this explanation largely relies on stereotypes of "cold" Puritans and "warm" evangelicals, Nylander is correct to look for an ideological or theological explanation. There must have been a metamorphosis of belief behind such material changes. As we have seen, worshipers desired a worship space that enhanced individual feeling and spiritual experience. But worship was also a significant *group* experience, so we must look to community dynamics to understand fully the changing meaning and purpose of the worship space. Why was "comfort" for all now desirable in the sanctuary?

One answer can be found in new ideas about Christian spiritual formation. Near the point where this study ends, there emerged out of the Hartford Congregational community the highly influential teachings of North (Park) Church's Reverend Horace Bushnell. Bushnell's ideas, particularly his beliefs about Christian nurture, are germane to questions about comfort in worship. Born in 1802 near New Preston, Litchfield County, he was raised in a Congregational community, although his parents were Methodist and Episcopal in background.[9] Bushnell, an eager and earnest student in childhood and at Yale College, struggled to find his proper course in life. His religious skepticism eventually melted away in a dramatic experience of grace during an 1831 revival at Yale, where he was a tutor. Following this epiphany, he studied at Yale Divinity School. In 1833 he was called, provisionally, to Hartford's North Church, where he served faithfully for twenty-six years. Bushnell, although not from an elite family, was a social conservative who believed fundamentally in the importance of raising virtuous republican citizens. He was also much affected by changing conceptions of child rearing. His most influential and widely read work was first published in 1847 as *Views on Christian Nurture*. In *Christian Nurture*, a highly controversial book among the Congregationalist clergy, Bushnell argued that it was possible to "grow up a Christian," raising a child in a loving, instructive "Christian atmosphere" with the result that the child would gradually and naturally adopt his parents' faith without the necessity of harsh discipline or a dramatic conversion from sinful ways.

Like Timothy Dwight and others who absorbed Scottish moral philosophy and associationism, Bushnell argued that environment was crucial to character formation. He believed that the way one reacted to behaviors, events, and images in life was dependent on associations already formed in one's mind. Bringing up children in a secure, moral, beautiful environment would ensure that they would seek those good things once they left the nest and would shrink intuitively from dangers that would challenge that virtue. Indeed, a proper notion of God's love and grace would simply arise from positive experiences in a nurturing, Christian environment. Reverend Bushnell was evidently in step with the times and the needs of his Hartford congregation, for they stuck with him throughout several intense theological controversies.

Such an understanding of Christian nurture had implications for churches and the worship environment. By extension, one's church home should be a gentle, nurturing, and beautiful environment. Material and documentary evidence indicates that these ideas predate Reverend Bushnell. Remember the poem for the 1815 dedication of Center Church, New Haven: the writer referred to the church as a "Modern Ark" that would "guide our footsteps to a world above" and "bear our souls afar." This was a gentle sort of instruction. The Bushnell family's congregation in New Preston built a new, neoclassical stone church in 1824, one of the loveliest in Litchfield County, and Bushnell preached his first sermon there in 1832. While at Yale, Bushnell would have frequently been inside Center and United Churches, as well as other fine religious structures in town. His 1827 Yale graduation, in fact, took place in Center Church. The Hartford congregation that called Bushnell invited him to preach in a beautiful 1824 brick neoclassical church with lamps, a pipe organ, and carpet on the floors, pulpit, and pulpit stairs.[10] Perhaps the pews were even padded: on March 26, 1827, B. Hudson and Co. advertised in Hartford's *Connecticut Mirror* that the firm was selling "church cushions." Writing in the 1840s, Bushnell did not institute those changes in church interiors. Perhaps he was responding intuitively to the cues of the worship environments he had experienced. For decades Connecticut's Christians had been showing, by the church interiors they created, that they wanted the place they met together to be an attractive, welcoming space that fostered the right kind of moral associations. Nothing was to be gained by preaching to miserable people sitting in uncomfortable pews in cold buildings. That would send the wrong messages about God's love and grace and about Christian concern for one another. Bushnell's ideas about environment and nurture articulated what was already felt among his parishioners.

Reverend Bushnell, along with many of his time, strongly believed in the special moral character of women and their crucial role in the home. This carried over into the sanctuary. Although prominent men still ran church affairs, women had significant and growing influence in the decoration of the worship space and the procurement of its fittings. Women had always participated in the giving of church plate. Of about eight hundred named donors in E. Alfred Jones's *The Old Silver of American Churches*, a compendium of colonial and early-nineteenth-century American church silver, approximately two hundred were women, most of them, like Mrs. Hillhouse, widows of prominent gentlemen.[11] After the Revolution evidence suggests that women—not just widows of wealthy men, but younger, even unmarried women—were giving gifts of church silver. Women donors gave four beakers to the church of Northford between 1814 and 1817: one in 1814 by Mrs. Mary Noyes; one in 1816 by her daughter Mary Ann; one in 1819 by Rebekah Hoadley, wife of a state representative; and another, also in 1819, by Martha Baldwin, widow of Deacon Phineas Baldwin who left twelve dollars for a beaker, which the church procured around 1817.[12]

Rather than an unlikely increase in economic power, the involvement of women in furnishing the communion table reflected a different sense of what was appropriate. Women, joining churches in greater numbers than men following early-nineteenth-century revivals, assumed a mantle of holiness that distinguished them from men. This special character made women suitable not only for furnishing and caring for domestic environments but for the house of God as well, a place that increasingly provided women an outlet for their energy and organizational skills.[13] Reverend Pitkin Cowles reminded the hearers of his 1823 dedication sermon in North Canaan that it was "those benevolent-hearted and pious daughters of Sion [sic], who have brought of their willingness, for the trimmings of the Sanctuary." "We would say," preached Cowles, "they have done virtuously."[14] Women may have been the vanguard of the comfort-conscious. In Morris, the 1842 records reveal that the congregation was busy with "building an organ loft, in front of the gallery and also the building of a porch within the doorway, also lowering the slips and sloping the backs as proposed by the Ladies Sewing Society."[15]

Women had a special role in procuring textiles for churches. Church textiles included a tablecloth and other linens for communion, seat cushions, a pulpit cushion for the Bible, and, increasingly, drapery behind the pulpit and in the pulpit window and carpeting on stairs and in the aisles. These textiles could be highly ornate. Recall Edward Kendall's surprise at finding a "modern" "pulpit of which the furniture is of green velvet, with cords of green and gold, fancifully entwined round the supporting columns" in Hartford's First Church.[16] The First Baptist Church of New Haven gave thanks in 1824 to "those ladies who presented the society with an elegant suit of drapery for the pulpit of this meeting house."[17] At the dedication of the Ellington church in 1807, Reverend Diodate Brockway mentioned that "the Ladies contributed a hundred and thirty-three dollars, for the rich trimmings with which the desk is attired."[18] Reverend Jeremiah Hallock, at the dedication of the meetinghouse in Canton in 1815, noted that "The dressing of the pulpit has been done by the free-will offering of the ladies."[19] "The ladies" clearly were exerting an influence on the look of Connecticut's church interiors, claiming a role commensurate with their place in the church family.

Besides softening the edges of the physical experience of worship, by the 1830s, many congregations were considering major changes to their interior architecture that suggest changing relationships between minister and people. Churches lowered their pulpits and galleries and, if not done already, altered pews into slips "in modern style like other houses recently built."[20] The church in Washington in 1831 asked that the "top of the desk be cut down as far as to make it convenient for the speakers."[21] The Roxbury Congregational Church debated in 1826 whether or not they would "cut off the pulpit." Hartford's First Church considered "the propriety of altering and lowering the pulpit" in 1815 and voted in 1831 to "remove the two canopies in or near the center" of the church (the governor's seats). On March 20, 1835, the congregation agreed to lower the galleries and the pulpit, and rearrange the seats, all for the sake of "convenience."[22]

These alterations greatly changed the spatial relationships inside. The pulpit was no longer a canopied box jutting out from the wall and towering over the congregation, but a small, elevated stage (figs. 45 and 46). A British visitor to New York in 1818 described one of these pulpits of "the more modern American fashion":

It consists of a platform, about four feet above the level of the floor, of pretty considerable extent, and with a flight of steps at each end; in front is a flat cushion, raised about three feet above the platform, terminated on each side by a low open railing, reaching to the steps. Against the wall are three mahogany dining room chairs the centre one of which has arms, and a considerable space intervenes between the chairs and the cushion.[23]

The traveler's impression was that this innovation was definitely a move in the right direction. "This form of a pulpit," he wrote, "is becoming very common in modern churches, and strikes me as an improvement upon the old ones, in which the minister is so completely boxed up."[24] As with other architectural elements, builders looked around to get a sense of what these new pulpits should be. In Connecticut, one of the earliest congregations to have such a pulpit was United Church, New Haven. In Samuel Belcher's 1815 contract to build the new Lyme church, the building committee specified "to finish the pulpit & stairs in the style of the N. Brick Meeting House in New Haven."[25] A lower pulpit necessitated additional changes, specifically the lowering of the galleries. The visitor's recognition of "mahogany dining room chairs" set against the wall is a blunt recognition of the domestic, comfortable character these spaces were assuming.

This alteration was in part the result of new preaching styles that were both more personal and more physically active.[26] One of the hallmarks of

45. High pulpit, Rocky Hill meetinghouse, Amesbury, Mass., c. 1785. Library of Congress, HABS Collection.

this style of pulpit was its width and openness. Older, elevated pulpits could contain formal, structured arguments and immobile preachers who read from a written text or detailed outline. In the mid–eighteenth century, Congregationalist ministers had already begun to show the influence of revivalists who used direct, practical, conversational preaching, complete with dramatic gestures. The popularity of such preaching grew amid early-nineteenth-century revivalism. In an article titled "The Pulpit," in the February 1835 issue of the *Religious Magazine*, the author argued that it was obvious that a minister was most effective "in the midst of his audience . . . surrounded by them, his sympathies are awakened . . . excited by a glow and a fervor of feeling, which he in vain endeavors to

46. Bookplate from the Theological Institute of Connecticut, 1833. Photo by Henry E. Peach. Courtesy of William L. Warren, Old Sturbridge Village.

attain, when in the isolation of his lofty eminence in the church." Newer pulpits, platforms reached by a curved stair on either side, presented "an air of ease and elegance and freedom" as well as refinement.[27]

The pulpit changes affected Episcopalians as well. The congregation of St. Peter's, Plymouth, for example, voted in 1837 to "rebuild the Desk, Pulpit and Slips after the Modern Style."[28] This similarity between denominations is important in that it shows that the change was not solely the result of doctrinal emphasis or evangelical methods, although such factors were part of the equation, too. The change, rather, was rooted in a fundamental cultural shift in the relationship between preacher and people. The old-style, triple-decker pulpit marked the ascendancy of the preacher, socially, intellectually, and spiritually, as he became God's spokesman. The pulpit dramatically increased the minister's ability to see what was going on in the high-walled pews and forced those in the pews to look up. What made the new slip and pulpit arrangement "convenient," as it was so often described? When seated in the new style of seat, front-facing slips, the audience had no visual impediment to overcome. The minister had fewer steps to climb to reach the pulpit and more freedom once there. "Convenient" seems at face value a rather weak term to describe the new relationship between minister and congregation. But, in this context, "convenient" meant "suitable" and "comfortable." With a growing comfort in church surroundings, the message sent from minister to people and back again was that they were friends working on the same projects. Ministers could be charismatic leaders, but physical and spiritual distance was no longer a dominant or even very useful strategy for getting one's message across. The new architecture of worship dramatically emphasized this different relationship between minister and congregation, facilitating a level of engagement and emotional connection not previously required.

There is little registered criticism about the outmoding of the triple-decker pulpit. The introduction of stoves, on the other hand, had its detractors. For the most part, congregations brought cast-iron stoves into their churches in the 1810s or 1820s, often by the private initiative and financing of a few individuals. The society records betray very little resistance to this new technology, perhaps in part because the issue was most often broached in December or January. Thomas Robbins noted in January of 1818 that the new "stove in the meeting-house makes it quite comfortable," a standard response.[29] The First Church of Hartford voted in December of 1815 that the "Society procures 2 suitable stoves for warming the Meeting house & cause the same to be set up in such manner as shall best comport with the ornament & safety of the house, and the accommodation of the Assembly."[30] The First Church of Canaan in December of 1827 decided "to give liberty to individuals without expense to the society to put a stove and pipe in this meeting house."[31] Harwinton Congregational Church voted in January of 1827, "Stoves may be placed in the meeting house provided that money can be obtained by subscription."[32] The people of the church of New Hartford decided in 1820 "at their own expense to erect a Stove or Stoves within the Meeting house for the purpose of warming the same on the Sabbath," agreeing that the stoves remain "so long as said Society does not order their removal — or the individuals whose property they are do not see cause to remove them."[33]

Stoves were not attractive additions to decor; unsightly pipes often appeared as spider legs, crisscrossing the interior from the stoves to their outlets on side walls (fig. 47). Recall the snide description of the Litchfield meetinghouse interior with its "stoves and stovepipes" resembling "the furnishings of the linto of an old iron-mongers shop."[34] Until stove technology improved, danger from fire, excessive smoke, heat, and the noisy

47. "Interior of East Church, Salem," drawn by D. M. Shepard, Bufford & Co. lithograph, Boston, c. 1847. Courtesy, Peabody Essex Museum.

Stoves and pipes were an unsightly addition to the worship space.

banging of pipes presented practical problems as well. New Haven's Harry Croswell "went up to the Church [Trinity] at 1/2 past 8" on the morning of December 8, 1822, "to instruct the sexton about making fires" in the church's new stoves. Unfortunately, the sexton "had already got the church well filled with smoke, by attempting to make the fire contrary to [Croswell's] former directions." Croswell recorded that they "expelled it as well as we could, and then begun anew, and succeeded tolerably well." The next Sunday followed an extremely cold night, and there were "no fires in the stove because they would not draw." The next Wednesday, Croswell wrote, I "set myself to work in the forenoon, to have something done about the stoves—and at length succeeded in getting a sufficient number of the committee together, to warrant my proceeding to employ the carpenter and tinker." Before the day was over, Croswell "had the satisfaction of seeing them earnestly at work." By the last Sunday in December the stoves were putting off welcome heat. Croswell gave two old sermons, convinced that they would not appear stale, for "as they had both been delivered in the first instance in cold churches, they were probably little remembered."[35]

There is no doubt that the old meetinghouses were extremely cold in the dead of winter. A speaker at the Litchfield centennial celebration of 1851 remembered ministers speaking in "great coat and thick gloves or mittens" while "the howling blasts of winter" blew through the cracks "fresh streams of ventilation."[36] Stories of frozen bread, seeing one's breath during services, and gloved and heavily cloaked ministers and worshipers are common. These tales are part of the lore of Puritan worship, how dreadfully dreary and uncomfortable—if quaint—it was. Noah Porter, in his 1882 historical lecture "The New England Meeting House," offered an especially melodramatic description of icy winter days in the meetinghouse.

Of a cold winter morning the breath of the worshipers not unfrequently would seem like smoke from a hundred furnaces as it came in contact with the frosty atmosphere. The walls which had been almost congealed into ice by the fierce northwesters of the preceding week, would strike a chill of death into the frame of many of the congregation. That they should come to such a place as this, on a snowy morning, plowing through unswept walks, and plunging through fearful drifts—man, woman and child—and sit with half frozen feet under long discourses on knotty doctrines, makes us shiver as we think of it, and say from the heart, "herein is the patience of the saints.[37]

Porter did concede that foot stoves, Sabbath Day houses, and warm hospitality made the cold bearable.

Looking back with mixed feelings toward their ancestors' preferences and practices, writers such as Porter, in memoirs and fiction, appreciated the intellectual rigor of their forebears and the physical discomfort endured by them, yet were obviously delighted they had progressed to softer, more accommodating times. A humorous genre of stove story came to illustrate the interaction of tradition, new technology, and generational conflict. By the middle of the nineteenth century these tales provided, via allegory, one means by which congregations could comprehend the changes recently made to the interior of Puritan worship space and to worship itself.

The Litchfield Congregational Church installed one stove late in 1816. The records of the society state simply that on October 18, 1816, the following petition was received by the society's committee:

An Association of Young men, inhabitants of the Town of Litchfield desire the first Ecclesiastical Society, by their committee to accept of a Stove & Pipe for their Meeting house. They request the committee would consult the Society & inform the undersigned where they would wish to have it placed.
Signed
John P. Brace, Hiram Wallace, L. Goodwin.[38]

The committee accepted the proposal and presented it to the society. The society, after approval, asked the committee to designate the place for the installation. Although the records betray no sign of conflict, the memory of several of the young men involved in the purchase tells a different story.

Payne Kenyon Kilbourne, in his *Sketches of the Town of Litchfield, Connecticut*, published in 1859, made reference to the controversy surrounding the introduction of stoves and the formation of the "anti-stove party." The source of the story appears to be not a period account, but a nostalgic after-dinner lecture given by Lyman Beecher's son Henry Ward Beecher in New York in December of 1853. Beecher rambled along, remembering the Sabbaths of his youth in Litchfield. "I do not say," Beecher cautioned, "that I should relish these old ideas of church-going, and sitting for two mortal hours of a Winter's morning, without a fire in the room—for a stove in a church, in those days, was understood to be a desecration, even if such a thing as a stove was conceived of."[39] Beecher proceeded to treat his audience to his reminiscences of the stove controversy in Litchfield:

When it was first proposed to introduce stoves in the church of my native place, Litchfield, Connecticut, there was a violent opposition made to it. A man said to one good old deacon—Trowbridge, I call him: "Deacon Trowbridge, why do you object to a stove?" " 'Cause it's desecration," said the deacon. "Well," said the man, "but does not Aunt Polly (that was the Deacon's wife) bring a foot stove with her?" "Well, I never thought of that," said the Deacon, the question was settled, and it was agreed that if it was right to have a foot stove it was right to have a stove all over.[40]

Beecher's story was picked up by the *Cleveland Herald*, which added first-person commentary by a former Litchfielder then residing in Cleveland "who remember[ed] all about that stove and its advent into the meeting house on Litchfield Hill."

Deacon Trowbridge was not the only one who opposed that innovation upon the good old ways. There was a Mrs. Peck, who was violent in her opposition to a *clos* stove, because she knew it would make them all sick. One Sunday, in particular, after meeting she was bitterly denouncing the stove; it had given her such a headache she was blind from pain, it was that awful kind of sick head-ache which nothing but stove heat could bring on! She felt the hot air plain as day clear over her side. When Dr. Beecher told the old lady that there had not been a spark of fire in the stove all day, she "gave in," and never after said a word about the stove.[41]

These two stories were retold by the *Hartford Courant*, January 17, 1854, together with remarks of the editor, who happened to be "one of the 7 young men who purchased a stove, and requested permission to be allowed to put it up in the Meeting House, on trial." "After much difficulty," he remembered, "the committee consented."

It was all arranged on Saturday afternoon, and on Sunday we took our seat in the Bass [gallery], rather earlier than usual, to see the fun. It was a warm Novem-

ber Sunday, in which the sun shone cheerfully & warmly into the old south steps
& into the naked windows. The stove sat in the middle aisle, rather in front of
the Tenor Gallery. People came in and stared. Good old Deacon Trowbridge, one
of the most simple hearted and worldly men of that generation, had, as Mr.
Beecher says, been induced to give up his opposition. He shook his head however
as he felt the heat reflected from it, and gathered up the skirts of his great coat,
as he passed up the broad aisle to the Deacon's seat. Old uncle Noah Stone, a
wealthy and worthy farmer of the West End, who sat near, scowled and muttered
at the effects of the heat of the stove, but waited until noon to utter his maledic-
tion over his nut-cakes and cheese at the intermission.

There had been no fire made in it—the day was too warm—and we knew it.
We were too much upon the broad grin to be very devotional, and smiled rather
loudly at the funny things we saw.—But when the editor of the village newspaper
came in, Mr. Bunce, who was a believer in stoves in churches, and with a most
satisfactory air, warmed his hands by the stove, keeping his great coat carefully
between his knees, we could stand it no longer and dropped invisible behind the
breastwork.

But the cap-sheaf of the whole, was as the Cleveland man says, when Mrs.
Peck went out in the midst of the sermon! It was the climax of the fun of the
whole, but was the means of reconciling the whole society to the innovation, for
after this first day, we heard no more of opposition to a warm stove in the Meeting
House![42]

At the start of his talk, Henry Ward Beecher had conceded that "when
viewed at a little distance" his impressions of his early life were colored
with nostalgia. Other remarkably similar accounts of "stove controversies"
increase the probability of these stories being in large part folklore, circulated and embellished like a game of telephone. In his history of the
United Church, New Haven, Simeon Baldwin told another "fainting
lady" story. "One lady, indeed, tradition says," related Baldwin, "on the
first Sunday after the vote to introduce stoves, felt so overcome by the
new kind of warmth that she was carried out of church in a fainting
condition. In fact, however, though the stoves had been purchased, they
had not been connected with the chimney, and no fire had been kindled
in them."[43] Yet another story, greatly embellished, Samuel Goodrich re-
layed in his 1856 *Recollections of a Lifetime*. "In a certain country town
within my knowledge," Goodrich wrote,

the introduction of stoves into the meeting-house, about the year 1830, threatened
to overturn society. The metropolis, which we will call H——, had adopted stoves
in the churches, and naturally enough some people in the town of E—— set about
introducing this custom into the meeting-house of their own village. Now, the
two master-spirits of society—the Demon of Progress and the Angel of Conservatism—somehow or other had got into the place, and as soon as this reform was
suggested, they began to wrestle. . . .[44]

Again, we find the "Stove Party" and the "Anti-stove Party," and once
more a woman, here "Mrs. Deacon P.," slid to the ground in a swoon.

Once revived, she complained of "the heat of those awful stoves." Predictably, her rescuers broke the news: "it's a warm day, you know, and there's no fire in them."[45]

While it is difficult to find the precise, literal truth in these accounts, broader readings are possible. The "Anti-stove" party in these stories had two objections: stoves were a health hazard, and they were sacrilegious. This health concern was not confined to churches. Early-nineteenth-century cast-iron stoves were cranky, awkward machines that smelled of hot iron and emitted a dry heat that many found uncomfortable and feared would lead to respiratory ailments. William Woolsey noted in 1820 that a female friend "took some cold the last Sabbath at Church it being sacrament day the exercise were long and the house crowded and heated."[46] Being cold when inside was an accepted fact of life for many New Englanders, who had inefficient fireplaces but no stoves in their homes until after the 1820s. Legends abound of water turning to ice in bedroom basins, ink freezing in inkwells, fingers sticking painfully to icy door latches, and women wearing woolen mittens to do their house-work.[47] People coped with the help of foot stoves such as Aunt Polly's, and warm clothing. The complaints of Mrs. Peck and old-timer Noah Stone were likely expressions of the fear of physical discomfort more than anything.

Deacon Trowbridge's protestations about desecration may point to a true theological complaint, but his fears were quickly assuaged, and in Litchfield and other congregations there is no sign that this was any real deterrent. More than anything, the Litchfield story suggests an intergenerational conflict over the introduction of new technology and the practical and philosophical question of whether or not worship needed to be "comfortable." Young men and newspaper editors were for it; hoary-headed farmers, old ladies, and deacons were not. By the time these stories crystallized, artificial heating was standard in religious buildings, no longer a luxury but a necessity. Physical warming, by then a safe issue, operated as a suitable metaphor for changes in worship and community; a laugh at the silliness of the conservative characters in "fainting lady" legends helped assuage any lingering doubts about the suitability or advisability of "progress," material or spiritual, in the house of worship. Such tales served to keep the romantic past alive (more alive than it ever was) but also touted progress; both ends built a sense of community identity.

Objects of Ritual and Gift Giving

The Sunday worship service was the primary event in the life of a congregation, and the shared sacrament of the Lord's Supper bound the people together. The Lord's Supper was the "seal" of the covenant God had made with his chosen people; direct participation in it was a reaffirmation of one's identity as a member of the body of Christ. It is a natural place to look for the meaning of Christian community. The communion service of New England's Puritans, unlike the Anglican Eucharist and Roman Catholic Mass, by design had always had a distinctive, domestic, simple cast to it. One of the major aims of the Reformers was to make the sacrament familiar and comfortable so that no mystery of setting or ritual would impede the communicant's ability to sense the presence of Christ at the table. There was no kneeling at the altar, and the mystical qualities of communion ostensibly were held to the belief that Christ was present in a special way with the congregation as they ate bread and drank wine symbolic of his sacrifice. Early Reformed congregations literally sat around a table, as at a meal. As time went on, common practice was for deacons and elders to take communion out to the communicants in the pews.[48]

By the late eighteenth century, New England Reformed churches typically owned a set of communion objects (called a communion "service") that included large vessels such as flagons or tankards for storing and pouring the wine, an assortment of smaller drinking vessels for the distribution, and possibly some plates or patens (footed plates) for either the distribution of the bread or the collection of an offering (fig. 48).[49] A baptismal basin, representative of the only other sacrament recognized by Reformed congregations, complemented the communion service, as did an altar cloth and other textiles for storage and protection. The actual number of objects varied with the size and wealth of the congregation. In the seventeenth century, plates and drinking vessels were primarily domestic forms—chalices, tankards, two-handled cups—that had been given to the church; hence there was little uniformity to a communion service. By the eighteenth century, congregations desired a uniformity of shapes and materials, so matched sets were most common.[50] Although the largest percentage of surviving colonial communion objects with clear provenance is silver, church records show that pewter was a frequent substitute, and glass and even wooden ware found occasional use.[51]

Even in the absence of formal liturgy, the Reformed communion ritual had rules of performance. In general it seems that those seated at the front of the church, often prominent members of the congregation, received

48. Communion plate of First Congregational Church, New Haven and Trinity
Church, New Haven, E. Alfred Jones, *The Old Silver of American Churches,* pl. XCIV.
Courtesy, The National Society of The Colonial Dames of America, Washington, D.C.

First Church's plate (*top*) included this 1735 Boston baptismal basin and eight caudle
(bulbous, two-handled) cups c. 1690–1724. Three additional matching cups (not pictured) were made from old silver in 1833. Trinity (*bottom*) used these two eighteenth-
century plates, a mid-eighteenth-century New York tankard (Mary Hillhouse's gift of
1822), and two beakers.

communion first. A 1724 excerpt from the diary of Samuel Sewall suggests that not only the order of communion but the vessel offered to the individual was coded. In Boston's First Church, Sewall wrote, "Deacon Checkly Deliver'd the cup first to Madam Winthrop, and then gave me the tankard. 'twas humiliation to me and I think put me to the Blush."[52] The humiliation may have stemmed from the preeminence of the cup over the tankard, but the situation was complicated by the fact that the widow Winthrop had refused Sewall's marriage proposal four years earlier. Sewall might have been embarrassed because the deacon served him immediately after serving the widow, thus symbolically joining their spirits. Obviously, sacred and secular meanings were hopelessly and wondrously entangled in the communion service. This passage from Sewall's diary is remarkable in that it sheds any light on the ritual at all, for Congregational church records and other documents rarely mention communion or the worship service. Unlike Anglicans, who constantly discussed their liturgy, Congregationalists preferred to examine doctrine and church organization.

In general nineteenth-century communion services continued the eighteenth-century trend toward uniformity, matched sets, and more appropriate forms, and the performance of the ritual appears to have changed very little. It is possible that the use of uniform vessels indicates a leveling of distinction among communicants and a desire for equality before God. More probably it reflects an aesthetic preference for symmetry and order that manifested itself in the accoutrements of domestic spaces: matched sets of chairs, teacups, and silver spoons, for instance. Communion services, in other words, were updated. Tankards, which had earlier fallen out of domestic use, now lost their place at the communion table to the smooth-walled beakers that had been popular in Connecticut churches since the early 1700s. In 1794 the Congregational Church of New London converted "Tankards belonging to the church into cups, as more convenient for the service of the table (fig. 49)."[53] Sets of smaller, simple chalices also had some popularity. In 1804, the Congregational Church of Derby sold "one Flagon & the cups formerly used by the Chh" and bought six new chalices made by New Haven silversmith Miles Gorham.[54] Some churches sold their old plate and bought entirely new sets. In 1802–03 the First Congregational Church of Hartford tendered "one old silver tankard" worth $30.55, one "silver 2 handle cup" worth $10, "two old silver cups" worth $18.67, plus some old pewter to Hartford silversmith Jacob Sargeant as partial payment for a new set of plated ware worth over two hundred dollars.[55]

Pewter of similar forms continued to be an acceptable substitute for silver, as was Brittania (a pewterlike alloy) and even tin, and congregations

49. Three silver beakers, First Congregational Church, New London, Conn., Cleveland & Post, c. 1819. Courtesy, Winterthur Library: Decorative Arts Photographic Collection, and First Congregational Church, New London.

Inscribed "Given to the First church, New London / By Harriet Lewis / Relict of James Lewis / 1819."

with limited resources often opted for these less expensive metals. In 1822 the Congregational Church of New Preston asked its committee to purchase "2 half gallon Flaggons, 10 cups without handles, 2 Platters, 1 Bason" to be "all of Brittania or Block Tin."[56] Soon after its organization, the Hartford Free Church received a set of pewter communion ware (2 flagons, 4 cups, 2 plates, and a baptismal basin) from its patron "Brother" Normand Smith, purchased of Thomas Danforth Boardman and Sherman Boardman, well-known Hartford area pewterers who also operated a retail shop in New York.[57] In 1824 the Baptist Church of New Haven held a subscription for the purchase of communion ware from New York: "One plated Flaggon Two plated cups & Three brittania plates."[58] Four pewter chalices, one pewter footed bowl, one pewter flagon, and two large pewter plates used by the East Granby Congregational Church are now at the Connecticut Historical Society.

In the process of remaking a set of communion plate, societies were often careful to preserve the historical associations of the old. If a society sold or refashioned a formerly donated object, it usually transferred the inscription memorializing the donor from the old object to the new. One of the New London church's tankards had been inscribed with the name of the donor, Governor Gurdon Saltonstall; the new beaker, made circa

1795, bore the inscription "The Gift of the Honble. / Gurdon Saltonstall Esqr. / to the first Church of Christ / in New london / 1725."[59] When the First Church of New Haven remade its plate in 1833, the inscription on four new caudle cups explained the metamorphosis: "Presented to the First Church in / New Haven by FRANCES BROWN / Rev. Mr. Noyes being Pastor. AND BY / Mrs. Sarah Diodate in 1762. made anew in / 1833."[60]

These inscriptions, prominent and common, raise questions about patronage and the meaning of these gifts of precious metal objects. The practice of leaving a legacy for the purchase of communion plate or donating an actual object, especially silver, had a long history in English and American churches. Anglican churches received silver from Queen Anne, King George, the Society for the Propagation of the Gospel, or local church leaders. Puritan congregations received gifts from their own local elite, such as Governor Saltonstall. Engraving of some sort—initials or full name of donor, coat of arms, age at death, or longer narrative description—appears on nearly all colonial-period gifted silver.[61] This was clearly the wish and expectation of the patron, and evidence suggests if anything that the church readily acquiesced. Churches frequently put monetary bequests toward an engraved communion vessel. Josiah Rogers left three pounds to the church of Northford "to be improved at the discretion of said Church" in 1783; the church applied the money to the purchase of a silver beaker made by Ebenezer Chittendon of New Haven and had it inscribed "A Gift / to the Church of Northford / by / Josiah Rogers their first Deacon."[62] Instructions for handling a monetary bequest could be much more explicit. In her 1771 will, widow Ruth Naughty left four pounds to the Guilford Congregational Church for a "Silver Cup for the use of the Lord's Table which shall have my name Engraven on the same."[63]

These giving practices continued well into the nineteenth century. An 1827 note in the records of the Second Church of Hartford mentions a bequest in William Stanley's will instructing the church "to purchase a Silver tankard of the Same Weight and dimensions as near as conveniently may be of that one formerly given said church by Mr. John Ellery, deceased" and to present it "to the Officers of Said Church to be kept forever."[64] Stanley asked his trustees "to cause my name, Coat of Arms, the time of my death, and my age thereon to be engraved." Mary Hillhouse, widow of prominent citizen (and Congregationalist) James Hillhouse, in her 1821 will bequeathed a silver tankard to Trinity Church (Episcopal), New Haven, of which she had become a member. In 1822 the rector "called on Mr. Smith, and on Mr. Doolittle [engravers] to give directions for engraving & acknowledgment on a silver tankard presented to the church by Mrs. Hillhouse."[65] The inscription on this circa 1730–40 tankard made by Cornelius Kiersted reads: "This cup / was bequeathed / with a Legacy of £200 / to Trinity Church New Haven / by Mrs. Mary Hillhouse / who died June 22, 1822 / aged 87 years" (fig. 48, tankard).[66]

These inscriptions appear to mark the invasion of worldly distinction and family pride into the practice of the sacrament. No doubt these benevolent gifts of church silver can partially be explained as what Robert St. George calls "calculated acts of largesse."[67] Silver was not a common commodity among the middling farmers and artisans of Connecticut, for whom communion plate provided an uncommon contact with a precious metal. With noblesse oblige wealthy citizens, usually but not always members of the congregation, could remind church members of the social hierarchy. Those who had economic and social power could display it with a highly visible gift and, by means of the engraving, continue to remind generations of communicants of their benevolence. Kevin Sweeney has argued that for the "River Gods" of southwestern New England, gifts of church silver served as one way of stretching tenuous family power into perpetuity.[68] This certainly seems to be an obvious reason behind the gifts to these Connecticut churches—they gave a family's name prominent status at an important community event. Inscriptions might even go so far as to express family genealogy; two circa 1797 two-handled cups given to the First Church in Killingworth display the message "MRS CATHERINE ATWATER LATE / WIFE OF / MR JEREMIAH ATWATER / OF NEW HAVEN / & DAUGHTER OF / DOCT. BENJ: GALE."[69]

These gifts, however, should not be dismissed simply as displays of elite power. The act of Christian communion, which demonstrated spiritual equality before God, on some level transcended distinctions and boundaries; artifacts used in the ritual cemented fellowship. A gift could be a token of genuine affection from a longtime parishioner, deacon, or a former minister. By leaving a bequest at the time of death, the giver made sure he or she would not be forgotten. Such remembrance was also the desire of congregations, for they often freely chose to apply undesignated monetary bequests to engraved communion articles. Communion vessels and their inscriptions were valued signs of congregational strength and reminded communicants that their assembly had a history. United Church of New Haven, for example, still has two caudle cups marked "White Haven Church."

The Lord's Supper forged a spiritual connection not only with others present in the church, but also with past saints, and with the whole "invisible" church, past, present, and future. As the communion service symbolized the body of Christ, so did the vessels. When the New Preston Congregational Church purchased a new set of plate in 1822, it subsequently voted that its "old church Furniture be committed to the care of Messrs. Sachets of [Warren], to present to the Church of C in [Boardman] Ohio, & in case sd. church is supplied with furniture to present it to some chrch. in that region destitute of furniture."[70] This congregation saw the gift of its old plate to a needy frontier church as a form of missionary activity, a symbolic extension of the hand of fellowship.

Although the practice of giving silver continued, nineteenth-century Connecticut churches were buying collectively a much greater percentage of their plate, either with funds out of the church treasury or with money raised by subscription. Bethlehem Congregational Church voted on May 16, 1795, "to procure two Flaggons & three small vessels & linnen for the use of the Lord's table."[71] The New Preston church in November of 1822 voted as a society to draw on the church treasury for some "new furniture" and appointed a committee "to superintend Purchase."[72] In 1830 the vestry of St. Andrew's Church in Northford voted "That the money that is in the Treasury be laid out for Communion Cups."[73] The Second Church in Hartford bought a flagon, a baptismal font, and four cups out of the proceeds of the sale of an old chapel two months before the dedication of their new church in 1827. Twelve years later three silver plates and six silver cups were purchased for $191.31, "of which $101 had been raised by subscription at the meeting October 6th 1839 and the balance by the avails of the old silver plate belonging to the church."[74] This new silver was engraved, simply, "Second Church of Christ Hartford Con. January 1840." We can assume congregations paid for many of the vessels that are either unmarked or engraved with the name of the church in similar fashion.

Urban churches often patronized local craftsmen. New Haven silversmiths Miles Gorham, Abel Buel,[75] and Ebenezer Chittendon all supplied silver to New Haven area churches. Rural congregations usually took their business to larger cities. Thomas Robbins, minister of the East Windsor church, traveled south to Bridgeport several times between 1817 and 1819 to purchase two communion cups of Barzillai Benjamin.[76] Two decades later, while serving the Mattapoisett (Rochester), Massachusetts, church, Reverend Robbins described the practical details of another such purchase: "Rode with Cpt. Freeman to Bedford, & procured our silver cups for the church. Nine, seven given by individuals. They cost $10.35 each. They are cheap and very good; made for $4.00 each [labor cost]."[77] Plated ware, such as that bought by the New Haven Baptists in 1824, might come from New York, but was also available from local silversmiths such as Jacob Sargeant of Hartford.

Because of a desire for uniformity, the choice of form and style was often a question of matching the vessel forms a congregation already owned. Hence, the Northford church continued to purchase beakers; the United Church in New Haven bought two circa 1817–26 caudle cups of Merriman & Bradley in New Haven to match cups made by Ebenezer Chittenden twenty years earlier. Sometime between 1817 and 1826, the North Haven congregation asked Merriman & Bradley to match its four two-handled, footed cups, purchased of another local silversmith, Abel Buel, around 1797.[78] Beakers—simple, slightly conical cups with an inset bottom and frequently decorative banding around the lower edge—increasingly outnumbered other types of vessels for the distribution of wine. They were among the simplest, least expensive forms manufactured, especially after the advent of rolling techniques.[79] Silversmiths regularly produced beakers for regional consumption; Connecticut churches acquired at least thirteen by Chittenden and another thirteen by Silas and Marcus Merriman alone. Rural congregations might not have had silver flagons, but they often had a set of silver beakers that would have passed through the hands of all the communicants.

The elusive dimension of taste in the purchase of communion articles is illuminated by the rare account of one particular shopping trip. United States Senator Benjamin Tallmadge, traveling to Washington, D.C., in 1806, took advantage of a layover in New York City to search shops for a new baptismal bowl for the Litchfield Congregational Church. In a letter to Julius Deming (once and future moderator of the Litchfield Ecclesiastical Society) he described his adventure:

When I was at N. York I was not unmindful of the Christening Bowl Wanted by our Church. I examined the principle [sic] stores where plaited ware is obtained and found that bowls of an inferior size to what I could have wished might be purchased for about 13 Dollars. As I did not like the Article I next examined the Silver Smiths Shops, Where I found several that suited me very well. These were solid silver & were from $27 to [——] apiece. The [funds in] my hand Amounting to only $16.12, I did not purchase one [but when I] reached this place [Washington] I mentioned the fact to Mr. Tracy who joined me in the opinion—that we had better try to purchase one of solid silver, in preference to a plaited one. Accordingly I have written to Oliver Wolcott esq. to inform him that if he would purchase one and contribute a certain Sum himself, Mr. Tracy & I would make up the residue, to which he has just replied and informed me that he would make inquiry for the article and contribute his full proportion . . . be Good Enough to Notify the Rev. Mr. Huntington of the same.[80]

Tallmadge and his friends were responding to a specific need. The bowl was "Wanted" by the Church, and they were looking outside of Litchfield. His chief consideration was not the style or size of the bowl, but the quality of the material. Apparently there had been some discussion in which it was decided that a silver-plated bowl would be the best option. But Tallmadge reacted coolly to the plated ware, strongly preferred solid silver, and proceeded to change the plan under his own initiative. He assumed that a small group of Litchfield's elite gentlemen—merchant Ebenezer Tracy, former Chief Justice Oliver Wolcott, himself, and possibly Julius Deming—would pay for it. In turn, these men seem to have assumed it was their responsibility to do so. Although the basin was for the church, its purchase was the project of a few and its appearance was determined by their taste.

Two decades later, in 1825, Tallmadge and Deming purchased an entire communion service for the Litchfield church. One Litchfield historian has suggested that minister "Lyman Beecher was irked by the air of patronage with which Colonel Tallmadge and Julius Deming presented a communion service to the church."[81] Unfortunately, the source of this tantalizing interpretation has not been found. Ministers often were instrumental in the acquisition of communion plate. Thomas Robbins went to Bridgeport to negotiate with Barzillai Benjamin; Harry Croswell took care of getting Mrs. Hillhouse's tankard engraved. Thus it would not be surprising if Beecher, himself a powerful man who enjoyed the limelight, felt that his own prerogative had been ignored.

Litchfield gentlemen did have the reputation for snobbish and condescending behavior. The details of the baptismal bowl transaction and Beecher's possible aggravation suggest that, not unlike the building of the churches themselves, the acquisition of church silver was directed more or less by the minister and a well-heeled few. These men were proficient in the ways of the marketplace and acted as brokers for the material interests of the congregation. Although the market culture changed the basis of relationships within the congregation somewhat, making them more voluntary, as with pew rental, the same people remained in control. Today, the Litchfield Historical Society displays one of the Congregational Church's communion beakers; ironically according to the label, its most significant feature is not who purchased it but the fact that it was used by the celebrated Reverend Lyman Beecher.

Doctrine, Identity, and Worship Space

Communities instinctively made mental associations between buildings, ministers, and the doctrine of the faithful. The practice of calling a church after a pastor, for example, "Mr. Merwin's house," or "Mr. Taylor's house" reflected the belief that the pastor presided over it. The heart of the building, the seat of the minister's control, was the pulpit. This is most graphically illustrated in an excerpt from Thomas Robbins's *Diary*. At the dedication of the new church in Norfolk in 1813, the church his father Ammi served for fifty-two years, Robbins noted, "Father's portrait was hung in the pulpit."[82] An often perplexing problem for a Christian community was the decision whether or not to open its pulpit to ministers of different persuasions. We have seen that churches were shedding their role as multipurpose meeting spaces as they became special, even "sacred." But they were still among the largest spaces in town, and had a convenient pulpit that every itinerant minister or lecturer of one brand or another seemed determined to occupy. There continued to be small rural congregations who actually shared buildings because one congregation alone could not bear the expense, and in such cases pulpit control by one congregation was not feasible. This was not, however, the preferred relationship between congregation and worship space. The growing concern churches displayed over the propriety of opening their doors to heresy shows that congregations increasingly saw buildings as the protected home of their own spiritual interests, rather than an open forum for city- or villagewide debate.

Some ministers made their pulpits available as long as they would have the opportunity, immediately following any presentation, to refute false doctrine. In a religious environment where new creeds constantly bubbled to the surface, this was a means of monitoring and controlling contrary opinion. Most congregations were willing to open their churches to other "Christian" preachers. The members of the Winchester Congregational Society, in 1795, agreed that "other denominations of Christians differing in sentiment from this society may have liberty to meet for religious worship in our meeting house on any day when the Society or Church does not want to use sd. meetinghouse."[83] But these are signs of interdenominational Christian cooperation—toleration *without* acceptance of opposing points of view. Many ministers leaned toward the sentiments of Reverend Bezaleel Pinneo, who, preaching at the dedication of the New Milford Congregational Church in 1811, insisted forcefully, "you would consider it a judgment of heaven, if any thing, but the true gospel of Christ should ever be heard within these walls."[84]

Even limited cooperation could be awkward for a congregation. In July of 1822, when the "famous Methodist preacher" Lorenzo Dow was to preach in St. Michael's Episcopal Church, Litchfield (or "Mr. Jones' meetinghouse"), one young girl expressed "a violent curiosity to see him" yet feared "it would not be proper" for her to go.[85] Dow's presence at St. Michael's is surprising, because, even though Methodism originated in the Anglican tradition, official Episcopal policy did not permit churches to share pulpits with any but other Episcopal ministers. Episcopalians took careful and even self-satisfied notice of the chaos open pulpits caused their neighbors. "We have seen something of the confusion wrought in other communions," wrote one correspondent for the *Episcopal Watch-man*, "by throwing open the doors of their houses of worship yielding up their pulpits, to every bold innovator in religion, and to the advocates of the most various and contrary doctrines." Once the deed was done, there was no drawing the line. "If a house of worship be opened to one preacher of a different denomination, it must be opened to all who apply, however heterodox they may be thought, or the denial becomes invidious, and may be taken as an affront." Congregational churches were particularly confused by their open-door policy, the writer remarked, and "it is a question for their consideration how far this license has contributed to the breaking up of their Societies, and the multiplication of religious sects."[86]

Congregational ministers were in a difficult spot, desirous of maintaining control of religious debate in their cities and towns, uncomfortable with the idea of rampant heresy, yet also wary of the label of intolerance. Congregationalists were trying to have it both ways: keeping their church as the community's primary intellectual marketplace, a comfortable, convenient lecture hall, while at the same time striving to establish their churches as "sacred" houses of worship for a specific church family bound by orthodoxy. No one solution to the problem appeared, although the growing number of lecture halls and Sunday school rooms owned and operated by churches provided more neutral, if smaller, spaces for debate.

The South Congregational Church in Hartford nearly split apart over a battle for control of its pulpit in 1821–22. A portion of the society that preferred the Universalist sentiments of the Reverend Richard Carrique challenged the pulpit hegemony of the Reverend Abel Flint. In 1821 Carrique gathered a congregation in the State House, and he and his followers began a campaign to take over the South Church pulpit. A letter to Reverend Dr. Flint from members Elisha Shepard and Sylvanus Wells, dated May 27, 1822, explained the circumstances. Because "a large proportion of the members of said society believing in the universality of the atonement and of the final restitution of all men, have expressed their desire that a clergyman agreeing with them in sentiment should be permitted to preach in the meeting house of the Society," they requested use of the church one-half of the Sabbaths. Those leaning toward Universalism felt that it was by virtue of their *society* membership, and particularly their ongoing financial support, that they had equal right to use the sanctuary for their own purposes. Because "they are members of the same society, and subject to the like burthen with their other Christian brethren, so also they are entitled to equal privileges, and of course have an equal claim with those who differ from them in sentiment."[87] Reverend

Flint did not agree. In a letter addressed to the society, dated May 29, 1822, he staked his claim to authority. First, as minister, his was the prerogative: "It is considered as the right, the privilege, and the duty of a minister, regularly ordained and installed, in a Church and Society, to have the control of the pulpit, belonging to the parish, on the Sabbath, and at such other times as he may have occasion to occupy it." Although free to offer the pulpit to visitors, Flint believed he was "bound by certain restrictions, a principal one of which is that he do not encourage that which he thinks fundamental errors to be taught to the people of which he has the charge." If preachers "who inculcate a system of religion materially different from that on which the church and society were founded" were allowed to speak at will, Reverend Flint would be failing his at his job of doctrinal gatekeeper. Allowing the Universalists to take over the church every other Sunday would effectively "drive several hundred people from the house where they have been accustomed to meet to worship." Reverend Flint was quick to insist that he was not intolerant, and had "no right to dictate to others what religious sentiments they may embrace." "All we ask," Flint maintained, "is to be left to the unmolested enjoyment of our own opinions, and to the occupancy of a house, for worship, which was built by our fathers, for persons of our general system of sentiments."[88]

Reverend Flint's strategy was to recall the original intent of the church *builders* (not the congregation's original founders) and claim that he and his followers were heirs to the building by virtue of orthodox (that is, traditional) theology. This line of argument was not always successful; today plenty of Unitarian-Universalist (formerly Congregational) New England churches testify to its failure. But Flint's remarks reveal significant new perceptions of how a religious community and its building might claim to be connected. Ownership in this instance was not based on society membership, or money contributed, or even a long history of association, although such claims clearly presented a threat. Entitlement, Flint insisted, came from a shared theology that matched that of the minister (himself, in this case) and the builders. It was a question of shared goals, history, and "sentiment." Following such a line of argument, the building belonged not to dues-paying society members, but to a community of like-minded individuals who, although ostensibly tolerant of other beliefs, chose to associate together and protect their pulpit from outsiders.

Some ministers were much less squeamish about allowing even heretics to preach in their pulpits. The deciding factor seems to be the threat posed to the minister's own congregation's stability and integrity. Ministers realized that itinerant preachers drew an audience and may well have used those occasions as an opportunity to assert the correct theology of the congregation in a public forum. It was certainly in the interest of Congregational ministers to keep the voice of orthodoxy in the public debate, and for that purpose a convenient pulpit was a handy tool.

The mixture of interest and fear generated by open pulpits, as predicted by the writer to the *Episcopal Watchman* cited above, appeared in New Haven in 1821. Nathaniel Taylor, minister of Center Church, was pressed into a corner when it became clear that an itinerant Universalist was going to preach in the city to a ready audience, either in a church, if granted him, or otherwise in the statehouse. Reverend Taylor made Center Church available "on condition that [he] be permitted to follow the preacher with an immediate refutation of his doctrine."[89] Taylor may have temporarily allowed the itinerant to use his pulpit, but he in no way relinquished control. Wanting to appear confident and tolerant, he allowed heresy in his church only for the opportunity to be able to expose it for the lie it was. There was, in this climate of religious diversity and innovations, simply no way for a preacher to prevent his parishioners from hearing a wide variety of religious opinions. This made regular Sunday worship all the more important, when the minister and the setting would together reassure worshipers of the truths of their particular creed.

The artifacts associated with religion—church buildings, pulpits, communion silver, even wood stoves—worked to put boundaries around each Christian community and ordered the lives of the faithful. One must not lose sight of the fact that for most Christians, interaction with these artifacts happened in the context of worship, filling material things with spiritual meaning. Buildings *did* stand for spiritual victory. Pulpits *did* stand for true doctrine. Beautiful, brand-new buildings could energize spiritual life, providing the opportunity for a renewed commitment to both creed and community. As Reverend Samuel Merwin eloquently stated, his New Haven flock "felt very happy" in their new building; it contributed both to the churchgoers' sense of spiritual urgency and to their sense of community. When St. John's Episcopal Society in Salisbury completed its new brick church in 1825, finally a match for the town's Congregational church of 1800, the effect was an electric charge through the spirit of the congregation. The consecration "dispensed a joy among the friends of our church, which it would be impossible for me to describe," related one member. "A new courage seemed to be inspired, and new hopes created, that the precious services of our Church might be long continued and preserved in that part of our Saviour's vineyard."[90] At the consecration of St. Andrew's, Marble Dale (Washington–New Preston), the congregation expressed a common wish that "what they have thus [given] the Lord will be repaid in blessings on themselves and their posterity."[91] A spokesman for United Church, New Haven, said nearly the same thing when he hoped that the new church might "prove a blessing, and a bond of union to the Society, and be the means of the future growth and peace and prosperity of the same."[92]

Houses of worship were intended to be agents of "social happiness," as Reverend Brockway expressed it in 1806.[93] Buildings represented and nurtured Christian community, and the building project itself could serve as a metaphor for the community that would grow inside. Scarcely a building project went by without someone commenting on the "unity and harmony" of the proceedings, or, occasionally, the lack thereof. "Behold how good and how pleasant it is for brethren to dwell together in unity," Joel Hawes told the Hartford Congregationalists assembled in the new North Church, directly quoting Psalm 133. "Strengthen, encourage, and quicken each other in the path of obedience and heaven," and "let this sacred and delightful example of Christian unity ever prevail among you."[94] We have seen that a new building was a material investment and carried a wide array of secular meanings and purposes. But far more intimate and perhaps more meaningful to the congregation was how it felt to worship in a slightly unfamiliar place, hoped for in its prayers and paid for by its labor. Pastor Aaron Hill, of New Haven's Baptist Church, was much relieved when his church was finally ready in 1824. "A great portion of the past year, like several which preceded it," he wrote, "was occupied by the church in painful anxiety concerning the final completion of their Meeting House."[95] No wonder the dedication service on July 27, and baptism and the Lord's Supper the following Sunday, were celebrated "with particular solemnity." The physical reality of the church was in one sense an end—the reward of persistence, generosity, and hard work—but it also was a fitting place to think anew about the meaning of spiritual community and, with suitable seriousness of sentiment, to make a fresh start.

Epilogue

By the 1840s Connecticut's elegant neoclassical churches were already becoming old-fashioned, eclipsed by a multiplicity of style choices. Even Congregationalists began building in an eclectic array of styles, including the formerly tainted Gothic.[1] Church architecture underwent further dramatic changes with the invention of the auditorium plan in the later nineteenth century, an architecture especially suited for large urban congregations who used their buildings to perform a growing number of spiritual and social functions.[2] Connecticut's churches dating from the mid–nineteenth century on show great variety in style and plan; there was no longer a clear regional style of ecclesiastical architecture. In the light of later buildings, the churches of the early republic came to look simple and restrained; neoclassical, rectangular buildings were no longer "modern." Many were adapted to new tastes by the introduction of stained glass and a richer use of colored textiles and paint.

A surprising number of Connecticut's federal-period churches have survived, however, largely because of fortuitous timing and location. J. Frederick Kelly described seventy-five 1785–1830 buildings when he wrote in the 1940s, and virtually all of these buildings are still standing. Most are Congregational, but nearly one-quarter are Episcopalian. These neoclassical or Gothic churches are primarily in rural villages where urban development did not threaten old town centers, buildings still were able to meet the needs of their congregations, or congregations simply could not afford to rebuild. In many of the nineteenth century's rapidly industrializing cities such as Waterbury or Bridgeport, no church buildings from this early period survive. Enduring urban buildings of this era, such as the brick churches of Hartford and New Haven, remained standing because of powerful congregations, substantial brick or masonry construction, and the gathering forces of nostalgia.

As industry and immigration changed the face of America, buildings such as these came to represent revered old New England village life and were therefore worthy of preservation. They became one of the most enduring icons of "authentic" America, a course initiated by boosters such as Reverends Thomas Robbins and Timothy Dwight at the time the churches first appeared. With their New England pride and moral mission, these enthusiasts gave neoclassical churches central place in the image they created of a second City on a Hill, rendering them right from the beginning romantic emblems of community morality, history, and taste. In this campaign they were enormously successful, especially since the New England of the early nineteenth century, its religious life in particular, was anything but tranquil. Revivalism, evangelicalism, and religious pluralism created an environment that was quite chaotic; religion was hotly contested terrain. Even in Connecticut, new ways of being religious powerfully challenged the old. Yet innovation and confusion are hardly what Americans think of when they look at an image of a "serene" white church in a bucolic setting.

One element in the making of this icon has been regional pride. Initially, this entailed belief among New Englanders that their region, on its best behavior, was the perfect model for America. We have seen how Thomas Robbins and Harry Croswell turned a critical eye to the religious landscape, or apparent lack thereof, in Philadelphia. Senator David Daggett saw the world through similar New England–colored glasses, measuring the character of a place by the visibility of religious life. Writing from Washington, D.C., to Susan Dwight in 1815, Daggett expressed pleasure at the religious improvements in New Haven, stating "If only a small portion of that excellent spirit which has done so much for honour of religion in N. H. [New Haven] could activate the people of Washington, this wilderness would become like a garden. . . ."[3] Daggett had sampled Washington's unsatisfactory religious offerings, including an Episcopal service and a Catholic mass.

New Englanders earnestly believed that religion was more beneficially present and influential in their region than in other parts of America. It was at the core of regional identity: "New England is my nation, Christ is my salvation," went a popular motto. Omnipresent church buildings substantiated that belief. Susan Smith's circa 1794 needlework picture of the First Baptist Church in Providence, Rhode Island, with its caption "Let Virtue be A Guide to thee," demonstrates this identity as internalized by a young girl (fig. 50). Church buildings embodied the virtue of an

50. Needlework picture, "Let Virtue be A Guide to thee," Susan Smith, Providence, R.I., c. 1794, linen/silk. Courtesy, Winterthur Museum, 1958.2879.

American middle class that celebrated both its untainted history and its controlled refinement. In 1835 the landscape painter Thomas Cole, in his *Essays on American Scenery*, put this concisely. He found both visual and moral beauty in these buildings that he already looked upon with some nostalgia: "from yonder dark mass of foliage the village spire beams like a star. You see no ruined tower to tell of outrage—no gorgeous temples to speak of ostentation; but freedom's offspring—peace, security, and happiness, dwell there. . . ."[4] Cole's nostalgia and pride are all the more striking because he was born in England in 1801 and did not come to America and see the American Northeast until 1819.

Especially in times of assault and moral confusion, many Americans (particularly Protestant, middle-class, white ones) have turned to this icon to shore up cherished beliefs about American history, values, and spirit. Following the physical and emotional upheaval of the Civil War, New Englanders actively promoted the image of the old-time village, with a "tree-shaded green surrounded by a tall, steepled church and white clap-boarded shops and dwellings."⁵ The church was at the center of this highly celebrated landscape, both literally and metaphorically. Local historian Josiah Temple wrote in 1887 about the symbolic force of this location: "When [a town's] roads radiate from a common centre to the circumference, and that center is the meeting-house, you will commonly find an intelligent, moral, and religious, as well as thriving community. The people have faith in God and faith in each other; are social and helpful; are mindful of individual prosperity, and the prosperity and position of the town."⁶ Temple's statement was not just about religion, but also about religion's place as the central cog in the well-oiled machine of "ideal" community. Out of the meetinghouse, out of a collective Christian faith, would come both good citizenship and well-being.

In the twentieth century the image has had equal power, particularly in the hands of proponents of the Colonial Revival, a post–Civil War celebration and promotion of the architecture, objects, and perceived ideals of early America. In towns that were—or were potentially—picturesque in old New England fashion, churches and meetinghouses received much attention. In 1907 Lyme, Connecticut, the site of a thriving art colony, lost another church building to fire, this time Samuel Belcher's 1816 structure. With much fanfare, the community rebuilt the church as closely as possible to original specifications, basing the reconstruction on drawings, photographs, and memories. In 1910 no less imposing a figure than Woodrow Wilson, then president of Princeton University, gave the dedication sermon. Several years later, in an astonishing near total make-over of the village of Litchfield, citizens once again turned their attention to their community's appearance. The Village Improvement Society transformed the town center into a park, removed signs of industry, and made rambling old homes conform to a "colonial" (white with dark shutters) appearance. The town needed an appropriate church on the green, of course, so first the improvers tore down an 1873 Gothic church; Victorian architecture and artifacts were anathema to the Colonial Revival vision. Next, they brought back what was left of the 1829 Congregational Church to its original site (it had been removed from the green in the 1880s, and subsequently used as a barn, theater, and gymnasium) and employed New York architect Richard Henry Dana, Jr., to supervise a ten-year "restoration." This 1929 church, ironically, is now one of the most photographed in all of New England. Like the town of Litchfield, many Connecticut communities and congregations in the twentieth century removed sub-

51. Cover, *Life* magazine Thanksgiving issue, 20 November 1944. Barnard Hoffman/
TimePix.

"Rural Thanksgiving," a photo by Barnard Hoffman, depicts the Congregational
Church in Tallmadge, Ohio, built by Lemuel Porter, 1826.

sequent additions to their churches in order to recover an "original" appearance.

In November 1944, toward the end of a long and bitter war, *Life
Magazine* chose a Barnard Hoffman photograph of an 1826 New England–style church for the cover of the Thanksgiving issue (fig. 51).[7] Inside
the magazine was an explanation: the church evoked a vision of America
that was good and admirable—small, tightly bound communities sharing
democratic values and a sure and steady faith in God. An editor wrote,
"New Englanders have always carried with them their faith in God and
their belief that Americans should be humbly grateful for the good things
they enjoy." This "New England" church was actually built in Tallmadge,
Ohio, by Lemuel Porter, who emigrated to this "New Connecticut" from
Waterbury and was one of many to spread the style westward. Three years

later another writer, in an architectural and social history of "churches of old New England," extended a similar plea: "if civilization as we have known it is to survive, it can only be by a return to the original ideals of this country, inseparable from the old moral and spiritual standards of the Christian churches."[8]

Cold War era uses for the icon were limitless. On a midcentury Christmas card, the Litchfield church stood as the central message: "Among surroundings rich in the traditions of early America, the Congregational Church in Litchfield, Connecticut, rears its graceful spire. Notable for its beautiful Doric portico and fine interior woodwork, visitors find it one of the most perfect examples of Colonial architecture in New England today." Christmas hymns in the old church recalled "an earlier time when the voices of men and women who helped build our nation joined there in thanks for holiday blessings in a free land" (fig. 52).[9] The use of the term "Colonial" shows the tendency to collapse the preindustrial past into one scene; this is a legacy of the Colonial Revival, which helps to explain why even now it is common to mistake these churches for Puritan meetinghouses.[10] Of course, most of the Litchfield church was built in the twentieth century.

Today, although we might imagine ourselves less susceptible to these unalloyed myths of our pastoral American heritage, the image continues to resonate. In January of 2002 Sotheby's, New York, sold a silver communion service belonging to the First Congregational Church in Milford, Connecticut. In the sale catalogue the church historian described the 1823 building rising "gracefully and proud" on its idyllic site. "In its picture postcard setting, this prim yet imposing edifice connotes an era of civic and social serenity when the church was the only force in the infant community."[11] This writer is by no means alone in her continuing assertion that these church buildings stand for "serenity" and "unity" and represent a preindustrial, peaceful past. After nearly two centuries, the historical reality matters little; these buildings mean what people want them to mean.

As the Sotheby's example illustrates, these church buildings can be useful tools for those wishing to sell "authentic" America. Thus they frequently appear in the employ of advertising or tourism. L.L. Bean, a company that prides itself on its commitment to old-fashioned American values of reliability, service, and quality, chose to use Maine artist Alfred Chadbourne's beautiful painting *Old Meeting House, Yarmouth, Maine* for the cover of its 1992 Christmas catalogue (fig. 53). This 1796 building, unusual for its subtle Gothic features, was originally a Baptist church; today it serves the town as a memorial hall. In 1995, the Litchfield County Tourist Board used an image of Trinity Episcopal Church, Milton (1802–

52. "When Christmas Comes," Christmas card featuring the Congregational Church of Litchfield, Brown & Bigelow, St. Paul, Minn. Courtesy, Litchfield Historical Society, 1981-09-128, gift of Mrs. D. J. Hack.

26), a small, white, wooden building with Gothic details, to market local attractions. The text for the ad read: "unwind in the unspoiled natural beauty of Connecticut's Historic Litchfield Hills." A tree or a mountain might have been a choice more in keeping with the actual words of the advertisement but would have been no more effective in conveying peace and serenity. This choice of an Episcopal building was unusual yet it worked, demonstrating that it is the basic elements of the building that matter (rectangular shape, white paint, steeple) and historical or even decorative details are largely irrelevant. To illustrate how completely this image dominates our perceptions of the New England rural landscape, try to imagine a similar advertisement with an irregular, dark, stone Gothic church.

As anyone who has driven the highways across the United States will

Shop Early
and
enjoy the
Holidays..

*Christmas
1992*

© 1992 L.L.Bean, Inc.

53. Cover, L.L. Bean Christmas Catalogue, 1992, Alfred Chadbourne, *Old Meeting House, Yarmouth, Maine.* L.L. Bean collection, Courtesy, L.L. Bean, Inc.

know, buildings of this type abound not only all over New England and the old Northwest Territory but from coast to coast. Particularly in rural or newly developed areas, the building, stripped to its basic elements — steeple, long-axis orientation, front-facing pews in a rectangular sanctuary — is ubiquitous. What has been most remarkable is the style's tremendous staying power. Even today, a building constructed around the skeleton of these basic ideas most cheaply and easily communicates "church" to a passerby. Modern inventions such as ready-made fiberglass steeples that arrive on a flatbed truck make the style even easier to reproduce. These simplified reproductions, however, rely heavily on the allusion to *something else* for their power. That "something else" is the recognizable form of the noble and graceful buildings of an earlier era.

As told here the hidden story of these buildings, and one reason their image has been so comforting, is because of the gentle way they taught Christians how to live in an expanding material world. They balanced the sacred and the secular in a particularly effective manner that did not suggest compromise. In the catalogue for the recent Smithsonian exhibition "Picturing Old New England," William Truettner and Thomas Denenberg, when considering Childe Hassam's 1905 painting of the 1816 Lyme Congregational Church, argued that New Englanders in history and art often referenced a mythical "spiritual (Congregational) past that was stern and self-denying."[12] There may have been such a self-denying spiritual past. Yet, as we have seen, *these* buildings were not about stoicism and self-denial. They assaulted the very definition of religion as "stern and self-denying" and challenged the faith to adapt to a culture of beauty and feeling.

What could not be said flat outright in theology—God loves a proper and genteel consumer—could be implied in subtly inflected dedication sermons and more forcefully argued in the not-so-subtle fashionable statements of church architecture and worship. In the end, the message was about Christianity's relationship to the material world. This is not to say that sincere and vital belief was usurped by a scheming elite itching to buy things. Connecticut's Congregationalists may have been enamored of material possibilities, yet many of them were anxious to hold a pure and fervent faith. Elegant buildings and artifacts of worship sacrificed neither concern; they were *both* fashionable and spiritually effective. In those spaces, with those things, Christians made connections between beauty, taste, elegance, and grace—grace both secular and spiritual. What made these buildings possible for Calvinists was the belief that Christianity, civility, and elegance were inextricably bound up together.

The fact that Americans have long looked back on these buildings as representative of an austere, traditional way of life says something not about the early republic but about the modern world and how far down the roads of extravagance and consumption we have traveled. Today most Christians consume comfortably at a level that would have shocked the premodern, pious soul. Andrei Condrescu, a Romanian poet who lives and teaches in Louisiana, is a sort of modern-day de Tocqueville. In his recent book *Road Scholar*, a description of his travels across America, Condrescu commented that he was particularly struck by two American traits: (1) how materialistic they are, and (2) how spiritual they are. The surprising thing is how easily Americans wear these two apparently contradictory attributes.[13] Jesus himself, after all, bluntly stated in the Sermon on the Mount (Matthew 7:24): "You cannot serve both God and Money." This was a problem for citizens of the early republic, too. They solved it by putting their money in the service of God—honorable, worshipful consumption that not only refined souls, but perhaps even saved them. The elegant, graceful churches of federal Connecticut were the perfect setting for this lesson.

Appendix

Salisbury Congregational Church Agreement for Building a Meeting House, November 21, 1798

(Direct transcription with eighteenth-century spelling)

Whereas the town of Salisbury in Litchfield County having agreed & Voted to Build Meeting House in said town of Salisbury of the form of the Meeting House Lately Erected in Richmond in Berkshire County [Massachusetts] and did by their Vote at an Adjourned Meeting Holden at sd. Salisbury in the 30th Day of April A. D. 1798 Appoint & Impower Messirs Lot Norton Esqr. Coll. Nathaniel Buel & John Whittlesey Esqr. a Commmittee to agree with & enter into Obligation in Behalf of the town to have Sd. Meeting Houses Built By Contract therefor [*sic*] this agreement or Covenant Made Between the sd. Lot Norton Esqr. Coll. Nathaniel Buel & John Whittlesey Esqr. all of Salisbury in their capacity as Committee on the one part & Capt. Thomas Dutton of Watertown in Litchfield County on the other part. Witnesseth (viz.) that we the above named committee do Agree to and with the sd. Thomas Dutton that there shall Bee Delivered to him for the purpose of Building the meeting house at the Place where Sd. House is to be erected as established by the Honble. Court of Common pleas for the Country of Litchfield Timber Boards Shingles Clap Boards Plank & Scantling at the Price hereafter named (viz.) Square Timber at Four Dollars & seventeen cents pr. Hundred feet Small Timber such as small Rafters & Sleepers at two Dollars & Nine Cents pr. Hundred feet Short braces & Scantling at Seven Dollars & fifty cents pr. thousand feet running measure Reckoning four Inches square to the Foot. sd. Timber is to be rough hewed except the sleepers which are to be hewed on one side and there is to be Delivered a sufficient quantity for the Frame of sd. Meeting Houses Porch Tower & Cupola by the first Day of May next. Shingles of the best quality at two Dollars & eighty three Cents pr. thousand. Pine Class Boards clear stuff at Eight Dollars pr. thousand Inch & quarter Plank white or yellow Pine of the best quality at Nine dollars pr. thousand. (Eight Hundred to be considered as a thousand) Inch & half Plank at thirteen Dollars & fifty cents pr. thousand. Board Measure Inch Boards Pine best kind at Nine Dollars pr. thousand Common Boards for Siding Roof &c. at five Dollars pr. thousand Lime slacked at seven Cents pr. thousand. Lath Boards Chestnut or hemlock at six

Dollars pr. thousand all the forgoing enumerated Articles to be Delivered at the Place where the House is to be built and in Suitable times & season so that the sd. Thomas Dutton or his Workmen employed in sd. Building shall not be put to any trouble Hindrance or Delay in prosecuting the Building of sd. House & We the under written Committee do Covenant & agree with the sd. Thomas Dutton that there shall be provided & laid at the Towns Expense a good & sufficient foundation of underpining [sic] under the Sills of sd. Houses with sufficient Pillars or Supports under the Body of the House by the fifteenth Day of June next & furthermore we agree that the Sd. Thomas Dutton & his hands such as Carpenters Joiners & the whole of his workmen shall be Boarded or found with Diet Washing &c. at the Price of one dollar per week for each Man during the time that he or they shall be employed upon the Building sd. Houses & also we do hereby promise and Covenant in our sd. Capacity of committee to give unto the sd. Thomas Dutton for Building sd. Meeting Houses of the form hereafter Described the sum of Three Thousand Seven Hundred Sixty Six Dollars and Sixty Seven Cents to be paid in the following manner (viz.) Four Hundred & Seventy five Dollars by the first Day of January next four Hundred & ten Dollars on the fifteenth Day of July next and by the fifteenth Day of November 1799 to make out and pay unto sd. Dutton the whole amount of his Labour & Expence on sd. Building to that time & we agree to furnish Nails for sd. Building when wanted at the Cash price or pay the Money to the Sd. Thomas Dutton to procure them demanded & the remainder to be paid Deducting for the timber Boards Plank Shingles Lime & other materials which shall be procured by the town of Salisbury and used by sd. Dutton in Buildings sd. Houses at the foregoing stipulated prices when the work is compleated or on the first Day of July in the year one thousand eight hundred. We also agree to furnish at the expense of sd. Town of Salisbury a sufficient Number of suitable hands to assist in raising sd. House and I the sd. Thomas Dutton do Covenant & agree to and with the sd. Lot Norton Esqr. Coll. Nathaniel Buel & John Whittlesey Esqr. the fore named committee in their sd. Capacity to execute or build a meeting House in sd. Salisbury of the following Dimensions (viz.) sd. House to be Sixty four feet in Length & forty Eight feet in width with a projection of eight feet for the Porch & twenty Six feet at the base the Posts of the House to be twenty six feet in length together with a tower sixteen feet square & cupola take the Timber rough hewed at the Place of Building Dress the same in suitable Manner frame the same with & sufficiently strong for such an House provide good and sufficient Ropes Blocks apparel & tackle to raise the same & carpenters that the frame shall attend & assist through the whole of the raising sd. frame sd. House is to be Boarded on the outside Studds before it is Clapboarded the floors above & below to be Plained and laid in good & workmanlike manner & I agree to provide glass to glaze sd. House twenty four squares in a window [   ] by 11 glass the tower windows to be 10 by 12 Glass to be painted and to find Oil and Paints to Lathe & Plaister the Same and Compleatly to finish said Meeting House from the sills and upwards finding all Necessary Hangings and Trimmings for Doors Pews & with a Decent Vane & Ball on the Top of the Cupola and a Conductor for Lightning and to Do Build Compleat and finish Said Meeting House in all things (the Bell & Necessary Apparatus excepted) upon the Same Plan & after the Model and with as good workmanship as the Meeting House in Richmond lately Built is Done for the Sum of three thousand Seven hundred Six Dollars Sixty Seven Cents to be paid to me as is hereafter in the agreement Expressed (viz.) in Timber Boards

Plank Singles Clapboards Lime and Scanting for sd. Building at the Prices therein expressed and I do hereby agree to give the sum of thirteen dollars and thirty three cents in addition for the large stick for the Collumns the Remainder to be Paid in Money at the Several times as is heretofore Expressed and I Do hereby agree and Covenant to and with the above named committee that the sd. House shall be compleated and finished by the first Day of July which will be in the year one Thousand Eight Hundred for the true performance of the foregoing Covenants Contract and agreement and every Part there of the Contracting Parties Do by these Present Bind themselves to Each other in witness whereof we have hereunto Interchangeable set our hands & Seals this 21st Day of November 1798 at Salisbury Signed Sealed and Delivered in Presence of

Charles [Layton]   *Lot Norton*
Eliphalet Whittlesey   *Nathaniel Buel*
                           John Whittlesey
                           Thomas Dutton

Notes

Preface

1. Rev. Henry M. Dexter, "Meeting-Houses Considered Historically and Suggestively," *Congregational Quarterly* 1 (April 1859): 194.

2. Throughout this study I will refer to these new buildings as "churches" to differentiate them from earlier "meetinghouses." Contemporaries, however, often used these terms interchangeably. Well into the nineteenth century, even when houses of worship looked nothing like plain-style meeting houses in either style or plan, some Reformed congregations continued to call them "meetinghouses."

3. Excellent recent examples of this type of scholarship include Colleen McDannell, *Material Christianity: Religion and Popular Culture in America* (New Haven: Yale University Press, 1995) and David Morgan, *Visual Piety: A History and Theory of Popular Religious Images* (Berkeley, Calif.: University of California Press, 1998). For studies in early American religious architecture the benchmark is Dell Upton, *Holy Things and Profane: Anglican Parish Churches in Colonial Virginia* (New York: Architectural History Foundation and M.I.T. Press, 1986).

4. See, for example, Nathan Hatch, *The Democratization of American Christianity* (New Haven: Yale University Press, 1989); David Waldstreicher, *"In the Midst of Perpetual Fetes": The Making of American Nationalism, 1776–1820* (Chapel Hill: Published for the Omohundro Institute of Early American History and Culture, Williamsburg, Virginia, by the University of North Carolina Press, 1997); Richard Bushman, *The Refinement of America: Persons, Houses, Cities* (New York: Knopf, 1991).

5. These were superbly documented by J. Frederick Kelly in his two-volume *Early Connecticut Meetinghouses* (New York: Columbia University Press, 1948). Kelly did an extraordinarily thorough job of measuring buildings, crawling around in attics and basements to investigate framing timbers, separating original elements from modern, and recording the techniques of the craftsmen who built these early-nineteenth-century structures. He looked extensively and carefully at all existing religious architecture in Connecticut documented as built before 1830 and went to the primary sources, particularly town or ecclesiastical records, for other information about the buildings. He also used, in some cases, less-substantiated sources such as undocumented church histories and local tradition. I rely heavily on Kelly's fieldwork, but have retraced his steps in the documents and add both information

about churches no longer extant and churches built between 1830 and 1840. Documentary sources also provide information about Baptist and Methodist worship environments, seats of the two other denominations with significant representation in Connecticut in this period.

Chapter 1. Builders and Building (pp. 1–39)

1. Salisbury Town Records, 8 January 1798.
2. Salisbury Town Records, 19 January 1797, 8 January 1798, and 19 February 1798.
3. Thomas Robbins, *Diary of Thomas Robbins, D.D., 1796–1854*, 2 vols. (Boston: Beacon Press, 1886), 12 June 1800. Robbins's *Diary* is an excellent source of candid remarks about the religious life of the period. He was an ardent Federalist and a Congregational minister from a prominent Connecticut clergy family. His father, Reverend Ammi Robbins, was the longtime minister of the Norfolk church. Thomas was ordained in Norfolk in 1803 and served as a missionary in "New Connecticut," the Ohio territory. He traveled frequently and extensively, and served several congregations, including East Windsor (1809–27) and Mattapoisett (Rochester), Massachusetts (1831–44). His remarks often concern the age of the house of worship where he is a visitor, its comforts or lack thereof, and the quality of worship, including many notices of music performed.
4. Hartford, First Congregational Society Records, 11 December 1804, microfilm, Connecticut State Library (hereafter noted as CSL mf).
5. Hartford, First Congregational Society Records, 22 March 1805, CSL mf.
6. Nathan Strong, *A Sermon Delivered at the Consecration of the New Brick Church in Hartford. December 3, 1807* (Hartford: Hudson & Goodwin, 1808). I discuss this sermon in chapter 4.
7. Winchester, First Congregational Society Records, 1 March 1796, CSL mf.
8. Roxbury, Congregational Society Records, 25 February and 13 April 1818, CSL mf.
9. In this study, when referring to a group of people, I use "church" to mean the covenanted body of "saved" church members; I use "society" to indicate the organization and its members legally responsible for the business affairs of the church. When referring to the body of worshipers, or those actively involved in the spiritual life of the church, I use "congregation."
10. In 1727 the Colony of Connecticut granted tax exemption to Episcopalians; Baptists and Quakers received similar exemption in 1729. But these acts were hardly indicative of general toleration. For one example, a dissenter still had to prove he lived within a short distance of an established dissenting congregation to avoid paying taxes to the Congregationalists, and these laws were not interpreted liberally.
11. *Public Records of the Colony of Connecticut*, vol. 9 (1744–50), October 1748, 398–400.
12. Plymouth, St. Peter's Episcopal Society Records, 31 January 1791, CSL mf. Note that by this date Congregationalists were sometimes referred to as "Presbyterians" by Episcopalians and dissenters.
13. Plymouth, St. Peter's Episcopal Society Records, 16 January 1793, CSL mf.
14. *Connecticut Journal*, 19 November 1812.

15. Sharon, Christ Episcopal Society Records, 5 February 1812, CSL mf.

16. Roxbury, Congregational Society Records, 23 December 1794, CSL mf.

17. Winchester, First Congregational Society Records, March 1796, CSL mf.

18. *Connecticut Journal*, 31 January 1814.

19. J. Ritchie Garrison, "Tramping and the Transformation of Early New England Architecture" (unpublished paper delivered at Asher Benjamin Symposium, Deerfield, Mass., November 1993). See also Garrison, *Two Carpenters: Architecture and Building in Early New England, 1799–1859*, forthcoming.

20. Report of the Contractors, New Haven First Congregational Society, dated 9 September 1815, reported 2 January 1818. Cited in Kelly, *Early Connecticut Meetinghouses*, vol. 2, 12–14.

21. Ibid.

22. The designer of First Church was Asher Benjamin; the records of the United Society include a receipt for payment of thirty dollars to Peter Banner, a Boston architect, for plans. Receipt dated 29 March 1813. United Society Records, loose docs., New Haven Colony Historical Society.

23. Building records are in the minutes of town meetings. In 1804, a separate ecclesiastical society formed; from then on building records no longer appear in the town meeting minutes.

24. *History of Litchfield County, with Illustrations and Biographical Sketches of its Prominent Men and Pioneers* (Philadelphia: J. W. Lewis & Co., 1881), 518–62.

25. Statistical significance is difficult to claim for this data because of the relatively small number of buildings and the diverse circumstances under which they were constructed. Some of them replaced well-built older buildings, but others were the first buildings of substance that a younger congregation erected. (Compiled from ecclesiastical society records.)

26. Salisbury Town Records, 2 November 1790, 14 July 1791, 2 October 1792, 16 September 1793, 26 October 1795, 27 March, and 10 April 1797.

27. Salisbury Town Records, 22 April 1793, 21 October 1794, and 19 January 1797.

28. Sterling's tax valuation in 1803 of $598.78 was the third highest in Salisbury (after Adonijah Strong, at $722.87). Vested property owners, wealthy and prominent townspeople, were almost always chief among those involved in such projects. 1803 Grand List, Salisbury Town Records.

29. Salisbury Town Records, 8 January 1798.

30. Ibid.

31. Of the 337 heads of household listed on the 1803 Grand List, 32, or less than 10 percent, had estates valued at more than three hundred dollars. Samuel Lee alone does not appear in this top 10 percent, although a Mylo Lee has a large estate, and the Esq. after Lee's name indicates certain privilege and status. 1803 Grand List, Salisbury Town Records.

32. Salisbury Town Records, 9 April 1798.

33. Salisbury Town Records, 8 January 1798.

34. "Agreement for building a meeting house," dated 21 November 1798. Connecticut State Library Archives. J. Frederick Kelly states that the master workman was, by local tradition, Moses Wells of Salisbury; while this is possible, I have been unable to find Kelly's documentation for that assertion. Kelly, *Early Connecticut Meetinghouses*, vol. 2, 176.

35. Morris, Congregational Society Records, 24 January 1785, CSL mf.

36. The Washington society recorded payment to "Mssrs. Thomas Dutton and Peter Powil for building a Meeting House" in its records for 2 November 1802. Cited in Kelly, *Early Connecticut Meetinghouses*, vol. 2, 257.

37. Winchester, First Congregational Society Records, third Monday in March 1796, CSL mf.

38. Edmund Sinnott tracks the Salisbury church to the Pittsfield example. Edmund Ware Sinnott, *Meeting House and Church in Early New England*. (New York: McGraw-Hill, 1963), 77. Richmond is about ten miles southwest of Pittsfield. See chapter 3 for a further discussion of these buildings.

39. See Kelly, *Early Connecticut Meetinghouses*, vol. 1, xl–xli.

40. See Ibid., xl–xlviii; Abbott Lowell Cummings, *Architecture in Early New England* (Sturbridge, Mass.: Old Sturbridge Village, 1958, 3d ed. 1984), 3–12; Cummings, *The Framed Houses of Massachusetts Bay* (Cambridge, Mass.: Harvard University Press, 1979), 52–95.

41. Robbins, *Diary*, 12 June 1813.

42. Charles Denison to David Daggett, 12 January 1814, Daggett Family Papers, Manuscripts and Archives, Yale University Library.

43. *Litchfield County Post*, 26 June 1828.

44. Morris, Congregational Society Records, 6 June 1785, CSL mf.

45. Winchester, First Congregational Society Records, 17 January 1785, CSL mf.

46. Salisbury Town Records, 19 February 1798.

47. "Salisbury Town Records, Agreement for building a meeting house," 21 November 1798.

48. Salisbury Town Records, 30 December 1799.

49. Kelly, *Early Connecticut Meetinghouses*, vol. 2, 177–80, and on inspection by author.

50. Kelly determined this by looking at the roof framing and its curved braces (*Early Connecticut Meetinghouses*, vol. 2, 180).

51. Roxbury, Congregational Society Records, 23 December 1794 and January 1795, CSL mf.

52. Watertown, Christ Church Episcopal Society Records, 12 December 1792, CSL mf.

53. See Kelly on roof framing, *Early Connecticut Meetinghouses*, vol. 1, xlii–xliii. Kelly considers roof framing the "most interesting aspect of Connecticut's early meetinghouses" and concludes from material evidence of great overbuilding that, unlike Hoadley and Town, "most of the early builders . . . had no exact knowlege of engineering." See also David T. Yeomans, "British and American Solutions to a Roofing Problem," *Journal of the Society of Architectural Historians* 50 (September 1991): 266–72. Yeomans notes that Asher Benjamin also recommended a divided tie beam, in his 1811 *American Builders' Companion*, and used a metal strap joining the two sides. Town and Damon's modified "scissor" truss was more effective at distributing the stresses.

54. Salisbury Town Records, 13 January 1800.

55. Robbins, *Diary*, 12 June 1800.

56. Salisbury Town Records, 19 May 1800.

57. James Hammond Trumbull, ed., *The Memorial History of Hartford County, Connecticut, 1633–1886* (Boston: E. L. Osgood, 1886), 208–9.

58. See Rockwell Harmon Potter, *Hartford's First Church* (Hartford, 1932), and George Leon Walker, *History of the First Church in Hartford, 1633–1883* (Hartford: Brown & Gross, 1883).

59. Not coincidentally, more people confessed their belief and joined the church during those years of Reverend Strong, particularly 88 who joined in 1808 and another 128 who joined as a result of the 1813–14 revival. Walker, *History of the First Church*, 356. Membership, of course, is not the same as attendance, and probably many more people worshiped in the church than church membership statistics indicate. In this case and many others, church membership rose after the construction of a new building.

60. Hartford, First Congregational Society Records, 22 March 1805, CSL mf.

61. Ibid.

62. Ibid.

63. These figures have been determined from a reconstituted membership roster in the society records that lists, for some members, date of death and age at death. The roster is found with the Hartford First Congregational Society Records, CSL mf. In the nineteenth century "pew" and "slip," although not always used consistently, generally designated different types of seats. A pew was a closed space that might have had benches facing several directions. "Slips" were like modern pews, long open bench seats that one could "slip" into.

64. Records of the City of Hartford, 5 August 1805.

65. Records of the New Haven Common Council, vol. 2, 220.

66. Harry Croswell, Diary, 10 May 1821, Manuscripts and Archives, Yale University Library.

67. Ibid.

68. From document "At a meeting of the Contractors to build a Meeting-House for the First Ecclesiastical Society in New-Haven, and of the special committee of said society, March 30th, 1813." Reproduced in *At a Meeting concerning the Burying-Ground in New-Haven, held at the County-House on the 31st. day of March, 1813* (New Haven, 1813), 2.

69. Ibid.

70. Peter W. Gallaudet, Account Book, Hartford, First Congregational Society Records, CSL mf (Hereafter, Gallaudet's Account). The account book has two parts. The first (section one) is arranged according to either name of account or materials; the second (section two) records disbursement of funds chronologically. A record of pew sales is also contained in section 2.

71. David Wadsworth was a very distant relation to prominent Hartford citizen Daniel Wadsworth, who was a member of the First Society; David's great-great grandfather was Daniel's great-great-great grandfather. See Lucius Barnes Barbour, *Families of Early Hartford, Connecticut* (Baltimore: Genealogical Publishing Co., 1977).

72. Gallaudet's Account, section 1, 6, entry dated 28 July 1806.

73. Hartford, First Congregational Society Membership Records, CSL mf.

74. Gallaudet's Account section 1, 6; section 2, 47.

75. Gallaudet's Account, section 1, 41.

76. Ibid., 42.

77. Ibid.

78. Ibid., 15.

79. Ibid., 32.

80. Other men who have only one name listed may also have been African-Americans: Hovey, Loomis, Perry, Skinner, William, and Jared. First Church did have several African-American members later: July 1815, "Brister March, black"; April 1820, "Rhoda Freeman (Black)"; and in August of 1821 two black African-

American women joined, "Polly A Freeman" and Jane Anderson. This should not be taken as equal status in the church, for they were assigned separate seats, and it was thought necessary to designate their race in the membership roster. James Lathrop was paid for work of George Olcott; Olcott may have been a slave, or he may have been a servant or under some sort of contract to Lathrop. After 1784 Connecticut practiced gradual emancipation. In 1803 there were about 900 slaves in Connecticut; by 1820 there were fewer than 100.

81. For some reason in this account labor is still valued at shillings/day, although all payments are converted into dollars. Payment is scattered throughout the book; see, for example, David Wadsworth's account in Gallaudet's Account, Section 1, 44.

82. Gallaudet's Account, section 2, 10 and section 1, 46.

83. Ibid., 9.

84. Ibid., 1.

85. Ibid., 2.

86. Ibid., 6.

87. Ibid., 26.

88. Ibid., 6. The names Robert J. Collins and Robert J. Collins junior appear frequently in the building record. They seem to be two carpenters, perhaps father and son.

89. *Connecticut Journal*, 20 March 1815.

90. *Connecticut Journal*, 5 April 1815, 11 September 1815.

91. Gallaudet's Account, section 1, 1.

92. Ibid., 8.

93. For an informative discussion of brick construction in the early nineteenth century, see Bernard L. Herman, "Kensey Johns and His Carpenters," in *After Ratification: Material Life in Delaware, 1789–1820*, edited by J. Ritchie Garrison, Bernard L. Herman, and Barbara McLean Ward, eds., (Newark, Del.: Museum Studies Program, University of Delaware, 1988), 65–77.

94. Gallaudet's Account section 2, 10. The work of the carpenters at this time was also called "raising," although it was nothing as dramatic as the erection of the frame for the Salisbury house.

95. Gallaudet's Account, section 1, 6.

96. Ibid., 33, 43.

97. Gallaudet's Account, section 2, 24–6, section 1 pp. 28, 32–33, 37, 41, 43. Abbott Cummings notes that it was common for masons to do plastering as well. See Cummings, *Architecture in Early New England*, 8.

98. Robbins, *Diary*, 3 December 1807.

99. Gallaudet's Account, section 2, 63–71.

100. Kelly, *Early Connecticut Meetinghouses*, vol. 1, 201.

101. Ibid., 200.

Chapter 2. Building Committees, Fund-Raising Schemes, and Churches as Capital (pp. 40–72)

1. David Kling estimates that 100,000 left the state in the 1790s alone, basing this figure on Gaspare Saladino, "The Economic Revolution in Late-Eighteenth-Century Connecticut" (Ph.D. diss., University of Wisconsin, 1964), 342. This outmigration began in the middle of the century and peaked between 1790 and

1820. David W. Kling, *A Field of Divine Wonders: The New Divinity and Village Revivals in Northwestern Connecticut, 1792–1822* (University Park: Pennsylvania State Press, 1993), 186, n. 58.

2. See Richard Purcell, *Connecticut in Transition, 1775–1818* (1918; reprint, Middletown, Conn.: Wesleyan University Press, 1963). Bushman, *From Puritan to Yankee*; Charles Roy Keller, *The Second Great Awakening in Connecticut* (New Haven: Yale University Press, 1942).

3. See Charles Sellers, *The Market Revolution: Jacksonian America, 1815–1846* (New York: Oxford University Press, 1991); Richard E. Ellis et al., "A Symposium on Charles Sellers, *The Market Revolution: Jacksonian America, 1815–1846,*" *Journal of the Early Republic* 12 (winter 1992): 445–76; Sean Wilentz, "Society, Politics, and the Market Revolution, 1815–1848," in *The New American History*, edited by Eric Foner (Philadelphia: Temple University Press, 1990); Michael Zuckerman, "Holy Wars, Civil Wars: Religion and Economics in Nineteenth-Century America," *Prospects* 16 (1991): 205-40. Zuckerman writes that "a smooth functional fit between the capitalists and the churches was functionally impossible. A close convergence between the marketplace and the meetinghouse was culturally impossible" (224). Zuckerman uses "meetinghouse" metaphorically; ironically, in literal terms religion and the marketplace intersected precisely at that meetinghouse.

4. Several scholars have recently looked at the problem of religion and capitalism in mid-eighteenth-century America. In his work on George Whitefield and the first "Great Awakening," Frank Lambert demonstrates how revivalists used the techniques of the marketplace, such as print advertising and advance teams, to promote revival. See Frank Lambert, *Inventing the "Great Awakening"* (Princeton, N.J.: Princeton University Press, 1999), and *"Pedlar in Divinity": George Whitefield and the Transatlantic Revivals, 1737–1770* (Princeton, N.J.: Princeton University Press, 1994). James German has argued that capitalism and Calvinism actually found a comfortable coexistence (Weber was right), and that eighteenth-century ministers recognized that self-love, in the form of desire to achieve and acquire, had social utility in a free market economy. See James German, "The Social Utility of Wicked Self-Love: Calvinism, Capitalism, and Public Policy in Revolutionary New England," *Journal of American History* 82, no. 3 (December 1995): 965–98. When church builders of the early republic turned to the market for ways to finance their projects, it did not necessarily require a revolution in their ideas about the morality or utility of the marketplace. It did, however, necessitate a new understanding of the symbolic and practical value of church buildings.

5. Literature on pews is scant, with the notable exception of two excellent articles: Robert Dinkin, "Seating the Meetinghouse in Early Massachusetts," in *Material Life in America, 1600–1860*, edited by Robert B. St. George (Boston: Northeastern University Press, 1988), 407–18; and Jonathan D. Sarna, "Seating and the American Synagogue," in *Belief and Behavior: Essays in the New Religious History*, edited by Philip R. Vandermeer and Robert P. Swierenga (New Brunswick, N.J.: Rutgers University Press, 1991), 189–206. Sarna chronicles a shift from pew assignment to pew rental that parallels that of Protestant churches, and also describes the later nineteenth-century movement for free seating.

6. J. G. Davies, *The Secular Use of Church Buildings* (New York: Seabury Press, 1968), 138.

7. For a view of the pew system in Massachusetts at this time, see William G. McLoughlin, "The Role of Religion in the Revolution: Liberty of Conscience and

Cultural Cohesion in the New Nation," in *Essays on the American Revolution* edited by Stephen G. Kurtz and James H. Hutson (Chapel Hill: University of North Carolina Press, 1973), 229–30. McLoughlin notes that pew rentals were allowed in Boston from colonial times because Boston was outside of any parish system. A 1755 Massachusetts law granted parishes the right to assess pews and sell them if renters failed to pay rent. McLoughlin, 229.

8. William Leffingwell, Diary, 1765–1834, Leffingwell Family Papers, Manuscripts and Archives, Yale University Library. Historians have found a majority of female members in colonial churches as well. See Patricia Bonomi, *Under the Cope of Heaven: Religion, Society, and Politics in Colonial America* (New York: Oxford University Press, 1986). For the nineteenth century, see, for example, Mary Ryan, *Cradle of the Middle Class: The Family in Oneida County, New York, 1790–1865* (New York: Cambridge University Press, 1981; Nancy Cott, *The Bonds of Womanhood: "Woman's Sphere" in New England, 1780–1835* (New Haven: Yale University Press, 1977); Barbara Welter, "The Femininization of American Religion, 1800–1860," in *Clio's Consciousness Raised: New Perspectives on the History of Women*, edited by Mary Hartman and Lois Banner (New York: Harper and Row, 1974): 137–57; and Zuckerman, "Holy Wars, Civil Wars." Zuckerman puts it succinctly: "The business of the marketplace was the business of men. And in the religious demography and ideological geography of the age, Christianity was within the sphere of women" (224). Church business brought men back into the religious circle, even if their experience remained distinct from that of women.

9. Other historians have noticed that nonchurch members were often actively involved in the life of their churches. John Brooke, in his work on Worcester County, Massachusetts, writes that in the aftermath of the (First) Great Awakening, many Congregationalists participated in the church, actively affirming its tradition and culture without ever experiencing a formal conversion. See John L. Brooke, *The Heart of the Commonwealth: Society and Political Culture in Worcester County, Massachusetts, 1713–1861* (Cambridge: Cambridge University Press, 1989), 93–96.

10. Hartford, First Congregational Society Records, 27 March 1808 (from 23 November 1807 sale); list of subscribers to 1802 fund, CSL mf. Wadsworth became one of the great benefactors of Hartford, particularly in his founding leadership and support of the Wadsworth Athenaeum, an important, early cultural institution devoted to the arts and history. Because of his reputation and involvement in the church, the architecture of the 1807 church has often been erroneously attributed to him.

11. Faith was pleased to take communion, at long last, with her husband and their "two aging mothers." Faith Wadsworth, Journal of Faith Trumbull Wadsworth, 5 February 1815, Wadsworth Family Papers, Manuscripts and Archives, Yale University Library.

12. For the changing relationship between towns and religious societies, see Kevin Sweeney, "Meetinghouses, Town Houses, and Churches: Changing Perceptions of Sacred and Secular Space in Southern New England, 1720–1850, *Winterthur Portfolio* 28 (Spring 1993): 59–93; Regarding the colonial period, see also Ola Winslow, *Meeting House Hill* (New York: W. W. Norton, 1952; 2d ed. 1972).

13. Still the most thorough account of this period in Connecticut's religious and political history is Purcell, *Connecticut in Transition*, 12, 48. Purcell tends to be overly critical of the Congregationalists. This problem is addressed by Jonathan Sassi in *A Republic of Righteousness: The Public Christianity of the New England*

Clergy (New York: Oxford University Press, 2001). Purcell attributes the rapid founding of dissenting congregations and the construction of their churches after 1784, especially among the Baptists, to the liberality of this act. See Purcell, 47.

14. Bruce Daniels, *The Connecticut Town: Growth and Development, 1635–1790* (Middletown, Conn.: Wesleyan University Press, 1979), 104.

15. These figures are from a map in Purcell, *Connecticut in Transition*, following page 64.

16. Churches found ecclesiastical funds useful for several reasons. First, after 1791, with the introduction of state and national banks, this money could be deposited at interest in one of these chartered organizations. Religious societies could legally purchase bank stock at par value and withdraw money on a short six-month notice. The stock itself was special in that it was not transferable and counted as over and above the maximum capital stock authorized by the state charter. Purcell, *Connecticut in Transition*, 71. These funds also provided a convenient way for the state to contribute to the support of religion, something the state was finding increasingly necessary for political purposes. See note 58 below. Church funds were important components of the financial stability of many congregations.

17. In 1804 the First Congregational Society at Lebanon underwent a similar divisive crisis when the building of a new church necessitated the destruction of the old. The sticking point was the location of the new house, and such contention ensued that respected persons on both sides of the issue had to be jailed. The disagreement eventually split the congregation into North and South Societies. See Kelly, *Early Connecticut Meetinghouses*, vol. 1, 267–78.

18. The Connecticut General Court finally recognized the independence of White Haven Society in 1759; Fair Haven Society was recognized in 1774. See Mary Hewitt Mitchell, *History of the United Society of New Haven* (New Haven: The United Church, 1942).

19. "Resolve Uniting the Societies of White Haven and Fair Haven" (October 1796), in *Resolves and Private Laws of the State of Connecticut, 1789–1836*, vol. 1 (Hartford: J. B. Eldridge, 1837), 556.

20. New Haven, United Society Records, 1807, CSL mf.

21. These protesters had no interest in the new building, yet faced the destruction of their shares in the old houses. Their "Report" is a lengthy gripe about improper procedure, hinging on technicalities of ownership. "Report of a Committee Respecting White-Haven Meeting-House" (New Haven, 1813), 4–5. This petition exists bound together with a document of similar tone protesting the desecration of the old burying ground by the imposition of Center Church's new building, indicating the probable common cause, if not common identity, of both sets of petitioners.

22. Ibid., 6–8.

23. Ibid.

24. Ibid., 8.

25. Ibid., 6.

26. This meetinghouse was called the "new brick" in church records as early as December 1812.

27. Ebenezer Foster to David Daggett, 21 December 1815, Daggett Family Papers, Manuscripts and Archives, Yale University Libary.

28. Charles Bostwick to David Daggett, 25 December 1815, Daggett Family Papers.

29. Simeon Baldwin to David Daggett, 7 January 1816, Daggett Family Papers.

30. New Haven, United Society Records, 5 January 1815, CSL mf.

31. Purcell, *Connecticut in Transition*, 17, 200–201.

32. *Connecticut Journal*, 19 December 1815.

33. New Haven, Trinity Episcopal Society Records, MS. Group B85, Box I:E, New Haven Colony Historical Society; *Connecticut Journal* 12 December 1815.

34. Shattuck's pew deed articulated the promise noted above, "The amount . . . paid towards the expense of building the New Church, and the interest . . . shall be considered as pledged . . . for the payment of the rent of any Pew." Trinity Church Pew Lease, 13 January 1816, MS. Group B85, New Haven Colony Historical Society.

35. *Connecticut Courant*, 16 May 1810.

36. *Connecticut Mirror*, 27 December 1824.

37. *Resolves and Private Laws*, vol. 1, 537. That people considered pews as other real estate is accentuated by the notation that for the society clerk's trouble, he was to receive the same fee that town clerks earned for recording other deeds.

38. The first was printed in the *Connecticut Journal*, 21 November 1814; see also *Resolves and Private Laws*, 21 November 1814; and *The Public Statute Laws of the State of Connecticut, revised and enacted by the General Assembly, May 1821* (Hartford: H. Huntington, Jr., 1824), 331.

39. On the main floor, one-fourth of the pews could be sold and half could be rented, the rest retained by the society. Half of the gallery pews were available for rental up to thirty years, and could be sold in fee simple only if the sale of the floor pews looked like it would fall short of covering the building costs. Hartford, First Congregational Society Records, Building Committee Report, 22 March 1805; Hartford, First Congregational Society Records, 11 January 1811, CSL mf. A complete list of renters is found in the records for March 1809.

40. Hartford, First Congregational Society Records, 11 January 1811, CSL mf.

41. Hartford, First Congregational Society Records, December 1815, CSL mf. Two years earlier, the society, recognizing that many nonsociety members worshiped in First Church without paying tax or pew rent, voted "to prefer [*sic*] a petition to the General Assembly praying that this Society may be vested, with a power, to tax in the same manner as they do members of said society, all persons who, or whose families, ordinarily attend public worship in the Meeting-house of sd. Society; so long as such persons or their familys [*sic*] shall ordinarily so attend public worship." This calls attention to an unanticipated result of new religious freedoms: people worshiping with a given religious community with no financial obligation to them whatsoever. A comprehensive system of pew rental could limit that possibility. Hartford, First Congregational Society Records, January 1813, CSL mf.

42. Hartford, First Congregational Society Records, 17 January 1826, CSL mf.

43. Ibid.

44. In 1838 the society clerk summed up the situation: "about the year 1822 many members of the society had become dissatisfied with the private ownership of seats in the meeting house and with the practice of raising money by taxation to defray the current expenses." It had seemed unfair "that former owners with few exceptions, continued to occupy their old pews and slips while others, for the most part, were practically limited to what were called the poorest seats." By the time of this 1838 record, the original thirty-year leases had expired, yet approximately one-quarter of the pews were still in private hands. The society recognized

two options to pay its still unruly bills: the annual sale of seats, or the taxation of members. In 1837 pew rents brought $4,700; in the same year a tax brought $533.88. Pew owners paid nothing on rent and a mere $34.88 in taxes. The society figured that rent on those pews would have brought in an additional $650. "The result of this individual ownership taken in the aggregate is that other members of this society defray the whole expenses of the minister, the music, warming, lighting, and care of and attendance of the place of worship." Furthermore, "it is obvious that those who own seats, and are not members of the society pay no tax; they pay nothing. Others keep their property in repairs, and defray all those expenses which makes the pews of such owners valuable or saleable at all." The society voted yet again to renew efforts to purchase the remaining pews; seven of the last owners sold back their pews between 1834 and 1840. Hartford, First Congregational Society Records, 14 February 1838, CSL mf.

45. Stuart Bruchey, *Enterprise: The Dynamic Economy of a Free People* (Cambridge, Mass.: Harvard University Press, 1990), 172 ff.

46. Petition dated February 1814, in Trumbull, ed., *History of Hartford County*, 333–35.

47. Kelly, *Early Connecticut Meetinghouses*, vol. 2, 26.

48. Ibid.

49. Loose document following entry for 17 February 1823. Hartford, North (Park) Congregational Society Records, CSL mf.

50. Undated document regarding 1825–27 building. Hartford, Second (South) Congregational Society Records, Connecticut Historical Society Library.

51. Ibid.

52. Ibid.

53. Report of Joint Committee on Subject of Free Church," 9 December 1831, Hartford, North (Park) Congregational Society Records, CSL mf.

54. Hartford, Second (South) Congregational Society Records, 12 March 1832, CSL mf.

55. Hartford, Christ Episcopal Society Records, 8 December 1807, CSL mf.

56. Petition dated 10 April 1807, Hartford, Christ Episcopal Society Records, CSL mf.

57. Hartford, Christ Episcopal Society Records, 29 July 1816, CSL mf.

58. On several occasions the state made restricted funds available to ecclesiastical societies. For example, although the sale of lands in the Western Reserve was designed to benefit schools, a 1795 act allowed individual districts, by a two-thirds majority, to use that money for the ministry (Kling, *Field of Divine Wonders*, p. 70 n. 122,). Furthermore, in 1816 the state passed an act appropriating a portion of the national refund of war expenses to ecclesiastical societies: one-third to the Congregationalists, one-seventh to the Episcopalians, one-eighth to the Baptists, one-twelfth to the Methodists, and one-seventh to Yale College. This act, sometimes called the Act for the Support of Literature and Religion, was more problematic than helpful, for the dispensation of funds was cumbersome and the allocation unfair. See *Report of the Committee on the Claims Against the United States* (Hartford, 1816). The Episcopalian share went into the Episcopal "Bishop's Fund." The state never delivered the $20,000 it promised to the Bishop's Fund after the chartering of the Phoenix Bank, and the ensuing scandal pushed the Episcopalians further away from the Congregational/Federalist government into the Republican/ Toletionist political party, a position they might never have filled if not for a desperate sense of discrimination. To placate them, in 1817 the General Assembly

allotted one-seventh of the national refund of the state's war expenses to the Bishop's Fund. See Purcell, *Connecticut in Transition*, 44. Another small percentage of this refund was to go to other denominations.

59. Purcell, *Connecticut in Transition*, 68.

60. Roxbury, Congregational Society Records, 23 April 1795.

61. Roxbury Congregational Society Records, Wednesday following 23 December 1794, CSL mf.

62. Roxbury, Congregational Society Records, 12 December 1796, CSL mf.

63. Roxbury, Congregational Society Records, 28 November 1796, CSL mf.

64. Roxbury, Congregational Society Records, 6 and 13 December 1802, CSL mf.

65. Roxbury, Congregational Society Records, 5 December 1803, CSL mf.

66. Roxbury, Congregational Society Records, 3 May 1804, CSL mf.

67. Roxbury, Congregational Society Records, 17 and 24 December 1821, CSL mf.

68. Roxbury, Congregational Society Records, 13 February 1826, CSL mf.

69. Roxbury, Congregational Society Records, 28 December 1836, CSL mf.

70. Morris, Congregational Society Records, 17 November 1815, CSL mf.

71. Morris, Congregational Society Records, 29 November 1819, CSL mf.

72. Morris, Congregational Society Records, 27 November 1820, CSL mf.

73. Morris, Congregational Society Records, 6 December 1820, CSL mf.

74. Morris, Congregational Society Records, 24 December 1826, CSL mf.

75. Winchester, First Congregational Society Records, 17 November 1814, CSL mf.

76. Winchester, First Congregational Society Records, 5 December 1814, CSL mf.

77. Winchester, First Congregational Society Records, 3 November 1828, CSL mf.

78. Washington, First Congregational Society Records, 14 November 1839, CSL mf.

79. Woodbury, First Congregational Society Records, 8 and 14 November 1841, CSL mf.

80. Ibid.

81. Woodbury, First Congregational Society Records, 7 January 1842, CSL mf.

82. Agreement between building committee (Bishop Stone Smith and Doolittle) and builders (James and Giles Kilbourn), Litchfield, St. Paul's in (Bantam) Episcopal Society Records, found in Account Book of Silvanus Bishop, 2 April 1796, Litchfield Historical Society.

83. Litchfield, St. Paul's (Bantam) Episcopal Society Records, 14 September 1799, Litchfield Historical Society.

84. Plymouth, St. Peter's Episcopal Society Records, 29 October 1792, CSL mf.

85. Kent, St. Andrew's Episcopal Society Records, historical note in vol. 1, n. p., CSL mf.

86. Thomaston (Plymouth Hollow), Congregational Society Records 31 August 1836, CSL mf.

87. Thomaston (Plymouth Hollow), Congregational Society Records 23 September 1836, CSL mf.

88. Goshen, North Congregational Society Records, 4 January 1830, CSL mf.

89. Bethlehem, Episcopal Society (Christ Church) Records, 26 July 1841, CSL mf.

90. Northfield (Litchfield), Congregational Society Records, 2 March 1801, CSL mf.

91. Litchfield, First Ecclesiastical Society Records, vol. 1, 18 November 1808, CSL mf.

92. Colebrook, First Congregational Society Records, October 1821, CSL mf.

93. Colebrook, Union Society Records, 26 April 1815, CSL mf.

94. Barkhamsted, First Congregational Society Records, 28 December 1849, CSL mf.

95. Plymouth, St. Peter's Episcopal Society Records, 1 September 1791, CSL mf.

96. John Samuel Ezell, *Fortune's Merry Wheel: The Lottery in America* (Cambridge, Mass.: Harvard University Press, 1960): 141–42. Ezell says between 1790 and the Civil War two hundred church groups in the United States were recipients of lotteries granted by Rhode Island and Connecticut in New England, all the middle states down to Georgia, Louisiana, Michigan and Kentucky. All societies participated except Quakers.

Lotteries Granted to Religious Societies in Connecticut, 1800–1818

1800	Danbury Episcopal	$1800 mhs [meetinghouse] repairs
	Goshen	$1800 mhs
1801	Norwich 1st	$3000 mhs
1803	Preston	$6000 mhs
	Voluntown	—
	Canterbury	—
	Winsted	—
1804	Canaan 1st	$2000 "discharge debts of building mhs"
	So. Lebanon	$3000 unspecified
1805	Ellsworth	$10,000
	Roxbury Episcopal	—
	Greenwich Episcopal	—
	Newtown	—
	W. Britain in Bristol	—
1806	Eastbury in Glastonbury	$4000 mhs
	Episcopal Society in Milford	—
1808	Bridgewater in New Milford	$1500 mhs
1809	Groton 2nd Soc.	$5000 "gospel ministry"
1813	Bridgewater	$500 another class for above
1815	Plainfield	$4000 mhs
1818	Fairfield Episcopal	$6000 unspecified

These data are from a document Secretary Thomas Day put together 28 May 1829 to get a handle on the unruly state of lottery grants. Lottery Papers 1763–1830, Connecticut State Library Archives.

97. Albert Van Dusen, ed., *Public Records of the State of Connecticut, May 1800–October 1801*, vol. 10 (Hartford: Connecticut State Library, 1965), 152–53.

98. Ibid., 258–59.

99. Christopher Collier, ed., *Public Records of the State of Connecticut, May 1802–Oct. 1803*, vol. 11 (Hartford: Connecticut State Library, 1967): 223–24.

100. "Authority of the State of Connecticut Fairfield Episcopal Society Lottery," broadside, Lottery Papers, Connecticut Historical Society Library.

101. *Danbury Recorder, 26 November 1828*; Fairfield Episcopal Society Lottery, broadside, Connecticut Historical Society Library; Ezell, *Fortune's Merry Wheel*, 84.

102. Loose documents relating to Norwich Meeting House lottery in Lottery Papers, 1763–1830, Connecticut Historical Society Library. A class one ticket sold for two dollars and class two for three dollars.

103. Samuel Trumbull to managers of Goshen Meeting House Lottery, 19 January 1800, Lottery Papers, 1763–1830 Connecticut Historical Society Library.

104. Ibid.

105. Lippitt Manufacturing Company, Providence, Rhode Island, Account Book (1819), Lottery Papers, 1763–1830, Connecticut Historical Society Library.

106. Canaan First Congregational Society Records, 1784-1801, CSL mf.

107. Osborn "Scheme of Canaan Meeting House Lottery," papers relating to lotteries chiefly in Connecticut, 1774–1824, Connecticut State Library Archives.

108. Canaan, First Congregational Society Records, January 1806, CSL mf.

109. Canaan, First Congregational Society Records, 22 November 1808, CSL mf.

110. Canaan, First Congregational Society Records, May 1812, CSL mf.

111. Canaan, First Congregational Society Records, 17 November 1828, CSL mf.

112. *Connecticut Evangelical Magazine and Religious Intelligencer*, (March 1811), cited in Ezell, *Fortune's Merry Wheel*, 195.

113. *American Mercury*, 3 May 1804.

114. Hudson & Goodwin to Mr. Thomas Fanning, 24 December 1801, Lottery Papers, 1763–1830, Connecticut Historical Society Library.

115. Petition, c. 1830, probably addressed to General Assembly, Lottery Papers, 1763–1830, Connecticut Historical Society Library.

116. Representatives of other religious traditions—Quakers, Catholics, Jews, and Unitarians, for instance—existed in small numbers in Connecticut in this period. But erecting their own buildings was not possible for most of them until the 1830s; financial records of such ventures, therefore, do not exist.

117. Watertown and Bethlehem, Methodist Episcopal Society Records, 1820–26, November 1820, CSL mf.

118. See Frank S. Bishop, *History of the First Baptist Church in New Haven: An Historical Address Delivered at the Centenary Celebration October 11, 1916* (New Haven: First Baptist Church, 1916).

119. New Milford Baptist Church Covenant, probably dates from formation of society in 1814, from 1825 transcript in New Milford, Northville Baptist Church Records, CSL mf.

120. New Haven, First Baptist Society Records, September 1821–December 1822, CSL mf.

121. New Haven, First Baptist Society Records, 27 December 1824, CSL mf.

122. New Haven, First Baptist Society Records, 15 January 1833, CSL mf.

123. New Haven, First Baptist Society Records, 7 August 1834, CSL mf.

124. Undesignated document, petition addressing the General Assembly, 15 May 1818, Hartford, Central Baptist Church Records, CSL mf.

125. Hartford, First Baptist Church Records, 18 February 1814, CSL mf.

126. Hartford First Baptist Church Records, 18 October 1830 and 27 May 1831, CSL mf.

127. Robert Emory, *History of the Discipline of the Methodist Episcopal Church to 1856* (New York: Carlton & Porter, 1857), 71.

128. Ibid., 205.

129. Ibid.

130. New Haven, Methodist Episcopal Society Records, CSL mf. Papers include 1822 and 1827 pew deeds.

131. Litchfield, First Methodist Episcopal Society Records, 17 July 1837, CSL mf.

132. Woodbury, Methodist Episcopal Society Records, 1 January 1840, 28 January 1841, 1851, CSL mf.

133. New Haven, Methodist Episcopal Society Records, loose document, n.d., CSL mf.

134. Ibid.

135. New Haven, Methodist Episcopal Society Records, loose document, 1827, CSL mf. An 1822 document certifies to the rental of pew number sixty-five, three dollars per year, to P. Isaac Gilbert.

136. Nathan Hatch discusses how the "allure of respectability" challenged traditional Methodist ideas about worship space. See Hatch, *Democratization of American Christianity*, 201–6.

137. Hartford, First Universalist Church Records, 14 March 1831, Connecticut Historical Society. This practice was not uncommon among American urban churches by the middle of the nineteenth century, but this is an unusually early example. *Geer's Hartford Directory* for 1852–53 illustrates several churches, including the Advent Church at 226 Main Street and the First Baptist Church, 229–35 Main Street, with shops at street level. This form suggests a comparison with some of northern New England's rural churches that were divided into two stories in the middle of the nineteenth century to create a bottom story for town offices or social spaces with a sanctuary above. For example, see the 1790 Federated Church in Thetford, Vermont, or the 1796 church in Rindge, New Hampshire. In some cases, this division of the building was completed in order to separate space from the sanctuary for other church functions. The Congregational Church in Plainfield, Connecticut, for example, was divided into two stories in 1849, with a sanctuary above and social and lecture rooms below. As congregations multiplied their functions and programs in the later nineteenth century, the early-nineteenth-century church plan often proved inadequate. See Jeanne Halgren Kilde, *When Church Became Theatre: The Transformation of Evangelical Architecture and Worship in Nineteenth-Century America* (New York: Oxford University Press, 2002).

138. In 1827 "Miss Beecher" paid $38.15 to use the room from 20 May through 20 October. Hartford, North (Park) Congregational Church Papers, CSL mf, noted in an 1828 report.

139. "Report of Joint Committee on Subject of Free Church," 9 December 1831, Hartford, North (Park) Congregational Church Papers, CSL mf.

Chapter 3. Architectural Style and Religious Identity (pp. 73–124)

1. A note about my use of the word "style." Architectural historians have adapted the language of sociologists and anthropologists in order to emphasize the complexity of design. In so doing, they have both enriched and complicated the lexicon. The idea of "restrictive" and "nonrestrictive" codes, for example, as developed by sociologist Basil Bernstein (see *Class, Codes, and Control*, vol. 1, *Theoretical Studies toward a Sociology of Language* [London: Routledge and Kegan Paul, 1971–75], 122–36) is used by Dell Upton, who calls these concepts "mode" and "style." See Upton, *Holy Things and Profane*. Catherine Bisher, Bernard Herman, and other students of vernacular architecture use this distinction as a way to describe more precisely design as a "language" to which some persons have more access than others. (See See Catherine W. Bishir, "Good and Sufficient Language for Building," in *Perspectives in Vernacular Architecture*, edited by Thomas Carter and Bernard L. Herman *Perspectives in Vernacular Architecture, IV* [Columbia: University of Missouri Press, 1991], vol, 4, 44–52; Upton, *Holy Things and Profane*; Bernard L. Herman, *The Stolen House* [Charlottesville: University of Virginia Press, 1992].) For these scholars, "style" is now a specific term meaning only the part of design that is easily comprehensible or "unrestricted." I am using "style" in a broader sense, the way it was used by building committees in the nineteenth century, that is, the totality of the building—ornament, construction, and the way the parts came together to form the whole.

2. Upton, *Holy Things and Profane*; see also Richard L. Bushman, *The Refinement of America: Persons, Houses, Cities* (New York: Knopf, 1992). For a somewhat different interpretation of Anglican buildings, one that takes Anglican spirituality into account, see Louis P. Nelson, "The Material Word: Anglican Visual Culture in Colonial South Carolina" (Ph.D. diss., University of Delaware, 2001).

3. Many historians have demonstrated the role of social status in the composition of local government of New England towns in the colonial period (see, for instance, Kenneth Lockridge, *A New England Town: The First Hundred Years* [New York: W. W. Norton, 1970]), and historians agree that New England was basically a hierarchical society, something that persisted, especially in rural areas. But economic opportunity and the lack of the stark division between rich and poor that existed in the Chesapeake made the northern colonies a reasonable to place to attempt to improve one's station.

4. Scholars of religion in the South have shown what chaos this sort of democratic spirituality brought to the social order. See for example Rhys Isaac, *The Transformation of Virginia, 1740–90* (Chapel Hill: Published for the Institute of Early American History and Culture by University of North Carolina Press, 1982); Christine Heyrman, *Southern Cross: The Beginnings of the Bible Belt* (New York: Knopf, 1997).

5. See Hatch, *Democratization of American Christianity*.

6. See Harold Turner, *From Temple to Meeting House: The Phenomenology and Theology of Places of Worship* (The Hague: Mouton Publishers, 1979); Mircea Eliade, *The Sacred and the Profane: The Nature of Religion* (San Diego: Harcourt, Brace, Jovanovich, 1959).

7. For general history of classicism, and classicism in America, see William H. Pierson, *American Buildings and Their Architects*, vol. 1, *The Colonial and Neoclassical Styles*, (Garden City, N.Y.: Doubleday, 1970), 444; Wendy A. Cooper, *The Classical Taste in America, 1800–1840* (New York: Abbeville Press for the Baltimore

Museum of Art, 1993); *Classical America, 1815–1845* (Newark, N.J.: The Newark Museum, 1963).

8. See Talbot Faulkner Hamlin, *Greek Revival Architecture in America* (London: Oxford University Press, 1944). See also Joseph J. Ellis, *After the Revolution: Profiles of Early American Culture* (New York: W. W. Norton, 1979), 1–21.

9. This early "Gothick" is not to be confused with the Gothic Revival that began in the late 1830s and had a deep, theoretical, scholarly base, favoring exact replication of medieval parish churches. See Phoebe B. Stanton, *The Gothic Revival and American Church Architecture: An Episode in Taste, 1840–56* (Baltimore: The Johns Hopkins University Press, 1968). For a wider consideration of Gothic influence on American religious architecture, see Peter W. Williams, "The Medieval Heritage in American Religious Architecture," in *Medievalism in American Culture: Papers of the Eighteenth Annual Conference of the Center for Medieval and Early Renaissance Studies*, edited by Bernard Rosenthal and Paul E. Szarmach (Binghamton, N.Y.: Medieval & Renaissance Texts & Studies, 1989), 171–91.

10. See Paul Jeffrey, *The City Churches of Sir Christopher Wren* (London: Hambelton Press, 1996); Geoffrey Beard, *The Works of Christopher Wren* (Edinbugh: John Bartholomew & Son Ltd, 1982).

11. See Terry Friedman, *James Gibbs* (New Haven: Yale University Press for the Paul Mellon Center for Study in British Art, 1984).

12. See Abbott Lowell Cummings, "An Investigation of the Sources, Stylistic Evolution, and Influence of Asher Benjamin's Builders Guides" (Ph.D. diss, The Ohio State University, 1950). See also Kenneth Hafertepe and James O'Gorman, eds., *American Architects and Their Books to 1848* (Amherst: University of Massachusetts Press, 2001).

13. Pierson, *American Buildings and Their Architects*, vol. 1, 444.

14. See Marian Card Donnelly, *The New England Meeting Houses of the Seventeenth Century* (Middletown, Conn.: Wesleyan University Press, 1968).

15. The design of colonial meetinghouses, however, would have been somewhat out-of-date compared with other buildings. Abbott Cummings has argued that religious architecture lagged behind domestic architecture in fashion until the Revolution, after which, primarily under the influence of Bulfinch and Benjamin, it led the way, introducing New Englanders to Adamesque (Federal) style. See Abbott Cummings, "Meeting House and Dwelling House: Interrelationships in Early New England," in *New England Meeting House and Church, 1630–1850*, edited by Peter Benes (Boston: Boston University for the Dublin Seminar for New England Folklife, 1979), 4–17.

16. See Peter Benes, "Sky Colors and Scattered Clouds: The Decorative and Architectural Painting of New England Meeting Houses, 1738–1834," in *New England Meeting House and Church*, 51–69.

17. Most churches of the later early national period seem to have been originally painted white, although there were some surprising flashes of color, and "white" was not the stark white we see today, but shades of off-white or light gray. The Roxbury church, for example, voted to give its new building three coats of paint: white on the building's facades and red on the roof. Roxbury Congregational Society Records, Wednesday following 23 December 1794, CSL mf. The congregation at Lyme asked its builder to paint the church "with a bright straw color [pale yellow] or white." See Samuel Belcher indenture for building the Lyme meetinghouse, Connecticut Historical Society.

18. An exception to this plan was found in scattered buildings with a "reverse

plan," in which the pulpit was between the front doors, pews facing. Philip D. Zimmerman discussed this in his dissertation, "Ecclesiastical Architecture in the Reformed Tradition in Rockingham County, New Hampshire, 1790–1860" (Ph.D. diss., Boston University, 1985). In my study such buildings include North Congregational, Hartford; First Baptist, New Haven; and the Southington, Cheshire, Derby, Milford, New Preston, Litchfield, and North Cornwall Congregational Churches. In most cases this plan was subsequently reversed, making it difficult to know the number of buildings originally employing the plan. It seems that churches with this plan often had a sloping floor. The reasons for this curious arrangement are obscure.

19. Roxbury, Congregational Society Records, 23 December 1794, CSL mf.

20. Washington Congregational Society Records, 1801, cited in Kelly, *Early Connecticut Meetinghouses*, vol. 2, p. 257.

21. Richard Bushman has recently argued that this architectural shift belies Puritan-Anglican, New World–Old World competition. Bushman draws on Donald Friary, "The Architecture of the Anglican Churches in the Northern American Colonies: A Study of Religious, Social, and Cultural Expression" (Ph.D. diss, University of Pennsylvania, 1971). See Bushman, *The Refinement of America*, 174–80.

22. The "meetinghouse to church" shift has often been read as the dissolution of the "Puritan plain style" in favor of something more fashionable and Anglican. This parallels "declension" theories offered by historians to explain broader shifts in Puritan society. For the "meetinghouse to church" paradigm, see Charles Place, "From Meeting House to Church in New England," *Old Time New England* 13 (October 1922): 69–77; 13 (January 1923): 111–23; 13 (April 1923): 149–64; 14 (July 1923): 3–26. See also Sinnott, *Meeting House and Church*. Regarding declension in seventeenth-century American Puritanism, see Perry Miller, *The New England Mind: The Seventeenth Century* (Cambridge, Mass: Harvard University Press, 1939). The interpretation of the colonial meetinghouse as "austere" and "plain" can also be traced to many stereotypes of Puritans as having an "entirely negative attitude . . . to all the sensuous and emotional elements in culture and religion" (Max Weber, *The Protestant Ethic and the Spirit of Capitalism*, 1904–5, translated and with an introduction by Anthony Giddens [New York: Charles Scribner's Sons, 1958], 105). Religious historians have repeatedly taken issue with the idea of declension. See, for example, Harry S. Stout, *The New England Soul: Preaching and Religious Culture in Colonial New England* (New York: Oxford University Press, 1986).

23. For a discussion of the "plain style" in rhetoric, see Miller, *The New England Mind*, 331–62.

24. See, for several examples among many, John Demos, *A Little Commonwealth: Family Life in Plymouth Colony* (London: Oxford University Press, 1970); Charles Hambrick-Stowe, *The Practice of Piety: Puritan Devotional Disciplines in Seventeenth-Century New England* (Chapel Hill: University of North Carolina Press, 1982); *New England Begins: The Seventeenth Century* (Boston: Museum of Fine Arts, 1981).

25. See John Calvin, *Institutes of the Christian Religion*, edited by John T. McNeill, translated by Ford Lewis Battles (Philadelphia: The Westminster Press, 1960). "Did [God] not," asked Calvin, "distinguish colors as to make some more lovely than others? . . . Did he not, in short, render many things attractive to us,

apart from their necessary use?" (book III.10.2). Because we have senses, Calvin argued, God uses them to teach us, imparting "spiritual things under visible ones," and beauty can be useful as long as it is employed "decently and in order" (book IV.14.3). For one of the few comprehensive treatments of Calvin's aesthetics see Leon Wencelius, *l'Esthetique de Calvin* (Paris: Société d'Edition "Les Belles Lettres," 1938).

26. Anthony Garvan, in an influential 1950 article, described what he thought to be the architectural heritage brought by the Puritans. "When, in 1630, the Great Migration to New England began," Garvan wrote, "its ships carried not only Puritan settlers and Puritan theology, but also a full-fledged Protestant esthetic. The meetinghouses of New England were not haphazard or accidental responses to the demands of the American forest," he insisted (here arguing with Kelly's recently published *Early Connecticut Meetinghouses*). "The non-liturgical floor plan, the box pew, the movable communion table, galleries, the two-story facade, the low ceiling, the elaborate pulpit, all were known to Protestant builders who, by 1630, had striven for almost a century to create a Plain Style of church architecture." Garvan allowed for regional variation in America, but argued that these buildings, nonetheless, followed basic principles of space, light, and ornament. Anthony Garvan, "The Protestant Plain Style before 1630," *Journal of the Society of Architectural Historians* 9 (October 1950): 4–13, quote p. 12. Garvan is not incorrect, but has so standardized the model that it fails to represent anything uniquely "Puritan"—most rules apply to Anglican buildings in Virginia just as well; he was talking about a common, Reformed architecture, and nothing specifically Calvinistic.

27. Robert Trent believes that the only thing truly "plain" about New England meetinghouses was found in the auditory spatial arrangements, not in ornament or design, and he finds no reason to assume any *theological* basis for the architecture. Based on the fine finish qualities of fragments of pews from Marblehead, Medfield, and Hingham, Massachusetts, and Bristol, Rhode Island, from the second quarter of the seventeenth century, Trent argues, "The earliest meetinghouses were not Protestant, but secular; not Plain, but heavily decorated; and not built in any one style, but subject to the regional origins of the builders, the needs of the individual community, and the changing uses to which the structures were put," p. 111 in Robert F. Trent, "The Marblehead Pews," in *New England Meeting House and Church*, edited by Benes, 101–11.

28. "Report of the Contractors," 9 September 1815, read and accepted 2 January 1818. "In the progress of the building it was thought best to face the tower with brick instead of stone as contracted for, to raise the side walls and tower higher, to paint the inside of the pews, to put down side steps, and to make a number of other alterations that were thought indispensable," cited in Kelly, *Early Connecticut Meeting houses*, vol. 2, 13.

29. Report of Building Committee, April 1828, Hartford, Second (South) Congregational Society Records, CSL mf.

30. See Jack Quinan, "Asher Benjamin and Charles Bulfinch: An Examination of Baroque Forms in Federal Style Architecture," in *New England Meeting House and Church*, edited by Benes, 18–29, and also Quinan, "Asher Benjamin and American Architecture," *Journal of the Society of Architectural Historians* 38, no. 3 (1978), 244–56.

31. Garrison, 'Tramping and the Transformation of Early New England Ar-

chitecture." See Kenneth Haftertepe, "The Country Builder's Assistant: Text and Context," in *American Architects and Their Books to 1848*, edited by Hafertepe and O'Gorman, 129–148.

32. Benjamin's design, and probably most of the earlier church-type buildings of the Connecticut River Valley, had old-style box pews. These pews were all front-facing, however, and most congregations replaced them with narrower "slips" within a few decades.

33. Cummings, "Meeting and Dwelling House," 14.

34. Reference to other buildings was common in English practice. See Catherine W. Bishir, "Good and Sufficient Language for Building."

35. Plymouth, St. Peter's Episcopal Society Records, 1 January 1795, CSL mf.

36. Plymouth, St. Peter's Episcopal Society Records, 4 October 1792, CSL mf.

37. Roxbury, Congregational Society Records, 28 June 1837, CSL mf. (This church replaced the one built in 1795 and noted in note 17.)

38. "Report of building committee," Hartford, North (Park) Congregational Society Records, early 1823 (exact date unclear), CSL mf. Today we use "plan" in reference to floor plans only; at this time "plan" also referred to elevations, roof framing, and other drawings.

39. It is tempting to see some sort of structuralism at work here, similar to what Henry Glassie found in the folk houses of Virginia (*Folk Housing in Middle Virginia: A Structured Analysis of Historic Artifacts* [Knoxville:University of Tennessee Press, 1975], for there is clear evidence that design was conceived of as large parts joined together from a limited design vocabulary. With the wide use of pattern books, and the awareness of transcontinental architectural style, another explanation is that it was easier for communities to process these buildings as parts. For the layman, an understanding of style began with recognizing gross features of form. It was up to the builders to fit those parts together as a whole, using knowledge of ornament and proportion to make it "decent."

40. See Jane Nylander, "Toward Comfort and Uniformity in New England Meeting Houses, 1750–1850," *New England Meeting House and Church*, edited by Benes, 86–100. Nearly all the older churches in the present study went through some extensive remodeling between the late 1820s and the 1840s, putting in slips to replace pews, lowering the galleries, putting in an organ, adding stoves, and in other ways making the interior more comfortable. Few changes were made to update the exteriors stylistically, although occasionally a temple front was placed over an older facade. I discuss this at length in chapter 6.

41. "Report of building committee," c. 1823, Hartford, North (Park) Congregational Society Records, CSL mf.

42. Cornwall, First Congregational Society Records, 25 January 1841, CSL mf.

43. Roxbury, Congregational Society Records, December 1794 (exact date unclear), CSL mf.

44. Morris, Congregational Society Records, 11 June 1784, CSL mf.

45. Woodbury, Methodist Episcopal Church Records, 19 January, 1839, CSL mf.

46. James Gibbs, *A Book of Architecture: containing designs of buildings and ornaments* (London: Printed for W. Innys and R. Hanby, J. and P. Knapton, and C. Hitch, 1728), ii–iii.

47. In her current research on academies and seminaries in New England in this era, Catherine Kelly has noted that, while girls were instructed in drawing and ornamental arts, boys often had an art curriculum that focused on learning

the rules of proportion and symmetry. This helps to explain why members of the building committee and their congregations were keenly interested in the overall dimensions of their buildings from stylistic, as well as practical, concerns. Catherine Kelly, Winterthur Scholars Seminar, unpublished paper, presented spring 2000.

48. Simeon Baldwin to son, 24 December 1812, Baldwin Family Papers, Manuscripts and Archives, Yale University Library. A further letter from his son, dated 27 January 1813, indicates that he sent actual plans "made by the artist who planned it which are accurate and handsome" back to his father.

49. Baldwin to Rev. J. H. Turner of Fayetteville, 6 March 1816, Baldwin Family Papers, Manuscripts and Archives, Yale University Library.

50. Theodonia Woolsey to James A. Hillhouse, 7 February 1813, Hillhouse Family Papers, Manuscripts and Archives, Yale University Library.

51. *Connecticut Journal*, 20 November 1815.

52. Hartford, Second (South) Congregational Society Records, undated loose documents, CSL mf.

53. Ibid.

54. Bushman, *The Refinement of America*.

55. See Nelson Rollin Burr, *The Story of the Diocese of Connecticut: A New Branch of the Vine* (Hartford: Church Mission Publishing Co., 1962), and James Shepard, *The Episcopal Church and Early Ecclesiastical Laws of Connecticut* (New Britain, Conn.: Tuttle, Morehouse, & Taylor Co., 1908).

56. Ezra Stiles, as cited in Burr, *Diocese of Connecticut*, 116. Connecticut's Anglicans were *not* necessarily upper crust, as Bruce E. Steiner has shown in "New England Anglicanism: A Genteel Faith?" *William and Mary Quarterly* 3rd ser. 27 (1970): 122–35.

57. Truman Marsh, manuscript history of St. Michaels Episcopal Church, n.d., written after his retirement in 1808, probably after 1825, Litchfield Historical Society.

58. Purcell, *Connecticut in Transition*, 31.

59. John Henry Hobart, *The United States of America as compared with some European countries particularly England*, discourse delivered October 1825, St. John's Chapel, St. Paul's Chapel, and Trinity Church, New York City (New York, 1825).

60. Ibid., 10–21.

61. *Journal of the Proceedings of the Annual Convention, Protestant Episcopal Church* (Middletown, Conn.), for 1828, 4.

62. The Rev. Samuel F. Jarvis, *An Address delivered in the city of New-Haven at the Laying of the Corner-Stone of Trinity Church, May 17th, 1814*. (New Haven: Oliver Steele, 1814), 12–13.

63. Ibid. Episcopalians by no means considered themselves Roman Catholics, yet, when convenient, they earnestly claimed that heritage as part of their own tradition—hence the reference to "fifteen hundred years at least."

64. Samuel Wheaton to Rev. Samuel Francis Jarvis, Newport, 28 August 1818, Connecticut Historical Society Library.

65. Theodonia Woolsey to James A. Hillhouse, New Haven, 16 August 1816, Hillhouse Family Papers, Manuscripts and Archives, Yale University Library.

66. Robbins, *Diary*, 25 December 1823.

67. Robbins, *Diary*, 25 December 1827.

68. Robbins, *Diary*, 15 June 1820.

69. Later buildings in the "grecian style" (Greek Revival) were constructed by Episcopalians in the 1830s—churches in New Milford, Chatham, Greenwich, New Canaan, and Middletown were all consecrated in 1834. It is interesting to note that Episcopalians began to build in the Greek Revival style just as other denominations were edging toward a full-blown Gothic Revival.

70. See Upton, *Holy Things and Profane*; Friary, "Architecture of the Anglican Churches."

71. Robbins, *Diary*, 7 June 1829.

72. Gothic details do appear occasionally on New England Congregational churches of this period, probably the first being Charles Bulfinch's 1809 Federal Street Church in Boston.

73. Litchfield, St. Paul's (Bantam) Episcopal Society Records, 2 April 1796, Litchfield Historical Society.

74. Harry Croswell, "Annals of Trinity Church," 48, Manuscripts and Archives, Yale University Library.

75. Jarvis, *Address at the Laying of the Corner-Stone*, 11.

76. Ibid.

77. Roger Sherman Baldwin to Ebenezer Baldwin, 9 January 1816, Baldwin Family Papers, Manuscripts and Archives, Yale University Library.

78. Daniel Wadsworth, "Architecture," *American Journal of Science and Arts* 24 (April–June 1833), 261–62.

79. Many changes were made to Trinity in the late nineteenth century. The tower was rebuilt in stone in 1870 and the chancel was extended twenty-five feet in 1884–85. Major interior repairs and redecoration were completed in 1905–7. Kelly, *Early Connecticut Meetinghouses*, vol. 2, 27–28.

80. Croswell, "Annals," 55.

81. Croswell, "Annals," 55. Ebenezer Foster informed David Daggett that when it came time for the United Church dedication "as many as seventeen hundred persons attended the exercises of the day." Letter dated 21 December 1815, Daggett Family Papers, Manuscripts and Archives, Yale University Library. Trinity's consecration, therefore, drew far more people. See also *Connecticut Journal*, 27 February 1816: "a considerable time before the service, the church was filled. The slips below, with the exception of a few seats reserved for the aged, were entirely taken up by ladies; the galleries seemed loaded with spectators—the aisles and avenues of the church, both in the galleries and below, and even the steps around the rails of the altar, were crowded with attentive hearers."

82. See *Journals of the Annual Convention of the Diocese of Connecticut from 1792–1820* (New Haven: Stanley & Chapin, 1842), in "parish reports" section.

83. Croswell, "Annals," 82.

84. Ibid.

85. Town had also worked on Hartford's new City Hall and the Phoenix (Episcopal) Bank. See Roger Hale Newton, *Town and Davis, Architects: Pioneers in American Revivalist Architecture, 1812–70* (New York: Columbia University Press, 1942), 56.

86. See Nelson Rollin Burr, *A History of Christ Church Parish and Cathedral, Hartford, Connecticut, 1762–1941* (Hartford: Church Mission Publishing Co., 1942); *Celebration of the Semi-centennial Anniversary of the Consecration of Christ Church, Hartford, Dec. 23, 1879* (Hartford: Case, Lockwood, & Brainard Co., 1879); *Contributions to the History of Christ Church, Hartford*, comp. Gurdon Russell (Hartford: Belknap & Warfield, 1895).

87. This petition raised $445 in subscriptions of $5–30 each. Hartford, Christ Episcopal Society Records, 7 December 1807 transcript of 10 April 1807 petition, CSL mf.

88. Recorded in *The Motto* 2 (10 November 1851).

89. Cited in *Celebration of the Semi-centennial Anniversary of the Consecration of Christ Church, Hartford*, 71.

90. Nathaniel Wheaton to Charles Sigourney, Cambridge, England, 9 December 1823, reprinted in *The Historiographer of the Episcopal Diocese of Connecticut* 16 (May 1956).

91. Nathaniel Wheaton to Charles Sigourney, 27 December 1823, reprinted in *The Historiographer of the Episcopal Diocese of Connecticut* 16 (May 1956).

92. Nathaniel Wheaton, London, 27 March 1824, reprinted in *The Historiographer of the Episcopal Diocese of Connecticut* (May 1950; letter's recipient unknown). These sentiments were repeated by Wheaton in the sermon he gave at the laying of the cornerstone for Christ Church in May of 1828: "It would be no wish of ours, were the thing possible, to build on the ruins of other denominations, who hold the essentials of the christian faith." "While we conscientiously differ from some of our Christian brethren, on points not unimportant; we desire to be united with all who love the Lord Jesus in sincerity." Unitarians, however, were explicitly outside this vision of cooperation. *Connecticut Mirror*, 19 May 1828.

93. *Episcopal Watchman*, 9 April 1827.

94. Ibid.

95. *Episcopal Watchman*, 26 March 1827.

96. Barksdale Maynard, in his provocative reassessment of the picturesque in America, shows how the neoclassical aesthetic of "plain but elegant" may be considered a picturesque category and argues that even the Greek Revival style was more picturesque than political. William Barksdale Maynard, "The Picturesque and American Architecture: A Reappraisal" (Ph.D. diss, University of Delaware, 1997), 490. This more expansive understanding of terminology may in turn explain the how contemporaries could use the term "elegant"—generally thought of in relation to the neoclassical—to describe *Gothic* style. See also William H. Pierson, Jr., *American Buildings and their Architects*, vol. 2, *Technology and the Picturesque, the Corporate and Early Gothic Styles* (New York: Oxford University Press, 1978), 9–148.

97. *Journal of the Proceedings of the Annual Convention*, 1823, 18.

98. *Episcopal Watchman*, 9 January 1830.

99. *Connecticut Mirror*, 19 December 1828.

100. Nathaniel Wheaton to Bishop Hobart, 29 December 1829. Wheaton File, Episcopal Diocesan House, Hartford.

101. Henry R. Cleveland, review of James Gallier, "The American Builder's General Price Book and Estimator; deduced from extensive Experience in the Art of Building," *North American Review* 93 (October 1836): 367.

102. Ibid., 370.

103. The *Hartford Courant* reported 24 February 1829 on the "ingenious" roof frame: "they [the frames] are put together with mortise and tenon; and although their weight, including that of the slating, is estimated at 80 tons, and they are unsupported from wall to wall, not the least tendency to spread can be observed." Other remarks in the article also considered raw construction: "strength and durability," thick walls, heavily timbered floors and galleries, projecting front bu-

tresses, and a "degree of strength scarcely to be paralleled in any building in this part of the country."

104. Nathaniel Wheaton to Bishop J. H. Hobart, 15 December 1829, Wheaton File, Episcopal Diocesan House, Hartford.

105. *Celebration of the Semi-centennial Anniversary of the Consecration of Christ Church, Hartford*, 14–16.

106. James Wells, Journal, 24 March 1833, 38, Connecticut State Library Archives.

107. Hartford, Christ Episcopal Society Records, 8 March 1830, CSL mf.

Chapter 4. The Sacred and the Sentimental (pp. 125–64)

1. Recommendation of Prof. Cogswell to Perkins and Marvin regarding new psalmody, letter dated 19 November 1832. Hartford North (Park) Congregational Society Records, section G (loose papers), CSL. Perkins might have been a church member; records show that there was a Thomas Perkins on the building committee in 1823.

2. Many scholars have acknowledged this puzzling "meetinghouse to church" transition. See Sinnott, *Meeting House and Church*; Philip D. Zimmerman, in "Ecclesiastical Architecture in the Reformed Tradition in Rockingham County," explains the shift as something that happened later in New Hampshire, and as a result of changing in preaching styles; Benes and Zimmerman, eds., *New England Meeting House and Church*; Kelly, *Early Connecticut Meetinghouses*; and Sweeney, "Meetinghouses, Town Houses, and Churches." Sweeney's article offers the most persuasive attempt to explain the shift from meetinghouse to church and focuses on the appearance of the town house in rural New England.

3. James White describes two different approaches to Protestant worship, either "work done in God's service" or "primarily a matter of feelings" (the sense that one is "getting something out of" worship). In early-nineteenth-century Connecticut churches the intention was to accomplish both ends. Several decades later, "the feelings of the worshiper really became the prime focus in worship," and that continues to this day in most Protestant denominations. James F. White, *Protestant Worship and Church Architecture: Theological and Historical Considerations* (New York: Oxford University Press, 1964), 3–25.

4. Kling, *Field of Divine Wonders*, 193. See also Sydney Ahlstrom, *A Religious History of the American People* (New Haven: Yale University Press, 1972), 415–17.

5. Kling, *Field of Divine Wonders*, 176–77.

6. Ibid., 170. In the latter portion of this period, Kling found the gender difference even more dramatic. From 1807 to 1822, twice as many women as men joined the Hartford and Litchfield County churches (179).

7. Ibid., 241, 243.

8. Ibid., 2.

9. See William Breitenbach, "Piety *and* Moralism: Edwards and the New Divinity," in *Jonathan Edwards and the American Experience*, edited by Nathan Hatch and Harry S. Stout (New York: Oxford University Press, 1988), 177–204. Breitenbach writes, "*Religious Affections* was perhaps the most important work in the development of Edwardsian "new" divinity" (183). Breitenbach argues that the theology in the *Affections* was Edwards's response to Arminians (those who argued that their own efforts were able to work salvation, hence encouraging legalism)

and Antinomians (those who claimed actions had nothing to do with salvation, leading to moral anarchy). Edwards, according to Breitenbach, found a middle ground. God alone changed hearts (and, consequently, human wills), which brought salvation in the first place, and that change of heart necessarily resulted in an intuitive attraction to the good. It asked Christians to focus on their heart feelings but brilliantly directed those feelings toward what was morally appropriate.

10. Terminology can be somewhat confusing because words like "sensible" or "sentimental" have numerous uses, both today and in the past. For the purposes of this study, "sentiment" is thought guided by emotion and having a moral purpose; "sensibility" is the capacity to have those feelings; and "sentimentality" is usually pejorative, referring to an indulgence in feeling for its own sake. I use "the culture of sensibility" to describe the general belief throughout the period of this study that right feelings were essential to proper moral character as revealed in political, religious, and social behavior.

11. Colin Campbell, *The Romantic Ethic and the Spirit of Modern Consumerism* (Oxford: Basil Blackwell, 1987).

12. Kenneth Charles Hafertepe, "The Enlightened Sensibility: Scottish Philosophy in American Art and Architecture" (Ph.D. diss., University of Texas at Austin, 1986).

13. Archibald Alison, *Essays on the Nature and Principles of Taste*, 1790, discussed in Campbell, *The Romantic Ethic*, 153 ff.; see also Hafertepe, "The Enlightened Sensibility."

14. See, for example, Jules Prown, "Style as Evidence," *Winterthur Portfolio* 15 (autumn 1980): 197–210; Alan Gowans, *Images of American Living: Four Centuries of Architecture and Furniture as Cultural Expression* (New York: Harper & Row, 1964); Cooper, *The Classical Taste in America*.

15. Neil Harris, *The Artist in American Society: The Formative Years, 1790–1860* (New York: George Braziller, 1966), 41; see also David L. Barquist, " 'The Honours of a Court' or 'the Severity of Virtue': Household Furnishings and Cultural Aspirations in Philadelphia," in *Shaping a National Culture: The Philadelphia Experience, 1750–1800*, edited by Catherine E. Hutchins (Winterthur, Del.: Henry Francis du Pont Winterthur Museum, 1991), and Kevin M. Sweeney, "High Style Vernacular: The Lifestyles of the Colonial Elite," in *Of Consuming Interest: The Style of Life in the Eighteenth Century*, edited by Cary Carson, Ronald Hoffman, and Peter J. Albert (Charlottesville: University Press of Virginia for the United States Capitol Historical Society, 1994), 1–58.

16. Charles Brockton Brown, *Wieland; or, The Transformation* (New York: H. Caritat, 1798).

17. David Kling explains how New Divinity ministers adapted these ideas into what he calls a "theology of proportionality." Recognizing an Enlightenment concern for order and balance, they emphasized that God's laws were absolutely logical, rational, and aesthetically satisfying. Kling, *Field of Divine Wonders*, 82–85.

18. Amos Townsend, "Religious Reminiscences from 1806 to 1826" (c. 1876), manuscript journal, 5, New Haven Colony Historical Society.

19. Kling discusses the importance of the lecture room setting to these revivals in *Field of Divine Wonders*, 68–69.

20. Townsend, "Reminiscences," 8

21. *Connecticut Evangelical Magazine* 2 (March 1809): 98.

22. Ibid., 99.

23. Ibid., 103.

24. *Connecticut Evangelical Magazine* 6 (May 1806): 431.

25. Sweeney, "Meetinghouses, Town Houses, and Churches." See also Davies, *The Secular Use of Church Buildings*.

26. William Ellery Channing, *Discourse preached at the Dedication of the Second Congregational Unitarian Church, New York, December 7, 1826* (New York: Second Congregational Unitarian Church, 1827), 4.

27. Ibid., 5.

28. Ibid.

29. Calvin, *Institutes*, book III.xx.30.

30. Ibid.

31. Davies, *The Secular Use of Church Buildings*, 115. For a helpful consideration of iconoclasm as a means of *asserting* the power of images, see Lee Palmer Wandel, *Voracious Idols and Violent Hands: Iconoclasm in Reformation Zurich, Strasbourg, and Basel* (Cambridge: Cambridge University Press, 1995).

32. See Andrew Landale Drummond, *The Church Architecture of Protestantism: An Historical and Constructive Study* (Edinburgh: T. & T. Clark, 1934); Keith Thomas, *Religion and the Decline of Magic* (New York: Scribner, 1971).

33. This is found particularly in older and art historical interpretations that rely on stereotypes of Puritans as dour or at least doctrinally tyrannical. See Noah Porter, "The New England Meeting House" (1882; reprinted in *Tercentenary Commission of the State of Connecticut* 1993, no. 17, 1–34); Arthur B. Mazmanian, *The Structure of Praise—a Design Study: Architecture for Religion in New England from the Seventeenth Century to the Present* (Boston: Beacon Press, 1970). Kevin Sweeney's more recent "Meetinghouses, Town Houses, and Churches" softens this in line with scholarship offering less severe interpretations of New England Puritans in general, such as Hambrick-Stowe, *The Practice of Piety*.

34. [Cotton Mather], *Thirty Important Cases, Resolved with Evidence of Scripture and Reason [Mostly] by Several Pastors of Adjacent Churches, Meeting in Cambridge, New-England* (Boston: Bartholomew Green and John Allen, 1699), 64. Cited in Sweeney, "Meetinghouses, Town Houses, and Churches," 60.

35. Sweeney, "Meetinghouses, Town Houses, and Churches," 60–61. See also James P. Walsh, "Holy Time and Sacred Space in Puritan New England," *American Quarterly* 32 (spring 1980): 79–95. Walsh makes no argument for meetinghouses, but does describe how Puritans sacralized their environment, in fact holding the belief that some places and times were more "holy" than others, despite theology to the contrary. This is precisely the same sort of simultaneous, apparently contradictory belief that I find in the culture surrounding these early-nineteenth-century buildings.

36. Hambrick-Stowe, *The Practice of Piety*, 51, 211–212.

37. Eliade, *The Sacred and the Profane*; see chapter 1, "Sacred Space and Making the World Sacred."

38. Mary Ellen Hern has suggested that these arched ceilings may have a stylistic or technical connection to the domed ceilings built somewhat earlier in regional tavern ballrooms, for example, the Haviland Tavern built in Rye, New York, c. 1779–84. This interesting idea, which would challenge sacred associations of this form, deserves further investigation.

39. See for example, John Wesley Cook, *Art and Religion: Faith, Form, and Reform*, Paine Lectures in Religion, 1984, edited by Osmund Overby (Columbia: University of Missouri–Columbia, 1986).

40. Robbins, *Diary*, 3 December 1807.

41. Strong, *Sermon*.

42. Ibid., 5, 6, 7, 8, 6.

43. Ibid., 8, 10.

44. Ibid., 9, 10, 9–10.

45. Ibid., 12, 14–15, 12.

46. Ibid., 5, 14, 20, 19–20.

47. Joel Hawes, *A Sermon Delivered at the Dedication of the North Congregational Church in Hartford, December 1, 1824* (Hartford: Goodwin & Co., 1825), 5.

48. Ibid., 11, 13, 14, 18.

49. The surprising use of the term "altar," which Hawes uses here to describe the communion table, is occasionally seen in other church records of the period, evidence of how far the language of sentiment had overtaken some older Puritan conventions.

50. Hawes, *Sermon*, 19, 20, 19, 25, 26, 29.

51. Joel Harvey Linsley, *A Sermon Delivered at the dedication of the Second or South Congregational Church in Hartford, April 11, 1827* (Hartford: D. F. Robinson, 1827), 6, 8.

52. Ibid., 7, 11, 15.

53. Ibid., 8, 21, 20–21.

54. Bushman, *The Refinement of America*. See especially chapter 6, "Ambivalence," and chapter 10, "Religion and Taste."

55. Rev. Elisha Atkins, *A Sermon delivered Nov. 18, 1818, at the Dedication of the Congregational Meeting House in the North Parish of Killingly* (Providence: Miller & Hutchins, 1819), 10–11.

56. Strong, *Sermon*, 9, 14.

57. Hawes, *Sermon*, 25.

58. "On the propriety of private religious meetings," *Connecticut Evangelical Magazine* 4 (May 1811): 181.

59. *Episcopal Watchman*, 7 June 1831.

60. Strong, *Sermon*, 9.

61. "On the sacredness of churches," *Churchman's Monthly Magazine* 4 (November 1806): 420–24.

62. Strong, *Sermon*, 14.

63. Hawes, *Sermon*, 10.

64. Linsley, *Sermon*, 8.

65. Jack Larkin briefly discusses the introduction of fancy church music in *The Reshaping of Everyday Life, 1790–1840* (New York: Harper & Row, 1988) 251–57.

66. Terry Bilhartz, in his study of Baltimore at this time, noted the gradual acceptance of organ music and claims it was used to maintain order and dignity in worship. Terry Bilhartz, *Urban Religion and the Second Great Awakening: Church and Society in Early National Baltimore* (Rutherford, N.J.: Associated University Presses, 1986).

67. See Horton Davies, *The Worship of the American Puritans* (Morgan, Pa: Soli Deo Gloria Publications, 1990), 124–45.

68. On the origins of Yankee singing schools, see Alan C. Buechner, "Thomas Walter and the Society for Promoting Regular Singing in the Worship of God: Boston, 1720–23," in *New England Music: The Public Sphere, 1600–1900*, edited by Peter Benes (Boston: Boston University for the Dublin Seminar for New England Folklife, 1998), 48–60.

69. Stephen Marini, "Evangelical Hymns and Popular Belief," *New England Music*, edited by Peter Benes, 117–26.

70. Hatch, *Democratization of American Christianity*, 147.

71. William Lyman, *The design and benefits of Instrumental Musick considered on a sermon, delivered at Lebanon-Goshen May 7, 1807, on the occasion of having an Organ introduced as an aid in the worship and melody of God's house* (New London: Ebenezer P. Cadt, 1807).

72. Ibid., 6.

73. Ibid., 6.

74. Ibid., 7–9. Many similar arguments were made in various lectures and sermons in New England in the first two decades of the nineteenth century. See, for example Daniel Dana, *An Address on Sacred Music Delivered at a public meeting of the Rockingham Sacred Music Society* (Exeter, N.H., 1814); William Bascom Fitchburg, *Discourse Delivered at a Singing Lecture* (Boston: Lincoln and Edmands, 1814); Samuel Worcester, *Address on Sacred Music delivered before the Middlesex Musical Society & the Handel Society of Dartmouth College* (Boston: Manning & Loring, 1811).

75. Lyman, *The design*, 14–18.

76. *Churchman's Monthly Magazine* 5 (May–June 1808): 175–77.

77. Hartford, First Baptist Church Records, 10 March 1809, CSL mf.

78. Hartford, First Baptist Church Records, 1 January 1811, CSL mf.

79. Hartford, First Baptist Church Records, 8 June 1811, CSL mf.

80. Mary Treadwell Hooker, Record Book, 19 February 1804, Connecticut State Library Archives. Hooker probably was worried about impropriety because of her advanced age. I am indebted to Paula Scott for this reference.

81. Harry Croswell, Diary, 29 August 1821, Manuscripts and Archives, Yale University Library.

82. Hartford, Second (South) Congregational Church Choir Records (1840–42), Connecticut Historical Society Library.

83. "Sacred Music," *Litchfield County Post*, 16 February 1827.

84. Lyman, "The design," 7–9.

85. Rev. Samuel Gilman, *Memoir of a New England Village Choir* (Boston: S. G. Goodrich, 1829), 32–33.

86. Robbins, *Diary*, 24 March 1799.

87. Winchester, First Congregational Society Records, 16 November 1809, CSL mf.

88. Hartford, First Congregational Society Records, December 1812, CSL mf.

89. The Rev. William Bentley, *Diary of William Bentley*, vol. 1 (Salem, Mass.: Essex Institute, 1911), 12 June 1791, 264. Bentley decried the lack of talent, the jealousies, and the financial problems that attended choirs.

90. Gilman, *Memoir of a New England Village Choir*, 44.

91. Bentley, *Diary*, vol. 3, 415–16 (12 February 1809).

92. Edwin Liemohn, *The Organ and Choir in Protestant Worship* (Philadelphia: Fortress Press, 1968), 111.

93. The Stratford Episcopal Church claims to have had the first organ in the colony, acquired from Gilbert Deblois of Boston for sixty pounds sterling, raised by subscription. The congregation used this organ until 1879. William H. Wicoxson, *The History of Stratford, Connecticut, 1639–1939* (Stratford: Stratford Tercentenary Commission, 1939), 459–60.

94. Receipt, New Haven, United Society Records, IV.A., New Haven Colony Historical Society.

95. Hartford, First Congregational Society Records, 1 June 1822, CSL mf.

96. Hartford, North (Park) Congregational Society Records, 6 February 1828, CSL mf.

97. James Jackson to J. D. Huntington, 24 July 1829. Litchfield Historical Society documents. Bill for the cost of transporting the organ from New York to Litchfield was itself $82.78. This must have been quite a production; Jackson asked Huntington to meet the steamboat with "3 waggons at least."

98. Robbins, *Diary*, 18 May 1825. The Norfolk organ was acquired in 1822; see Kelly, *Early Connecticut Meetinghouses*, vol. 2, 70.

99. Salisbury Town Records, Meeting Minutes, 13 April 1801.

100. Hartford, North (Park) Congregational Society Records, 1829 (unspecified day), CSL mf.

101. Harry Croswell, Diary, 22 May 1822. Manuscripts and Archives, Yale University Library.

102. *Connecticut Mirror*, 19 September 1825.

103. See Leigh Eric Schmidt, " 'A Church-going People are a Dress-loving People': Clothes, Communication, and Religious Culture in Early America," *Church History* 58 (March 1989): 36–51. Schmidt suggests that churchgoers communicated in a variety of ways, arguing against logocentric interpretations of early American religious experience. "Gesture, deportment, posture, and procession, as well as architectural settings, objects, and emblems—all these and more were employed to carry religious messages" (37).

104. "Directions for a devout and decent behavior in the Public Worship of God," *Churchman's Monthly Magazine* (August 1804): 113–16.

105. Ibid.

106. "On the Manner of Divine Worship," *Churchman's Monthly Magazine* (July 1805): 154

107. *Episcopal Watchman*, 12 January 1833.

108. *Litchfield Enquirer*, 13 August 1829.

109. *Episcopal Watchman*, 19 January 1833. Taken from the "Cincinnati Standard" (probably *The Standard*, a Cincinnati Baptist publication running from 1831 to 1832).

110. Morris, Congregational Church Records, 10 December 1819, CSL mf.

111. *Memoir of Miss Eliza Brainard who Died in Haddam, November 30, 1820* (Middletown, Conn.: Clark & Lyman, 1821), 9.

112. Ibid., 16.

113. Hartford, First Congregational Society Records, December 1807 (exact day unclear), CSL mf.

114. Hartford, Second Congregational Society Records, 6 April 1818, CSL mf. This vote was reversed the following month, reversed again a year later, and finally reconsidered in March of 1820. Clearly there was some disagreement. Hartford Second (South) Congregational Society Records, 5 May 1818; 22 April 1819; 3 March 1820, CSL mf.

115. Roxbury, Congregational Society Records, 23 December 1794, CSL mf.

116. Roxbury, Congregational Society Records, 5 December 1803, 3 May 1804, CSL mf.

117. Roxbury, Congregational Society Records, misc. docs., petition dated 1821, CSL mf.

118. Ibid.

119. Zuckerman, "Holy Wars, Civil Wars," 215.

120. *Connecticut Courant*, 16 October 1826, printed a hymn for the cattle fair:

"To Thee, O God, the Shepherd King . . . God of Nature . . . smile upon our festive rite."

121. Poem written for dedication of new building of First Congregational Society, New Haven. *Connecticut Journal*, 2 January 1815.

122. Poem by "Alumnus," *New England Magazine* 1 (August 1831): 149–50.

123. "Consecration of a Church," *Episcopal Watchman*, 26 December 1829.

124. Theodonia Woolsey to James A. Hillhouse, 17 February 1813, Hillhouse Family Papers, Manuscripts and Archives, Yale University Library.

125. "Farewell to an Ancient Church," *Episcopal Watchman*, 26 December 1829.

126. "A New England Village," *Litchfield County Post*, 4 July 1826.

127. "Old Parish Church," *Connecticut Courant*, 20 March 1826.

128. "Dedication of First Congregational Church, New Haven," *Connecticut Journal*, 2 January 1815.

129. "New England Village," *Litchfield County Post*, 4 July 1826.

130. "On Entering Church," *Episcopal Watchman*, 10 December 1827.

131. "On Opening a New House of Worship," hymn 343 in Nathan Strong and Abel Flint, *The Hartford Selection of Hymns*, 3d ed. (1799; Hartford: P. B. Gleason, 1810).

132. "Consecration of a Church," *Episcopal Watchman*, 26 December 1829.

133. "New England Village," *Litchfield County Post*, 4 July 1826.

134. L. H. S. (Lydia Huntley Sigourney), "The Lonely Church," *Episcopal Watchman*, 4 August 1832.

135. Ibid.

136. Ibid.

137. Ibid.

138. An excellent discussion of girls' education in Hartford is found in Joan D. Hedrick, *Harriet Beecher Stowe: A Life* (New York: Oxford University Press, 1994).

139. Jane Austen, *Mansfield Park*, 1814 (reprint; New York: Penguin Books, 1979), 69.

140. *Episcopal Watchman*, 2 February 1833.

141. Dedication 1 September 1836. Hymn written for the occasion by John H. Collins. Cited in Elbert S. Richards, *History of the West Goshen, Methodist Church* (1877), Goshen, West Goshen Methodist Church Records, CSL. This is probably another expression of the sort of "mainstreaming" of former outsider denominations that Nathan Hatch describes in *The Democratization of American Christianity*.

142. Edward. A. Kendall, *Travels through the Northern Parts of the United States in the years 1807 and 1808* (New York: I. Riley, 1809), 131.

Chapter 5. Religious Architecture and Republican Community (pp. 165–97)

1. See Walsh, "Holy Time and Sacred Space."

2. Sassi, *A Republic of Righteousness*. Sassi's work is a study of the clergy of southern New England (Massachusetts and Connecticut) with a concentration on Worcester County, Massachusetts. By emphasizing the individualism and democratizing impulses of this period, Sassi argues, previous scholarship has largely missed the active participation of and important contributions made by Congregational clergy. Using Jonathan Edwards's notion of "disinterested benevolence,"

these ministers forcefully shaped the "public Christianity" of New England and set the stage for the era of moral reform to follow. Sassi uses the term "public Christianity" meaning "the ways in which ministers tried to make religious beliefs and values speak to the problems of life in society" (10).

3. These ideas are discussed by Donald Scott in chapter 3 of *From Office to Profession: The New England Ministry, 1750–1850* (Philadelphia: University of Pennsylvania Press, 1978). See also Donald G. Mathews, "The Second Great Awakening as an Organizing Process, 1780–1830," *American Quarterly* 21 (spring 1969): 23–43. Mathews argues that the first Great Awakening (mid-eighteenth-century revivals) was a reorganization of authority inside the churches; the second, on the other hand, was concerned with expansion and had a strong "recruiting impulse."

4. Reports from approximately half the towns in Connecticut are being edited for publication by the Connecticut Historical Society and the Connecticut Academy of Arts and Sciences. A companion volume will contain interpretive essays. See Carolyn Cooper, ed., *Voices of the New Republic: Connecticut Towns 1800–1832* (New Haven: Yale University Press, forthcoming).

5. Circular letter printed in Timothy Dwight, *A Statistical Account of the City of New Haven* (New Haven: Walter & Steele, 1811), vi–xi.

6. David D. Field, *A Statistical Account of the County of Middlesex, in Connecticut* (Middletown, Conn.: Clark & Lyman, 1819).

7. David D. Field, "Narrative Account of Middlesex County," typescript provided by Connecticut Academy of Arts and Sciences, 15.

8. For a thorough treatment of civil religion, see Robert Bellah, *Varieties of Civil Religion* (San Francisco: Harper & Row, 1980). I am using "civil religion" to mean a collection of values (here with a Protestant cast) that, although moral, are not specifically doctrinal but are closely tied to national identity and the political beliefs of the ruling classes.

9. See Harry S. Stout, "Rhetoric and Reality in the Early Republic: The Case of the Federal Clergy," in *Religion and American Politics from the Colonial Period to the 1980s*, edited by Mark A. Noll (New York: Oxford University Press, 1990), 62–76. Stout explained the ability of clergy to live in different "rhetorical worlds" that existed in tension. On the one hand, they had an "identity as Christian people" and inherited the covenant responsibility of the Puritans to make sure that America was a Christian nation. Yet they also participated in a republican polity that valued the separation of church and state. That republican state depended on virtue, and these thinkers could not imagine virtue existing without regular Christian observance and instruction. Using Timothy Dwight and other New England divines/cultural critics, Stout argued that in the end, political thinking evolved to a point where "individual salvation was not required at all, but corporate morality was" (70).

10. For an older interpretation, see Arthur M. Schlesinger, Jr., *The Age of Jackson* (Boston: Little, Brown, 1945), 137–143. Schlesinger claimed the Sabbatarians were marginal to more important political issues of the day.

11. Richard R. John, "Taking Sabbatarianism Seriously: The Postal System, the Sabbath, and the Transformation of American Political Culture," *Journal of the Early Republic* 10 (winter 1990): 517–67, quotation, 530; James Rohrer, "Sunday Mails and the Church-State Theme in Jacksonian America," *Journal of the Early Republic* 7 (spring 1987): 53–74.

12. John, "Taking Sabbatarianism Seriously," 531.

13. Elbridge Gerry, Jr., *The Diary of Elbridge Gerry, Jr.* (reprint; New York:

Brentano's, 1927). The 1813 journey by the son of Vice President Elbridge Gerry; 7 May 1813 visit to Hartford, n.p.

14. Mary G. Camp, Journal, June 1818–January 1834, Connecticut State Library Archives.

15. *Connecticut Courant*, 17 January 1810.

16. Ibid.

17. See Robert Handy, *A Christian America: Protestant Hopes and Historical Realities* (New York: Oxford University Press, 1971), 21–56.

18. David Daggett to Wealthy Ann Daggett, 20 December 1815, Daggett Family Papers, Manuscripts and Archives, Yale University Library.

19. Timothy Dwight, *Travels in New England and New York*, vol. 4 *The Establishment of the public worship of God in Connecticut* (New Haven, 1822), 390.

20. Ibid., 391.

21. Ibid., 390.

22. Raymond Williams, *Keywords* (New York: Oxford University Press, 1983), 313–15.

23. Dwight argued that taste may come from within, and proper instruction could develop that innate sense of taste, which could then lead one toward religious truth. For Edwards, a sense of Christian taste was an important *result* of sanctification, emanating from a spiritual source and constantly drawing one back to that source and to all good things.

24. Dwight, *Travels*, vol. 2, 473.

25. *Connecticut Mirror*, 17 December 1823.

26. Bushman, *The Refinement of America*. See especially chapter 5, "Cities and Churches," and chapter 10, "Religion and Taste."

27. Dwight, *Travels*, vol. 2, 473.

28. Ibid., 474.

29. Ibid., 475.

30. Elizur May, *The Spiritual Presence of the Lord Jesus Christ in his house of worship its greatest glory* (Hartford: Ebenezer Watson, 1772), 24.

31. Jarvis, *Address*.

32. Hawes, *Sermon*, 13.

33. Norbert Elias discussed the concept of "civilization" as it grew in western Europe after the Middle Ages in *The Civilizing Process: The History of Manners* (Basel, 1939; English translation, New York: Urizen Books, 1978), 3–50. According to Elias, civilization became a self-conscious concept in the West, one with distinct nationalistic overtones after the French Revolution. Implicit was a belief in cultural superiority. After the French Revolution, "civilization" came to mean more particularly the "Western Powers" (30). "Civilization" described an ongoing process, as Elias noted (4), and Americans perceived themselves as part of this movement of "civilization." More weight was added to American shoulders when it appeared they were being handed the cultural baton from the decaying European civilizations as art and power moved westward. See Ellis, *After the Revolution*, chapter 1, "Premonitions: An American Athens," 3–21.

34. *Churchman's Monthly Magazine* (September 1806): 9.

35. Dwight, *Travels*, vol. 3, 126.

36. For a discussion of the importance of the landscape itself to early Americans, see Karol Ann Peard Lawson, "An Inexhaustible Abundance: National Landscape, 1780–1820," *Journal of the Early Republic* 12 (fall 1992): 303–330.

37. "WESTERN CANAL," *Danbury Recorder*, 7 March 1826, 4. These terms were also used by Joel Hawes in *An Address Delivered at the request of the citizens of Hartford, on the 9th of November, 1835*, 6. Hawes wrote, "instead of savage tribes, we behold communities of civilized men; instead of the murky Indian hut, we behold comfortable houses and splendid public edifices . . . ," 6.

38. Joel Hawes, *Address*, 51–52.

39. David Austin, *The Rod of Moses upon the Rock of Calvary; or the mountains of fire, and of blood, a Dedicatory Discourse at the opening of a place of worship, west-parish of Franklin, December 21, 1815* (Norwich: Russell Hubbard, 1816), 23–24.

40. Dwight, *Travels*, vol. 4, 511.

41. Timothy Dwight, *Greenfield Hill: a poem, in seven parts* (New York: Childs and Swaine, 1794), 1: 155; 7: 40; 1: 342–45.

42. See Nancy J. Brcak, "Country Carpenters, Federal Buildings: An Early Architectural Tradition in Ohio's Western Reserve," *Ohio History* 98 (summer–autumn 1989): 131–46.

43. Frederick Marryat, *Diary in America with Remarks on its Institutions* (New York: William H. Colyer, 1839), 204–14.

44. Pitkin Cowles, *A Sermon Preached at the Dedication of the Church in North Canaan, February 19th, 1823, by the late Rev. Pitkin Cowles, Pastor* (Hartford: Elihu Geer, 1823), 13.

45. Diodate Brockway, *A Sermon, Delivered in Ellington, June 25, 1806, at the dedication of the New Meeting House in that place.* (Hartford: Lincoln Gleason, 1807), 23.

46. Robbins, *Diary*, 18 March 1825.

47. *Connecticut Mirror*, 12 June 1830. During the period of this study Catholics were a very minor presence and therefore not much of a threat; there was not even a settled priest in Connecticut until the late 1820s. Purcell, *Connecticut in Transition*, 61.

48. *Connecticut Journal*, 27 February 1816.

49. William Leffingwell, Diary, 1765–1834, 22 November 1815, Leffingwell Family Papers, Manuscripts and Archives, Yale University Library.

50. *Connecticut Journal*, 27 November 1815.

51. See Henry T. Blake, *Chronicles of the New Haven Green from 1638 to 1862* (New Haven, 1898), 11. New Haven's central space was first called "the green," rather than "market place," in a 1759 *New Haven Gazette* advertisement; by 1784 the city sometimes referred to the green as the "public square."

52. In 1785 the Connecticut General Assembly had granted New Haven incorporation as a city.

53. Sophos Staples to Emily [   ], 20 August 1814, Baldwin Family Papers, Manuscripts and Archives, Yale University Library.

54. See Jonathan G. Lowett, "The Elms of Elm City," *Journal of the New Haven Colony Historical Society* 38 (fall 1991): 47–63.

55. *Connecticut Journal*, 27 November 1815.

56. *Connecticut Mirror*, 16 April 1827.

57. Ibid.

58. James T. Pratt to [   ], 12 June 1823. Typescript copy, Connecticut State Library Archives.

59. Payne Kenyon Kilbourne, *Sketches and Chronicles of the Town of Litchfield,*

Connecticut: Historical, Biographical, and Statistical (Hartford: Press of Case, Lockwood and Co., 1859). According to this source, the 1820 census recorded a population of 4,610.

60. William Williams to his wife (Litchfield to hometown of Utica, N.Y.), 18 May 1818, Connecticut State Library Archives.

61. Ibid.

62. Elmer Booth to Nicholas B. Booth, 31 January 1831, Connecticut State Library Archives.

63. William Butler, "Another City upon a Hill: Litchfield, Connecticut, and the Colonial Revival," in *The Colonial Revival in America*, edited by Alan Axelrod (New York: W. W. Norton, 1985), 26–27. Butler concluded that the meetinghouse was red based on microscopic analysis and Ralph Earl portraits showing a red meetinghouse with a white steeple in the background. An 1817 sketch by Mary Anne Lewis also shows the meetinghouse red.

64. Stowe's *Reminiscences* cited in George T. Peck, "The Meeting House on the Hill," in *A History of the First Congregational Church in Litchfield, Connecticut, on Its 126th Anniversary and 25th Anniversary of Its Restoration* (Litchfield, 1955), 8.

65. Kendall, *Travels*, vol. 1, 236.

66. New American Standard translation.

67. Connecticut's Presbyterians and Congregationalists formed a loose association at this time, hence the blurring of denominational lines. The Litchfield congregation remained technically Congregational.

68. *Litchfield County Post*, 29 August 1826.

69. Regarding the society's decisions, see Kelly, *Early Connecticut Meetinghouses*, vol. 1, 279; *Litchfield County Post*, 26 June 1828 and 3 July 1828.

70. *Hartford City Directory* (Hartford: Price & Lee, 1828; reprint, Price & Lee Co., 1937). See also John Warner Barber, *Hartford Historical Collections: History and Antiquities* (New Haven and Hartford, 1836; reprint, Hartford Architectural Conservancy, 1976). This religious profile was typical for towns in western Connecticut: Congregationalists remained the majority, followed by Episcopalians and increasingly challenged by Baptists, Methodists, and Universalists (Unitarians were scarce in western Connecticut at this time). In eastern Connecticut there were proportionately more Baptists and fewer Episcopalians, but with the Congregationalists still dominant and an equal range of religious options.

71. See *Centennial Memorial of the First Baptist Church of Hartford, Connecticut* (Hartford: Christian Secretary, 1890); also Hartford, First Baptist Church Records and Hartford, Central Baptist Church Records, CSL mf. The addition of one hundred new members in 1832 led to the formation of a new congregation, South Baptist (*Centennial Memorial*, 28).

72. Glenn Weaver, *Hartford: An Illustrated History of Connecticut's Capital* (Woodland Hills, Calif. : Windsor Publications for the Connecticut Historical Society, 1982), 68.

73. James T. Pratt to [   ], 12 June 1823, Connecticut State Library Archives. Pratt mentions, "the Universal Church is progressing. It is as large on the ground as the Brick Church in this city."

74. Croswell, Diary, 8 August 1821.

75. "Plan For the disposing of the Pews in the New Episcopal Church," 1815. New Haven, Trinity Episcopal Church Records, New Haven Colony Historical Society Archives.

76. Croswell, Diary, 9 April 1821. See also 12 April 1821. Croswell's lectures to

African-Americans happened with some regularity. See also Carol V. George, *Segregated Sabbaths* (New York: Oxford University Press, 1973).

77. Kendall, *Travels*, vol. 1, 141.

78. See Ellsworth Strong Grant and Marion Hepburn Grant, *The City of Hartford, 1784–1984: An Illustrated History* (Hartford: Connecticut Historical Society, 1984).

79. Town Votes, Hartford, December 1816, cited in Mary Talcott, "The town since 1784," in Trumbull, ed., *History of Hartford County*, 361.

80. *Connecticut Courant*, 19 June 1826.

81. Ibid.

82. This location placed them off Main Street toward the river, east of the 1830 Catholic Church also on Talcott Street. It is worth noting that these two marginal religious groups were neighbors and not located on Main Street.

83. *Connecticut Courant*, 12 November 1827.

84. *Litchfield County Post*, 29 November 1827.

85. The Talcott Street Congregational Church became so symbolic of the African-American community in Hartford that it was targeted for violence by white racists in 1835. The *Hartford Courant*, 15 June 1835, reported that while the members gathered for worship, a white gang assembled outside, attacking the worshipers as they left.

86. "Report of Joint Committee on Subject of Free church," 9 December 1831. Hartford North (Park) Congregational Society Records, Treasurer's Reports (1830–55), CSL mf. Some Free Church records are filed with those for the North Church.

87. Hartford, Fourth (Free) Congregational Society Records, n.d., CSL mf.

88. Hartford, North (Park) Congregational Society, Treasurer's Reports (date of this document is unclear), CSL mf.

89. Ibid.

90. Hartford, Fourth (Free) Congregational Society Records, 12 April 1833, CSL mf.

91. The previous summer lightning had burned to the ground the congregation's former church. "Outline of ceremony at laying of cornerstone Old Lyme Congregational Church meeting house June 10, 1816," Connecticut Historical Society (ms 74676). This new Lyme church, not atypically for a rural congregation, had a rather high (although new-style) pulpit and pews with doors until 1850. See George Francis Marlowe, *Churches of Old New England: Their Architecture and Their Architects, Their Pastors and Their People* (New York: The Macmillan Co., 1947), 132.

92. Beginning in the late 1820s, notices of religious paintings on exhibition appeared in newspapers. For example, in Hartford, 1827, "The Bearing of the Cross," by Dunlap, and a "copy of da Vinci's Last Supper done by Mr. Parker of Connecticut," were on display in the Hartford State House. *Connecticut Mirror*, 12 November 1827. On 25 September 1830, the *Connecticut Mirror* noted that a "Celebrated painting of Christ Healing the Sick in the Temple is now exhibiting for a few days only, at the Masonic hall." This copy of West's original was purportedly "equal in the whole and superior in some points of view to the original." For an insightful essay on the Protestant appreciation of Catholic art, see John Davis, "Catholic Envy: The Visual Culture of Protestant Desire," in *The Visual Culture of American Religions*, edited by David Morgan and Sally M. Promey, (Berkeley: University of California Press, 2001), 105–28.

93. *Connecticut Mirror*, 23 April 1827.

94. *Episcopal Watchman*, 2 May 1829 (excerpt from *American Monthly Magazine*).

95. Eliade, *The Sacred and the Profane*, 59.

96. Croswell, Diary, 9 October 1821.

97. Susan G. Davis, *Parades and Power: Street Theatre in Nineteenth-Century Philadelphia* (Philadelphia: Temple University Press, 1986), 159.

98. I have found no evidence in church records or elsewhere that these buildings were ever used for African-American coronation festivals, although we do know that these took place in Hartford and New Haven in the late eighteenth and early nineteenth centuries. See Melvin Wade, " 'Shining in Borrowed Plumage': Affirmation of Community in the Black Coronation Festivals of New England, c. 1750–1850," in *Material Life in Early America, 1600–1860*, edited by Robert B. St. George (Boston: Northeastern University Press, 1988), 171–82.

99. Leffingwell, Diary, 8 September 1815.

100. *Connecticut Journal*, 18 September 1815.

101. Kendall, *Travels*, vol. 1 3–4.

102. Ibid.

103. Ibid.

104. Robbins, *Diary*, 4 May 1831.

105. Robbins, *Diary*, 13 June 1806.

106. Croswell, Diary, 1 November 1821. Another New Englander, Timothy Bigelow, noted in his 1815 *Diary* (Boston, 1880) "but *two* steeples!" in all of Philadelphia. One must assume, from these several references, that Philadelphia was a particularly significant opponent in this matter.

Chapter 6. Church Interiors and Christian Community (pp. 198–228)

1. Samuel Merwin to David Daggett, 5 May 1816, Daggett Family Papers, Manuscripts and Archives, Yale University Library.

2. Episcopalians were much more cautious in their ecumenical connections with other groups, although in principle they sympathized with the purpose of moral societies. Episcopalians, as explained in the previous chapter, quite naturally thought of their churches as both sanctuaries and a refuge from the Congregational order. Hence, my assertions here about changes in the notion of Christian community and its relationship to buildings already applied to Episcopalians.

3. The word appears most frequently, not surprisingly, in poetry and dedication sermons. See, for example, Brockway, *Sermon*.

4. Reverend Solomon Stoddard of Northampton, Massachusetts, in the seventeenth century daringly experimented with "open" communion, but the large majority of congregations resisted this change.

5. Morris, Congregational Church Records, vol. 2, 1 July 1827, CSL mf. The exact timing of this change in communion practice is not clear and the question deserves more study.

6. John E. Crowley, *The Invention of Comfort: Sensibilities and Design in Early Modern Britain and Early America* (Baltimore: The Johns Hopkins University Press, 2001). Crowley claims the "culture of sensibility identified the phenomenon of *discomfort*" (168) and "made physical comfort an objective problem" (204).

7. Nylander, "Toward Comfort and Uniformity."

8. Ibid., 86.

9. Robert L. Edwards, *Of Singular Genius, of Singular Grace: A Biography of Horace Bushnell* (Cleveland: The Pilgrim Press, 1992).

10. North Hartford, (Park) Congregational Church Records, 1 November 1824 subscription list, CSL mf. In the records 26 November 1824 is a receipt for green silk, orange silk, and "silk velvit."

11. E. Alfred Jones, *The Old Silver of American Churches* (Letchworth, England: Privately printed for the National Society of Colonial Dames of America at the Arden Press, 1913), lxvij, lxxx.

12. Peter Bohan and Philip Hammerslough, *Early Connecticut Silver, 1700–1840* (Middletown, Conn.: Wesleyan University Press, 1970), 185, 191–93.

13. See Cott, *The Bonds of Womanhood;* Ann Douglas, *The Feminization of American Culture* (New York: Knopf, 1977).

14. Cowles, *Sermon*, 13.

15. Morris, Congregational Society Records, 20 August 1842, CSL mf.

16. Kendall, *Travels*, 131 ff.

17. New Haven, First Baptist Society Records, 4 August 1824, CSL mf.

18. Brockway, *Sermon*, 23 ff.

19. Jeremiah Hallock, *A Sermon delivered at the Dedication of the Meeting House in Canton*, 5 January, 1815 (Hartford: Peter B. Gleason & Co., 1815), 11.

20. Washington, First Congregational Society Records, 8 November 1842, CSL mf.

21. Washington, First Congregational Society Records, "Second Monday" of November, 1831, CSL mf.

22. Roxbury, Congregational Society Records, 18 December 1826, CSL mf; Hartford, First Congregational Society Records, December 1816, 15 January 1830, 15 and 18 January 1834, 20 March 1835, CSL mf. Carl Lounsbury has pointed out that similar discussions about comfort and convenience were being made in the mid–eighteenth century, although with much less frequency and limited results in practice (communication with Dr. Lounsbury, March 1997).

23. John M. Duncan, *Travels through part of the United States and Canada in 1818 & 1819* (Glasgow: Printed at the University Press for Hurst, Robinson, & Co., London, 1823), vol. 2, 352.

24. Ibid.

25. Samuel Belcher contracts, 23 December 1815, Connecticut Historical Society. In Belcher's notebook, also at the Connecticut Historical Society, is a pulpit plan for an 1816–17 church, probably the church at Lyme. The pulpit was rectangular with a built-in seat at the rear. Stairs curved up seven feet from the bottom to doors leading to the platform. His sketch looks very much like the pulpit in figure 46, although it is still quite high, as some of these earlier Connecticut pulpits were.

26. The origins of this type of preaching can be seen in Harry S. Stout's excellent biography of George Whitefield, the great British revivalist of the eighteenth century. Stout argues that borrowing techniques from the theater, Whitefield revolutionized Protestant preaching. Harry S. Stout, *The Divine Dramatist: George Whitefield and the Rise of Modern Evangelicalism* (Grand Rapids, Mich.: Eerdmans, 1991). See also Hatch, *Democratization of American Christianity.*

27. Philip D. Zimmerman makes this argument in "Ecclesiastical Architecture," 330–43. The article "The Pulpit," cited by Zimmerman, was written by "the Mssrs. Abbott," and first appeared in the *Religious Magazine* 2:5, 203–4.

28. Plymouth, St. Peter's Episcopal Society Records, 16 January 1837, CSL mf.
29. Robbins, *Diary*, 11 January 1818.
30. Hartford, First Congregational Society Records, December 1815, CSL mf.
31. Canaan, First Congregational Society Records, 9 December 1827, CSL mf. Vote included directions to place the stove in the twenty-sixth pew, with the pipe running across the room and then toward the front of the meetinghouse.
32. Cited in Kelly, *Early Connecticut Meetinghouses*, vol. 1, 224.
33. Cited in ibid., 328.
34. *Litchfield County Post*, 29 August 1826.
35. Croswell, Diary, 8, 18, 29 December 1822.
36. *Litchfield County Centennial Celebration* (Hartford: Edwin Hunt, 1851), 121.
37. Porter, "The New England Meeting House," 10.
38. Litchfield, Congregational Society Records, 18 October 1816, CSL mf.
39. *Hartford Daily Courant*, 17 January 1854.
40. Ibid.
41. Ibid.
42. Ibid.
43. Cited in Kelly, *Early Connecticut Meetinghouses*, vol. 2, 38.
44. Samuel Griswold Goodrich, *Recollections of a Lifetime* . . . (New York: Arundel Print, 1856), 134–36, reprinted in Nylander, "Toward Comfort and Uniformity," 88–89,
45. Ibid.
46. William Woolsey to Charles Chauncy, 14 March 1820, Woolsey Family Papers, Manuscripts and Archives, Yale University Library.
47. See Elizabeth Donaghy Garrett, *At Home: The American Family, 1750–1870* (New York: Harry N. Abrams, 1990), 183–191; Jane C. Nylander, *Our Own Snug Fireside: Images of the New England Home, 1760–1860* (New York: Alfred A. Knopf, 1993), 74–102.
48. See Philip Zimmerman, "The Lord's Supper in Early New England: The Setting and the Service," in *New England Meeting House and Church*, edited by Benes, 124–34; Barbara McLean Ward, " 'In a Feasting Posture': Communion Vessels and Community Values in Seventeenth- and Eighteenth-Century New England," *Winterthur Portfolio* 23 (spring 1988): 2–24; Horton Davies, *Worship and Theology in England: From Watts and Wesley to Maurice, 1690–1850* (Princeton, N.J.: Princeton University Press, 1961), 30–31, 101–6, 204–9.
49. The large, shallow dishes that appear in church plate in the colonial and early national periods have most often been called "alms basins" by twentieth-century collectors, curators, and church members. E. Alfred Jones, for example, in *The Old Silver of American Churches*, uses the term indiscriminately. The use of "alms basins" to describe these objects in Reformed congregations may be an anachronistic. While the Anglican service typically included an alms basin of this type that was placed on the altar, Congregationalists and Presbyterians more often had either a "Deacon's Box," placed in a stationary position toward the rear of the church, or used long poles with a cloth bag on the end to collect an offering in the pews. The purpose of this offering was the support of the poor in the parish (the deacon's responsibility) or payment for the bread and wine for the communion table. (As we have seen, the primary source of church operating funds was not the weekly offering.) During the period of this study, some churches did begin passing the plate during worship services, but that was clearly a departure from previous practice (see, for example, the records of New York's Collegiate/Dutch

Reformed Church, 1791, Presbyterian Historical Society, Philadelphia). The function of these large dishes—whether for passing the bread or taking an offering—is still unclear and deserves further study.

50. See Barbara Ward, " 'In a Feasting Posture,' " 24.

51. The Connecticut Historical Society has a pair of large wineglasses (Accession #1955.1.1–2), English, 1740–50. An old note indicates they were used by the Congregational Church of Groton, brought from England about 1690, but the style indicates this cannot be true.

52. M. Halsey Thomas, ed., *The Diary of Samuel Sewall, 1674–1729*, vol. 2 (New York: Farrar, Straus, and Giroux, 1973), 1023, cited in Ward, " 'In a Feasting Posture,' " 12.

53. Bohan and Hammerslough, *Early Connecticut Silver*, 130. These tankards were converted into three circa 1795 beakers made by New London silversmith John Proctor Trott.

54. Ibid., 150–51.

55. Hartford, First Congregational Society Financial Records 1801–1913, 3 June 1802, June 1803, 21 June 1803, 5 August 1806, CSL mf. This new set included four flagons, six cups, three two-handled cups, four platters, and one basin.

56. New Preston, Congregational Society Records, 25 November 1822, CSL mf.

57. Hartford, Fourth (Free) Society Records, c. 1832–33 (n.d.), 17, CSL mf.

58. New Haven, First Baptist Society Records, 5 May 1824, CSL mf. Unlike the doctrine and practice of baptism, Baptist communion practice did not differ considerably from the Congregationalist. Methodists, especially after a congregation was somewhat settled and financially secure, invested in communion silver. But because these congregations were generally poor at this time, few artifacts from this period remain.

59. Bohan and Hammerslough, *Early Connecticut Silver*, 130.

60. Jones, *The Old Silver of American Churches*, vol. 2, 306.

61. Although church pewter was often engraved with the name of the church, it was much less frequently a gift.

62. Bohan and Hammerslough, *Early Connecticut Silver*, 103.

63. Ibid., 64. The beaker was made by Samuel Parmelee, Guilford silversmith.

64. Hartford, Second (South) Congregational Society Records, vol. 2, copied excerpt from William Stanley's will, n.p., CSL mf.

65. Croswell, Diary, 30 November 1822.

66. Bohan and Hammerslough, *Early Connecticut Silver*, 31.

67. Robert B. St. George, "Artifacts of Regional Consciousness in the Connecticut River Valley, 1700–1800," in *The Great River: Art and Society of the Connecticut River Valley, 1635–1820* (Hartford: Wadsworth Atheneum, 1985), 35. Barbara Ward, in " 'In a Feasting Posture,' " and Dell Upton, in *Holy Things and Profane*, similarly argue—almost to the exclusion of other interpretations—that communion silver and the ritual served to preserve hierarchical social relationships and reify the power of the elite.

68. Kevin M. Sweeney, "Mansion People: Kinship, Class, and Architecture in Western Massachusetts in the Mid–eighteenth Century," *Winterthur Portfolio* 19 (1984): 231–95.

69. Bohan and Hammerslough, *Early Connecticut Silver*, 94–95.

70. New Preston, Congregational Society Records, 7 September 1823, CSL mf.

71. Bethlehem, Congregational Society Records, 16 May 1795, CSL mf.

72. New Preston, Congregational Society Records, November 1822, CSL mf.

73. Cited in Bohan and Hammerslough, *Early Connecticut Silver*, 195

74. Hartford, Second (South) Congregational Society Records, 2 February 1827, 5 January 1840, CSL mf.

75. Abel Buel, the silversmith, was not the same Buel who carved capitals for the First Congregational Church in Hartford.

76. Robbins, *Diary*, 15 July 1817 and 23 February 1819.

77. Robbins, *Diary*, 16 March 1836.

78. Bohan and Hammerslough, *Early Connecticut Silver*, 94, 138, 188.

79. Martha Gandy Fales, *Early American Silver* (New York: E. P. Dutton, 1973), 44–45, 205. Fales notes that by 1790 mill-rolled silver was available by sheet in several thicknesses. This saved the silversmith the time and effort of raising beaker walls by hand.

80. Huntington was the Reverend Dan Huntington, pastor from 1798 to 1809. Benjamin Tallmadge to Julius Deming, Esq., 10 January 1806, facsimile copy at Litchfield Historical Society.

81. James G. McGivern, *Pillars of Litchfield* (Spokane, Wash., 1971), 65.

82. Robbins, *Diary*, 30 August 1814.

83. Winchester, First Congregational Society Records, 10 December 1795, CSL mf.

84. Bezaleel Pinneo, *A Sermon Preached April 17, 1811 at the Dedication of the New Meeting House in New Milford* (New Haven: Sidney's Press, 1811), 11. Phineas Cooke, addressing the church of Acworth, New Hampshire, in 1822, was even more forceful: "that this pulpit should ever become the vehicle of heresy . . . is a reflection too painful to be indulged." Cooke, *To the Congregational Church in Acworth, New Hampshire, at the Dedication of the New Meeting-House* (Bellows Falls, Vt., 1822).

85. Cited in Mary B. Brewster, *St. Michael's Parish, Litchfield, Connecticut, 1745–1954* (Litchfield, 1954). Reverend Isaac Jones was rector of St. Michael's, a Yale graduate with a previous stormy career as a Congregationalist minister. He had served as assistant to Reverend Truman Marsh at St. Michael's.

86. *Episcopal Watchman*, 4 August 1832.

87. Letter cited in Edwin Pond Parker, *History of the Second Church of Christ in Hartford, 1633–1885*, (Hartford, 1885), 182.

88. Hartford, South Congregational Church Records, loose letter dated 29 May 1822, Connecticut Historical Society Library.

89. Croswell, Diary, 30 August 1821. Croswell, typically, ascribes the whole event to the "itching ears" of New Havenites.

90. Account of the consecration of St. John's, Salisbury, in a letter from Stephen Beach, missionary to Litchfield County, *Journal of the Proceedings of the Annual Convention* (1825).

91. Washington (Marble Dale), St. Andrew's Society Records, 2 June 1824, CSL mf.

92. New Haven, United Society Records, vol. 2, 1815 (exact date is unclear), p. 4, CSL mf.

93. Brockway, *Sermon*, 18.

94. Hawes, *Sermon*, 29.

95. New Haven, First Baptist Society Records, 31 December 1824, CSL mf.

Epilogue (pp. 229–38)

1. While some of these buildings were stone structures that represented the historically accurate Gothic Revival, many were "Carpenter Gothic," that is, wooden buildings of various forms decorated with milled elements that gave them a rather fanciful appearance.

2. See Kilde, *When Church Became Theatre*.

3. David Daggett to Susan Dwight, 25 December 1815, Daggett Family Papers, Manuscripts and Archives, Yale University Library.

4. Thomas Cole, "Essays on American Scenery," in *American Art 1700–1960* edited by John McCoubrey, (Englewood Cliffs, N.J.: Prentice-Hall, 1965), 109.

5. Joseph Wood, *The New England Village* (Baltimore: The Johns Hopkins University Press, 1997). As Wood points out, most of these New England villages emerged in the early national period out of former meetinghouse greens and relatively undeveloped town centers.

6. Josiah Temple, *History of Framingham, Massachusetts, 1640–1880* (Framingham, Mass.; By the Town, 1887), cited in Wood, *New England Village*, 105.

7. *Life*, 20 November 1944. I am grateful to Peter Williams for alerting me to this image.

8. Marlowe, *Churches of Old New England*, 219.

9. Card printed by Brown & Bigelow, St. Paul, Minn., n.d., Litchfield Historical Society.

10. In 1947, George Francis Marlowe wrote: "It has been the custom to describe all the work of this time [late eighteenth and early nineteenth centuries] as "Colonial," including many buildings of the years after the Revolution, for which Early Republic or Federal would be a more correct term." This seems to imply that the usage of the term fifty years ago did not necessarily indicate a misapprehension of dates. Marlowe, *Churches of Old New England*, 1.

11. Rutheva Baldwin Brockett, in Sotheby's *One Hundred Years of American Silver, 1690–1790*, sale 19 January 2002 (New York, 2002), 9.

12. William Truettner and Thomas Andrew Denenberg, "The Discreet Charm of the Colonial," in *Picturing Old New England: Image and Memory* edited by Truettner and Roger B. Stein, (New Haven: Yale University Press for National Museum of American Art, 1999), 99.

13. Andrei Condrescu with David Graham, photographer, *Road Scholar: Coast to Coast Late in the Century* (New York: Hyperion Books, 1993).

Bibliography

Secondary Sources

Archer, John. "Puritan Town Planning in New Haven." *Journal of the Society of Architectural Historians* 34 (May 1975): 140–49.

Barber, John Warner. *Hartford Historical Collections: History and Antiquities*. New Haven and Hartford, 1836. Reprint, Hartford Architectural Conservancy, 1976.

———. *History and Antiquities of New Haven, Conn.* 3d. ed. New Haven: Barber and Punderson, 1870.

Barnes, Howard A. *Horace Bushnell and the Virtuous Republic*. Metuchen, N.J.: The American Theological Library Association and The Scarecrow Press, 1991.

Barney, Frances Bishop. *History of St. Paul's Parish, New Haven, 1830–1930*. New Haven: Quinnipiac Press, 1930.

Beard, Geoffrey. *The Works of Christopher Wren*. Edinburgh: John Bartholomew & Son, 1982.

Beardsley, Eben Edwards. *The History of the Episcopal Church in Connecticut*. 2d ed. 2 vols. New York: Hurd & Houghton, 1869.

Bellah, Robert. *Varieties of Civil Religion*. San Francisco: Harper & Row, 1980.

Benes, Peter, ed. *New England Meeting House and Church, 1630–1850*. Boston: Boston University for the Dublin Seminar for New England Folklife, 1979.

Benes, Peter, and Philip D. Zimmerman, eds. *New England Meeting House and Church, 1630–1850*. Boston: Boston University for the Currier Gallery of Art and the Dublin Seminar for New England Folklife, 1979.

Benes, Peter, ed., *New England Music: The Public Sphere, 1600–1900*. Boston: Boston University for the Dublin Seminar for New England Folklife, 1998.

Bickford, Christopher P., and J. Bard McNulty, eds. *John Warner Barber's Views of Connecticut Towns, 1834–36*. Hartford: The Connecticut Historical Society, 1990.

Bilhartz, Terry. "Sex and the Second Great Awakening: The Feminization of American Religion Reconsidered." In *Belief and Behavior: Essays in the New Religious History*, edited by Philip R. Vandermeer and Robert P. Swierenga, 117–135. New Brunswick, N.J.: Rutgers University Press, 1991.

———. *Urban Religion and the Second Great Awakening: Church and Society in Early National Baltimore*. Rutherford, N.J.: Associated University Presses, 1986.

Birdsall, Richard. "The Second Great Awakening and the New England Social Order." *Church History* 39 (September 1970): 345–64.

Bishir, Catherine. "Good and Sufficient Language for Building." In *Perspectives in Vernacular Architecture*, vol. 4, edited by Thomas Carter and Bernard L. Herman, 44–52. Columbia: University of Missouri Press, 1991.

Bishop, Frank S. *History of the First Bapist Church in New Haven: An Historical Address Delivered at the Centenary Celebration October 11, 1916*. New Haven: First Baptist Church, 1916.

Blake, Henry T. *Chronicles of the New Haven Green from 1638 to 1862*. New Haven: 1898.

Bohan, Peter, and Philip Hammerslough. *Early Connecticut Silver, 1700–1840*. Middletown, Conn.: Wesleyan University Press, 1970.

Bonomi, Patricia. *Under the Cope of Heaven: Religion, Society, and Politics in Colonial America*. New York: Oxford University Press, 1986.

Brainerd, Newton C. *The Hartford Statehouse of 1796*. Hartford: Connecticut Historical Society, 1964.

Brcak, Nancy J. "Country Carpenters, Federal Buildings: An Early Architectural Tradition in Ohio's Western Reserve." *Ohio History* 98 (summer–autumn 1989): 131–46.

Breitenbach, William. "Piety *and* Moralism: Edwards and the New Divinity." In *Jonathan Edwards and the American Experience*, edited by Nathan Hatch and Harry S. Stout, 177–204. New York: Oxford University Press, 1988.

Brooke, John L. *The Heart of the Commonwealth: Society and Political Culture in Worcester County, Massachusetts, 1713–1861*. Cambridge: Cambridge University Press, 1989.

Brown, Elizabeth Mills. *New Haven: A Guide to Architecture and Urban Design*. New Haven: Yale University Press, 1976.

———. *The United Church on the Green, New Haven, Connecticut: An Architectural History*. New Haven: United Church, 1965.

Bruchey, Stuart. *Enterprise: The Dynamic Economy of a Free People*. Cambridge, Mass.: Harvard University Press, 1990.

Burns, Martha Dennis. "The Power of Music Enhanced by the Word: Lowell Mason and the Transformation of Sacred Singing in Lyman Beecher's New England." In *New England Music: The Public Sphere, 1600–1900*, edited by Peter Benes, 139–50. Boston: Boston University for the Dublin Seminar for New England Folklife, 1998.

Burr, Nelson Rollin. *A History of Christ Church Parish and Cathedral, Hartford, Connecticut, 1762–1942: An Historical Sketch*. Hartford: Church Mission Publishing Co., 1942.

———. *The Story of the Diocese of Connecticut: A New Branch of the Vine*. Hartford: Church Mission Publishing Co., 1962.

Bushman, Richard L. *From Puritan to Yankee: Character and the Social Order in Connecticut, 1690–1765*. Cambridge, Mass.: Harvard University Press, 1967.

———. *The Refinement of America: Persons, Houses, Cities*. New York: Knopf, 1992.

Butler, Jon. *Awash in a Sea of Faith: Christianizing the American People*. Cambridge, Mass.: Harvard University Press, 1990.

Butler, William. "Another City upon a Hill: Litchfield, Connecticut, and the Colonial Revival." In *The Colonial Revival in America*, edited by Alan Axelrod, 15–51. New York: W. W. Norton, 1985.

Cameron, Kenneth Walter. *Vanished and Vanishing Episcopal Churches of Early Connecticut: A Pictorial Record*. Hartford: Transcendental Books, 1984.

Campbell, Colin. *The Romantic Ethic and the Spirit of Modern Consumerism*. Oxford: Basil Blackwell, 1987.

Celebration of the Semi-centennial Anniversary of the Consecration of Christ Church, Hartford, December 23, 1879. Hartford: Case, Lockwood, & Brainard Co., 1879.

Centennial Memorial of the First Baptist Church of Hartford, Connecticut. Hartford: Christian Secretary, 1890.

Cherry, Conrad. "Nature and the Republic: The New Haven Theology." *New England Quarterly* 51 (December 1978): 509–26.

Classical America, 1815–1845. Newark, N.J.: The Newark Museum, 1963.

Collier, Christopher. "Steady Habits Considered and Reconsidered." *Connecticut Review* 5 (April 1972): 28–37.

Contributions to the History of Christ Church, Hartford. Comp. Gurdon Russell. Hartford: Belknap & Warfield, 1895.

Coons, Paul Wakeman. *The Achievement of Religious Liberty in Connecticut*. New Haven: Yale University Press, 1936.

Cooper, Wendy A. *The Classical Taste in America, 1800–1840*. New York: Abbeville Press for the Baltimore Museum of Art, 1993.

Cott, Nancy. *The Bonds of Womanhood: "Woman's Sphere" in New England, 1780–1835*. New Haven: Yale University Press, 1977.

Crowley, John E. *The Invention of Comfort: Sensibilities and Design in Early Modern Britain and Early America*. Baltimore: The Johns Hopkins University Press, 2001.

Cummings, Abbott Lowell. *Architecture in Early New England*. Sturbridge, Mass.: Old Sturbridge Village, 1958. Rev. ed. 1984.

————. *The Framed Houses of Massachusetts Bay, 1625–1725*. Cambridge, Mass.: Harvard University Press, 1979.

————. "An Investigation of the Sources, Stylistic Evolution, and Influence of Asher Benjamin's Builders Guides." Ph.D. diss., The Ohio State University, 1950.

Daniels, Bruce. *The Connecticut Town: Growth and Development, 1635–1790*. Middletown, Conn.: Wesleyan University Press, 1979.

Davies, Horton. *Worship and Theology in England: From Watts and Wesley to Maurice, 1690–1850*. Princeton, N.J.: Princeton University Press, 1961.

————. *The Worship of the American Puritans*. Morgan, Pa.: Soli Deo Gloria Publications, 1990.

Davies, J. G. *The Secular Use of Church Buildings*. New York: Seabury Press, 1963.

Davis, Natalie Z. "The Sacred and the Body Social in Sixteenth-Century Lyon." *Past and Present* 90 (February 1981): 40–70.

Davis, Susan G. *Parades and Power: Street Theatre in Nineteenth-Century Philadelphia*. Philadelphia: Temple University Press, 1986.

Dexter, Rev. Henry Martin. "Meeting-Houses: Considered Historically and Suggestively." *Congregational Quarterly* 1 (April 1859): 186–214.

Dinkin, Robert. "Seating the Meetinghouse in Early Massachusetts." in *Material Life in America, 1600–1860*, edited by Robert B. St. George. Boston; Northeastern University Press, 1988.

Donnelly, Marion Card. *The New England Meeting Houses of the Seventeenth Century*. Middletown, Conn.: Wesleyan University Press, 1968.

Dorsey, Stephen Palmer. *Early English Churches in America, 1607–1807*. New York: Oxford University Press, 1952.

Drummond, Andrew Landale. *The Church Architecture of Protestantism: An Historical and Constructive Study*. Edinburgh: T. & T. Clark, 1934.

Edwards, Robert L. *Of Singular Genius, of Singular Grace: A Biography of Horace Bushnell*. Cleveland: The Pilgrim Press, 1992.

Eliade, Mircea. *The Sacred and the Profane: The Nature of Religion*. San Diego: Harcourt, Brace, Javonovich, 1959.

Elias, Norbert. *The Civilizing Process: The History of Manners*. Basel, 1939. English translation, New York: Urizen Books, 1978.

Ellis, Joseph J. *After the Revolution: Profiles of Early American Culture*. New York: W. W. Norton, 1979.

Ellis, Richard E., et al. "A Symposium on Charles Sellers, *The Market Revolution: Jacksonian America, 1815–1846.*" *Journal of the American Republic* 12 (winter 1992): 445–76.

Emory, Robert. *History of the Discipline of the Methodist Episcopal Church to 1856*. New York: Carlton & Porter, 1857.

Ezell, John Samuel. *Fortune's Merry Wheel: The Lottery in America*. Cambridge, Mass.: Harvard University Press, 1960.

Fales, Martha Gandy. *Early American Silver*. New York: E. P. Dutton, 1973.

Fennimore, Donald. "Religion in America: Metal Objects in Service of the Ritual." *American Art Journal* 10 (November 1978): 20–42.

Finney, Paul Corby, ed. *Seeing beyond the Word: Visual Arts and the Calvinist Tradition*. Grand Rapids, Mich.: W. B. Eerdmans Publishing Co., 1999.

Fisher, Samuel H. *An Account of the Congregational Church at Litchfield, Connecticut, and Its Restoration, 23 October 1930*. New Haven, 1931.

Foster, Stephen. "A Connecticut Separate Church: Strict Congregationalism in Cornwall, 1780–1809." *New England Quarterly* 39 (September 1966): 309–33.

Friary, Donald. "The Architecture of the Anglican Church in the North American Colonies: A Study of Religious, Social, and Cultural Expression." Ph.D. diss., University of Pennsylvania, 1971.

Friedman, Terry. *James Gibbs*. New Haven: Yale University Press for the Paul Mellon Center for Study in British Art, 1984.

Garfinkel, Susan. "Letting in the World: 'Re' interpretive Tensions in the Quaker Meeting House." In *Perspectives in Vernacular Architecture* vol. 5, edited by Thomas Carter and Bernard L. Herman, [78–92]. Columbia: University of Missouri Press, 1991.

Garrett, Elizabeth Donaghy. *At Home: The American Family, 1750–1870*. New York: Harry N. Abrams, 1990.

———. "The Protestant Plain Style before 1630." *Journal of the Society of Architectural Historians* 9 (October 1950): 4–13.

Garrison, J. Ritchie. *Two Carpenters: Architecture and Building in Early New England, 1799–1859*. Forthcoming.

Garvan, Anthony N. B. *Architecture and Town Planning in Colonial Connecticut*. New Haven: Yale University Press, 1951.

George, Carol V. *Segregated Sabbaths*. New York: Oxford University Press, 1973.

German, James. "The Social Utility of Wicked Self-Love: Calvinism, Capitalism, and Public Policy in Revolutionary New England." *Journal of American History* 82, no. 3 (December 1995): 965–98.

Gilmore, William J. *Reading Becomes a Necessity of Life: Material and Cultural Life in Rural New England, 1780–1835*. Knoxville, Tenn.: University of Tennessee Press, 1989.

Glassie, Henry. *Folk Housing in Middle Virginia: A Structural Analysis of Historic Artifacts*. Knoxville: University of Tennessee Press, 1975.

Goen, Clarence C. *Revivalism and Separatism in New England, 1740–1800: Strict Congregationalists and Separate Baptists in the Great Awakening*. Middletown, Conn.: Wesleyan University Press, 1987.

Gould, Nathaniel. *Church Music in America*. Boston: A. N. Johnson, 1853.

Gowans, Alan. *Images of American Living: Four Centuries of Architecture and Furniture as Cultural Expression*. New York: Harper & Row, 1964.

Grant, Ellsworth Strong, and Marion Hepburn Grant. *The City of Hartford, 1784–1984: An Illustrated History*. Hartford: Connecticut Historical Society, 1984. *The Great River: Art and Society of the Connecticut River Valley, 1635–1820*. Hartford: Wadsworth Atheneum, 1985.

Green, M. Louise. *The Development of Religious Liberty in Connecticut*. 1905. Reprint, Freeport, N.Y.: Books for Libraries Press, 1970.

Hackett, David G. *The Rude Hand of Innovation: Religion and Social Order in Albany, New York, 1652–1836*. New York: Oxford University Press, 1991.

Hafertepe, Kenneth Charles. "The Enlightened Sensibility: Scottish Philosophy in American Art and Architecture." Ph.D. diss., University of Texas at Austin, 1986.

Hafertepe, Kenneth, and James F. O'Gorman, eds. *American Architects and Their Books to 1848*. Amherst: University of Massachusetts Press, 2001.

Hambrick-Stowe, Charles. *The Practice of Piety: Puritan Devotional Disciplines in Seventeenth-Century New England*. Chapel Hill: University of North Carolina Press, 1982.

Hamlin, Talbot Faulkner. *Greek Revival Architecture in America*. London: Oxford University Press, 1944.

Handy, Robert. *A Christian America: Protestant Hopes and Historical Realities*. New York: Oxford University Press, 1971.

Hatch, Nathan O. *The Democratization of American Christianity*. New Haven: Yale University Press, 1989.

Hawks, Francis L., and William Stevens Perry. *Documentary History of the Protestant Episcopal Church in the U. S. A. containing hitherto unpublished documents concerning the church in Connecticut*. 2 vols. New York: James Pott, Publishers, 1863–64.

Henretta, James A. *The Evolution of American Society, 1700–1815: An Interdisciplinary Analysis*. Lexington, Mass.: D. C. Heath and Co., 1973.

Herman, Bernard L. "Kensey Johns and His Carpenters." In *After Ratification: Material Life in Delaware, 1789–1820*, edited by J. Ritchie Garrison, Bernard L. Herman, and Barbara McLean Ward, 65–77. Newark, Del.: Museum Studies Program, University of Delaware, 1988.

———. *The Stolen House*. Charlottesville: University of Virginia Press, 1992.

Historical Catalogue of the First Church in Hartford, 1633–1885. Hartford, 1885.

History of Litchfield County, with Illustrations and Biographical Sketches of its Prominent Men and Pioneers. 2 vols. Philadelphia: J. W. Lewis and Co., 1881.

A History of the First Congregational Church in Litchfield, Connecticut on its 126th Anniversary and 25th Anniversary of Its Restoration. Litchfield, 1955.

Jeffrey, Paul. *The City Churches of Sir Christopher Wren*. London: Hambleton Press, 1996.

Jenkins, Thomas E. "The Character of God in America." Ph.D. diss., Yale University, 1991.

John, Richard R. "Taking Sabbatarianism Seriously: The Postal System, the Sabbath, and the Transformation of American Political Culture." *Journal of the Early Republic* 10 (winter 1990): 517–67.

Johnson, Paul. *A Shopkeeper's Millennium: Society and Revivals in Rochester, New York, 1815–37*. New York: Hill & Wang, 1978.

Jones, E. Alfred. *The Old Silver of American Churches*. 2 vols. Letchworth, England: Privately printed for the National Society of Colonial Dames of America at the Arden Press, 1913.

Keller, Charles Roy. *The Second Great Awakening in Connecticut*. New Haven: Yale University Press, 1942.

Kelly, J. Frederick. *Early Connecticut Meetinghouses*. 2 vols. New York: Columbia University Press, 1948.

Kerber, Linda. *Women of the Republic: Intellect and Ideology in Revolutionary America*. Chapel Hill: University of North Carolina Press for the Institute of Early American History and Culture, Williamsburg, Virginia, 1980.

Kilbourne, Payne Kenyon. *Sketches and Chronicles of the Town of Litchfield, Connecticut: Historical, Biographical, and Statistical*. Hartford: Press of Case, Lockwood and Co., 1859.

Kilde, Jeanne Halgren. *When Church Became Theatre: The Transformation of Evangelical Architecture and Worship in Nineteenth-Century America*. New York: Oxford University Press, 2002.

Kirker, Harold. *The Architecture of Charles Bulfinch*. Cambridge, Mass.: Harvard University Press, 1969.

Kling, David. W. *A Field of Divine Wonders: The New Divinity and Village Revivals in Northwestern Connecticut, 1792–1822*. University Park: Pennsylvania State Press, 1993.

Lambert, Frank. *Inventing the Great Awakening*. Princeton, N.J.: Princeton University Press, 1999.

———. *"Pedlar in Divinity": George Whitefield and the Transatlantic Revivals, 1737–1770*. Princeton, N.J.: Princeton University Press, 1994.

Larkin, Jack. *The Reshaping of Everyday Life, 1790–1840*. New York: Harper & Row, 1988.

Lawson, Karol Ann Peard. "An Inexhaustable Abundance: National Landscape, 1780–1820." *Journal of the Early Republic* 12 (fall 1992): 303–30.

Lewis, Jan. *Pursuits of Happiness: Family Values in Jefferson's Virginia*. Cambridge: Cambridge University Press, 1983.

Liemohn, Edwin. *The Organ and Choir in Protestant Worship*. Philadelphia: Fortress Press, 1968.

Liscombe, R. W. "A 'New Era in My Life': Ithiel Town Abroad." *Journal of the Society of Architectural Historians* 50 (March 1991): 5–17.

Lowett, Jonathan G. "The Elms of Elm City." *Journal of the New Haven Colony Historical Society* 38 (fall 1991): 47–63.

Marini, Stephen A. "Evangelical Hymns and Popular Belief." In *New England Music: The Public Sphere, 1600–1900*, edited by Peter Benes, 117–26. Boston: Boston University for the Dublin Seminar for New England Folklife, 1998.

Marlowe, George Francis. *Churches of Old New England: Their Architecture and Their Architects, Their Pastors and Their People*. New York: The Macmillan Co. 1947.

Mathews, Donald G. "The Second Great Awakening as an Organizing Process, 1780–1830: An Hypothesis." *American Quarterly* 21 (spring 1969): 23–43.

May, Henry F. *The Enlightenment in America*. New York: Oxford University Press, 1976.

Mazmanian, Arthur B. *The Structure of Praise — a Design Study: Architecture for Religion in New England from the Seventeenth Century to the Present*. Boston: Beacon Press, 1970.

McAleer, J. Philip. "St. Mary's (1820–30) Halifax: An Early Example of the Use of Gothic Revival Forms in Canada." *Journal of the Society of Architectural Historians* 45 (June 1986): 134–47.

McDannell, Colleen. *Material Christianity: Religion and Popular Culture in America*. New Haven: Yale University Press, 1995.

McGivern, James G. *Pillars of Litchfield*. Spokane, Wash., 1971.

McLoughlin, William G. "The Role of Religion in the Revolution: Liberty of Conscience and Cultural Cohesion in the New Nation." In *Essays on the American Revolution*, edited by Stephen G. Kurtz and James H. Hutson, 197–225. Chapel Hill: University of North Carolina Press, 1973.

Melton, Julius. *Presbyterian Worship in America: Changing Patterns since 1787*. Richmond, Va: John Knox Press, 1967.

Merrill, David O. "Isaac Damon and the Architecture of the Federal Period in New England." Ph.D. diss., Yale University, 1965.

Miles, Margaret. *Image as Insight: Visual Understanding in Western Christianity and Secular Culture*. Boston: Beacon Press, 1985.

Mitchell, Mary Hewitt. *History of the United Church of New Haven*. New Haven: The United Church, 1942.

Morgan, David. *Visual Piety: A History and Theory of Popular Religious Images*. Berkeley: University of California Press, 1998.

Neale, John Mason. *A History of Pews*. Cambridge: At the University Press, 1841.

Newton, Roger Hale. *Town and Davis, Architects: Pioneers in American Revivalist Architecture, 1812–70*. New York: Columbia University Press, 1942.

Nichols, Frederick Doveton. *Palladio in America*. New York: Rizzoli International Publications, 1978.

Noll, Mark. *One Nation under God? Christian Faith and Political Action in America*. San Francisco: Harper & Row, 1988.

Nylander, Jane C. *Our Own Snug Fireside: Images of the New England Home, 1760–1860*. New York: Alfred A. Knopf, 1993.

———. "Toward Comfort and Uniformity in New England Meeting Houses, 1750–1850." In *New England Meeting House and Church*, edited by Peter Benes and Philip Zimmerman, 86–100. Boston: Boston University for the Dublin Seminar for New England Folklife, 1979.

Ochse, Orpha. *The History of the Organ in the United States*. Bloomington: Indiana University Press, 1975.

Osterweiss, Rollin G. *Three Centuries of New Haven, 1638–1938*. New Haven: Yale University Press, 1953.

Parker, Edwin Pond. *History of the Second Church of Christ in Hartford, 1633–1885*. Hartford, 1885.

Peck, George T. "The Meeting House on the Hill." In *A History of the First Congregational Church in Litchfield, Connecticut, on Its 126th Anniversary and 25th Anniversary of Its Restoration*. Litchfield, 1955.

Piersen, William. *Black Yankees: The Development of an African-American Subculture in Eighteenth-Century New England*. Amherst: University of Massachusetts Press, 1988.

Pierson, William H., Jr. *American Buildings and Their Architects*. Vol. 1, *The Colonial and Neoclassical Styles*. Garden City, N.Y.: Doubleday, 1970.

————. *American Buildings and their Architects*. Vol. 2, *Technology and the Picturesque, the Corporate and Early Gothic Styles*. New York: Oxford University Press, 1978.

Place, Charles. "From Meeting House to Church in New England." *Old Time New England* 13 (October 1922): 69–77; 13 (January 1923): 111–23; 13 (April 1923): 149–64; 14 (July 1923): 3–26.

Porter, Noah. "The New England Meeting House." 1882. Reprinted in *Tercentenary Commission of the State of Connecticut* 1933, no. 17, 1–34.

Potter, Rockwell Harmon. *Hartford's First Church*. Hartford, 1932.

Prown, Jules. "Style as Evidence." *Winterthur Portfolio* 15 (autumn 1980): 197–210.

Purcell, Richard. *Connecticut in Transition, 1775–1818*. 1918. Reprint, Middletown, Conn.: Wesleyan University Press, 1963.

Quinan, Jack. "Asher Benjamin and American Architecture." *Journal of the Society of Architectural Historians* 38, no. 3 (1978): 244–66.

Rabinowitz, Richard. *The Spiritual Self in Everyday Life: The Transformation of Personal Religious Experience in Nineteenth-Century New England*. Boston: Northeastern University Press, 1989.

Randall, Catherine. *Building Codes: The Aesthetics of Calvinism in Early Modern Europe*. Philadelphia: University of Pennsylvania Press, 1999.

Rohrer, James. "Sunday Mails and the Church-State Theme in Jacksonian America." *Journal of the Early Republic* 7 (spring 1987): 53–74.

Rose, Harold W. *The Colonial Houses of Worship in America*. New York: Hastings House, 1963.

Roth, David M. *Connecticut: A Bicentennial History*. New York: Norton, 1979.

Rothman, David J. *The Discovery of the Asylum: Social Order and Disorder in the New Republic*. Boston: Little, Brown, and Col., 1971.

Ryan, Mary. *The Cradle of the Middle Class: The Family in Oneida County, New York, 1790–1865*. New York: Cambridge University Press, 1981.

Sarna, Jonathan. "Seating and the American Synagogue." In *Belief and Behavior: Essays in the New Religious History*, edited by Philip R. Vandermeer and Robert P. Swierenga, 189–206. New Brunswick, N.J.: Rutgers University Press, 1991.

Sassi, Jonathan. *A Republic of Righteousness: The Public Christianity of the New England Clergy*. New York: Oxford University Press, 2001.

Schlesinger, Arthur M., Jr. *The Age of Jackson*. Boston: Little Brown, 1945.

Schmidt, Leigh Eric. " 'A Church-Going People Are a Dress-Loving People': Clothes, Communication, and Religious Culture in Early America." *Church History* 58 (March 1989): 36–51.

Scott, Donald. *From Office to Profession: The New England Ministry, 1750–1850*. Philadelphia: University of Pennsylvania Press, 1978.

Sellers, Charles. *The Market Revolution: Jacksonian America, 1815–186*. New York: Oxford University Press, 1991.

Seymour, Charles. "The Episcopal Church in Litchfield County." Typescript, Litchfield (Conn.) Historical Society Collections.

Shepard, James. *The Episcopal Church and Early Ecclesiastical Laws of Connecticut*. New Britain, Conn.: Tuttle, Morehouse, & Taylor Co., 1908.

Shiels, Richard D. "The Connecticut Clergy in the Second Great Awakening." Ph.D. diss., Boston University, 1976.

———. "The Feminization of American Congregationalism, 1730–1835." *American Quarterly* 33 (spring 1981): 46–62.

———. "The Second Great Awakening in Connecticut: Critique of the Traditional Interpretation." *Church History* 49 (December 1980): 401–15.

Sinnott, Edmund Ware. *Meeting House and Church in Early New England.* New York: McGraw-Hill, 1963.

Snyder, K. Alan. "Foundations of Liberty: The Christian Republic of Timothy Dwight and Jedediah Morse." *New England Quarterly* 56 (September 1983): 382–97.

Stanton, Phoebe B. *The Gothic Revival and American Church Architecture: An Episode in Taste, 1840–56.* Baltimore: The Johns Hopkins University Press, 1968.

Steiner, Bruce E. "New England Anglicanism: A Genteel Faith?" *William and Mary Quarterly,* 3d ser., 27 (January 1970): 122–35.

Stillman, Damie. *English Neoclassical Architecture.* 2 vols. London: A. Swemmer, 1988.

Stokes, Charles J. *Historic Churches of Fairfield County.* Westport, Conn.: County Books, 1969.

Stout, Harry S. *The New England Soul: Preaching and Religious Culture in Colonial New England.* New York: Oxford University Press, 1986.

———. "Rhetoric and Reality in the Early Republic: The Case of the Federal Clergy." In *Religion and American Politics from the Colonial Period to the 1980s,* edited by Mark A. Noll, 62–76. New York: Oxford, University Press, 1990.

Stout, Harry S., and Catherine A. Brekus. "Declension, Gender, and the 'New Religious History'." In *Belief and Behavior: Essays in the New Religious History,* edited by Philip R. Vandermeer and Robert P. Swierenga, 15–37. New Brunswick, N.J.: Rutgers University Press, 1991.

Sutton, William R. "Benevolent Calvinism and the Moral Government of God: The Influence of Nathaniel William Taylor in the Second Great Awakening." *Religion and American Culture: A Journal of Interpretation* 2 (winter 1992): 23–47.

Sweeney, Kevin M. "Mansion People: Kinship, Class, and Architecture in Western Massachusetts in the Mid–eighteenth Century." *Winterthur Portfolio* 19 (1984): 231–55.

———. "Meetinghouses, Town Houses, and Churches: Changing Perceptions of Sacred and Secular Space in Southern New England, 1720–1850." *Winterthur Portfolio* 28 (spring 1993): 59–93.

Todd, Janet. *Sensibility: An Introduction.* London: Methuen, 1989.

Townshend, Henry H. "The Grove Street Cemetery." *New Haven Colony Historical Society Papers.* vol. 10 (1951): 119–46.

Truettner, William, and Roger B. Stein, eds. *Picturing Old New England: Image and Memory.* New Haven: Yale University Press for National Museum of American Art, 1999.

Trumbull, James Hammond, ed. *The Memorial History of Hartford County, Connecticut, 1633–1886.* Boston: E. L. Osgood, 1886.

Tuan, Yi-Fu. "Sacred Space—Explorations of an Idea." In *Dimensions of Human Geography: Essays on Some Familiar and Neglected Themes,* edited by Karl Butzer, 84–99. Chicago: University of Chicago Press, 1978.

Turner, Harold. *From Temple to Meeting House: The Phenomenology and Theology of Places of Worship.* The Hague: Mouton Publishers, 1979.

Tyler, Bennett. *New England Revivals, as they existed at the close of the eighteenth and the beginning of the nineteenth centuries.* Boston: Massachusetts Sabbath School Society, 1846.

Umbel, William Thomas. "The Making of an American Denomination: Methodists in New England Religious Culture, 1790–1860." Ph.D. diss., The Johns Hopkins University, 1992.

Upton, Dell. *Holy Things and Profane: Anglican Parish Churches in Colonial Virginia.* New York: Architectural History Foundation and M.I.T. Press, 1986.

Wade, Melvin. " 'Shining in Borrowed Plumage': Affirmation of Community in the Black Coronation Festivals of New England, c. 1750–1850." In *Material Life in Early America 1600–1860,* edited by Robert B. St. George, 171–82. Boston: Northeastern University Press, 1988.

Waldstreicher, David. *"In the Midst of Perpetual Fetes": The Making of American Nationalism, 1776–1820.* Chapel Hill: University of North Carolina Press for the Omohundro Institute of Early American History and Culture, Williamsburg, Virginia, 1997.

Walker, George Leon. *History of the First Church in Hartford, 1633–1883.* Hartford: Brown Gross, 1883.

Walsh, James P. "Holy Time and Sacred Space in Puritan New England." *American Quarterly* 32 (spring 1980): 79–95.

Wandel, Lee Palmer. *Voracious Idols and Violent Hands: Iconoclasm in Reformation Zurich, Strasbourg, and Basel.* Cambridge: Cambridge University Press, 1995.

Weaver, Glenn. *Hartford: An Illustrated History of Connecticut's Capital.* Woodland Hills, Calif.: Windsor Publications for the Connecticut Historical Society, 1982.

Welter, Barbara. "The Feminization of American Religion, 1800–1860." In *Clio's Consciousness Raised: New Perspectives on the History of Women,* edited by Mary Hartman and Lois Banner, 137–57. New York: Harper & Row, 1974.

Wencelius, Leon. *l'Esthetique de Calvin.* Paris: Société d'Edition "Les Belles Lettres," 1938.

White, Alan C., comp. *The Bi-Centennial Celebration of the Settlement of Litchfield, Connecticut, August 1–4, 1920.* Litchfield, Conn.: Enquirer Print, 1920.

White, James F. *Protestant Worship and Church Architecture: Theological and Historical Consideration.* New York: Oxford University Press, 1964.

Wilentz, Sean. "Society, Politics, and the Market Revolution, 1815–1848." In *The New American History,* edited by Eric Foner, 51–63. Philadelphia: Temple University Press, 1990.

Williams, Peter W. *Houses of God: Region, Religion, and Architecture in the United States.* Urbana: University of Illinois Press, 1997.

———. "The Medieval Heritage in American Religious Architecture." In *Medievalism in American Culture: Papers of the Eighteenth Annual Conference of the Center for Medieval and Early Renaissance Studies,* edited by Bernard Rosenthal and Paul E. Szarmach, Vol. 55, 171–191. Binghamton, N.Y.: Medieval & Renaissance Texts & Studies, 1989.

———. "Religious History and Landscape." In *Encyclopedia of the American Religious Experience,* edited by Charles Lippy and Peter W. Williams. New York, 1988.

Wilson, John D. "Religion under the State Constitutions, 1776–1800." *Journal of Church and State* 32, no. 4 (autumn 1990): 753–73.

Winslow, Ola. *Meetinghouse Hill, 1630–1783.* New York: Macmillan, 1952.

Wood, Gordon S. *The Radicalism of the American Revolution*. New York: Vintage Books, 1991.

———. "The Significance of the Early Republic." *Journal of the Early Republic* 8 (spring 1988): 1–19.

Yeomans, David T. "British and American Solutions to a Roofing Problem." *Journal of the Society of Architectural Historians* 50 (September 1991): 266–72.

Zimmerman, Philip D. "Ecclesiastical Architecture in the Reformed Tradition in Rockingham County, New Hampshire, 1790–1860." Ph.D. diss., Boston University, 1985.

Zuckerman, Michael. "Holy Wars, Civil Wars: Religion and Economics in Nineteenth-Century America." *Prospects* 16 (1991): 205–40.

Primary Sources, Published

Andrews, Frank D., comp. *1799 Hartford City Directory*. Vineland, N.J.: privately printed, 1910.

"Architecture." *American Journal of Science and Arts* 17 (January–June 1830): 99 ff.; 18 (July–December 1830): 11 ff., 212 ff.

Atkins, Rev. Elisha. *A Sermon delivered November 18, 1818 at the Dedication of the Congregational Meeting House in the North Parish in Killingly*. Providence: Miller & Hutchens, 1819.

Austin, Rev. David. *'The Rod of Moses upon the Rock of Calvary; or the mountains of fire, and of blood,' a Dedicatory Discourse at the opening of a place of worship, west-parish of Franklin, December 21, 1815*. Norwich: Russell Hubbard, 1816.

Austin, Samuel. *Address to the Calvinist Society in Worcester, Mass., October 15, 1823*.

Bascom, William. *Discourse delivered at a Singing Lecture*. Boston: Lincoln & Edmands, 1814.

Beecher, Lyman. *The Autobiography of Lyman Beecher*. Edited by Charles Beecher. 2 vols. New York: Harper & Bros., 1864.

Benjamin, Asher. *American Builders Companion*. 6th ed. 1827. Reprint, New York: Dover Publications, 1969.

———. *Country Builders' Assistant*. Greenfield, Mass.: Thomas Dickman, 1798.

Bennett, James. *Religion of the Closet*. Hartford, 1820.

Brockway, Diodate. *A Sermon, Delivered in Ellington, June 25, 1806, at the dedication of the New Meeting House in that place*. Hartford: Lincoln & Gleason, 1807.

Brownell, Bishop Thomas Church. *Charge to the Clergy of the Protestant Episcopal Church*. New Haven, 1832.

Calvin, John. *Institutes of the Christian Religion*. Edited by John T. McNeill. Translated and indexed by Ford Lewis Battles. Philadelphia: Westminster Press, 1960.

Channing, William Ellery. *Discourse preached at the Dedication of the Second Congregational Unitarian Church, New York, December 7, 1826*. Second ed. New York: Second Congregational Unitarian Church, 1827.

Chapin, Rev. A. B. *A Sermon Delivered in Christ Church, West Haven, on the Hundredth Anniversary of the Foundation of the Church*. New Haven, 1839.

Cooper, Carolyn, ed. *Voices of the New Republic: Connecticut Towns 1800–1832*. New Haven: Yale University Press, forthcoming.

Cowles, Pitkin. *A Sermon Preached at the Dedication of the Church in North Canaan,*

February 19th, 1823 by the late Rev. Pitkin Cowles, pastor. Hartford: Elihu Geer, 1841.

Crane, Rev. John. *Discourse delivered at Upton, at Grafton, and at Sutton at public meetings of a number of singers.* Sutton Mass.: Sewall Goodridge, 1811.

Daggett, David. *Steady Habits Vindicated or a Serious Remonstrance to the People of Connecticut, against changing their Government.* Hartford: Hudson and Goodwin, 1805.

Dana, Daniel. *An Address on Sacred Music Delivered at a public meeting of the Rockingham Sacred Music Society.* Exeter, N.H., 1814.

Dana, James D. D. *A Discourse delivered at Kensington, Thursday December 1, 1774. On occasion of the first assembling for religious worship in the newly erected SANCTUARY in said place.* New Haven: Thomas & Samuel Green, 1775.

Dwight, Timothy. *Greenfield Hill: a poem, in Seven parts.* New York: Childs and Swaine, 1794.

———. *A Statistical Account of the City of New Haven.* New Haven: printed and sold by Walter and Steele, 1811.

———. *Travels in New England and New York.* 4 vols. New Haven, 1822.

———. *The true means of establishing public happiness.* New Haven, 1795.

Emmons, Nathanael. *Discourse delivered April 11, 1806, at a Publick Meeting of a Number of Singers who were improving themselves in church music.* Providence: D. Heaton, 1806.

Ensign, Ariel. *1828 Hartford City Directory.* Facsimile printed with 1937 Price & Lee City Directory.

Field, David. D. *A Statistical Account of the County of Middlesex, in Connecticut.* Middletown, Conn.: Clark & Lyman, 1819.

Foster, Rev. John. *Discourse on Church Music.* Brighton, Mass.: D. Bowen, 1811.

Gardner's Hartford City Directory for 1838. Hartford: printed by Case, Tiffany & Co., 1838.

Gerry, Elbridge Jr. *The Diary of Elbridge Gerry, Jr.* 1813. Reprint, New York: Brentano's, 1927.

Gibbs, James. *A Book of Architecture.* London: printed for W. Innys and R. Manby, J. and P. Knapton, and C. Hitch, 1728.

Gilman, Rev. Samuel. *Memoir of a New England Village Choir.* Boston: S. G. Goodrich, 1829.

Hallock, Jeremiah. *A Sermon delivered at the Dedication of the Meeting House in Canton.* 5 January 1815. Hartford: Peter B. Gleason & Co., 1815.

Hawes, Joel. *An Address Delivered at the request of the citzens of Hartford, on the 9th of November, 1835. The close of the second century from the first settlement of the city.* Hartford: Belknap & Hamersley, 1835.

———. *A Sermon Delivered at the Dedication of the North Congregational Church in Hartford, December 1, 1824.* Hartford: Goodwin & Co., 1825.

Hobart, John Henry. *The Moral Efficacy and the Positive Benefits of the Gospel. A Sermon Preached at the Consecration of Trinity Church, New Haven, 21 February, 1816.* New Haven, 1816.

———.*The United States of America as compared with some European countries particularly England. Discourse delivered October 1825, St. John's Chapel, St. Paul's Chapel, and Trinity Church, New York City.* New York, 1825.

Jarvis, The Rev. Samuel F., *An Address delivered in the city of New-Haven at the Laying of the Corner-Stone of Trinity Church, May 17th, 1814.* New-Haven: Oliver Steele, 1814.

Journal of the Proceedings of the Annual Convention, Protestant Episcopal Church. Middletown, Conn., 1823–32.

Journals of the Annual Convention of the Diocese of Connecticut from 1792–1820. New Haven: Stanley & Chapin, 1842.

Kendall, Edward A. *Travels through the Northern Parts of the United States in the years 1807 and 1808*. Vol. 1. New York: I. Riley, 1809.

King, Rev. Dr. William (Late Bishop of Londonderry). *A Discourse concerning the Inventions of Men in the Worship of God*. New Haven, 1811.

Linsley, Joel Harvey. *A Sermon Delivered at the dedication of the Second or South Congregational Church in Hartford, April 11, 1827*. Hartford: D. F. Robinson, 1827.

Lyman, William. *The design and benefits of Instrumental Musick considered on a sermon, delivered at Lebanon-Goshen May 7, 1807, on the occasion of having an Organ introduced as an aid to the worship and melody of God's house*. New London: Ebenezer P. Cadt, 1807.

Memoir of Miss Eliza Brainard who Died in Haddam, November 30, 1820. Middletown, Conn.: Clark & Lyman, 1821.

Memoirs of Miss Mary Lyon of New Haven, Connecticut. New Haven, 1837.

Marryat, Frederick *Diary in America with Remarks on its Institutions*. New-York: William H. Colyer, 1839.

Mills, Samuel John. *The Nature and Importance of the Duty of Singing*. Litchfield, Conn., 1775.

Morris, James. *A Statistical Account of Several Towns in the County of Litchfield*. New Haven, 1815.

The Musical Olio. Hartford: Gleason and Co., 1811.

New Directory and Guide Book. Hartford: I. N. Bolles, 1841.

Pearson, Hugh. *A Sermon Preached at the Consecration of the King's Chapel annexed to his Majesty's Pavilion at Brighton, January 1, 1822*. London, 1822.

Pinneo, Bezaleel. *A Sermon Preached April 17, 1811, at the Dedication of the New Meeting House in New Milford*. New Haven: Sidney's Press, 1811.

Proceedings of the City of New Haven in the Removal of Monuments from its Ancient Burying Ground and in the Opening of a new Ground for Burial. New Haven, 1822.

Robbins, Thomas. *Diary of Thomas Robbins, D.D., 1796–1854*. Edited by Increase Tarbox. 2 vols. Boston: Beacon Press, 1886.

Silliman, Benjamin. "Sketches of a tour in the counties of New-Haven and Litchfield in Connecticut." *American Journal of Science and Arts* vol. 2, no. 2 (November 1820): 199–235.

Skinner, A. N. *Report of the Committee Appointed to Inquire into the condition of the New Haven Burying Ground and to propose a plan for its improvement*. New Haven, 1839.

Skinner, Newton. *Sermon Delivered at the Dedication of the new Congregational Meeting House at Berlin*. Hartford, 1823.

Smith, Rev. William. *An Assistant to the Evangelical Psalmodist, in setting forth the most worthy praise of almighty God*. New Haven: Connecticut Herald, 1816.

Strong, Nathan. *A Sermon Delivered at the Consecration of the New Brick Church in Hartford. December 3, 1807*. Hartford: Hudson & Goodwin, 1808.

Strong, Nathan, and Abel Flint. *The Hartford Selection of Hymns*. Hartford, 1799.

Terry, Ezekiel. *Memoirs of the Life and Character of the Late Reverend George Atwater*. Palmer: printed by Ezekiel Terry, 1815.

Tyler, Bennet. *Memoir of the Life and Character of Asahel Nettleton*. 2d ed. Hartford: Robins & Smith, 1845.

Wadsworth, Daniel. "Architecture." *American Journal of Science and Arts* 24 (April–June 1833): 257–63.

Willard, Samuel A. A. S. *A Sermon Preached at the Dedication of the New Meeting House in the First Parish in Deerfield, December 22, 1824*. Greenfield, Mass.: Ansel Phelps, 1825.

Worcester, Samuel. *Address on Sacred Music delivered before the Middlesex Musical Society & the Handel Society of Dartmouth College*. Boston: Manning & Loring, 1811.

The Writings of Nancy Maria Hyde of Norwich, Connecticut, connected with a Sketch of her life. Norwich: Russell Hubbard, 1816.

Yale, Cyrus. *Life of Jeremiah Hallock late pastor of the Congregational Church in Canton, Connecticut*. New York: John R. Haven, 1828.

Primary Sources, Unpublished

Baldwin Family Papers. Manuscripts and Archives, Yale University Library.

Camp, Mary. Manuscript journal kept by Mary Camp of Durham, Connecticut, June 1818–January 1834. Connecticut State Library Archives.

Croswell, Harry. Papers, including Diary and "Annals of Trinity Church," c. 1858. Manuscripts and Archives, Yale University Library.

Daggett Family Papers. Manuscripts and Archives, Yale University Library.

Day Family Papers. Manuscripts and Archives, Yale University Library.

Day, Jeremiah. Miscellaneous letters to Jonathan Miler, theological exchange, 1804–5. Connecticut Historical Society.

Hillhouse Family Papers. Manuscripts and Archives, Yale University Library.

Leffingwell, William. Diary. Manuscripts and Archives, Yale University Library.

Lottery Papers, 1763–1830. Connecticut Historical Society Archives.

Marsh, Truman. "History of St. Michael's Episcopal Church." Manuscript, n.d., Litchfield Historical Society.

Osborn papers relating to lotteries chiefly in Connecticut, 1774–1824. Connecticut State Library Archives.

Townsend, Amos. "Religious Reminiscences from 1806 to 1826." Manuscript journal, c. 1876, New Haven Colony Historical Society.

Wadsworth Family Papers. Manuscripts and Archives, Yale University Library.

Wells, Edward W. Manuscript journal of Edward Wells, 1832–33. Connecticut State Library Archives.

Williams, James. "School Boy Recollections of Hartford, Connecticut, 1829–1832." Manuscript, Connecticut State Library.

Woolsey Family Papers. Manuscripts and Archives, Yale University Library.

Connecticut Colony, State, and City Records

Connecticut Ecclesiastical Affairs. 2nd ser. 1666–1820, vols. 1–6. Microfilm, Connecticut State Library.

Public Records of the Colony of Connecticut. Edited by Charles J. Hoadley vols. 7–

14 (1726–1776). Hartford: Press of the Case, Lackwood & Brainard Company, 1868–90.

Public Records of the State of Connecticut. Vols. 1, 5–12 (1776–78; 1783–1805). Hartford, 1894–1986.

The Public Statute Laws of the State of Connecticut, as revised and enacted by the General Assembly, in May 1821. Hartford: H. Huntington, Jr., 1824.

Records of the City of Hartford. Hartford City Clerk's Office.

Records of the City of New Haven, 1784–1835. New Haven City Clerk's Office.

Records of the New Haven Common Council, 1812–21. New Haven City Clerk's Office.

Resolves and Private Laws of the State of Connecticut, 1789–1836. Vol. 1–2 (1789–1836). Hartford: J. B. Eldridge, 1837.

Salisbury Town Records, 1780–1810. Salisbury Town Hall.

Periodicals and Newspapers

American Eagle (Litchfield), 1822–25.

Christian Secretary (several 1820s and 1830s issues in the collections of the Connecticut Historical Society).

The Churchman's Monthly Magazine (scattered issues, vols. 1–4, 1804–8).

Connecticut Courant (1820–30).

Connecticut Evangelical Magazine and Religious Intelligencer (1808–12).

Connecticut Journal (1805–17).

Connecticut Mirror (1820–30).

The Episcopal Watchman (1827–1833).

Litchfield County Post (4 July 1826–11 June 1829).

Litchfield Enquirer (1829–30).

New England Magazine vol. 1 (July–December 1831). Boston: J. T. & E. Buckingham.

Church Records

Unless otherwise noted, these records are on microfilm at the Connecticut State Library. In the period of the study, congregations made a distinction between ecclesiastical "society" records and "church" records; society records yield the most useful information about buildings, interiors, and finances. Below I list the general title for each congregation's document collection at the State Library. Note that although this modern title is generally "church records" following the current name of the congregation, earlier society records are included as well.

Barkhamsted, St. Paul's Church at Riverton Records, 1828–1835.

Barkhamsted, First Congregational Church Records, 1781–1837.

Bethlehem, Christ Church Records, 1807–1845.

Bethlehem, Congregational Society Records, 1738–1850.

Bridgeport, United Congregational Church Records, 1784–1840.

Canaan, First Congregational Society Records, 1785–1840.

Canaan, Norfolk, and New Marlborough Baptist Society Records, 1819–1840.

Colebrook, Congregational Church Records, 1787–1842.
Colebrook, Union Church Society of Colebrook River Records, 1815–1849.
Cornwall, First Church of Christ Records, 1790–1840.
Danbury, First Baptist Church Papers, 1787–1840.
Danbury, Methodist Church Records, 1811–1840.
Goshen, First Congregational Church Records, 1791–1840.
Goshen, North Congregational Church Records, 1828–1840.
Goshen, West Goshen Methodist Church Records, 1832–1837.
Hartford, Blue Hills Baptist Church Records, 1810–1840.
Hartford, Central Baptist Church Records, 1789–1840.
Hartford, Christ Church Cathedral Papers, 1795–1815.
Hartford, Christ Church Cathedral Parish Register (Society Minutes), 1795–1840.
Hartford, First Baptist Church Records, 1789–1840.
Hartford, First Church of Christ (Congregational) Records, 1785–1840.
Hartford, First Congregational Church Papers, 1784–1840.
Hartford, First Methodist Church Records, 1824–1840.
Hartford, First Universalist Church Papers, 1825–1840, Connecticut Historical So-
     ciety.
Hartford, Fourth (Free) Congregational Church Records, 1832–1833.
Hartford, North (Park) Congregational Church Records, 1823–1842.
Hartford, North (Park) Congregational Church Papers, 1823–1840.
Hartford, Second (South) Congregational Church Records, 1790–1840.
Hartford, South Congregational Church Records, Connecticut Historical Society.
Hartford, Universalists of Connecticut, Hartford County Association, 1832–1840.
Kent, Congregational Church Records, 1785–1840.
Kent, St. Andrew's Episcopal Church Records, 1808–1872.
Litchfield, First Congregational Church Records, 1768–1848.
Litchfield, First Methodist Episcopal Church Records, 1790–1840.
Litchfield, St. Michael's Episcopal Church Records, 1784–1840.
Litchfield, St. Paul's (Bantam) Episcopal Church Records, 1796–1897. Records
     found in Account Book of Sylvanus Bishop, Litchfield Historical Society.
Milton (Litchfield) Congregational Church Records, 1785–1840.
Morris, Congregational Church Records, 1783–1827.
Morris, Congregational Church Treasurer's Book, 1797–1844.
New Hartford, Bakerville Methodist Episcopal Church Records, 1827–1840.
New Haven, First Baptist Church Records, 1824–1852.
New Haven, First Congregational Church Archives, CSL Archives.
New Haven, First Congregational Church Records, 1750–1840.
New Haven, First Congregational Church Seating Plans c. 1810–1840.
New Haven, First Methodist Church Papers, Connecticut Historical Society.
New Haven, Methodist Episcopal Church Records, 1808–1840.
New Haven, Trinity Episcopal Church Records, 1767–1840.
New Haven, Trinity Episcopal Church Records, New Haven Colony Historical
     Society.
New Haven, United Congregational Church Records, 1790–1840.
New Milford, First Congregational Church Records, 1784–1840.
New Milford, Northville Baptist Church Records, 1814–1838.
New Milford, St. John's Episcopal Church Records, 1784–1849.
New Preston, Congregational Society Records, 1757–1845 (with Washington Con-
     gregational Church Records).

Northfield (Litchfield), Congregational Church Records, 1795–1840.
Plymouth (Northbury), Congregational Church Records, 1758–1840.
Plymouth, St. Matthew's Episcopal Church Records, 1791–1841.
Plymouth, St. Peter's Episcopal Church Records, 1784–1840.
Roxbury, Christ Church Episcopal Records, 1806–1840.
Roxbury, Congregational Church Records, 1794–1840.
Salisbury, Congregational Church Records, 1785–1810.
Salisbury, Congregational Church Agreement for Building a Meeting House, 21
    November 1798.
Salisbury, St. John's Episcopal Church Records, 1823–1860.
Sharon, Christ Church Episcopal Records, 1809–1842.
Sharon, Congregational Church Records, 1800–1840.
Thomaston (Plymouth Hollow), Congregational Church Records, 1836–1840.
Torrington (Torringford), Congregational Church Records, 1783–1868.
Warren, Congregational Church Records, 1790–1840.
Washington, First Congregational Church Records, 1800–1852.
Washington, St. John's Episcopal Church Records, 1796–1851.
Washington (Marble Dale), St. Andrew's Episcopal Church Records, 1791–1824.
Watertown, Christ Church Episcopal Records, 1787–1840.
Watertown, First Congregational Church Records, 1784–1840.
Watertown and Bethlehem, Methodist Episcopal Church Records, 1820–1840.
Winchester, First Congregational Church Records, 1771–1842.
Winsted, First Congregational Church Records, 1784–1850.
Woodbury, First Congregational Church Records, 1785–1842.
Woodbury, Methodist Episcopal Church Records, 1838–1840.
Woodbury, St. Paul's Episcopal Church Records, 1785–1840.

Index